The New Golden Land

THE NEW GOLDEN LAND

European Images of America

from the Discoveries to the Present Time

by

HUGH HONOUR

PANTHEON BOOKS

A Division of Random House, New York

Copyright © 1975 by Fleming Honour Ltd.

All rights reserved under International and Pan-American Copyright Conventions. Published in the United States by Pantheon Books, a division of Random House, Inc., New York, and simultaneously in Canada by Random House of Canada Limited, Toronto.

Excerpt of fifteen lines of poetry on page 187 from *The Complete Poems of D. H. Lawrence*, edited by Vivian de Sola Pinto and F. Warren Roberts. Copyright © 1964, 1971 by Angelo Ravagli and C. M. Weekley, Executors of the Estate of Frieda Lawrence Ravagli. All rights reserved. Reprinted by permission of The Viking Press, Inc.

Library of Congress Cataloging in Publication Data
Honour, Hugh.
The New Golden Land.
Includes bibliographical references and index.
   1. United States in art. 2. Art, European.
I. Title.
N8214.5.U6H58 1976   704.94'9'973   75-22463
ISBN 0-394-49773-2
ISBN 0-394-73084-4 pbk.

Manufactured in the United States of America

Design by Kenneth Miyamoto

FIRST EDITION

Contents

ACKNOWLEDGMENTS vii
1. FIRST IMPRESSIONS 3
2. FROM THE NEW GOLDEN LAND 28
3. TRUE MEN 53
4. A LAND OF ALLEGORY 84
5. THE SAVAGE PEOPLE OF AMERICA 118
6. THE LAND OF LIBERTY 138
7. THE EXOTIC SOUTH 161
8. THE PREJUDGED LAND 190
9. GOOD INDIANS 219
10. LAND OF THE FUTURE 248

NOTES 271
LIST OF ILLUSTRATIONS 283
INDEX 293

ACKNOWLEDGMENTS

THE WRITING OF THIS BOOK has been a voyage of adventure, both enjoyable and exciting, and I have incurred very many debts during its lengthy course. Above all I am grateful to Sherman E. Lee whose timely invitation to organize an exhibition, "The European Vision of America," made the whole project possible. To him and his assistants at the Cleveland Museum, especially William S. Talbot, I am deeply indebted, as also to Carter Brown at the National Gallery, Washington, and Pierre Rosenberg at the Louvre. My publishers, André Schiffrin and Myriam Portnoy in New York and Peter Carson and Christopher Collier in London, have helped and encouraged me most warmly and I owe much to their support.

Without the published works of the writers and scholars mentioned in the bibliographical notes between pages 271 and 282 I could not, of course, have even begun to write this book and I gratefully acknowledge my debt to them. Several have also helped me personally, with information and advice, and to them and other friends who have patiently and kindly borne with my importunate questioning I am extremely grateful. I should particularly like to thank Detlef Heikamp not only for many stimulating discussions but also for a great deal of invaluable information — not to mention the loan of photographs; William C. Sturtevant for kindly allowing me to read his paper "First Visual Images of Native America" before publication; Elisabeth Dhanens for information and photographs from Belgium; John Wilmerding for allowing me to read in typescript parts of his forthcoming book on American painting in the Pelican History of Art; David Hockney, Reyner Banham, and Mario Amaya for discussions to which I owe much in the final pages of my book; Nikos Stangos and David Plante for many long remembered hours of talk; and, for help in many and various ways, Hans Aurenhammer, Carlos de Azevedo, A. W. A. Boschloo, C. R. Boxer, Ayres de Carvalho, K. Edsall, Everett Fahy, Federico del Forno, Wilma George, Myron Gilmore, John Golding, Ian Graham, Andreina Griseri, Carmen Gronau, John Hale, Eileen Harris, James Holderbaum, John Hopkins, Irene Hueck, Paul Hulton, Rachel Ingalls, H. W. Janson, James Joll, A. Kamber, Gerdt Kutscher, Myron Laskin, Jr., Michael Levey, Fred Licht, Hans Lüthy, Georgina Masson, John R. Martin, Henry P. McIlhenny, Klaus Mugden, John Muir, Benedict Nicolson, Linda Nochlin, Götz Pochat, Theodore Reff, Robert Rosenblum, Gertrude Rosenthal, Xavier de Salas, Willibald Sauerländer, Meyer Schapiro, Gert Schiff, Robert C. Smith, Craig Hugh Smyth, Dorothea von Stettin, Marvin Trachtenberg, Ross Watson.

Throughout I have had the unflagging assistance of Alastair Laing. But my greatest debt of all is to John Fleming, my co-pilot in the voyage, without whose constant help and encouragement the book would never have been written at all.

May 1975 —HUGH HONOUR

The New Golden Land

CHAPTER I

First Impressions

WHEN A EUROPEAN sets out on his first journey to America he knows, or thinks he knows, not only where he is going but what he will find when he arrives. So did Columbus. When he sailed from Palos on Friday, August 3, 1492, he was bound for Cathay, the land of fabulous wealth described by Marco Polo and Mandeville. He took with him a letter from the King and Queen of Spain addressed to the Great Khan and enrolled among his few companions a man learned in Arabic to act as interpreter. Many Europeans had traveled to China in previous years and his voyage differed from theirs in only one, all important, respect: he took a westerly course. As he wrote in the dedication of his logbook to Ferdinand and Isabella:

> Your highnesses ordained that I should not go eastward by land in the usual manner but by the western way which no one about whom we have positive information has ever followed.

To reconcile what he found with his expectations became his main preoccupation on arrival and on his three subsequent voyages.

In his wake thousands upon thousands of Europeans have crossed the Atlantic equally laden with preconceptions which they have often been forced to modify but rarely persuaded to jettison. For the relationship between Europe and America has always been a "special" one. From a very early period America seemed almost a creation or extension of Europe—in a way which Asia and Africa could never be. And with time this relationship became ever more involved as Europeans increasingly tended to see in America an idealized or distorted image of their own countries, onto which they could project their own aspirations and fears, their self-confidence and sometimes their guilty despair.

In a celebrated sentence Francisco López de Gómara described the discovery of the Indies as "the greatest event since the creation of the world, excepting the Incarnation and Death of Him who created it"—but that was not until sixty years after Columbus made his landfall. At the time of Columbus's death at Valladolid in 1506—an event, incidentally, which went unmentioned by the official chronicler of that city—no one knew quite what he had discovered. But a few Europeans had already begun to form a mental picture of the Indies which was in due course to dominate that of the whole American continent. It seems to have been composed, initially, of two superimposed images which took their form from European art and literature and only their coloring from the newly discovered lands. One was classical and related to the West; the other medieval and related to the East.

Before these are described, however, something should be said about the myths and traditions concerning the Western Straits and what lay beyond them, especially the legendary islands. One of them was Atlantis which, according to Plato who recounted the story as no more than an instructive fable in the *Timaeus,* was inhabited by a warlike people who invaded Africa and Europe, were defeated by the Athenians and their allies, driven back, and went into a decline. As the tale culminates with Atlantis

[3]

being swallowed up by the ocean in a single day and night, it hardly encouraged exploration beyond the Mediterranean. Nor did the fable of the Isles of the Blest or Hesperides, also set in the Western Ocean, for they were by definition inaccessible to the living. But accounts of them were, as we shall see, to have some influence on writers who described the Caribbean. A Christianized version of the Hesperides figures in the tenth-century account of the voyages of an Irish abbot, St. Brendan, who died in about 577, a very popular piece of medieval hagiography of which more than 120 manuscript copies are recorded. Its author seems to have had some knowledge of Iceland, perhaps Newfoundland, and some more southerly islands, probably the Azores. But the promised land of the Saints which Brendan and his monks visit after calling at many other Atlantic islands — and which Irish writers have attempted to identify with the Bahamas — is simply an idealized Ireland with a milder climate, abundant fruit, and precious stones. Whether or not St. Brendan crossed the Atlantic, his biographer was unable to provide an image of a distinctly new world. An appealing air of medieval fantasy pervades the book, which includes the story of the Irishman landing and lighting a fire on a floating island which proved to be a whale.

We are on firmer ground with the Norsemen. Icelandic sagas tell of an attempt made early in the eleventh century to colonize the district called "Vinland" on account of its wild "grapes" (probably red currants). It was given up partly because of the hostility of the local population (there was as yet no superiority in European weapons over those of Eskimos or Indians) and partly because it was insufficiently profitable. Vinland has been convincingly identified as the northern tip of Newfoundland. But the story of its brief colonization remained locked in sagas which were inaccessible to most Europeans until long after the area had been rediscovered. And even if it were to prove that Columbus was not, strictly speaking, the first European to set foot on American soil, that would be of little, if any, import to either the European vision of America or the late fifteenth- and early sixteenth-century exploration of the continent.

The twelfth-century cosmographer Vincent de Beauvais — followed by several other learned clerics including a fifteenth-century Florentine, Lorenzo Bonincontri — argued that Africa must be balanced on the other side of the Atlantic by a land mass of equal size, the Antipodes. This theory was probably known to Columbus, but he was seeking neither such a continent nor the Atlantic islands when he sailed westward.

> Your highnesses decided to send me, Christopher Columbus, to see these parts of India and the princes and the peoples of those lands . . .

he wrote in the dedication of his logbook. It was for Asia that he was bound in 1492. And in any case, his miscalculation of both the circumference of the world and the extent of Asia — he believed "Quinsay" (Hangchow) to be only some 3,550 nautical miles west of the Canary Islands whereas the real distance is 11,766 — left no room in his view of the world for a separate Antipodean continent.

Europeans had long been aware of the strangeness as well as the riches of the Far East. It had been described by Marco Polo and still more vividly by "Sir John Mandeville," whose enormously popular mid-fourteenth-century geographical fantasy abounded in islands in the Indian Ocean inhabited by men with no heads but eyes in their shoulders, people with ears so long that they hung down to their knees, with the heads of dogs or the feet of horses, and so on. As his logbook reveals, Columbus kept a weather-eye open for similarities between the islands he discovered and those which had previously been described; and in his letter which was printed in 1493 and spread the news of his voyage throughout Europe, he remarked: "I have not found the human monstrosities which many people expected." But he found much to confirm him in his belief that he had reached the Indian Ocean. Mandeville's Amazonia was peopled with women "who will not suffer men amongst them, to be their sovereigns," and Columbus reported that on the island of Matremonio there were no men but only women "who do not follow feminine occupations but use cane bows and arrows like those of the men." On "the great and fair isle called Nacumera," according to Mandeville, "the men go all naked except a little clout and are large men and warlike . . . and if they take any man in battle they eat him." Columbus was soon to find man-eaters—to be called cannibals, a corruption of the word Caribbean—

> people who are regarded in all the islands as very ferocious and who eat human flesh; they have canoes with which they range all the islands of India and pillage and take as much as they can; they are no more malformed than the others except that they have the custom of wearing their hair long like women.

No less striking affinities were to be found between the more docile inhabitants as well. "A good and true people" dwelt on Mandeville's Isle of Bragman: "and of good living after their belief, and of good faith, and although they are not christened, yet by natural law they are full of virtue and eschew all vice," caring "not for possessions or riches." Columbus noted that the Indians knew "neither sect nor idolatry, with the exception that all believe that the source of all power and goodness is in the sky." And although he had "been unable to learn whether they hold private property," it appeared to him that "all took a share in anything that one had, especially victuals."

But Columbus looked in vain for many of the more prominent elements in the traditional picture of the Indies. There were no very great riches, no great cities whatsoever, and no Great Khan. He went on searching, however, during his subsequent voyages. And when, in 1498, he finally set foot on the American mainland, he recognized at once that he had found "a very great continent, until today unknown," even possibly, he thought, the terrestial paradise which had always been located in the East. For by this time (his third voyage) he had begun to view his discoveries apocalyptically—as offering the possibility of converting all the races of the world, of global Christianity. He was dazzled by the vision of Christianity becoming not only dogmatically but geographically world-wide. And it was in a strain of Messianic, almost mystical, exaltation that he identified the Orinoco with one of the four rivers which went out of the Garden of Eden, perhaps the Pison, "which compasseth the whole land of Havilah, where there is gold; and the gold of that land is good: there is bedellium and the onyx stone."

It was not, however, of the Biblical so much as the classical landscape that readers of Columbus's first letter must have been reminded. Of Cuba he wrote:

> Its lands are lofty and in it there are many sierras and high mountains. . . . All are most beautiful, of a thousand shapes, and all accessible and filled with trees of a thousand kinds and tall, and they seem to touch the sky; and I am told that they never lose their leaves, which I can believe, for I saw them as green and beautiful as they are in Spain in May, for some of them were flowering, some with fruit and some in another condition, according to their nature. And there were singing the nightingale and other little birds of a thousand kinds in the month of November, there where I went. There are palm trees of six or eight kinds, which are a wonder to behold on account of their beautiful variety, and so are the other trees and fruits and herbs; there are marvellous pine groves, and broad fertile plains, and there is honey. There are many kinds of birds and varieties of fruit.

Mixed woods, a varied terrain, spontaneous fertility and bird-song, are the essential elements in the ideal poetic landscape from Homer onward. In the gardens of Alcinous there were trees that bore

> Fruit in his proper season all the year.
> Sweet Zephyr breathed upon them blasts that were
> Of varied tempers. These he made to bear
> Ripe fruits, these blossoms. Pear grew after pear,
> Apple succeeded apple, grape the grape,
> Fig after fig came, . . .
> And all th'adorned grounds their appearance made
> In flower and fruit. . . .

The translation is by George Chapman, who was later to write a description of British Guiana (*De Guiana. Carmen Epicum*, 1596) in very similar phrases. This fecund land also provided the background to life in the happy springtime of the human race, the Golden Age, when, according to Horace and Ovid, men had no need of iron to fight or to plough, when the untilled land yielded corn, the unpruned vine and fig tree were always in fruit, and honey flowed from the hollow oak. That the inhabitants of the newly found lands had "no iron or steel or arms, nor are they capable of using them," would not therefore have greatly surprised educated Europeans. They may indeed have read a good deal of Columbus's letter with a faint sense of *déjà vu,* visualizing the Bahamas and Cuba as being not unlike the background to Botticelli's *Primavera* or Jan van Eyck's vision of a Mediterranean paradise in which the palm, the pine, and fragrant orange flourish side by side while the ground is eternally bright with spring flowers.

This classical vision of the Indies was given its definitive form by Peter Martyr, an Italian humanist at the court of Ferdinand and Isabella and a friend of Columbus, in his *Decades de Orbe Novo* (of which the first part appeared in pirated editions in 1505 and 1511, before its official publication in 1515). Their inhabitants, he wrote, "seem to live in that golden world of which old writers speak so much, wherein men lived simply and innocently without enforcement of laws, without quarrelling, judges and libels, content only to satisfy nature." He pictured naked girls dancing "all so beautiful that one might think he beheld those splendid naiads or nymphs of the fountains, so much celebrated by the ancients." More than a century later Michael Drayton was to write of Virginia, where the "golden Age / Still Natures lawes doth give," and Andrew Marvell of the Bahamas with its "eternal Spring" in phrases which hark back to Horace and Ovid.

Sixteen editions of Columbus's letter were printed in the fifteenth century, and as none of these is known by more than one or two copies which have by chance survived, there may have been others. The first, a simple broadsheet in Spanish, was published in Barcelona in late April 1493 very shortly after Columbus went there with his cargo of parrots and Indians and gold and specimens of plants, to pay homage to Ferdinand and Isabella. Later that year a translation into Latin was printed in Rome, providing the text for further Latin editions issued in Paris, Basel, and Antwerp. A translation into Italian verse by Giuliano Dati also appeared before the end of 1493 in Florence and was reprinted four times in the next two years. So far as the vision of the new golden land is concerned, this is the most significant of all, for Dati incorporated Columbus's letter into a sixty-eight-stanza poem written in the newly fashionable *ottava rima*, which Boiardo had used for his chivalrous

1. Frontispiece to the first illustrated edition of Columbus's letter, Basel 1493

2. *Columbus Landing in the Indies.* Frontispiece to Giuliano Dati's *Lettera*, 1493

[6]

3. Detail of *The Story of Paris,* late fifteenth century. Florentine

epic *Orlando Innamorato*, and thus set the Indies in the context of Romance.

To illustrate the Latin version of the letter the Basel publisher used, with slight modifications, woodcuts which had previously been issued with accounts of Mediterranean voyages—one inscribed *Insula hyspana* shows figures going ashore from a forty-oared galley wholly unsuitable for transatlantic travel [1]. Dati's poem was provided with a frontispiece which seems to have been specially commissioned: a king (presumably Ferdinand) is seated in the foreground watching ships approach an island on which a palm tree grows and naked figures are dancing [2]. Reminiscent of contemporary Florentine *cassone* paintings, such as *The Story of Paris* [3], it might equally well have served to embellish a Renaissance version of the Troy legend or some tale of love and adventure like *Orlando Innamorato*.

While the letter in which Columbus had proclaimed the news of his discovery was gradually being diffused across Europe, the men who accompanied him on his second voyage were checking the realities they found against the expectations he had aroused. Columbus himself was distressed to find, on his return to the Indies, that the natives were less docile than they had at first seemed. Cannibalism was much more prevalent than he had supposed. And an Italian, better versed in natural history than he, noted that the flora not only differed from that of the Mediterranean but included plants with tempting fruits which proved to be virulently poisonous. But larger supplies of gold were found and sent back early the next year to Spain together with parrots and twenty-six Indians. Spices, the main object of trade with the Indies at this date, were also sent back but met with a less than enthusiastic reception from members of the Spanish court who sampled them—one complained that they included "so-called cinnamon, only it tasted like bad ginger; strong pepper but not with the flavour of Malayan pepper; wood said to be sandal-wood only it wasn't." At the same time reports revealed that life on Hispaniola was anything but idyllic: the explorers were in need of drugs, clothes, firearms, and even food. This was not widely publicized, however. Only one brief account of the second voyage seems to have been printed before the end of the century, by N. Scillacio in a book which also described eastward voyages, *De insulis meridiani atque indici maris nuper inventis* (Pavia, 1496).

In 1500 Pedro Álvares Cabral, in command of a Portuguese fleet bound for India by the Cape route, accidentally discovered Monte Pascoal on the Brazilian coast, decided that it was another island, stayed only long enough to find that the natives were friendly, and set his course for Calicut. But other navigators had already begun to exploit Columbus's discovery. Seeking another western route to the Indies, John Cabot sailed from Bristol in 1497 and Gaspare Corte Real from Lisbon in 1500, and both reached Newfoundland. No reports of these discoveries were printed for a few years (a brief letter about Corte Real is in Fracanzio da Montalboddo's *Paesi novamente retrovati*, Vicenza, 1507) but contemporary manuscript accounts, describing what they found, provide a striking contrast to Columbus's letter. They had found waters abounding in codfish, a land heavily forested with tall pine trees, and many animals and birds similar to those of Northern Europe. The inhabitants, some of whom were brought back to Lisbon in 1500 and (by Bristol merchants) to London in 1501, aroused some curiosity. They were "clothid in beastys skinnys," an English chronicler reported, "ete Rawe Flesh," and had the manners of "bruyt bestis." Alberto Cantino, ambassador of the Duke of Ferrara in Lisbon, not only saw but "touched and examined these people" and found them well formed, but noted the strange tattooing on their faces and remarked that their speech though unintelligible "was not harsh but almost human." However, they had "the most bestial manners and habits, like wild men." Clearly, the land they came from, though useful for stockfish and timber, would never nourish a vision like that of the Indies.

Cantino had a map made to record the new discoveries and mark the line which, by the Treaty of Tordesillas, determined the Portuguese and Spanish zones [1]. Here Newfoundland appears as an island with tall trees set in mid-Atlantic just to the east of the dividing line. To the south lies Brazil, an exotic country of mixed forests and swampy lagoons animated with brilliantly colored parrots (already clearly and correctly distinguished from those of Africa). Another map of 1502 (in the Staatsbibliothek, Munich) depicts a Brazilian cooking a human being—the first of many visual images of American cannibals. A distinct picture of South America was beginning to emerge and was soon given definitive literary expression in Vespucci's *Mundus Novus*, first published in Latin in Paris in 1503, translated into five modern languages, and reissued in some thirty editions before 1515, in England, Italy, Germany, the Netherlands, and Portugal.

Vespucci was not strictly truthful about himself. He antedated by two significant years his first voyage of 1499 and claimed to have been in command of it. And much of what he says of Brazil and its inhabitants seems to be the product of a fertile imagination, though perhaps as much that of his translator as his own, for the original text of the letter from which the *Mundus Novus* is derived is unfortunately lost. But he gave European readers the kind of information they wanted. Whereas Columbus had been cautious, vague, and on the sexual mores of the Indians, reticent, Vespucci was emphatic, explicit, and salacious. But like Columbus, he also set the New World (as he called it) in the context of the European classical tradition. Of the region he named Venezuela (because the villages built on piles in the water reminded him of Venice), he declared the climate to be so temperate that there were neither cold winters nor hot summers. The inhabitants lived without private possessions, laws, kings, or lords; they had no churches and were not idolaters.

> What more can I say? They live according to nature, rather as Epicureans so far as they can, than Stoics.

But despite all this, it is the exotic element that predominates in his account of the Indians. He revealed to a wondering Europe that they were not merely naked and wholly unashamed but had no hair on their bodies. The women were sexually attractive, even after childbirth, and also extremely libidinous. To satisfy their excessive lasciviousness they enlarged the penises of their lovers by the application of venomous insects—sometimes with fatal consequences. On the subject of cannibalism, to which Columbus had merely alluded in his published letter, Vespucci provided gruesomely circumstantial details.

> I met a man who told me that he had eaten more than three hundred human bodies. And I spent twenty seven days in a town where I saw cured human flesh hung up in the houses as we hang up hams in ours. They are amazed that we do

1. American section of the Cantino world map, 1502

Circulus articus.

Occeanus occidentalis

Terra del Rey de portuguall

Esta he o mar o q antre castella e portuguall

has antilhas del Rey de castella

Toda esta terra he descoberta p mandado del Rey de castella

A linha equinocialis

Mar occeanus

Tropicus capricorni.

Pollus antarticus.

THE NEW GOLDEN LAND

not eat our enemies and use their flesh for food which, they say, is very tasty.

Another longer publication, *Lettera di Amerigo Vespucci delle Isole Nuovamente Trovate*—known as the "Soderini letter" from the name of its recipient—first printed in Florence in 1505 and promptly translated into German, provided a still more vivid account of life among the Indians (and may depart still further than the *Mundus Novus* from Vespucci's original text). Here they were said to have no riches apart from brightly colored feathers and necklaces of fish bones and small stones. They did not trade and neither cultivated the land nor kept domesticated animals for food. Without regular mealtimes, they ate when they pleased from the floor. They obeyed no one, had no system of justice, and

4. (ABOVE) Frontispiece to Vespucci's *De ora antarctica (Mundus Novus)*, Strassburg, 1505

5. Illustrations to Vespucci's letter to Soderini, Strassburg, 1509

[10]

did not even chastise their children. Although they had no inhibitions about urinating publicly—in the course of a conversation if need be—they were pleasantly reticent about defecating and washed frequently (rather more, one suspects, than Europeans of the day). At night they slept in nets, soon to be known in Europe by their Carib name: hammocks. The strange wildlife of South America was described—the brilliance of the flowers, the diversity of the birds, and a reptile called *basilisco* or dragon, which is recognizably an iguana. This publication also gave an account of Vespucci's hair-raising adventures on his "four" (in fact, only three) expeditions.

To illustrate the Soderini letter, the Florentine printer copied the frontispiece to Dati's poetic version of Columbus's letter, while a Milanese reprinted a woodcut previously used for an edition of Mandeville. But in Germany, where Vespucci seems to have been particularly popular, much more elaborate illustrations were provided for it and for the *Mundus Novus*. Curious naked figures apparently playing some childlike game appear on the title page of the *Mundus Novus* printed in Strassburg [4]. And an early German edition of the Soderini letter, published in the same city in 1509, has woodcuts depicting several incidents described in it. A group of savages is shown conversing while one of them urinates and in the background a butcher chops up human limbs. In another, a wild naked woman swings a club to kill a European who is chatting with other members of her tribe [5]. The combination of nudity and a light-colored skin, together with their outlandish behavior, characterize these figures as natives of the New World. In some editions, however, the natives are merely naked Europeans—occasionally even with long, curly Düreresque beards and hair [6].

6(a). (LEFT) Illustration to Vespucci's *Mundus Novus*, probably Rostock, 1505

6(b). Illustrations to Vespucci's *Mundus Novus*, Dutch translation, c.1506–10

[11]

7. *The People of the Islands Recently Discovered...*, c.1505. German, probably Augsburg or Nuremberg

From these descriptions and the more vivid prints a single dominant image of America began to emerge and soon found further visual expression. On a broadsheet printed by Jan van Doesborch in Antwerp, describing the many discoveries made on behalf of the King of Portugal, the people of America are represented by a group of naked cannibals. Another sheet, published in Germany (probably Augsburg or Nuremberg) in about 1505, consists of a large woodcut [7] and several lines of text neatly summarizing the European conception of the New World at this date.

> The people are thus naked, handsome, brown, well-formed in body, their heads, necks, arms, privy parts, feet of women and men are slightly covered with feathers. The men also have many precious stones in their faces and breasts. No one owns anything but all things are in common. And the men have as wives those that please them, be they mothers, sisters or friends, therein they make no difference. They also fight with each other. They also eat each other even those who are slain, and hang the flesh of them in smoke. They live one hundred and fifty years. And have no government.

Though based almost word for word on Vespucci, this shows how much the New World still formed part of the Orient of Mandeville, in whose island of Lamary it was

> the custom for men and women to go all naked.... And they marry there no wives, for all the women are common.... And all land and property also is common, nothing being shut up, or kept under lock, one man being as rich as another. But in that country there is a cursed custom for they eat more gladly of man's flesh than any other flesh.

The newly found territories were still called islands, but Vespucci had discovered "what we may rightly call a New World . . . a continent more densely peopled and abounding in ani-

[12]

mals than our Europe or Asia or Africa." Very soon afterward, in 1507, Martin Waldseemüller, a young professor of geography at the college of Saint-Dié in Lorraine, delineated the New World as a vast continent in his edition of Ptolemy. Making what can have been no more than a guess—but a very intelligent guess—he created a single geographical entity by joining up the discoveries of Columbus with those of Vespucci in the south and of Cabot and Corte Real in the north. Since this fourth part of the world had "been discovered by Americus Vesputius," he wrote, "I do not see why there should be any objection to its being called after Americus the discoverer, a man of natural wisdom, Land of Americus or America, since both Europe and Asia have derived their names from women." On his map he placed the name *America* far down in the south—below a parrot symbolizing its natural products—and within half a century *America* was being used to designate the whole continent by most Europeans—apart, that is, from Spaniards who obstinately persisted in calling it *Las Indias*.

Yet despite Waldseemüller, who separated the new continent from China by a fairly wide stretch of water, most Europeans (including the cartographers) continued for many years to see America as the farthest extension of Asia. Similarly, no distinctions were as yet generally drawn between the West and East Indies. (Vasco da Gama had opened up the sea route to Calcutta in 1497–99, attracting rather more contemporary attention than Columbus.) Thus, in the early sixteenth century, the Portuguese painter of an Epiphany represented one of the Wise Men from the East as a Brazilian [43]. Still more significantly, the artists who depicted the "people of Calicut" in the pictorial triumphal procession devised by the Emperor Maximilian I in 1512 showed them in the guise of American Indians. A German artist, perhaps Albrecht Altdorfer, in his gilded and exquisitely colored paintings on vellum gave them headdresses, skirts, and leg bands of feathers [II].

Brazilians had been brought back to Europe from at least as early as 1505—when Binot Palmier de Gonneville returned with the son of a Tupinamba chief, Essomericq—and one of them or specimens of their accouterment must have reached Germany by 1515, for in that year no less an artist than Albrecht Dürer drew an Indian with an accurately depicted Tupinamba feather cap and scepter in the margin of a Book of Hours he decorated for Maximilian I [8]. Together with an Oriental leading a camel on the next page, he illustrates the Twenty-fourth Psalm: "The earth is the Lord's and all that therein is: the compass of the world and they that dwell therein." Drawn with Dürer's exquisite linear sensitivity, this is incomparably the most beautiful sixteenth-century depiction of an Indian, although he looks more like a snub-nosed German youth dressed up for a Nuremberg pageant than a genuine Tupinamba.

That such figures were still associated indiscriminately with the East or the West is shown

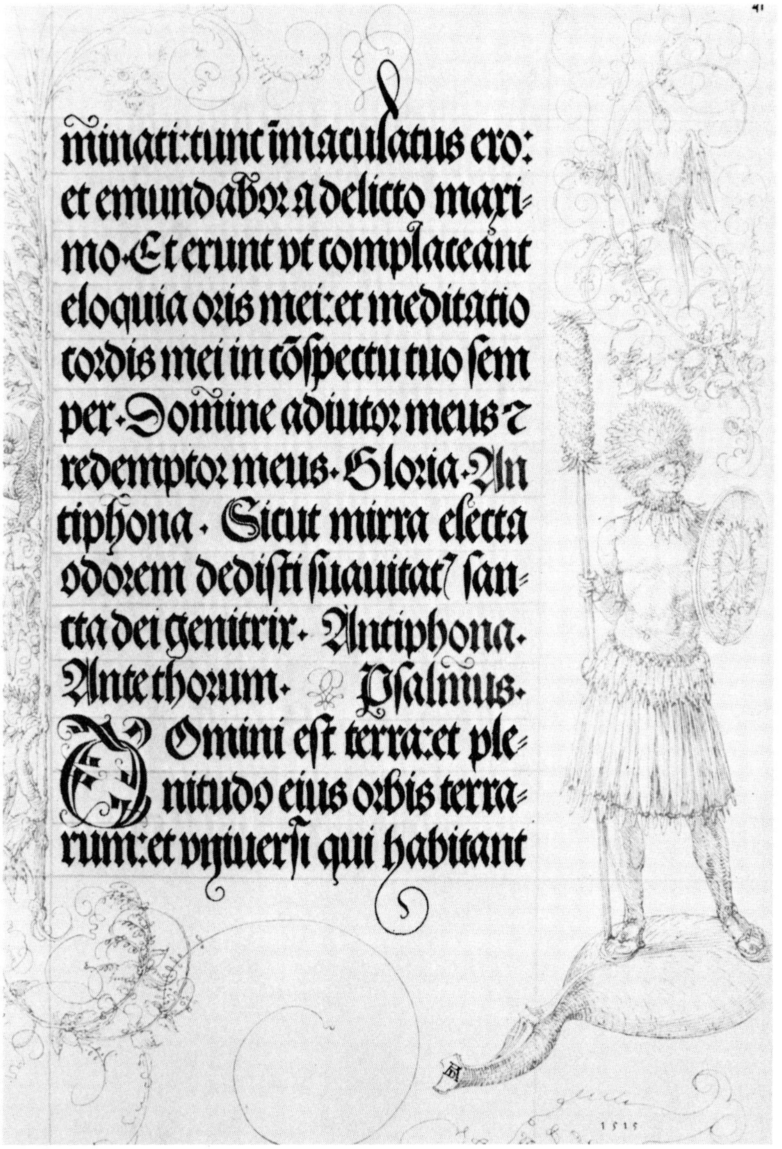

8. Page from the Prayer Book of Maximilian I, 1515. Albrecht Dürer

9(a). Detail from *The Triumph of Maximilian I*, 1526. Hans Burgkmair

by Jorg Breu's illustrations to the 1515 Augsburg edition of Lodovico de Varthema's book of Eastern travels, *Die ritterliche Reise*, in which he depicted the inhabitants of Sumatra clad in feather caps and skirts. Similarly in Burgkmair's *The Triumph of Maximilian I* (drawn in about 1516 but not printed until 1526) the "people of Calicut" include feather-clad figures mingling with women and children, some totally naked apart from a few bangles, others carrying parrots, monkeys, baskets of tropical fruit, and heads of Indian corn (the first in European art) and accompanied by the garlanded cows and fat-tailed sheep of Asia [9a]. Another German artist in the same circle, or perhaps Burgkmair, made two drawings of similar figures, one of whom carries a Mexican shield which could not, of course, have been seen or known in Europe until after 1519 [9b].

9(b). *Indian Holding a Mexican Shield*, post 1519. Attributed to Hans Burgkmair

FIRST IMPRESSIONS

11. *The Triumph of Maximilian I*, 1512–16. Attributed to Albrecht Altdorfer

Between 1519 and 1522 two events which were to transform the idea of the newly discovered lands took place contemporaneously: the circumnavigation of the world and the conquest of Mexico. Both helped to dissociate America from Asia, but in different ways. For while the one demonstrated the vast extent of the Pacific Ocean, the other revealed the potentialities of the New World, its barely credible riches and the existence in it of a civilization totally dissimilar from those of Asia with which Europeans had for centuries been familiar. It is perhaps significant that the Mexicans sent over to Europe by Cortés aroused far greater curiosity than Colum-

[15]

bus's Indians, for they could be recognized as the denizens of a wholly New World rather than just as savages or members of some very remote Asiatic tribe [46–48]. Nevertheless, it was the circumnavigation that seems to have had the more immediate influence.

The aim of Ferdinand Magellan, admiral in charge of this first journey around the world on which he lost his life, was to find a westerly route to the Spice Islands, believing them to be "no great distance from Panama and the Gulf of San Miguel" sighted by Balboa in 1513. After discovering the straits which were to be named after him and sailing up the southwest coast of America, Magellan was completely unprepared for a journey of eighty-eight days before reaching the Philippines—more than twice as long as Columbus's first crossing of the Atlantic. The narrative of the voyage by one of the few survivors, Antonio Pigafetta, first published in 1525 and frequently reprinted in the following years, left readers in no doubt about the width of the Pacific and thus the magnitude of Columbus's error. It also added some details to the picture of America—notably the giants of Patagonia, who performed a strange trick of swallowing arrows and pulling them out again without hurting themselves (as they were to be shown doing on many maps and prints). South America, however, became simply a hazard encountered on the way to the fabulously rich East Indian islands which Pigafetta described with far greater enthusiasm. The cargo of spices picked up there and brought home on the *Victoria* yielded more than enough money to pay for the equipment of the five ships which had set off in 1519. (The coat of arms which the Castilian heralds prepared for its captain, Elcano, bore two crossed cinnamon sticks, three nutmegs, and twelve cloves with Malay kings—not Patagonians—as supporters).

"America was discovered accidentally," Admiral Morison has recently remarked: "when discovered it was not wanted; and most of the exploration for the next fifty years was done in the hope of getting through or around it." The northern coast was investigated mainly in the hope of finding a passage less roundabout and perilous than that through the Straits of Magellan to what Giovanni da Verrazzano called "the happy shores of Cathay." With this as his objective he explored the coast from Cape Fear (in what is now North Carolina) to Maine on behalf of the King of France in 1524. "I did not expect to find such an obstacle of new land as I have found," he wrote; "and if for some reason I did expect to find it, I estimated there would be some strait to get through to the Eastern Ocean." Between 1534 and 1545 Jacques Cartier pursued the search further north, finding the St. Lawrence in the process. As the size and impenetrability of the continent was revealed a still more northern passage was sought, especially by the English who convinced themselves of its existence. In 1566 Sir Humphrey Gilbert confidently declared that "any man of our country that will give the attempt, may with small danger passe in Cataia" by this route and reach "all other places in the East, in much shorter time than either the Spaniard or the Portingale doth."

The picture of North America which emerged from accounts of these voyages was hardly enticing. "I am inclined to regard this land as the one God gave to Cain," Jacques Cartier wrote of the barren coast of Labrador in 1534. And a member of Frobisher's expedition to the Northwest in 1577 remarked:

> In place of odiferous and fragrant smells of sweet gums, and pleasant notes of musical birds, which other countries in more temperate zones do yield, we tasted the most boisterous Boreal blasts mixed with snow and hail in the months of June and July, nothing inferior to our intemperate winter.

And this is fully borne out by a contemporary drawing of one of their encounters with the Eskimos in those icy solitudes [III], perhaps that at Bloody Point on August 1, 1577, when Frobisher observed a "number of small things fleeting in the sea afarre off" which he supposed to be porpoises or seals until coming nearer he "discovered them to be men in small boats made of leather." The terrain in what was later to become the southern United States was much more attractive. Verrazzano named part of the coast "Archadia" because of the beauty of the trees which seems to have reminded him of Arcady as described by Virgil or, more recently,

III. *English Sailors in a Skirmish with Eskimo, 1577.* By or after John White

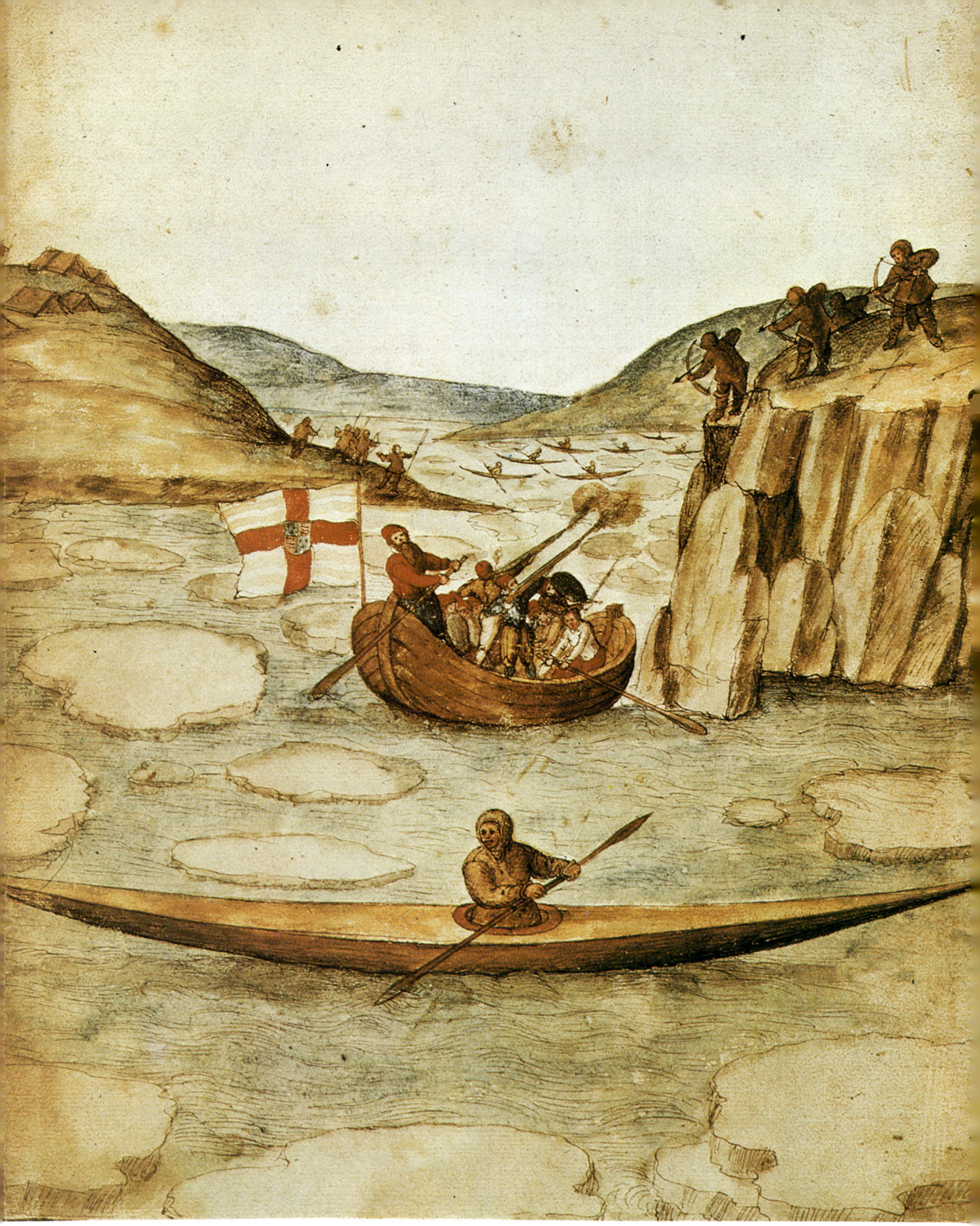

Jacopo Sannazaro. Just such a landscape is delicately delineated on a Portuguese map, probably drawn in 1525 by Lopo Homem, where it is labeled *Terra Bimene*, the fabulous island of the fountain of youth which Ponce de León was seeking when he discovered Florida [IV]. But its wildlife is distinctly northern—birds like those of Europe, bears, deer, and a fox—in striking contrast with the balancing vignette of the South American scene where naked savages dig for gold.

"It is to the South, not to the icy North, that everyone in search of fortune should turn," wrote Peter Martyr in 1525; "below the equator everything is rich." Some explorers persisted, however, in hoping to find in the north another empire as rich as those of the Aztecs and the Incas. Cartier sought the mythical Kingdom of Saguenay of which Indians had told him. An English sailor David Ingram boasted of finding near the Penobscot estuary the city of Norumbega with streets larger than any of those in London and inhabitants who wore hoops of gold and silver "garnished with pearls, divers of them as big as one's thumb." Expeditions were dispatched to this wholly imaginary place which was even marked on maps. Martin Frobisher claimed to have discovered gold in the far north in 1576, though it turned out to be only iron pyrites.

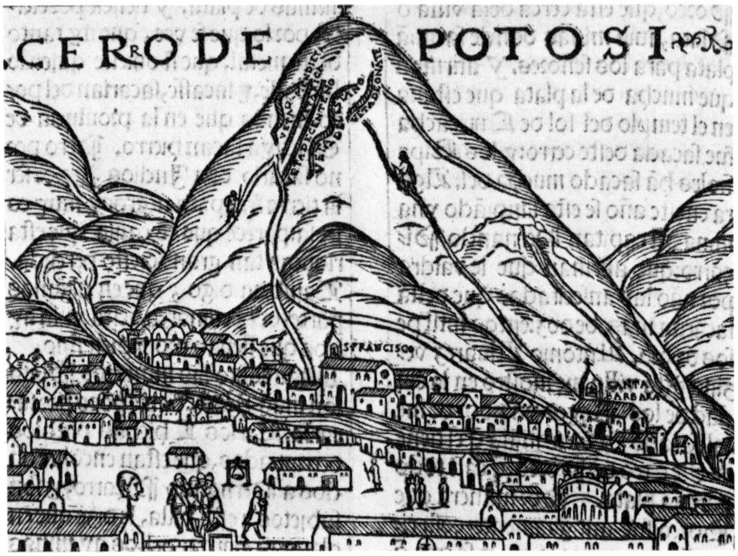

10. *The Silver Mines of Potosí*, from Cieza de León, Chronica del Peru, 1553

The story of Norumbega and the hope of finding gold mines in the North were, of course, inspired by the accounts of Mexico and Peru which gradually focused attention on America for its own sake and not merely as an obstacle in the passage to the Orient. "How much the richest empire in the world is that of these Indies," wrote Fernández de Oviedo in 1535, and many other similar comments could be quoted. Gold was the magnet which drew men to explore the new continent. Yet the interest which sixteenth-century Europeans took in America, even with its promise of gold, should not be exaggerated. In an age when travel literature flourished, with such compendia of voyages as those edited by Fracanzio da Montalboddo in Vincenza and by Ramusio in Venice and Hakluyt in England, the discovery of America played by no means the most prominent part. Many more books were written about other parts of the world. In France between 1480 and 1609 twice as many books and ten times as many pamphlets were devoted to the Islamic lands.

That Charles V should have made no allusion to his American empire in his memoirs (even though the book is a political apologia rather than an autobiography) is also very striking. No less so is the fact that whereas a great series of tapestries was woven to commemorate his conquest of Tunis in 1535, which seems a relatively trivial incident in retrospect, no official works of art were commissioned to record the conquest of Peru the previous year. The main reason for this neglect seems to have been economic. Not until after the chance discovery of the silver mines of Potosí in 1545 and the settlement of the wars between the colonists in Peru a decade later did Hispanic America begin to yield substantial profits to the Spanish Crown [10]. In 1554 America was producing no more than 11 percent of the Spanish Crown's total income, and this did not swell to as much as 25 percent until the 1590s, partly because of a decline in other sources of wealth. At the same time increased production in Peru, made possible by a new technique of treating the ore introduced in 1571, substantially reduced the relative value of silver itself. These sobering facts were known only to

IV. Western Hemisphere of the "Miller" world map, 1525. Attributed to Lopo Homem

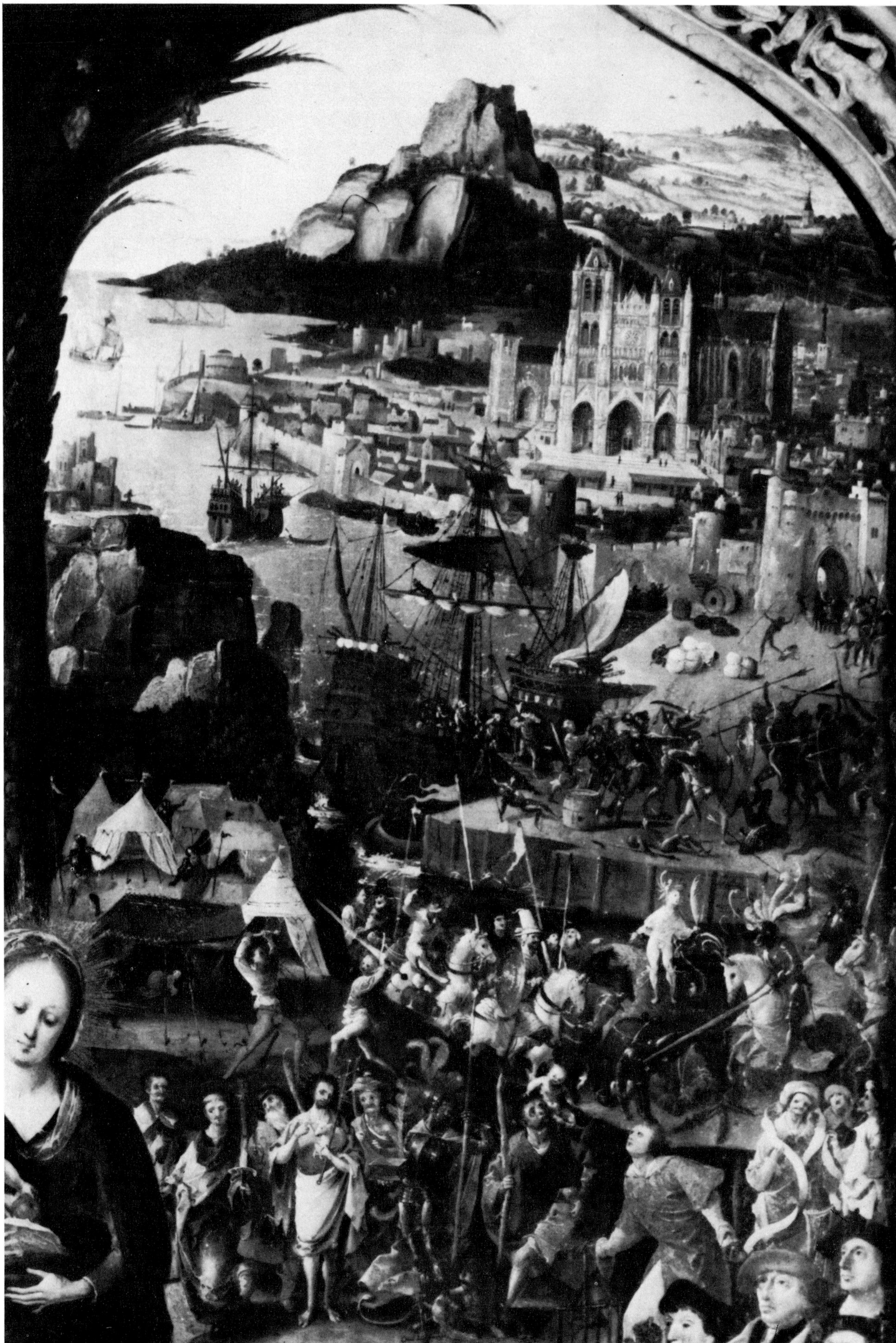

the Crown officials, of course. Tales of vast fortunes made by individual conquistadors and exaggerated contemporary estimates of the amount of gold and silver shipped to Spain (some of which was captured en route and diverted to England) were, however, on everyone's lips and played a major part in the formation of the late sixteenth-century American image. Describing the supposed wealth of Guiana in 1595, Sir Walter Raleigh wrote:

> Although these reports may seem strange, yet if we consider the many millions which are daily brought out of Peru into Spain, we may easily believe the same: for we find that by the abundant treasure of that country the Spanish King vexeth all the princes of Europe, and is become, in a few years, from a poor King of Castille, the greatest monarch of the World.

Other imports from the New World — mainly beaver pelts, dried cod, and dyewood — could not as yet compete with the spices of the East Indies.

Of course, gold had glittered in the vision of America from the very beginning, in the accounts of Columbus and Vespucci, but it became much more prominent after the conquest of Mexico and Peru. Almost simultaneously, however, a new image was superimposed on those of the classical Golden Age and fabulous East. Once again it took its form from a long established European literary tradition — that of the *chansons de geste*, especially those which recounted the deeds of Christian knights humbling the proud paynims. This transposition was due perhaps, in the first place, to the coincidence that the centuries-long war to drive the Moors out of Spain had ended, as Columbus himself pointed out in the dedication of his logbook, on the very eve of the discovery of America. And some of the energy previously expended on it was diverted to the conquest of the New World. Cortés referred to the Aztec temples as "mosques" and there can be little doubt that he saw himself as a champion of Christendom waging a holy war against the infidel. His accounts of combats between his men, shouting the time-honored battle cry *Señor Santiago,* and vast hordes of Mexicans seem almost to have been modeled on descriptions of those between the Spaniards and Moors. After one of them he knighted a converted Indian ally on the field. And Bernal Diaz, a soldier who served under Cortés, invoked the famous romance of *Amadis de Gaul* to describe his first sight of Tenochtitlán. The riches and luxury of this city, with its teeming markets, its handsome palaces and gardens, were very much of the kind previously associated with Islam; as were the manners and tastes of Montezuma and his courtiers, so reminiscent of the caliphs. (Polygamy and paederasty were common to both societies.) On the map of Tenochtitlán, illustrating a Nuremberg edition of the letters of Cortés published in 1524 (and copied elsewhere), a bold inscription marks Montezuma's *domus ad voluptate,* presumably his seraglio, the only explicitly Aztec features on the map being the central square with temples inscribed "where they sacrifice." In this way the conquest of Mexico was readily absorbed into the late medieval view of the world, and it is very tempting to see an allusion to it in a peculiar battle scene between Europeans in armor and naked, dark-skinned savages in the background of a votive picture of the *Virgin of the Palm* (or Victory) painted for Amiens Cathedral in 1520, the year in which news of Cortés's exploits first reached Europe [11].

The conquest of Mexico was also interpreted apocalyptically, almost as a confirmation of Columbus's mystical interpretation of his discovery. For the speedy conversion of the Mexicans could be seen as the fulfilment of one of the prophecies of the Apocalypse, as one of the events which were to precede the millennial kingdom of Christ. In his farewell sermon to the first twelve friars sent there, the minister-general of the Franciscans quoted the parable of the laborers in the vineyard, adding: "The day of the world is already reaching the eleventh hour; you of the Father of the family are called to go to the vineyard." Later in the century another Franciscan, Gerónimo de Mendieta, was to prophesy the imminent creation of an ideal theocratic state — a true City of God — in the New World, more than compensating for the Church's losses to Protestantism in the Old, which he dismissed as the City of Man. He and others believed in the westward spread of Christianity, initiating the idea that was to be

11. Detail of *The Virgin of the Palm,* 1520. School of Amiens

THE NEW GOLDEN LAND

extended by Bishop Berkeley in the eighteenth century ("Westward the course of Empire . . .") and, as we shall see, completely transformed by Karl Marx in the nineteenth.

A very different view of the *Conquista* is presented in a picture probably dating from the 1540s and certainly from before 1555–56 when the artist, Jan Mostaert, died [V]. This remarkable work depicts an imaginary scene of the conquest, not any specific incident. (Several schol-

v. *A West Indian Scene*, c.1540–50. Jan Mostaert

ars have tried to find evidence to the contrary but none is convincing.) The pastoral landscape, similar to that which Mostaert provided for Adam and Eve in another painting, is such as European readers of Columbus might well have imagined to exist in the Indies. And the stark naked figures with the lithe, athletic, well-proportioned bodies of Greek and Roman warriors drawn by Mantegna, Pollaiuolo, and others accord perfectly with the Indians as seen through the spectacles of a Renaissance humanist. Only the strange straw huts and a monkey squatting on a tree stump are manifestly exotic. It is a vision of the Golden Age of the Indies glimpsed at the moment when it is shattered by Spanish steel. While sheep and cows browse impassively on this fresh, green breast of the New World, the naked inhabitants, clutching primitive weapons, streak across the panel to encounter a posse of Europeans with pikes and halberds and cannon remorselessly advancing from the shore where they have beached their boats. Mostaert no doubt had personal experience of the behavior of Spanish soldiers and the picture may well allude, if only obliquely, to their activities in his native Low Countries. But more generally, it is a visual parable on the innocence and peace of unspoilt nature and the destructive urge of civilized man—a parallel to his painting of Eve banished from the pastoral dream of Eden, with Cain killing Abel nearby. It is a theme which was to echo down the ages in America.

The Black Legend of Spanish cruelty, which has a long medieval history, acquired still darker tones after the conquest of America. The man mainly responsible for adding them was himself a Spaniard. Bartolomé de las Casas, who had gone to the Indies as an adventurer, acquired an *encomienda* (a feudal grant of land with Indians to work it), but took holy orders, was suddenly struck with revulsion at the treatment of the native population by his fellow *encomienderos,* and devoted the rest of his life to its protection. In the early 1540s he wrote his *Brévissima relación de las destrucción de las Indias,* a bitter denunciation of the principles and practice of Spanish imperialism which was intended only for the eyes of officials but seems to have circulated widely in manuscript. (Mostaert may well have known of it.) The work was seized on by Europeans who were generally less concerned with the plight of the Indians in the New World than with the pretensions of Spain in the Old. And the fact that its author was a member of the Dominican Order, which staffed the hated and feared Inquisition, gave it a special significance

12. *The Spanish Treatment of Fugitive Black Slaves,* from T. de Bry, *America,* Part V, 1595

for Protestants in the Hapsburg lands. It was translated into Flemish in 1578, French in 1579 (as *Tyrannies et cruautés des Espagnols*), English in 1583, and German in 1597.

The cruelties of the Spaniards were also described in lurid detail by Girolamo Benzoni, a native of Milan (under Spanish rule from 1535), in his *Historia del mondo nuovo,* which was first published in 1565 and enjoyed success both widespread and enduring (outside Italy thirty-two editions were printed before the end of the eighteenth century). Providing a pocket history of America from the arrival of Columbus to the conquest of Peru, interspersed with lively anecdotes of Benzoni's own experiences in the Spanish colonies, this book denounced the treatment meted out not only to Indians but also (and for the first time in print) to the black slaves imported from Africa. But if the Spaniards are the villains of this piece, the Indians and Africans are no more than hapless victims. The same could be said of the accounts of American voyages published by Richard Hakluyt from 1582, though they also are provided with white Anglo-Saxon Protestant heroes who here make their bow on the American scene.

Benzoni's history fills three of the ten fully illustrated volumes in the collection of books on America issued by a Frankfurt publisher and engraver, Theodor de Bry, from 1590 to 1618. In them we can watch the gradual superimposition of one American image over another unfold before our eyes. It begins serenely in the pastoral paradise of Thomas Hariot's *Briefe and true report of the new found land of Virginia* (1590), illustrated by engravings after John White's watercolors made on the expedition, and it proceeds to an account of the brief golden age of happy relations between the French and Indians in Florida. Menacing clouds appear over the horizon in the third volume, which reprints Hans Staden's narrative of his adventures among the cannibals of Brazil. Then come the three Benzoni volumes vividly illustrating the atrocities committed by the gold-obsessed Spaniards [12] and also the gangsterism among themselves [13]. A later volume, taken over from Hakluyt, is devoted to the predominantly anti-

13. *The Assassination of Pizarro,* from T. de Bry, *America,* Part VI, 1596

THE NEW GOLDEN LAND

Spanish activities of Drake and Raleigh. The Indians are thus gradually reduced to the role of "extras" in the great drama of European expansion. And when they reappear more prominently in illustrations to a digest of John Smith's *General History of Virginia, New England and the Summer Isles*, they figure as little more than an inconvenient hindrance to the establishment of a Protestant colony.

In such ways, despite the steadily increasing interest they held for philosophers and missionaries, and the fear they continued to inspire in settlers, the Indians were steadily pushed to the back of the European picture of America. Sometimes they were almost pushed out of it altogether. When the first large-scale works of art on American subjects were finally commissioned in Spain in the early 1630s—as part of a series celebrating recent victories, notable mainly because it includes Velázquez's *Surrender of Breda*—Eugenio Caxés painted *The Recovery of San Juan de Puerto Rico* (from the Dutch) and *The*

14. *The Recovery of Bahia in Brazil*, 1635. Juan Bautista Maino

[26]

Recovery of the Island of San Cristobal (from the English) and Juan Bautista Maino, *The Recovery of Bahia in Brazil* (from the Dutch) [14]. The figures in these enormous canvases are all Europeans except in the third where two diminutive Indians may be dimly discerned on the beach in the background.

Thus, little more than a century after its discovery, America had already become, in fact and not just in a literary sense, an extension of Europe. In 1516 Thomas More had described Utopia as an island near those recently discovered by Vespucci, and its wise inhabitants were indigenous. But later dreams of an ideal state were usually located in a New World populated exclusively by Europeans. Nor were they merely fantasies. Sir Humphrey Gilbert—a reader of *Utopia*—drew up plans for a colony which he hoped to establish, ruled by a governor with an elected council, free housing provided for poor immigrants, land set apart for the support of a hospital, "learning, lectures, scholars and other good and godely uses," with all the colonists enjoying the rights of free-born Englishmen. And the chronicler of his voyages complacently remarked that it seemed "as if God has prescribed limits unto their Spanish nation which they might not exceed," apparently reserving North America for the English!—a land fit for English settlers!—"Earth's onely Paradise," as in Michael Drayton's Virginia of 1606:

> Where Nature hath in store
> Fowle, Venison and Fish,
> And the Fruitfull'st Soyle,
> Without your Toyle,
> Three Harvests more,
> All greater than your Wish.

CHAPTER 2

From the New Golden Land

"I SAW THE THINGS which have been brought to the King from the new golden land," Albrecht Dürer wrote in his diary on the August 27, 1520:

> a sun all of gold a whole fathom broad, and a moon all of silver of the same size, also two rooms full of the armour of the people there, and all manner of wondrous weapons of theirs, harness and darts, wonderful shields, strange clothing, bedspreads, and all kinds of wonderful objects of various uses, much more beautiful to behold than prodigies. These things were all so precious that they have been valued at one hundred thousand gold florins. All the days of my life I have seen nothing that has gladdened my heart so much as these things, for I saw amongst them wonderful works of art, and I marvelled at the subtle *ingenia* or men in foreign lands. Indeed, I cannot express all that I thought there.

These objects had been sent to Cortés, shortly after his arrival in Mexico in 1519, by Montezuma, who hoped thereby to satisfy his greed and deter him from advancing on the capital—they had, of course, precisely the opposite effect—and were promptly forwarded to the Queen of Spain Joan the Mad and her son Charles V by Cortés in order to justify his wholly unauthorized activities on the American mainland. Dürer saw them displayed in Brussels where Charles halted for a while on his way to be enthroned as Holy Roman Emperor in Aix-la-Chapelle.

American artifacts had been imported into Europe during the previous seventeen years, including hammocks and canoes (two Carib words which entered the European languages together with "hurricanes" and "cannibals"). But Montezuma's gift comprised objects of far superior quality, ingeniously wrought out of rare and precious materials. Before they were shipped from Vera Cruz an inventory was made listing the gold collars encrusted with precious stones, a large alligator's head modeled in gold, shields covered with plates of gold, and what Dürer described as "a sun" (probably an Aztec calender)—"a large wheel of gold, with figures of strange animals on it, and worked with tufts of leaves; weighing three thousand eight hundred ounces." Many other objects were decorated with the plumes of gaudy birds—"a fan of variegated feather-work, with thirty seven rods plated with gold," a "box of feather-work embroidered on leather with a large plate of gold in the midst," and "two birds made of green feathers with feet, beaks and eyes of gold—and in the same piece with them, animals of gold resembling snails." A hundred ounces of gold ore were also sent "that their Highnesses might see in what state the gold came from the mines." Among objects of less value there were pieces of embroidered cotton and "two books such as the Indians use."

The official historian of the Indies, Peter Martyr, also examined with astonishment this glittering cargo soon after it reached Seville and described it in detail, paying attention to the pictographic codices in which he saw evidence of a civilization similar to that of ancient Egypt. He was at a loss to describe the featherwork, however:

> It is not so much the gold or the precious stones I admire, as the cleverness of the artist and the workmanship, which much exceed the value of the material and excite my amazement. I have examined a thousand figures which it is impossible to describe. In my opinion I have never seen anything which for beauty could more delight the human eye.

Like Dürer, he seems to have been bewildered

by what he saw. And it is very difficult to know how or how much he appreciated it. Certainly it would be a mistake to read either his or Dürer's comments literally. To some extent their terms of praise are conventional, though this is less so with Dürer. His words have the ring of truth about them. But it is odd, and perhaps significant, that he who was so seldom without a pen or pencil or brush in his hand should not, apparently, have made a single drawing or sketch of any of the outlandish Mexican objects he saw in Brussels—even though he had drawn a Brazilian Indian five years earlier [8]. The reactions of Charles V and his ministers are easier to ascertain. They had little, if any, appreciation of these things. The gold and silver were melted down and the precious stones extracted. Of all the items described by Dürer and Peter Martyr only one seems to have survived—a codex (now in the National Library of Austria) which had no instrinsic value and was preserved merely as a curiosity. Further hoards of Mexican booty were, however, sent to Europe in the following years and some of it can still be traced—hardstone carvings of human and animal heads [15], masks decorated with turquoise mosaic [16], and most impressive of all, six pieces of featherwork, a headdress and fan and four shields [17].

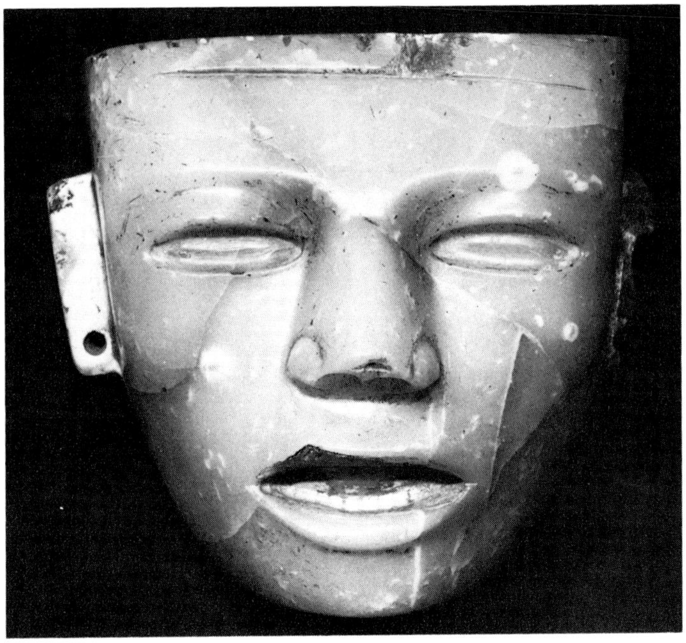

After Pizarro's invasion of Peru in 1533, Europeans encountered the products of another an-

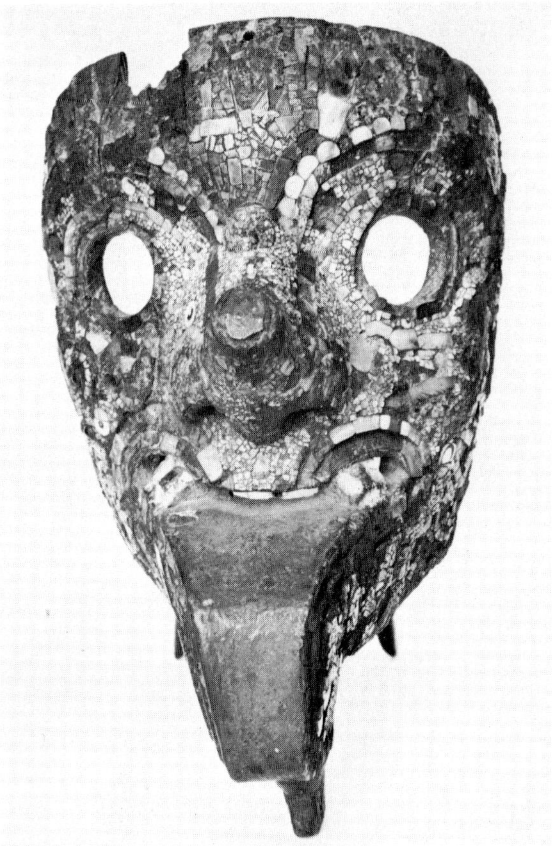

15. (LEFT) Mexican greenstone mask, fifth–sixth century, Formerly Medici collection
16. (ABOVE) Mexican turquoise-encrusted mask, Mixtec and Puebla Culture. Formerly Aldrovandi collection
17. (BELOW) Mexican featherwork shield, probably sent to Europe by Cortés. Formerly Hapsburg collection

cient American civilization. The Conquistadors were astonished by the sheer quantity of gold and silver they found and some of them recorded their admiration for the workmanship displayed in intricately wrought vessels, models of plants, and a group of golden animals surrounding a fountain which sent up a jet of gold wire. Several of the finest pieces were taken by Hernando Pizarro to Europe and presented to Charles V in January 1534. They included a life-size gold idol, a head of maize with silver leaves and golden grains and tassels, thirty-four golden vases, and more than a hundred pieces of silver. The Emperor is said to have been suitably impressed: but he sent the whole lot straight to the melting pot. An inventory of his possessions drawn up shortly after his death shows that of the vast quantity of rich and strange objects sent to him from his dominions in the New World all that survived intact were a few pieces of gold and silver, some examples of featherwork, and such oddities as a "pair of shoes of the Indians of Peru."

If Mexican and Peruvian works of art were described with apparent enthusiasm by the historians of the Indies and by some of the Conquistadors themselves, very few other Europeans showed any aesthetic appreciation of them. (A few early sixteenth-century collectors, notably the Hapsburgs and the Medici, acquired examples but they did so almost certainly as "curiosities" rather than as works of art, though one may wonder why Tommaso de' Cavalieri, the friend for whom Michelangelo made some of his finest drawings, included Mexican featherwork among the antique marbles in his collection in Rome.) They appear, in any event, to have had no influence whatsoever on the arts of Europe. This may seem strange if it is recalled how easily fourteenth-century artists had assimilated into the repertory of Gothic ornament the strange and exotic motifs they saw on Chinese silks and porcelain. But by the early sixteenth century Europeans had become too much obsessed with their classical past to respond to the products of cultures as different from their own as the Maya, Aztec, and Inca. Such objects seemed to them still more barbarous than those in the Gothic style from which they had just shaken themselves free.

Only the materials used by American craftsmen and their technical proficiency in handling them won wholehearted approval; thus, well-meaning missionaries often provided European designs for featherwork pictures and vestments intended for export to Europe, where many still survive, greatly outnumbering those in indigenous Mexican styles.

American objects aroused much more European interest scientifically or humanly than artistically and many found their way into collections of the type known in Germany as *Wunderkammer*. Providing a kind of humanist counterpart to medieval treasuries of holy relics, the *Wunderkammer* displayed both the wonders of creation and the works of man. Their contents ranged from ostrich eggs, the horns of narwhals, chunks of quartz, dried flowers, stuffed birds and reptiles (an alligator or crocodile suspended from the ceiling was almost obligatory) to Egyptian "idols," Chinese porcelain, Japanese lacquer, and such examples of European ingenuity as miniscule carvings in wood or ivory. The wonders of the New World—hammocks and canoes, Brazilian clubs and rattles, Mexican featherwork and hard-stone carvings—were eagerly welcomed, as well as the codices which enabled Europeans to see how their fellow men on the other side of the Atlantic lived and worked and worshipped. It was in these dusty and overcrowded chambers that anthropology was born.

The Emperor Ferdinand I (died in 1564, younger brother of Charles V) seems to have been the first European to collect Mexican objects, and his interest in them was inherited by his sons Archduke Karl of Steiermark and Archduke Ferdinand II of Austrian Tyrol (who owned the three magnificent examples of featherwork now in the Museum of Ethnology in Vienna [17]). The Emperor Rudolf II in Prague and Duke Albrecht V of Bavaria in Munich, both of whom were famous patrons of the most refined and sophisticated Mannerist goldsmiths and jewelers, acquired several Mexican hard-stone carvings. But no hunters after *curiosa* were more avid collectors of Mexican objects than the Medici in Florence. By 1539 Cosimo I had assembled no fewer than forty-four pieces of featherwork

VI. *A Mexican Chieftain with His Entourage*, 1588. Lodovico Buti

including various garments, and by 1553 he had several wooden masks covered with turquoise and some animal heads carved out of semiprecious stones. A few of the more striking of these objects were later put on show in the Tribuna of the Uffizi and the rest mingled with the hoard of weapons, exotic costumes, and natural history specimens in the adjoining Armory where in 1588 Lodovico Buti frescoed the ceiling with Indian warriors and American birds to accompany them [18, VI]. Later, a greenstone Mexican mask was similarly "acclimatized" by being set in an Italian silver mount [19].

Before the end of the sixteenth century, private citizens had also begun to form cabinets of curiosities and sometimes to enrich them with Amerindian artifacts. The great naturalist Ulisse Aldrovandi built up one of the most notable in Bologna, including in it a very fine turquoise-

19. Mexican greenstone mask in an early seventeenth-century European mount, probably part of the dowry of Vittoria della Rovere, 1634

18. Detail of frescoed ceiling, Uffizi, Florence, 1588. Lodovico Buti

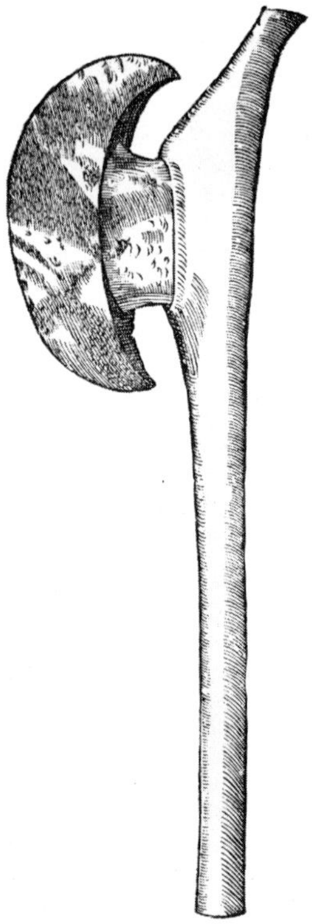

20. Brazilian axe in Aldrovandi's collection, from U. Aldrovandi, *Musaeum metallicum*, 1648

encrusted Mexican mask [16] now one of the most famous possessions of the Museo Pigorini in Rome, a Mexican knife with an obsidian blade, a Brazilian axe [20], and several smaller objects. In England the learned Dr. John Dee, astrologer to Queen Elizabeth I, mystagogue and hermetic philosopher—a polymath in the true sense of the word—who was also involved in early attempts to find the Northwest Passage, owned a Mexican obsidian disc which he is reputed to have used to conjure up spirits: it was known as "the Devil's Looking-glass." Also in London, Walter Cope, a merchant who had traveled to the West Indies, had several specimens of Americana in his apartment which was said to be "stuffed with queer foreign objects in every corner." A German traveler, Thomas Platter, visited him in 1599 and noted, in addition to Chinese porcelain, Roman coins, and the bauble and bells of Henry VIII's fool, "beautiful Indian plumes . . . an Indian stone axe like a thunderbolt . . . Indian stone shears . . . a Madonna made of Indian feathers . . . two beautifully dyed Indian sheepskins with silken sheen. . . . A long narrow Indian canoe, with the oars and sliding planks, hung from the ceiling of this room." But Mr. Cope seems to have indulged in travelers' tales for he showed Platter some "flies which glow by night in Virginia instead of lights, since there is often no day there for over a month!" The appearance of such a collection is recorded in an engraving of Ole Worm's museum in Copenhagen some years later [21].

In the "cabinets of the curious," as they were called, natural history specimens far outnumbered the artifacts. Three of those which included Americana were, in fact, formed by distinguished naturalists—Aldrovandi, Worm, and John Tradescant (whose collection, with its Indian arms and "Powhattan's cloak," passed to the

21. Ole Worm's museum at Copenhagen, from *Museum Wormianum*, Leyden 1653

Ashmolean Museum, Oxford, in 1683). It was the natural, not the manmade, products of the New World which first caught and continued to hold European attention. They included, of course, pearls and precious stones—and gold and silver. Las Casas described a gold nugget as being as big as the three-pound loaves of bread they bake in Seville, calling it a "unique marvel of nature" and "a remarkably beautiful piece." Featherwork was admired as much for the beauty of the plumes as for the skill with which patterns and pictures were made from them, and from the moment of discovery, gaily colored birds played a prominent part in the visual image of the New World. They were mentioned by Columbus in his first letter and brought back to Europe by him in 1493: Brazil was often called "the land of parrots" in the early 1500s. That America should have been represented mainly by featherwork in these *Wunderkammen* of natural and artificial curiosities was therefore wholly appropriate. And it is hardly surprising to find illustrations of Indian women wearing nothing but toucan feathers in Aldrovandi's book on ornithology [22].

The first century of American exploration coincides with the early development of scientific natural history. During these years the medieval bestiary and herbal gave way, if only slowly, to manuals of ornithology, zoology, and botany based less on the authority of the ancients and hearsay than on direct observation. This may, indeed, be more than a coincidence, for the sudden influx of birds, beasts, fishes, and plants unknown in the Old World stimulated interest in those that were already familiar. And although notable botanists were to discuss, as late as 1620, whether the potato could be identified with plants described by Dioscorides and Theophrastus, such inquiries were increasingly recognized to be anachronistic. Natural history had been transformed into an empirical study aided by—just as it encouraged—the development of more accurate techniques of drawing flora and fauna.

It has often been suggested that the first European zoological and botanical gardens were directly inspired by the gardens of Montezuma. Cortés certainly wrote in his published letters

22. *A Woman of Florida*, from U. Aldrovandi, Ornithologia, 1599

with evident wonder of the numerous ponds in which every type of waterfowl were kept, overhung by balconies from which they might be watched, of the large cages for birds of prey and animals, and of the six hundred men employed to attend to them.

> For the sea birds there were pools of salt water, and for the river birds, of fresh water. . . . Each species of bird is supplied with the food natural to it, which it feeds upon when wild. Thus fish is given to the birds that usually eat it; worms, maize and the finer seeds, to such as prefer them. . . .

There were menageries in Europe but none organized on this scale. Cortés and his companions had less to say about the gardens of herbs and flowers; but it is perhaps significant that the first European botanical garden should have been established in 1545 in Padua—the university city for Venice where very keen interest was taken in the new geographical discoveries. Even if the influence of Montezuma's gardens remains unproven, there can be no doubt about the tonic effect the new flora and fauna, and the need to study and categorize them, had on the development of European science. Aldrovandi, who founded the Orto Botanico in Bologna in 1568 and established in his own house what was virtually the first European museum of natural history, had a special interest in America, as we have already seen. Indeed, he planned a scientific expedition to the Indies with the support, he hoped, of the Grand Duke of Tuscany who—in addition to his Mexican works of art—also boasted American flora and fauna in his gardens and menagerie.

Of all living creatures the birds of the West Indies and South America were those that most impressed the early explorers—not without reason. The parrots particularly appealed for they were both larger and more colorful than the African species already prized in Europe. As we have seen, a group of them—with orange-red, yellow, and green plumage—was used to characterize the fauna of South America on the Cantino planisphere of 1502 [I]. Within an amazingly short time they began to appear in Renaissance painting. A large parrot in the center foreground of one of Carpaccio's series of pictures of the legend of St. George, painted in 1507, must have been brought to Venice from the West Indies [23]. Several more, completely assimilated into classical style *grotesque* decorations, perch on delicate festoons in the Loggetta of the Cardinal of Bibbiena in the Vatican, painted in 1516, probably by Giovanni da Udine, under the

23. Detail of *St. George Baptizing the Gentiles*, 1507. Carpaccio

VII. *A Parrot (Psittacus Araucana)*, 1580s. Jacopo Ligozzi

eye of Raphael [24]. Two or three years later, also in the Vatican, hummingbirds and Mexican quails were introduced into the similar painted decorations in the Logge of Raphael. Sailors brought stuffed specimens of the more colorful South American birds to Europe and three of them (including a toucan) are described and illustrated together with a handsome macaw in Pierre Belon's pioneering study of ornithology of 1555. But the Grand Duke of Tuscany's aviary seems to have boasted live macaws and curassows which were depicted in exquisite watercolors by Jacopo Ligozzi, who supplied copies to Aldrovandi [VII].

The explorers were also fascinated by turkeys. They are indigenous to North America but were domesticated as far south as Veragua where they were first seen, and apparently tasted, by Columbus and his companions in 1502. Information about them was diffused by Peter Martyr who had evidently seen some live specimens in Spain for he gives an extraordinarily vivid description of how they "preen themselves before their females" like peacocks,

> and from time to time at regular intervals, after taking four or more steps, they shiver like the victims of a strong fever when their teeth chatter from cold. They display the different coloured feathers about their necks, sometimes blue, sometimes green or purplish according to the movements of their body.

This behavior was later to strike Shakespeare. "Contemplation makes a rare turkey-cock of

24. Loggetta of Cardinal of Bibbiena in the Vatican, 1516. Raphael and Giovanni da Udine

[37]

Mar occanus occidentalis

El estrecho d'magallanes

him," Fabian says to Malvolio: "how he jets under his advanced plumes." Turkeys (like muscovy ducks, another American species) owe their Eastern name to the fact that they were imported into Europe while the West Indies were still supposed to lie off the shore of Asia. They had probably been imported and bred for some time in Spain before 1525 when they are first recorded in England. But although they had been used to symbolize the fauna of North America on early maps, by Desceliers and others, naturalists—even such learned ornithologists as Gesner and Belon—went on writing that they came from India. And thus the turkey came to regarded as an exotic rather than as a specifically American creature—described as "rich and royal" food by Rabelais in 1542, incorporated into a cartoon for a tapestry representing *Spring* by Agnolo Bronzino in 1549, modeled by Giovanni da Bologna in about 1567 [25], and illustrated by Georg Höfnagel in the magnificent missal he decorated for the Archduke Ferdinand of Tyrol in the 1580s. In the next century the turkey finally found its way to India and into Mughal miniatures. So apart from parrots the only birds which remained "American" in European eyes were those rarely seen alive, even in menageries: the toucan prized for its beak and feathers [26], hummingbirds, and from the far south, the penguin.

While parrots and toucans represented the brilliance and beauty of nature in the New World, the four-footed animals revealed its strangeness. The armadillo soon attracted attention: it was mentioned very briefly by Martín Fernández de Enciso in 1518 and described in bewildering detail by Roger Barlow in his *Brief Summe of Geographie* (1540):

> Ther is a kynde of small beastes no bigger than a pigges of a moneth olde, and the fete the hede and the eares be like a horse, and his bodie and his head is all covered saving his eres with a shell moche like the shell of a tortuga, but it is the very proportion of an armed horse for this shelle hangeth downe by his sides and afore his brest moving as it were hanged by gynowes hinges, or moche like the lappes of a complete harneis. It is an admiration to behold it. Hit fedeth like a horse and his tale is like a pigges taile, saving it is straight.

As a small piglike creature, probably drawn from a description, it appears among the fauna on Diego Ribero's world map of 1529. And it

VIII. American section of a world map, 1551. Sancho Gutiérrez

25. (LEFT) *A Turkey*, c.1567. Giovanni da Bologna
26. (BELOW) *A Toucan*, from A. Thevet, *Les Singularités de la France Antarctique*, 1558

was frequently to be seen on maps and prints later in the century [27] when stuffed specimens had become available, though illusions about its size persisted—perhaps as a result of remarks like that by Walter Raleigh who wrote that it "seemeth to be barred over with small plates somewhat like to a rhinoceros." Eventually it waddled its way into pre-Bellocian verses written by a Dr. Powis toward the end of the seventeenth century:

> This animal is arm'd with Scale
> As if it wore a Coate of Maile
> In shape and snout he is a swine
> And like to him doth grunt and whine.
> But if you view his scaly skin
> Hees Fish without and Swine within
> A creature of Amphibious nature
> And lives both in and out of water. . . .

The opossum, the first marsupial creature ever seen by Europeans, also aroused great curiosity. Vicente Yáñez Pinzón caught a female which he took back to Spain, but the description he wrote of it in 1499 might have been the result of a game of consequences:

> A strange monster, the foremost part resembling a fox, the hinder a monkey, the feet were like a man's, with ears like an owl; under whose belly hung a great Bag, in which it carry'd the young, which they drop not, nor forsake till they can feed themselves.

A very odd creature on Waldseemüller's map of 1516 is clearly based on such a description [28]. By a similar process of comparison with the animals of the Old World, Peter Martyr struggled to give an account of the tapir. "One animal in particular has Nature created in prodigious form," he wrote in his second *Decade* (1516):

> It is a large as a bull, and has a trunk like an elephant; and yet it is not an elephant. Its hide is like a bull's, and yet it is not a bull. Its hoofs resemble those of a horse, but it is not a horse. It has ears like an elephant's, though smaller and drooping, yet they are larger than those of any other animal.

The llama also strained descriptive powers. They were first mentioned in 1525—with the "head and ears of the size of a mule, and the neck and body of the fashion of a camel, the legs of a deer and the tail that of a horse"—in Pigafetta's account of the circumnavigation of the world. Strange beasts answering his description make their first graphic appearance in the Tierra del Peru on a map drawn by Alonzo de Santa Cruz in 1540 (British Museum). By 1551, however, the three types of llama—pacos, which yield alpaca wool, silky-haired vicuñas, and guanacos, which also served as beasts of burden—seem almost to have been distinguished from one another on a world map by Sancho Gutiérrez [VIII]. The value of these animals was soon appreciated and they were imported into Europe from at least as early as 1558 when one is recorded in Antwerp. In 1562 the Italian sculptor Gianpaolo Poggini, in Madrid, protrayed another as the emblem of Peru on the reverse of a medal of Philip II. "I have included it because it is a rare animal and a useful one," he wrote to a friend in Italy; "it gives wool, milk and meat, and it bears loads like an ass."

Some of the creatures which explorers encountered in North America were, of course, already familiar to them, notably the beavers which were so highly prized for their pelts; and several of those of South America could be asso-

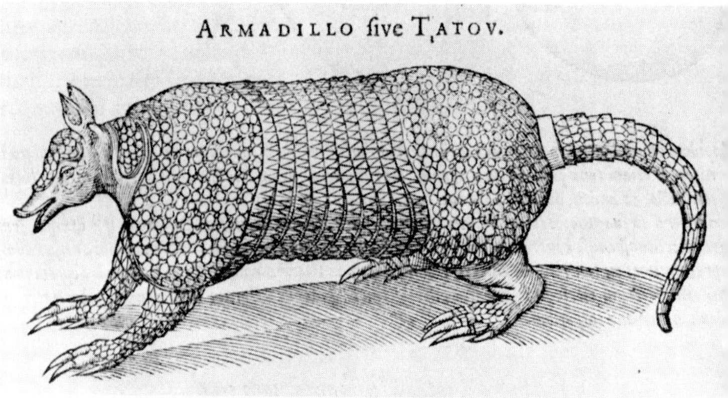

27. *An Armadillo*, from N. Monardes, *Auctarium ad Exoticorum libros*, 1605

28. *An Opossum and Cannibals*, from M. Waldseemüller's *Carta Marina*, 1516

ciated with Old World animals—alligators with crocodiles and peccaries with wild boar. The monkeys did not at first appear so very different from those already known, though Oviedo claimed to have heard of a peculiar one: the upper part of its body was covered with many-colored feathers, the lower with smooth reddish fur, and it sang in tones like those of a nightingale or lark "when it felt inclined." To the early sixteenth-century reader such a creature would have seemed no more fantastic than an armadillo, opossum, llama, or, for that matter, an iguana [29], so like (according to early descriptions) the dragons roaring and romping through late medieval paintings. But, slowly, distinctions were sharpened not only between fabulous and real beasts but also between the denizens of the Old and New Worlds, by artists as well as writers. Thus, in the 1580s, Ligozzi made his remarkably faithful drawings of American birds and even such inconspicuous beasts as the agouti in Florence, for the Grand Duke and for Aldrovandi [30]. At about the same time Stradanus must also have found in the Tuscan Grand Ducal collections the models for the sloth and anteater which he incorporated into his otherwise fantastic evocation of the discovery of America [81]. Monsters might still be associated with the New World, however, even as late as 1671 when several of the oddest were portrayed in the account of the *Nieuwe Weereld* by Arnoldus Montanus [31].

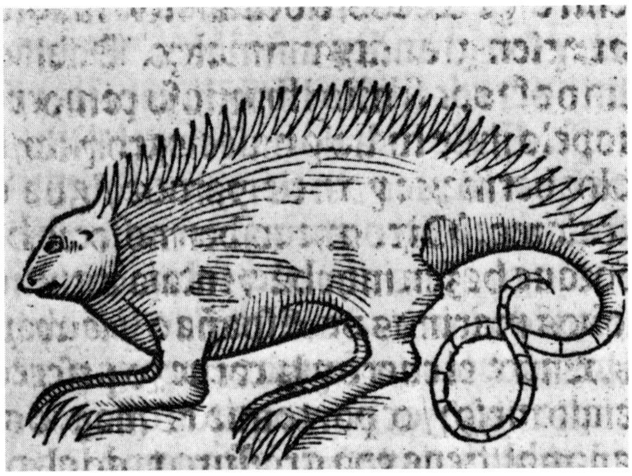

American plants were destined to play a much more important part in the life of Europe than American animals and birds. On his first voyage Columbus seems to have noticed only those which he could associate with Old World species—"palm-trees of six or eight kinds which are a wonder to behold on account of their beautiful variety" and groves of pines. He mistook agaves or yuccas for aloes, the West Indian *Bursera gummifera* for the Levantine mastic tree, *Canella alba* for the cinnamon tree of Southeast Asia, and goodness-knows-what for rhubarb. His botanical observations of the second voyage were more accurate, thanks to the advice of an Italian companion, Guglielmo Coma, who wrote the first description of maize published in 1494. From seed which he brought or sent back, maize was soon being cultivated in Spain and elsewhere in Europe. Indeed, it had been so well established before Magellan's voyage that it was supposed (like the turkey) to come from the Far East, even by botanists. It is still called *granoturco* (Turkish grain) in Italy where, of course, it eventually transformed agriculture and indeed the whole economy of the country.

Maize could easily be associated with types of grain cultivated in the Old World, but tobacco was a complete novelty both in appearance and in the use to which it could be put. On his first voyage Columbus remarked in his logbook on the dried leaves which Indians appeared to value highly. And nearly all subsequent travelers

29. (ABOVE) *An Iguana*, from G. F. de Oviedo, *Coronica de las Indias*, 1547

30. (BELOW) *An Agouti*, 1580s. Jacopo Ligozzi

31. *South American Wildlife*, from A. Montanus, De Nieuwe en Onbekende Weereld, 1671

gave an account of the strange practice of "drinking smoke" [32], the most vivid being that of Benzoni (1565) translated by Hakluyt:

> The smoke goes into the mouth, the throat, the head, and they retain it as long as they can, for they find a pleasure in it, and so much do they fill themselves with this cruel smoke, that they lose their reason. And there are some that take so much of it that they fall down as if they were dead, and remain the greater part of the day or night stupified. Some men are found who are content with imbibing only enough of this smoke to make them giddy, and no more. See what a pestiferous and wicked poison from the devil this must be!

By the time this was printed the tobacco habit had caught on throughout Europe. The growing of tobacco in Europe is not, however, known to have begun before 1554 when Konrad von Gesner raised some plants from seed and had one of them recorded in a watercolor drawing [33].

Monardes, in his account of American plants published in 1565 and "Englished by John Frampton" as *Joyfull Newes out of the Newe Founde Worlde*, remarked on the tobacco plant:

> Within these few yeeres there hath beene brought into Spayne of it, more to adornate Gardens with the fairnesse thereof, and too geve a plesaunt sight, than that it was thought to have the mervellous medicinable vertues which it hath....

Its leaves might be applied externally, he said, as a remedy for numerous complaints, "any griefe of the body, griefe, of the stomake, the stone and griefe of winds," bad breath, toothache, and chilblains. But it was surely for its fairness that Georg Höfnagel included a nicotiana among the exotic and homely flowers with which he adorned the margins of a prayerbook illuminated for Albrecht V of Bavaria in 1570 [34].

FROM THE NEW GOLDEN LAND

Of all American plants imported into Europe in the sixteenth century, the potato had the most extraordinary riches-to-rags career, beginning as a rare and exotic luxury and eventually becoming the staple diet of the poor. In 1493 Columbus brought back from Hispaniola sweet potatoes which were grown successfully in Spain and were imported in greater quantities in subsequent years, being much prized for both their taste and their supposed aphrodisiac effect. This plant, correctly called *Ipomoea*

32. *The Evil Effects of Tobacco*, from G. Benzoni, *La Historia del Mondo Nuovo*, 1565

33. (BELOW, LEFT) *A Tobacco Plant*, c.1554–55. Konrad von Gesner

34. (BELOW) Page from the Prayer Book of Albrecht V of Bavaria, 1570. Georg Höfnagel

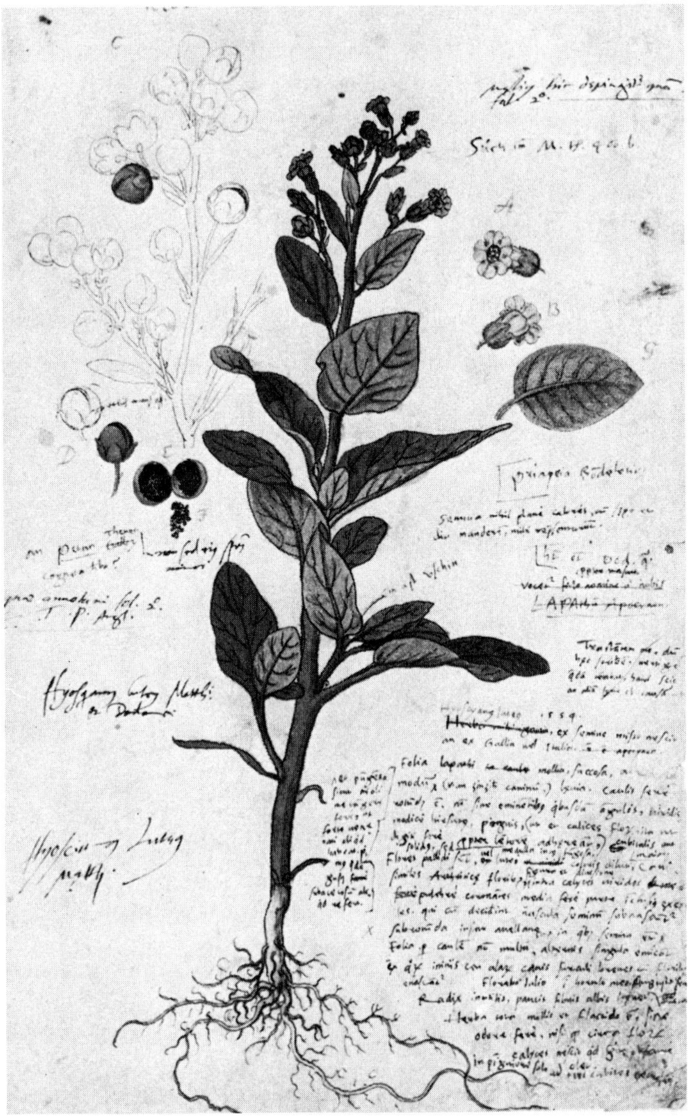

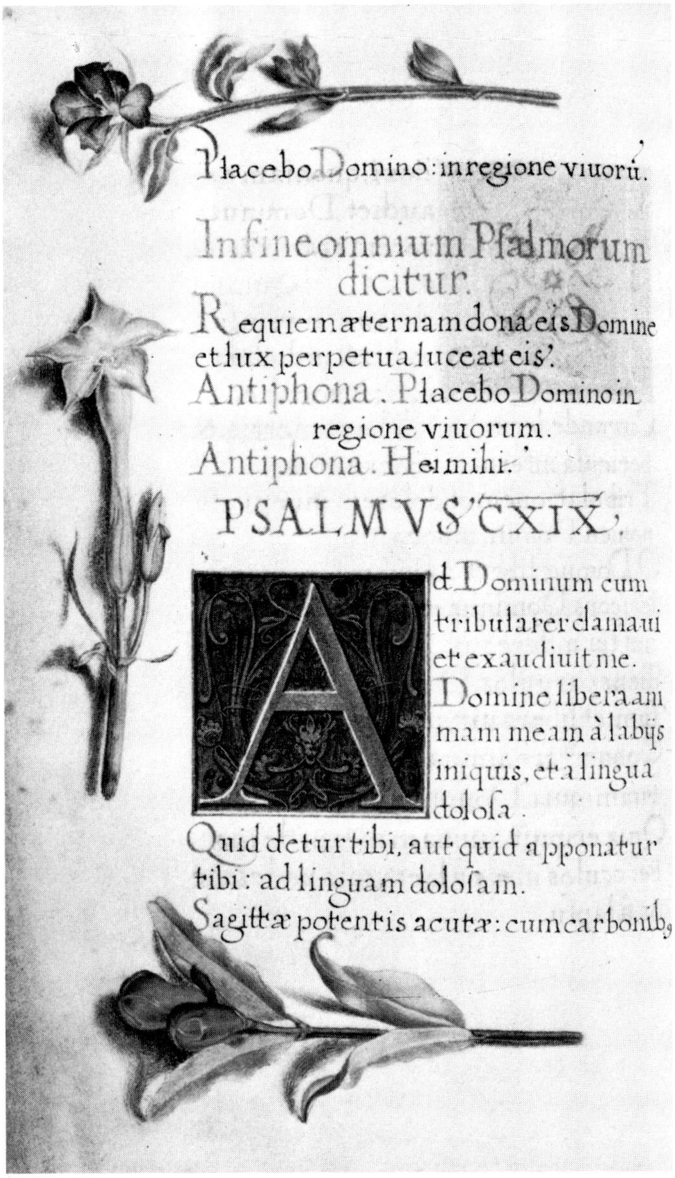

[43]

Batatas (a relation of the morning-glory), is botanically distinct from the common potato, *Solanum tuberosum*, which no European seems to have encountered until 1536 when Gonzalo Jiménez de Quesada led an expedition to the interior of Colombia and took the capital of the Chibcha kingdom, Bogotá. The inhabitants of this high plateau were found to live on maize and beans and what one of the invading party called "truffles," produced by plants with scanty flowers of a dull purple color and floury roots which, he said, were "of good flavor, a gift very acceptable to Indians and a dainty dish even for Spaniards." Two years later Pedro Cieza de León found potatoes near Popayán and was responsible for the first published description of the plant whose roots, he said, "are almost like truffles though they have no firm envelope and these when cooked have a soft pulp like a cooked chestnut." Nevertheless, the Conquistadors seem to have been wary of eating them even in Chile where they were a staple crop.

When the potato was finally introduced into Spain in about 1570 its success was immediate. Other countries soon followed and by the early 1580s it had ceased to be an exotic luxury. In Italy it was already a garden vegetable in 1588. But as a crop it remained relatively uncommon for many years and attempts made to further its cultivation in the late seventeenth century, by the Royal Society in England, for example, met with little success. Not until the mid-eighteenth century was its food value recognized by the peasants of Scotland and Ireland—with disastrous results when the crop failed because of disease in 1845. That a potato famine should have driven thousands of Irish families to emigrate to America is one of the ironies of history.

Clusius, who published the first full account of the potato in 1601, remarked that "they are flatulent, and therefore some use them for exciting Venus," apparently transferring to them an attribute previously given to the sweet potato. Thus Falstaff in *The Merry Wives of Windsor*, embracing Mistress Ford:

> My doe with the black scut?—Let the sky rain potatoes; let it thunder to the tune of *Green Sleeves*; hail kissing-comfits, and snow eringoes; let there come a tempest of provocation, I will shelter me here.

Still stronger sexual "provocation" was supposedly to be derived from tomatoes, introduced from Mexico in the mid-sixteenth century but known in England as "love-apples" until well into the nineteenth (only the latter word is to be found in Johnson's Dictionary). This libidinous association was quickly lost in Italy, however, where the tomato was so widely grown from the seventeenth century onward that it brought about a revolution in the kitchen. Two other American products, vanilla and chocolate, were also credited with aphrodisiac powers. A taste for chocolate was acquired by the Spaniards from the Mexicans at the time of the conquest and by the late eighteenth century cocoa had become one of the main items in the Hispano-American economy.

Among other American products imported into Europe from a very early period, the most notable was a wood which yielded a dye similar to that obtained from the bresel or brasel tree of the East Indies. It was after this tree that a large part of South America was named *terra de brasil*—land of the red dyewood—not the other way round. Brazilians are depicted cutting it on several sixteenth-century maps and also on some handsome mid-sixteenth-century carvings which once decorated a house in Rouen, one of the main French ports for trade with America [35]. (An even brighter red dye of New World origin, made from the cochineal insect found on some types of cactus and bred by the Mexicans, was also introduced into Europe in the sixteenth century.)

Plants used by the natives of America naturally intrigued the explorers. Cassavas, which provided staple foodstuffs, seemed to be the strangest, for while the sweet variety (*Manihot dulcis*) can be eaten raw as a vegetable, bitter cassava (*M. utilissima*) has a root which yields both a virulently poisonous sap and an eminently wholesome flour—tapioca or Brazilian arrowroot. Both need tropical conditions and not even the product of the latter was imported into Europe until the late seventeenth century (though it was to become the bane of many an English child's life from the nineteenth). But they were often confused with yuccas (whose dried roots were eaten by Indians in what is

35. *Dyewood Gatherers in Brazil*, c.1550. Anonymous, French

now the southwestern United States), which were grown as ornamental plants in Europe from the sixteenth century. The agave also caught the eye of early visitors to America, though they usually confused it with the Mediterranean aloe. The Mexicans wove its fibers into fabrics, including a kind of paper, or twisted them into ropes, and from its sap made pulque and the still more violently intoxicating mescal. It was promptly introduced into Europe and grown as an exotic (a specimen was drawn in Florence by Ligozzi in the 1580s [36]). But it remained a rarity until the eighteenth century when it became naturalized on the Mediterranean coast. Another American plant destined to transform the South European litoral was the prickly pear *(Opuntia ficus-indica)* said to have been brought back by Columbus himself [37]. When it first arrived it must have

36. *An Agave*, 1580s. Jacopo Ligozzi

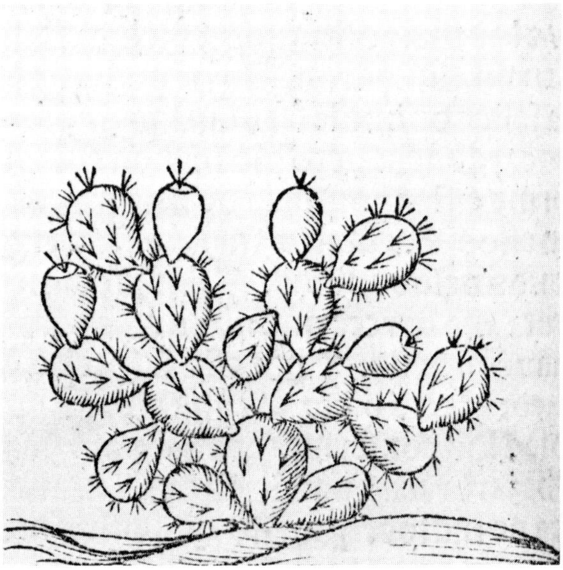

37. *A Prickly Pear*, from G. F. de Oviedo, *Coronica de las Indias*, 1547

THE NEW GOLDEN LAND

astonished Europeans who had previously seen no form of cactus—an exclusively American family of plants and one which epitomized for them the strangeness of the New World [38].

The American fruit which aroused most interest was the pineapple. A consignment was sent to Spain early in the sixteenth century and Peter Martyr reports that King Ferdinand found it superior in taste to all other fruit—adding, sadly, "I have not tasted it myself, for it was the only one which arrived unspoiled, the others having rotted during the long voyage." A century and a half later, John Evelyn had better luck and was given by Charles II—off his own plate—a piece of pineapple sent from Barbados. "It falls short of those ravishing varieties of deliciousness" which travelers had described, the

38. *A Cactus*, from G. B. Ramusio, *Navigationi et Viaggi*, 1565

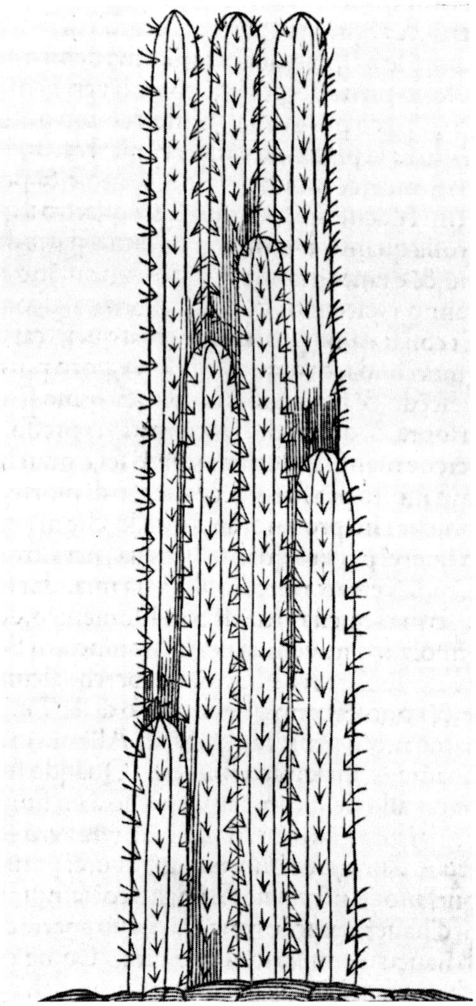

diarist wrote, "but possibly it might, or certainly was, much impaired in coming so far; it has yet a grateful acidity." The impossibility of describing its taste, which one writer likened to "a compound of Strawberye, Claret wine, rose

39. *A Pineapple*, 1580s. Jacopo Ligozzi

water and sugar"—became proverbial. Of this Locke made a philosophical point before the end of the century:

> If a child were kept where he never saw but black and white, he would have no more idea of scarlet, than he that never tasted a pineapple has of that peculiar relish.

The plant could easily be grown under glass in Spain or Italy [39]. But in England artists commemorated the presentation of an imported specimen to the King almost as if it were some outsize, precious jewel and, in 1720, the supreme horticultural achievement of raising one in England [40].

In the meantime many American plants of a purely decorative kind had been introduced into Europe and so easily acclimatized in gardens that their origin was often forgotten. The common sunflower *Helianthus annuus* from Florida, for example, which was a novelty when Monardes wrote of it in 1565 and retained its exotic status when illustrated in the *Hortus Floridus* of 1614 by Crispijn de Passe who listed the variety of names it had already acquired—*Chrysanthemum Peruvianum maius, Tromba d'Amore* (trumpet of love), *Gigante, Groote sonne blome* or *Sonnenkron,* and *Indian Golde sonne*—but had become quite naturalized by about 1633 when Van Dyck used it in his self-portrait to represent the royal patronage of Charles I beaming on him [41]. Its relative *Helianthus tuberosus,* first seen on Cape Cod by Champlain in 1605 and introduced into France between 1609 and 1617, reached England under the double disguise of a "Jerusalem artichoke."

Other sixteenth-century imports from America which have become very familiar throughout Europe included the nasturtium (*Tropaeolum majus*), the morning-glory (*Ipomoea purpurea*), and spiderwort (*Tradescantia virginiana*)—all of which appear among the poppies and crocuses in the margins of Albrecht V's prayer book

40. *The First Pineapple to Fruit in England,* 1720. Theodorus Netscher

41. *Self-Portrait*, 1633. Anthony Van Dyck

illuminated by Georg Höfnagel. Here we also find *Mirabilis jalapa* which, although it was absorbed into the common-or-garden flora of France as *belle de nuit,* preserved its transatlantic nationality in England where it is less easy to grow. In "The Mower against Gardens" Andrew Marvell wrote:

Another World was search'd, through Oceans new,
To find the *Marvel of Peru.*

And it is still known under this attractive soubriquet which is more accurate than its Latin name for it does not, in fact, yield the purgative jalap (derived from a Mexican plant *Ipomoea purga*) [IX].

"We are all devoted to the love of exotic plants, especially those from America," wrote Linnaeus in 1737. America was, indeed, the main source for *exotica* until the nineteenth century when botanists were first able to explore Central Asia, China, and Japan. Moreover, coming from the high lands of the tropics and the temperate zone, American exotics could easily be acclimatized in Europe, unlike most introductions from Africa and India. Dogwood (*Cornus florida*) and the first of the passion flowers (*Passiflora caerulea*) arrived before the end of the seventeenth century, the stately *Magnolia grandiflora* with its glossy leaves and huge lemon-scented blossoms in the early eighteenth, and gaudy dahlias with quilled petals, which had been hybridized in Aztec gardens, in the 1790s. Such a steady supply of outstanding horticultural novelties could hardly fail to keep alive the image of America as a land of unequaled natural riches.

As very few European students of natural history were able to go to America, most were obliged to study imported specimens and rely on the reports of travelers, few of whom had much scientific knowledge. In 1565 Monardes was able to describe only those American plants which were growing in Seville, and seventy years later Jacques Philippe Cornut based his pioneer flora of Canada — *Canadensium Plantarum* — on what he could see in the gardens of Paris. A properly equipped scientific exploration of the New World was clearly needed. Philip II dispatched an expedition to study the natural history of New Spain under physician and naturalist Francisco Hernández in 1571. But its discoveries remained unpublished until 1651. Hence the outstanding importance of Count Johan Maurits of Nassau-Siegen who organized a team of scientists and artists to study and record all aspects of the natural history of Brazil, while he was Dutch colonial governor there between 1638 and 1644.

The best known of the artists employed by Count Maurits is Frans Post, who made numerous records of the landscape on the spot, went on painting it from notes and memory long after he returned to Holland, and even used a Brazilian setting, complete with cactus and armadillo, for an Old Testament picture — the Sacrifice of Manoah, now in the Boymans–van Beuningen Museum, Rotterdam. His task seems to have been the representation of general aspects of the terrain, the natural scene as a whole, with its strange animals and plants, but also the relics of Portuguese rule and the new buildings and plantations of the Dutch [X]. Albert Eckhout specialized in painting the inhabitants [69–73, XIV] — Indian, European, African, and mixed — as well as the birds and plants. In a series of enormous still-life paintings he assembled pine-

IX. *Marvel of Peru (Mirabilis Jalapa),* 1580s. Jacopo Ligozzi

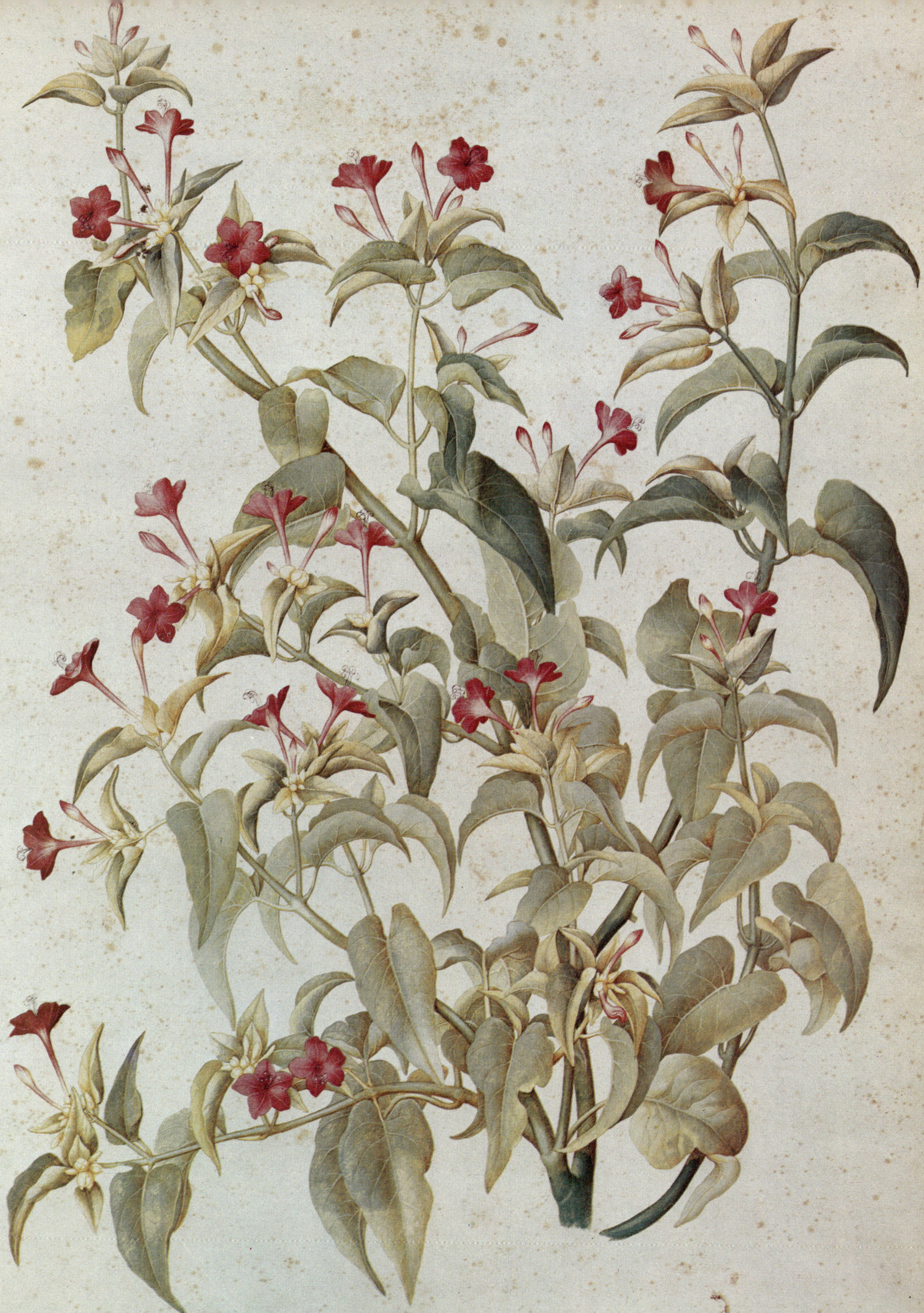

apples, melons, various types of gourd, brightly colored peppers, passion fruit, and the nuts of the coconut palm, all depicted over life-size and very close-up so that they almost overpower one with their succulence. He alone of all the artists who went to America succeeded in capturing the sense of wonder which these strange vegetable products excited in Europeans [42]. The scientists in the group included William Pies, better known as Piso, who was mainly concerned with botany and the more talented Georg Marcgrave who was engaged as an astronomer but, equally interested in terrestial matters, executed numerous careful watercolors of flora and fauna. The results of their combined researches were published in Leiden in 1648 at the expense of Count Maurits and provided the first full and accurate account of the natural history of any part of the New World—and one that was to remain a standard work for a century and a half.

42. *Brazilian Fruits*, 1640–43. Albert Eckhout

Books on other aspects of American natural history appeared in steadily increasing numbers from the late seventeenth century—Charles Plumier's on plants (with a volume devoted to ferns), Maria Sibylla Merian's account of the insects of Surinam (with scientifically accurate illustrations and a mystical text), Mark Catesby's *Natural History of Carolina, Florida, and the Bahama Islands*, and so on. They all demonstrated, some more explicitly than others, the difference between nature in the New World and the Old. Introducing the work of Marcgrave and Piso, the publisher remarked that they had "established that the quadrupeds, birds, snakes, fishes and insects of America, though related to those of the Old World are nonetheless distinct." The difference had, of course, been noticed already by writers unaware of the niceties of taxonomy—by poets such as Mellin de Saint-Gelais in 1556, for example. And while Drayton contrived to mention only one indigenous American plant in his poem on Virginia, "Earth's onely Paradise," Edmund Waller later worked several into his account of Bermuda: the "candid plantanes and the juicy pine," potatoes, "sweet palmette . . . leaves as ample as the broadest shield," and even the "fair Papah."

It was not until the mid-eighteenth century, however, that the great systematist Buffon published what he considered a deduction from the accumulated store of evidence, and one of which he was extremely proud:

> The greatest fact, the most general, the least known to all naturalists before me; this fact is that the animals in the southern part of the Old World are not to be found in the New, and reciprocally those of South America are not to be found in the old continent.

Nor was he content with this! He went on to claim that the animals of America were genetically inferior to those of the Old World, comparing the "ridiculous" tapir, no larger than a mule, with the elephant, the llama with the camel, and the "cowardly" puma with the noble lion. All domestic animals when transported to America, he wrote, declined in vigor and size, with the solitary exception of the pig. On the other hand, reptiles and insects flourished there as nowhere else. The reason for this state of affairs he found in the climate, for America, he believed, had emerged from the waters of the flood later than the continents of the Old World and was therefore still somewhat humid!

> Let us see why such large reptiles, such huge insects and such small quadrupeds and frigid men are found in the New World. It is to be attributed to the quality of the earth, the condition of the sky, the degrees of heat and humidity, to the situation, to the height of the mountains, to the quantity of flowing and stagnant water, to the extent of the forests, and above all to the raw state of nature.

This preposterous theory was to be widely popularized and repeated, as we shall see, times out of number by European writers in the course of the next century and a half. And it was to be no less frequently contradicted by numerous Americans.

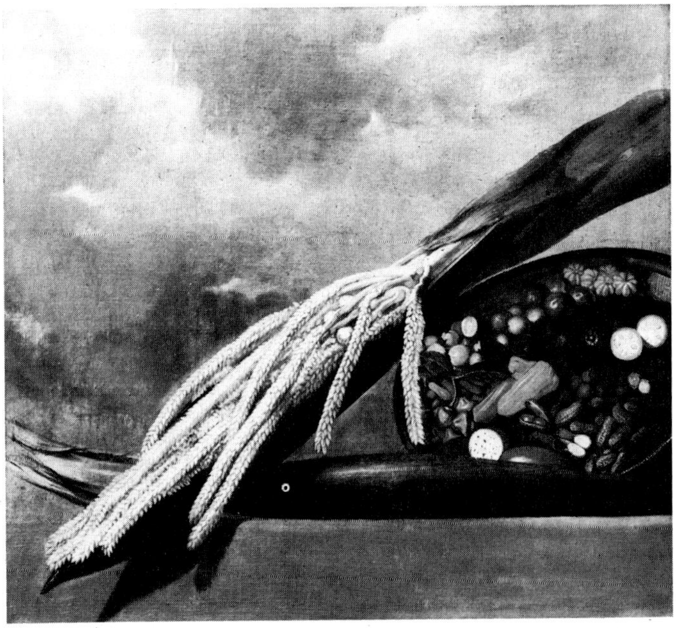

x. *Panorama in Brazil*, 1652. Frans Post

CHAPTER 3

True Men

IN A PORTUGUESE PAINTING of the *Adoration of the Magi*, probably dating from the first decade of the sixteenth century, the place traditionally occupied by the black Magus has been taken by a coppery-skinned Brazilian [43]. He wears a feather headdress—like those worn by the people of "Calicut" in the *Triumph of Maximilian I* [9a]—gold earrings, bracelets, and anklets, and a pearl necklace. In one hand he carries a bowl made from half a coconut and filled with gold nuggets, and in the other a wooden weapon with a flattened blade such as Brazilians were known to use. Only in one respect does he differ from the image of the American Indian which was soon to become conventional—his nakedness is covered with a richly patterned shirt and breeches, presumably to make him presentable to the Holy Family. Few savages could appear more gentle, courteous, and eminently human. But in another Portuguese religious painting, of about half a century later, a similar feather headdress and mantle of featherwork are worn by the Devil himself, presiding over the torments of the damned [44, XI].

These two pictures are divided from one another by more than just an interval of fifty years. The charming notion that one of the Wise Men might have followed the star all the way from Brazil to Bethlehem could hardly survive—even in a poetic sense—the discovery that the New World was not a part of Asia but a separate continent. Nor could first impressions of the Brazilians remain unmodified by later experience. The two pictures reflect these contrasting views of them—as they appeared at first sight and on closer acquaintance. The figure in the *Adoration*

43. *Adoration of the Magi*, c.1505.
The Master of Viseu

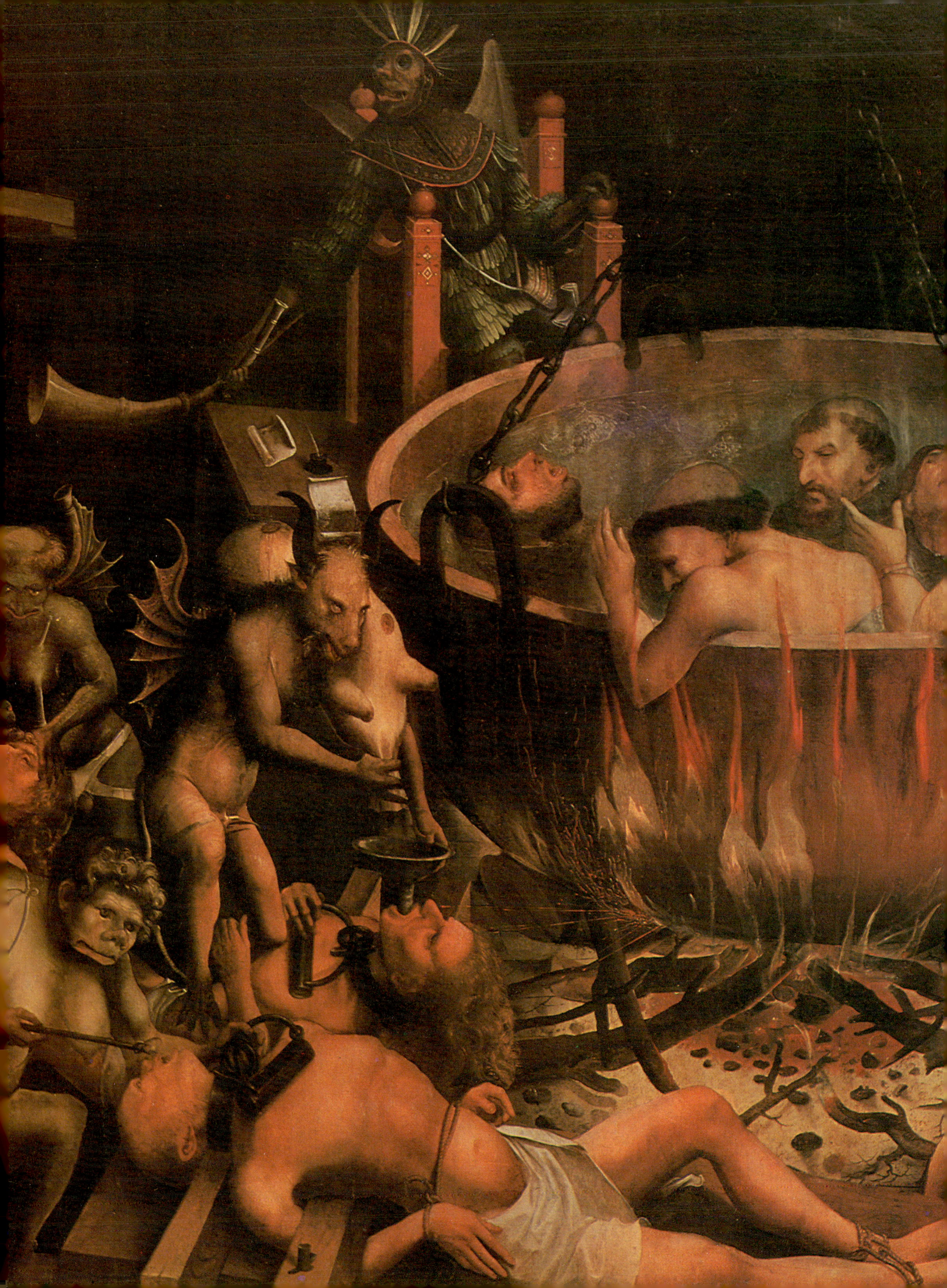

44. *Inferno*, c.1550. Anonymous, Portuguese

of the Magi might almost illustrate the first written description in Pedro Vaz de Caminha's eyewitness account of Cabral's discovery of Brazil in 1500:

> They seem to me to be people of such innocence that, if we could understand them and they us, they would soon become Christians.... For it is certain that this people is good and of pure simplicity, and there can easily be stamped upon them whatever belief we wish to give them. And furthermore, Our Lord gave them fine bodies and good faces as to good men, and He who brought us here, I believe, did not do so without purpose.

The same favorable view was to be taken by some later visitors to the same region, notably Jean de Léry who joined the short-lived French colony established there by Villegagnon in 1555. But familiarity often bred distaste. Two months in Brazil sufficed to convince the Franciscan missionary André Thevet that despite some good qualities, the natives lacked both the power of reason and the knowledge of God and hence were irredeemably given over to the Devil. Villegagnon, in a letter to John Calvin, dismissed them as "beasts in human form."

Such contrary opinions illustrate the difficulties experienced by sixteenth-century Europeans in coming to terms with the population of the New World. It confronted them with far more perplexing problems than the flora and fauna—problems both practical and theoretical, religious and philosophic. For they found themselves obliged to determine the place of the American Indians (or Amerindians as the indigenous races of the New World were later called) not only in a European colony but in the Christian Church and Christian community and, ultimately, in Creation. And this raised several central, challenging questions of morals and religion.

The whole issue was complicated by the belief that the majority of American Indians them-

XI. Detail of *Inferno*, c.1550. Anonymous, Portuguese

selves had no political or social organization, religious creed, or moral system. They lived, as Vespucci remarked, "according to nature," without kings, priests, or laws—*sans roi, sans loi, sans foi*, as sixteenth-century French writers seldom failed to remark. This led to two conflicting attitudes toward them—either that their prelapsarian state of innocence was such that they had no need for kings, priests, or laws; or, as most settlers held, that they were merely brutes, like the beasts of the jungle. The former view, which associated them with the Golden Age, could hardly be maintained when more became known about them, especially about their state of perpetual warfare, their cannibalism, and their sexual license. Indeed, their way of life helped to dispel the myth of the Golden Age itself. Yet the latter view, linking them with the cruel, lascivious, bestially hirsute, and deformed savages or "wild men" of medieval and Renaissance literature (the German *wilder Mann* who lived in a cave or under trees like a wild beast, naked and covered with hair) seemed to be denied by their physical appearance, by their hairless, smooth, and well-proportioned bodies which some, including Verrazzano who was eventually to be eaten by them, even went so far as to liken to Greek and Roman statues! However they were considered, the Indians were intractable: they broke whatever pattern Europeans tried to fit them into.

The great debate on the status and nature of the American Indians, which raged throughout the sixteenth century, began with a purely practical issue. As soon as Columbus decided to colonize Hispaniola and not merely build trading stations, like those of the Portuguese on the African coast, the way in which it was to be organized had to be decided. The Spanish Crown opted for a simple extension of the feudal system, treating the settlers as lords to whom grants of land were made with native Indian "serfs" to work them. This proved disastrous. The Indians of Hispaniola had neither the inherited subservience nor the physical capacity for labor of European villeins and they soon began to die off. Though probably due mainly to their inability to resist germs and infections imported from Europe, their decimation was generally ascribed to the cruelty of their Spanish taskmasters and, to save them from further exploitation and provide an alternative labor force, Queen Isabella was persuaded in 1503 to issue a decree restricting enslavement to "a certain people called Cannibals." Whether this was intended to refer strictly to man-eaters or merely to the less docile inhabitants of other Caribbean islands, it was interpreted as a license to enslave any Indian from any of the islands suspected of cannibalism. However, they too proved to be unsatisfactory laborers and from 1518 African slaves were imported in ever increasing numbers.

In their relations with the less friendly tribes—and later with the Aztec and Inca empires—the Spaniards reverted to European precedents. According to a decree issued by King Ferdinand in 1513 no conquests were to be made unless the local population failed to respond to an injunction formally read to them in the presence of witnesses. This preposterous document began by declaring that Pope Alexander VI "gave these islands and mainland" to the sovereigns of Spain and went on to demand that the natives should "recognize the Church and its highest priest, the Pope, as rulers of the universe, and in their name the King and Queen of Spain as the rulers of this land, allowing the religious fathers to preach the holy faith to you." Should the Indians resist, they were to be treated as "disobedient vassals"—in other words, as rebels rather than as enemies according to the code of medieval warfare. In this way the New World was ranked, legalistically, as a remote province of Spain; and in future the *conquista* was to be referred to as the *pacificación*.

As this document reminds us, the occupation of the islands and the American mainland was undertaken in the name of the Church as well as the State. The missionaries who began to arrive in 1502 were soon attributing their conspicuous lack of success to the way in which the Indians were being treated. So long as the settlers were massacring, or enslaving the men and debauching the women, the religious fathers could hardly expect to make many converts. They therefore appealed to the Catholic sovereigns to protect their new subjects. The substance of their complaint was not purely humanitarian: it arose because they were being impeded in their mission of saving Indians' souls. But as the conflict between them and the colonists developed, it took on a wider significance. Both parties were obliged to question whether the Indians could be regarded as normal subjects of the Crown, as members of the Church, or even as human beings—and the resulting division of opinion was no longer the simple one of that between the laity and the clerics.

At this time man was commonly believed to have been set apart from the rest of creation by two criteria: his rationality and his receptivity to divine grace. The former, a classical conception derived mainly from Aristotle, excluded beings so nearly bestial that they seemed fit only to be slaves of rational men. The latter, which was Christian, cut out associates of the devil. To many of the first settlers and even to some missionaries the Indians were beyond the pale on both counts, for their way of life seemed bestial, their indulgence in cannibalism and other "unnatural" practices (especially sodomy) diabolical. The prevalence of this view can nowhere be more clearly seen than on early maps of the New World, so beautifully and often so revealingly decorated. The American Indian is almost always shown either as a simple gatherer of brazilwood or as a cannibal, chopping up another Indian and preparing a fire and spit to barbecue him [45]. The civilizations of Mexico and Peru were of course recognized as superior to the primitive cultures of the islands and southwest coast, but their religious rites, involving human sacrifice, were perforce construed as devil worship.

A member of the Spanish royal council declared in 1517 that the American Indians were so low in the scale of humanity that they were incapable of receiving the faith; and in 1528 a Dominican father, Domingo de Betanzos, said that their bestiality condemned them providentially to a rapid and well-deserved extinction. In fact, they were not to be regarded as human beings at all. The belief that they had incurred the curse of God was widespread. His hand was seen in the overthrow of the Aztecs—a just punishment for their crimes—and all Indians came under the condemnation of the Dominican Tommaso Ortiz whose remarks on them were widely diffused in Peter Martyr's *Decades* (1515):

45. Detail from the Grynaeus world map, 1555

> They eat human flesh on the mainland; they are more given to sodomy than any other race; there is no sense of justice among them. . . . They are bestial and vaunt their abominable vices . . . they understand neither teaching nor punishment . . . they are wholly inimicable to religion . . . up to the age of ten or twelve they seem as if they might eventually acquire some beliefs and virtues, but growing up they change into brute beasts.

He ended by remarking that he would never have believed that God should have created a race at once so obstinate in its viciousness and bestiality and so lacking in any redeeming virtues.

To some extent such comments reflect, no doubt, the opinion of settlers who wanted to enslave the Indians or had some other interest in denigrating them. But their origins were deeper and more complicated, and their implications wider. As early as 1520 reports of the Indians inspired that bold thinker Paracelsus to assert the plurality of the races of mankind. For although the people who had been found "in the out-of-the-way islands" were fashioned in God's image, no one, he wrote,

> will easily believe that they are of the posterity of Adam and Eve, for the sons of Adam by no means departed into out-of-the-way islands. It is most probable that they are descended from another Adam. For no one will easily prove that they are allied to us by flesh and blood.

In another passage he suggested that they had been born

> after the deluge, and perhaps they have no souls. In speech they are like parrots. . . .

This theory of polygenesis was, of course, heretical and no other writer of the sixteenth century is known to have committed such bold thoughts to paper. But the frequency of references to the unashamed nakedness of the Indians, their toil-free way of life, and the astonishing ease with which their women gave birth suggests that it may have occurred to others besides Paracelsus that they might not have been descended from Adam and Eve. Even for those who thought they were, their unashamed, prelapsarian nakedness remained for long a very perplexing problem. As John Donne was to write in 1598:

> That unripe side of the earth, that heavy clime
> That gives us man up now, like *Adams* time
> Before he ate; mans shape, that would yet bee
> (Knew they not it, and fear'd beasts companie)
> So naked as this day, as though man there
> From Paradise so great a distance were,
> As yet the newes could not arrived bee
> Of *Adams* tasting the forbidden tree;
> Depriv'd of that free state which they were in,
> And wanting the reward, yet beare the sinne.

Francisco de Vitoria, Bartolomé de Las Casas, and others who sought to protect the Indians from the settlers maintained that reports of cannibalism and other vices were grossly exaggerated. They also denied that the Indians lived without religion or laws. Vitoria in 1532 descried "a certain method in their affairs," an institution of marriage, a system of barter which called for the use of reason, and even "a kind of religion." Las Casas found in the human sacrifices of the Aztecs evidence of a misguided religious sense which could, he believed, be rectified by Christian teaching. And as for cannibalism: had not the Irish practiced it in their unregenerate days before the arrival of Christian missionaries?

Appeals to the Crown to protect the Indians seemed to have little effect, so the higher authority of the Papacy was invoked. The first of several reports was sent to Leo X in 1517. But it was not until 1535 that the Bishop of Tlaxcala wrote to Paul III praising the intelligence of the Indians and describing them as "neither turbulent nor ungovernable," "but reverent, shy and obedient to their teachers." The suggestion that they were incapable of receiving the doctrines of the Church had, he said, "surely been prompted by the devil himself." Two years later a Dominican missionary, Bernadino de Minaya, who had worked in Mexico and Nicaragua, went to Rome to state the case of the Indians in person. The result was the bull *Sublimis Deus* promulgated by Paul III on June 9, 1537, declaring the Indians to be "true men" capable and desirous of receiving the Catholic faith. They were not to be treated as "dumb brutes created for our service": that was an idea inspired by "the enemy of the human race."

> The said Indians and all other people who may later be discovered by Christians, are by no means to be deprived of their liberty or the possession of their property, even though they may be outside the faith of Jesus Christ . . . nor should they be in any way enslaved.

This was an authoritative statement which no Catholic could ignore, but the dispute continued nevertheless and the Indians went on being exploited. In the very year the bull was promulgated Gonzalo Fernández de Oviedo issued the second part of his *Historia general y natural de las Indias* containing the fullest and most lurid account of their way of life, with many salacious details about their deviant sexual practices. By this time so many contradictory notions about them were current that a public debate was ordained by Charles V which opened at Valladolid in 1550 and lasted for more than a year. The report fills some 870 folio pages. The disputants were J. G. de Sepúlveda, a formidable theologian and classical scholar, and Las Casas. The former, taking much of his information from Oviedo, argued that the Indians were "natural slaves" in the Aristotelian sense. Las Casas, in his rebuttal, held the Indians to be physically weak but intelligent (the very opposite of Aristotle's definition of slaves), extolled their virtues, and even compared them with the ancient Greeks and Romans. In the fervor of the debate he was carried away by righteous indignation and rose above the immediate issue to a magnificent condemnation of the whole institution of slavery as an outrage against the dignity of man. As he wrote soon afterward:

> All the men of the world, however barbarous and bestial they may be, necessarily possess the faculty of reason and are capable of all things pertaining to man, and thus of being taught and improved.

But in 1550 the great debate seemed inconclusive to the judges, and the Indians of Hispano-America continued to be treated as slaves in fact if not in legal terms until long after the end of the century.

While discussion raged around the status of the Indians many Europeans had opportunities to inspect live specimens. Columbus had brought some back with him from his first voyage, as we have already seen, and by the end of the fifteenth century quite large numbers were being taken to Spain as slaves. But few of them survived for long and their importation was found unprofitable. Very soon it was officially prohibited. As they were generally regarded, in these early years, merely as savages living on

46(a). *Mexicans*, 1529. Christoph Weiditz

THE NEW GOLDEN LAND

the fringe of Asia and therefore not greatly unlike the Asiatics with whom Europeans had long been familiar, they aroused relatively little attention. In 1525 when a ship docked at Corunna and word spread that it carried a cargo of cloves (*clavos*), high hopes were dashed by the discovery that it brought nothing more glamorous than slaves (*esclavos*), illegally captured in North America. They were promptly released by the port officials.

Far greater curiosity was aroused by the Mexicans brought to Spain by Cortés in 1528, for they were not only inhabitants of a New World known by then to be completely separate from Asia, but were representatives of the Aztec empire of which such barely credible stories were already circulating. They included two princes, eight jugglers, and twelve ballplayers. Christoph Weiditz, a draftsman and medalist from Augsburg, saw them perform before Charles V in Toledo and recorded their appearance and antics in a fascinating series of drawings which brings them vividly before us—in motion, too, for to depict one of their antics he used a strip-cartoon technique. Keenly observant, a few swift strokes of his pen were enough to delineate their recognizably Mexican features and the strange way in which jewels were set in the skin of their cheeks and lips and foreheads. On two pages a pair play a game with small pieces of wood which reminded Weiditz of *morra* as seen in the streets of Italy [46b]; another two

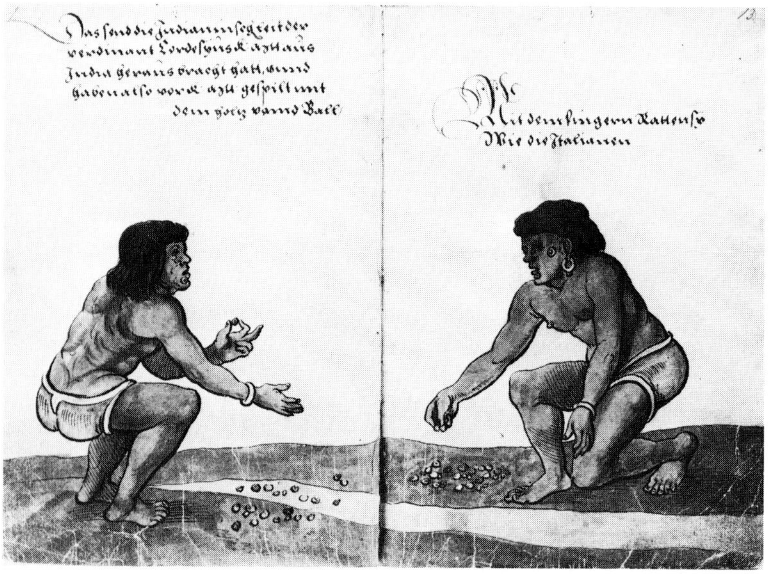

46(b). *Mexicans*, 1528. Christoph Weiditz

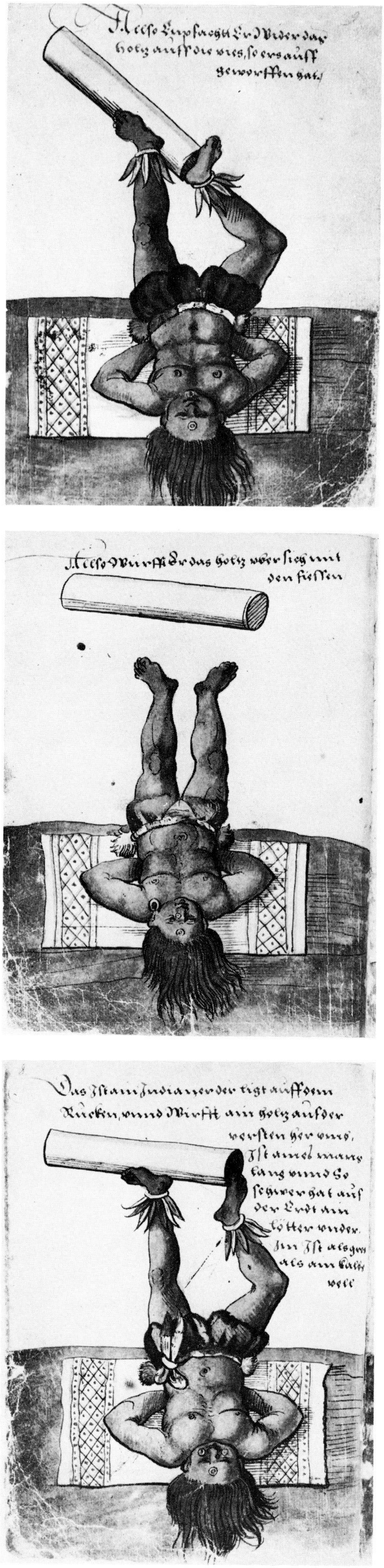

47. *Mexican Jugglers*, 1528. Christoph Weiditz

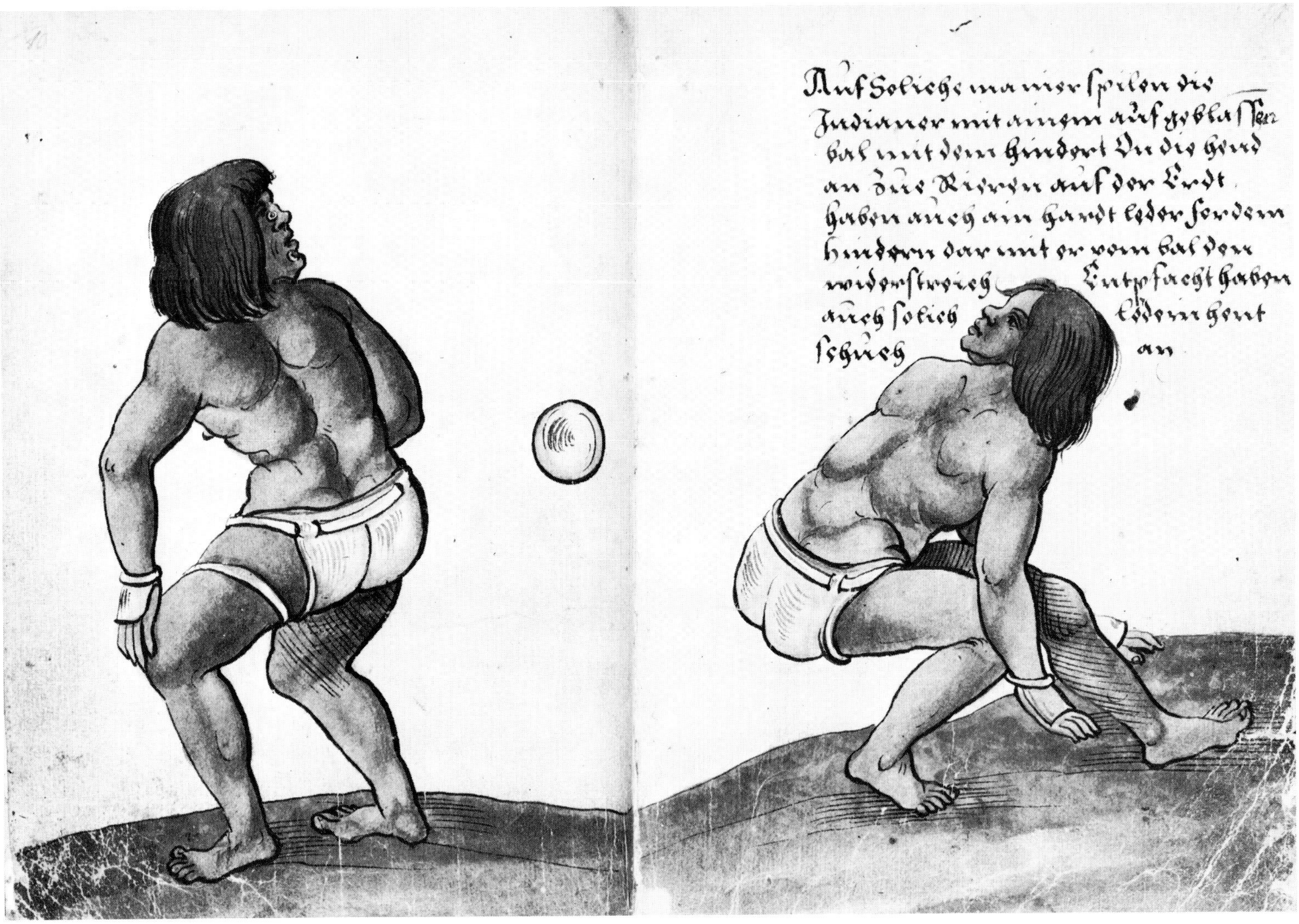

48. *Mexican Ball Players*, 1528. Christoph Weiditz

sheets are devoted to their much more bizarre back-to-front ball game [48]. But three sheets were needed to show how they juggled a log with their feet, tossing it up, spinning, into the air and catching it again [47]. Some of these Mexicans were sent down to Rome by Cortés in 1529 and they "juggled the stick with their feet" before Clement VII who was simply delighted with them and said that "he thanked God that such countries had been discovered in his days." It seems likely that they also visited the Low Countries, for their features appear on carved capitals of about this date in the courtyard of the episcopal palace in Liège, wearing Aztec headdresses and fiercely confronting one another or staring out through leaves of acanthus [49].

49. Capitals in the Episcopal Palace, Liège, c.1529

50. *Mexican Woman*, c.1550. Anonymous

must surely have been working under their influence.

It was, however, from more primitive tribes that most Europeans derived their impressions of the Indians. As we have already seen, a few of those from Newfoundland were taken both to Portugal in 1501 and to England in 1502. Others from Cape Breton reached France in 1508. These were of "a sooty colour," according to a contemporary chronicler, "with black hair like a horse's mane, having no beard . . . they have a speech but no religion." However, the idea of the American savage was to be dominated (outside Spain) by the Tupinamba of Brazil, brought back with cargoes of dyewood to Portugal, France, and England. In 1505 Binot Palmier de Gonneville came back with one, the son of a chief, named Essomericq, whom he had instructed in the Christian faith and married to his daughter. Returning to England from a South American voyage in 1532 William Hawkins pre-

51. *A Man from Acapulco*, c.1550. Anonymous

Mexicans of a more dignified bearing, fully measuring up to accounts of them by Las Casas, appear in six drawings, by an European (probably Spanish) artist, attached to a codex painted in the Valley of Mexico in the early 1550s. They have, indeed, an entirely European, almost classical, poise. A woman wearing a long striped garment is shown pouring liquid from a ewer into a cup with a sacramental gesture, another carries a basket on her head [50], while a third delicately holds a flower in her hand. A male figure dressed in sandals, tunic, and cloak might be mistaken for an ancient Roman were it not for the inscription identifying him as an *yndio de mexico*. Another, "from Acapulco on the South Sea," carrying a bow and arrow reveals his "savagery" only in his scanty garb—loincloth, arm and wrist bands, bangles, and the square cloak called a *tilmantli* [51]. If the artist was not himself one of the missionaries who followed Las Casas in protecting the Indians, he

sented to Henry VIII a Brazilian chief, at the sight of whom—so Hakluyt records,

> the King and all the nobility did not a little marvel, and not without cause: for in his cheeks were holes made according to their savage manner, and therein small bones were planted, standing an inch out of the said holes, which in his own country was reputed for a great bravery. He had also another hole in his nether lip, wherein was set a precious stone about the bigness of a pea; all his apparel, behaviour and gesture, were very strange to the beholders.

At this date the trade in dyewood was very actively pursued by the French. Dieppe was one of the main ports for it and here in the 1520s Jacques Ango, the *corsaire* and the owner of a fleet of merchantmen, had Brazilian figures carved on a frieze to decorate his family chapel in the parish church of Saint-Jacques (all but obliterated nowadays but still recognizable in a nineteenth-century print). In Rouen, the main market for the dyes, a merchant decorated his house with carvings of Brazilians hewing wood and carrying it to waiting ships [35]. When Henri II paid a state visit to Rouen in 1550 a Brazilian jungle village was put up on the banks of the Seine where some fifty natives were to be seen dancing, fighting, shooting at birds with bows and arrows, climbing trees, and paddling canoes while a crowned couple looked on from a hammock. The extraordinary scene was both described and illustrated in a book published to commemorate the visit [52]. Five years later Villegagnon established the French colony in Brazil, and more natives were brought to France and some of them (or Frenchmen dressed to resemble them) took part in several of the enter-

52. *Brazilian Fête at Rouen*, 1551. Anonymous, French

tainments devised for Charles IX when he made state visits to provincial capitals—in Rouen in 1563 (when Montaigne, a member of his court, spoke with them), in Troyes in 1564, when they defiled past him, some mounted on asses, others on goats—"chose fort plaisante a veoir," a chronicler remarked—and at Bordeaux in 1565.

Partly as a result of the French enterprise, Brazil was better known, or at any rate more talked about, than any other part of America at this period, and inspired three notable travel books. The first and in many ways the most interesting is that by a German mercenary in the Portuguese service, Hans Staden, vividly titled a "Truthful History and Description of a Landscape of Wild, Naked, Cruel Man-Eating People in the New World of America" (*Wahrhaftiger Historia und beschreibung einer Landtschaft der Wilden Nacketen Grimmigen Menschenfresser Leuthen in der Newenwelt America*), which was first published in 1557 and soon became a best-seller. Written in a brisk, direct manner and illustrated with woodcuts after his own amateurish but very revealing drawings, it remains a prime source of ethnological information about the Tupinamba as they were only shortly after they first came into contact with the Europeans, describing their religious beliefs, marriage customs, methods of agriculture, hunting, and fishing, and the ways in which they adorned their naked bodies with pigments, shells, stones, and feathers. But this was not Staden's intention, of course. His aim was to recount how God preserved him, a Lutheran, after he had been taken prisoner by them. They stripped him down to their own state of nudity and led him to their village, forcing him to announce his arrival by crying out: "Here I come, food for you" [53]. Once he learned their language sufficiently, he overheard his captors coolly discussing which of them was to eat which part of his body. Cannibalism is therefore the main subject of his book and he recorded its rites in great and gruesome detail. But while appreciating that the Indians eat their captives "not for hunger but for great hatred and jealousy," he admitted that they were not uninfluenced by gourmandise. On one occasion he boldly reproached the great chief Quoniambec who was gnawing on a human leg, saying "not even unreasoning beasts eat each other." The chief replied that he was a jaguar and the flesh had a good flavor.

53. *Hans Staden among the Brazilian Cannibals*, 1557. Anonymous, after Hans Staden

54. *Brazilian Indians Making Fire*, from A. Thevet, *Les Singularités de la France Antarctique*, 1557

André Thevet's *Les Singularités de la France Antarctique autrement nomée Amérique* (1557), though based on less harrowing experiences — he was safely ill in bed for much of his two months in Brazil — provided an equally unappealing picture of the same tribe, filled out with much information about flora and fauna (sometimes fanciful). It was widely read and played an important part in forming the French vision of the Brazilians, especially through its illustrations which showed them as classical figures, apart from the odd panaches with which they adorned their buttocks [54]. Strangely, Jean de Léry's much more favorable account, *Histoire d'un voyage faict en la terre du Brésil* (1578), has less idealized illustrations, one of which ingeniously combines a man and woman and their child, with all their hairless nudity in a hammock, an oddly rendered pineapple, and a plate of avocado pears [55]. Whereas Thevet was shocked by the nakedness of the people, crossly remarking that they could as easily have woven themselves shirts as hammocks, Léry delighted in it. "It should not be supposed that the nakedness of the women excites lust among the men," he remarked more than once: on the contrary, the elaborate clothes and jewels worn by Parisian ladies were "without comparison the source of greater evils than the ordinary nudity of the savage women who in their natural state are not a whit less beautiful." He was also charmed by their strange features and gestures,

> so different from ours that I must admit my inability to represent them in words or in pictures. To enjoy the real pleasure of them, you will have to go and visit them in their country.

Yet despite the wealth of new information about America published shortly after the mid-century, Europeans still clung tenaciously to their old ideas about the Indians derived from Vespucci and Peter Martyr. Thus, Pierre de Ronsard, who had read Thevet's *Singularités*, continued nevertheless to believe that the Brazilians were "now living in their golden age." In his *Complainte contre Fortune* (1559) he told "pauvre Villegagnon" that he was making a great mistake in wishing to change the lives of a people who "wander innocently, completely savage and completely naked, as free from clothes as from malice, who know not the words 'virtue' and 'vice', 'senate' and 'king,' who live according to their pleasure, satisfying their appetites and who have in their hearts none of that terror of the law which makes us live in fear." Their only master is Nature, they have no private property. Leave them in that happy state, he begged, untormented by bitter ambition:

> Ils vivent maintenant en leur âge doré.

Writing in a moment of disillusionment with worldly ambitions, Ronsard was probably thinking as much of the golden age of his own boyhood in the Vendée (a recurrent theme in his work) as of the life of the Tupinamba in the Brazilian jungle. But his poem played an important part in idealizing the happy and natural life of the American savages.

The roseate vision of the Brazilians was given still wider currency by Michel de Montaigne in

55. *Brazilians*, from J. de Léry, *Histoire d'un voyage faict en la terra du Brésil*, 1578

his famous essay *Des Cannibales*, first published in 1580. "In my opinion," he wrote,

> what we actually see in these nations not only surpasses all the pictures which the poets have drawn of the Golden Age, and all their inventions in representing the then happy state of mankind, but also the conception and desire of philosophy itself.

He seems to have read a good deal more about the American Indians than had Ronsard and, as we have seen, he had conversed with Brazilians through an interpreter in Rouen in 1563, had tasted their cassava bread, and acquired some of their artifacts—a hammock, sword-club, wrist guard, and stamping tube. Certain unpleasant and unwelcome facts he therefore had to accept, but he was at pains to rationalize them. Describing how the Brazilians fattened up their prisoners of war and ate them, sending some chops to absent friends to denote "the last degree of revenge," he commented:

> I think there is more barbarity in eating a man alive than when he is dead; in tearing a body limb from limb, by racks and torments while it has the sense of feeling, in roasting it by degrees, in causing it to be bit and worried by dogs and swine (as we have not only read but lately seen, not between veteran enemies, but between neighbours and fellow citizens, and what is worse under the pretence and piety of religion) than of roasting it after it is dead.

The contrast between the natural savagery of the Indians and the refined cruelty of the Spaniards, on which Las Casas, Benzoni, and others had enlarged, is here given more general significance; and another, more important and original, lies beneath. Whereas previous writers, following classical and theological usage, had opposed the state of nature to law, order, and religion, Montaigne drew a distinction between nature and the "artificiality" which frustrated legitimate expression of natural impulses and prohibited the attainment of true civilization. *Des Cannibales* is, in fact, an attempt to define civilization, not barbarism—"Chacun appelle barbarie ce qui n'est pas de son usage," he wrote. In the process, and with wide-ranging consequences in the history of European thought, Montaigne provided an American location for the good savage of classical literature (he had been a Scythian in Cicero's letters and a German in Tacitus), using him as a vehicle for satirizing luxury-loving European society and endowing him with positive natural virtues.

The readers of Montaigne included Shakespeare, who probably owned a copy of John Florio's translation of the *Essais* published in England in 1603. (His signature is on a copy now in the British Library.) In *The Tempest*, first performed in 1611, Gonzalo paraphrases Montaigne on America almost word for word when describing the commonwealth he would create if he had the "plantation of this isle":

>   no kind of traffic
> Would I admit; no name of magistrate;
> Letters should not be known; riches, poverty,
> And use of service, none; contract, succession,
> Bourn, bound of land, tilth, vineyard, none;
> No use of metal, corn, or wine, or oil;
> No occupation; all men idle, all;
> And women too, but innocent and pure:
> No sovereignty. . . .
> All things in common Nature should produce
> Without sweat or endeavour: treason, felony,
> Sword, pike, knife, gun, or need of any engine,
> Would I not have; but nature should bring forth,
> Of its own kind, all foison, all abundance,
> To feed my innocent people. . . .
> I would with such perfection govern, sir,
> T'excell the Golden Age.

But whereas Montaigne had ascribed this happy way of life to the Brazilians, Gonzalo makes it the basis of an ideal republic, apparently for Europeans. It has been implausibly suggested that Shakespeare was satirizing Montaigne in this passage—though Gonzalo is a consistently admirable character and in no wise a figure of fun. The play as a whole suggests that he agreed with the essential meaning of *Des Cannibales*, accepting the inferences to be drawn from it though rejecting Montaigne's idealization of the savage. For Caliban, who owes his god Setebos to Pigafetta's account of Patagonia and other characteristics to Thomas Hariot's *Briefe and True Report of Virginia*, is an irredeemable American "salvage" no better than the degenerate, villainous nobleman, Antonio. Prospero's attempt to educate him brings forth only the "briers and darnell of appetites." Raw nature, Shakespeare seems to be suggesting in his depiction of Caliban, may not be improved by the arts of civilization but, on the other hand, they must maintain contact with nature lest they become mere artifice. Furthermore, he hints, a temporary return to nature helps to make the civilized man more truly civilized. Thus, the savage people of the New World prompted him, like Montaigne and other thinkers of the time, to reconsider what was then called "civility."

Although *The Tempest* is not to be regarded as an allegory of colonialism, it touches on many of the problems then confronting members of the Virginia Company, with some of whom (including the Earls of Pembroke and Southampton) Shakespeare was acquainted. And the lascivious Caliban who begins by being so helpful to Prospero but then turns treacherous, like the Indians at the first Virginia colony described by Hariot and depicted by John White, surely reflects the English settlers' view of them. To them even his "Golden Age" virtues could be turned to disadvantage, as in John Smith's *Generall Historie of Virginia* (1624):

> We chanced in a land even as God made it, where we found only an idle, improvident, scattered people, ignorant of the knowledge of gold and silver, or any commodities, and careless of anything but from hand to mouth, except baubles of no worth.

In England, as in France, this image coexisted with that of the handsome, simple, and naturally virtuous savage. As we shall see, dancers fancifully dressed as Indians wholly different from Caliban were soon to make their bow in court masques, and in 1616 Pocahontas arrived as if to confirm it. For she, after all, was a princess. Indeed, James I is said to have been rather shocked that a commoner, John Rolfe, should have had the presumption to marry her!

Trinculo says that in England "when they will not give a doit to relieve a lame begger, they will lay out ten to see a dead Indian." By this time the English had, in fact, had several opportunities to see live Indians also, though of a different kind from those of whom they had read in Vespucci and Peter Martyr. For these were mainly North American and made of sterner stuff than those of the sultry and enervating South. That they too went naked or nearly so might be attributed to their hardiness. They seemed to have some political system. Cannibalism was rare. And whereas the South was so notorious as the land of free love, polygamy, incest, and sodomy, the frigid North soon had a reputation for sexual rectitude. In fact the further north, the more clothes people wore, the better their morals became. George Best was very favorably impressed by the propriety of a male and female Eskimo brought back from Baffin Island to England by Frobisher in 1576. "Albeit they live continually togither, yet they did never use as man and wife," he wrote.

> I think it worth the noting the continencie of them both; for the man would never shift himself, except he had first caused the woman to depart out of his cabin, and they both were most shamefast lest anye of their privie parts should be discovered, eyther of themselves or any other body.

Lucas de Heere, a Dutch artist who was in England in 1576, made a drawing of the Eskimo man dressed in his sealskin coat [56a]. The following year he drew another, brought back by

56(a). *An Eskimo*, 1576. Lucas de Heere

Frobisher, paddling his kayak and shooting duck with a spear on the Avon at Bristol—though he substituted a more appropriate, rocky piece of coast for the Avon and included an Eskimo woman with her baby on her shoulder, a dogsled, and a sealskin tent. Prints after this drawing were published in both France and Germany. John White, who seems to have accompanied Frobisher on his second voyage to Baffin Bay and illustrated one of its incidents, also portrayed male and female Eskimos, emphasizing the Mongolian features which encouraged explorers to suppose that they were near the shores of China [56b]. These figures later found their way into an allegory of America in company with some feather-clad Indians and parrots. But the Eskimo was to play no more than a very minor role in the vision of an America where the sun always shone and the people went naked. And White is better known for the drawings he made at Roanoke, the first Virginia colony in what is now North Carolina.

The drawings and paintings by Jacques Le Moyne of Florida in 1564 and John White of "Virginia" in 1585–87 constitute the first and by far the fullest visual account of America, especially of the North American Indian. Both men seem to have been cartographers by training, at a time when maps were expected to show something of the flora and fauna of newly discovered lands as well as their geography. Le Moyne was a native of Dieppe and was certainly influenced by, if not indeed trained in, the great school of French map-making which flourished there in the early sixteenth century. Several of the finest and most lavishly decorated maps showing the New World were made there—such as the "Harleian map" now in the British Library and another world map, both made for Henri, Dauphin of France, between 1536 and 1547, and the extraordinary Portuguese atlas of c. 1540 executed in France with pictorial decorations by a French painter. Guillaume Le Testu was among the Dieppe School's more distinguished members and Le Moyne was probably taken to Florida on Laudonnière's expedition specifically in order to document the region more fully and accurately than Le Testu had done—very beautifully but rather fancifully—a decade earlier [57a, b]. Unfortunately, only one of Le Moyne's original American paintings survives and it was almost certainly made after his return to France [XII]. Showing a key incident in the story of the expedition, the meeting of Laudonnière with the Indians who explain that the column his predecessor had erected as a symbol of French possession was not only intact but had become an object of veneration, it is a reminder that the colony failed for no want of native friendliness. (It was in fact, wiped out by the Spaniards.) The rest of Le Moyne's views of Florida and the Flor-

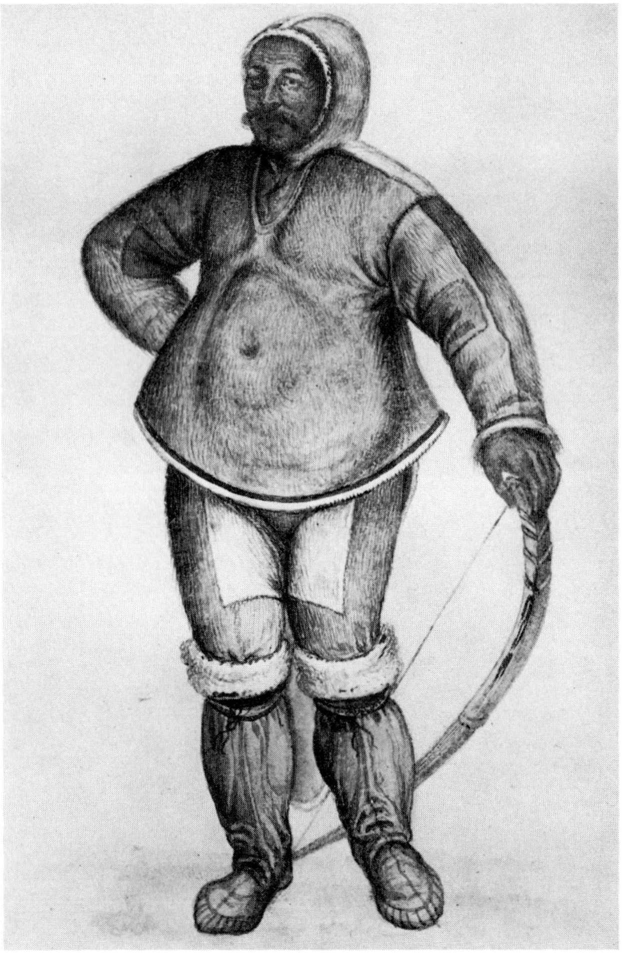

56(b). *An Eskimo*, 1576–77. John White

57(a). "Peru," from *Cosmographie Universelle*, 1555. Guillaume le Testu

TRUE MEN

TERRE DES Grantz
hommes

TERRE DV PERV

57(b). "Brazil," from *Cosmographie Universelle*, 1555. Guillaume Le Testu

idians are known only from watercolor copies by John White [58] and engravings after them published by de Bry, who freely altered and "improved" the originals [59]. Thus while White's copies retain unmistakably Indian features, the faces and figures in de Bry's prints are no less unmistakably European, however strange their hair styles and painted ornaments.

In a cartographical manner Le Moyne showed how the French arrived on the coast of Florida, explored the rivers, and built a fort on an island in one of them. He also illustrated the daily life of the inhabitants, at peace and at war—how they took advice from a sorcerer before beginning a campaign, how they declared war, marched to battle [59], dismembered and scalped the slain, and celebrated victory to the sound of rattle and drum beneath the glory trophies of the fight. Other plates are devoted to their methods of cooking, the administration of justice, and religious and other rites, including the sacrifice of first-born children to the chief. In the text accompanying the engravings Le Moyne described such extraordinary procedures as that of hunting alligators (which he calls crocodiles):

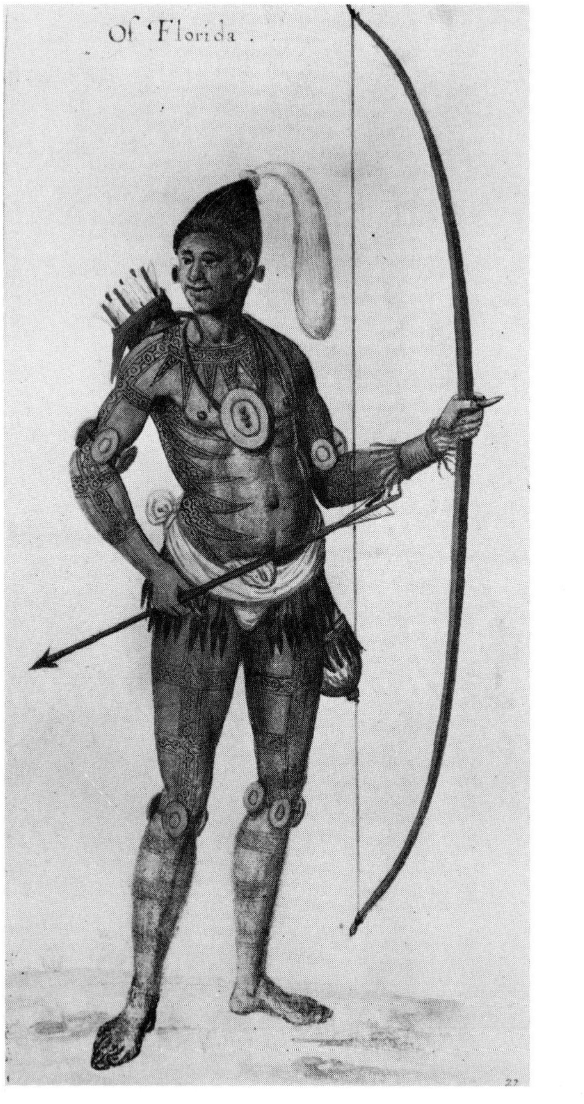

58. *A Man of Florida*, c.1588. John White, after Jacques Le Moyne

XII. *René de Laudonnière and Chief Athore*, 1564. Jacques Le Moyne

They put up near a river, a little hut full of cracks and holes, and in this they station a watchman, so that he can see the crocodiles and hear them, a good way off; for, when driven by hunger, they come out of the rivers, and crawl about on the islands after prey, and, if they find none, they make such a frightful noise that it can be heard for half a mile. Then the watchman calls the rest of the watch, who are in readiness; and, taking a portion, ten or twelve feet long, of the stem of a tree, they go out to find the monster, who is crawling along with his mouth wide open, all ready to catch one of them if he can; and with the greatest quickness they push the pole, small end first, as deep as possible down his throat, so that the roughness and irregularity of the bark may hold it from being got out again. They then turn the crocodile over on his back, and with clubs and arrows pound and pierce his belly, which is softer; for his back especially if he is an old one, is impenetrable, being protected by hard scales.

John White's drawings are far more convincing, ethnographically, than de Bry's engravings after Le Moyne. Yet they too give a distinctly favorable impression of life in this part of America, as does the scientist and surveyor Thomas Hariot's *A Briefe and True Report of the New Found Land of Virginia* (1588) which was later republished by de Bry with engravings after White's drawings—and from which, as we have seen, Shakespeare probably drew some touches for Caliban's more amiable characteristics (building dams for fish, identifying springs of fresh water, etc.). Both White and Hariot were, it should be remembered, personally interested in the success of the first Virginia colony—White became governor in 1587—and were naturally anxious not to discourage settlers from

[71]

59. *Outina on a Military Expedition.* After Jacques Le Moyne, from T. de Bry, *America*, Part II, 1591

60. (BELOW) *The Flyer or Medicine Man*, 1585–87. John White
61. (RIGHT) *Indian Woman and Child*, 1585–87. John White

going there. Thus White averted his eyes, or at least his pencil, from the more distressingly primitive aspects of Indian life. One would never suspect, from his drawings, that when he returned to the colony in 1590 not a living soul was to be found. Their fate was only too clear.

XIII. *A Camp-Fire Ceremony*, 1585–87. John White

In this respect White is a less candid observer than Le Moyne, for the latter had recorded such ceremonies as those for the sacrifice of first-born children whereas White concentrated on more innocent and homely scenes—sitting round the village fire [XIII] or dancing the "green corn ritual" of which Hariot also gave a reassuringly innocuous description. The posts around which the "fayrest Virgins" dance were, Hariot said, carved with heads like the "faces of Nuns covered with their veils." Both White and Hariot seem to have been concerned to demonstrate that contrary to common reports of the shameless nudity of the Indians, those of Virginia were clad in such a way as to spare the blushes of the settlers' tenderest wife or daughter. Even the medicine men, of whom White gives a very jolly impression [60], wore "a skinne which hangeth down from their girdle and covereth their privities," while the chief men "cover themselves before and behynde, from the navel unto the midds of their thighes as the women doe with a deered skynne handsomely dressed and fringed" [61]. And the "virgins of good parentage" were almost coy:

> Their haire is cutt with two ridges above the foreheads, the rest is trussed opp on a knott behinde, they have broade mowthes, reasonable fair black eyes: they lay their hands often uppon their Shoulders, and cover their brests in token of maydenlike modestye.

62. *The Village of Secoton*, 1585–87. John White

The country where these people lead their idyllic lives was, according to Hariot, "soe fruit full and good, that England is not to bee compared to it," and this is borne out by White's depiction of the village of Secoton [62]. He even gave to Indian cooking a far better press than it had ever had before, noting down a recipe which makes a striking contrast with the nauseating brews prepared farther south. But he felt bound to add a moralizing comment, perhaps to scotch rumors of the privations which the settlers were in fact suffering:

> Yet are they moderate in their eatinge wher by they avoide sicknes. I would to god wee would followe their exemple. For wee should bee free from many kynes of diseasyes which wee fall into by sumtwous and unseasonable banketts, continually devisinge new sawces, and provocation of gluttonye to satisfie our unsatiable appetite.

The subtly significant modifications which de Bry made when engraving John White's watercolors were relatively slight—an occasional touching up of facial features, the adjustment of gestures, the addition of a few plants, including some perfectly appropriate sunflowers to the village of Secoton, for instance, but these were enough to tame and "civilize" the savages White had observed and recorded with such freshness. Nor did he make more radical adjustments to Le Moyne's paintings, so far as may be judged from the only original which survives, though it is to be presumed that he was responsible for the classical proportions and poise of the svelte nude figures in some of the other scenes, such as that which shows the youth of Florida at their exercises like young Spartans [63]. But when de Bry came in 1592 to publish Hans Staden's narrative of life among the Brazilian cannibals as *America tertia pars* he was confronted with a much more difficult problem. The scratchy woodcuts after Staden's naïve drawings, quite oblivious of the rules of composition and perspective, had to be entirely redrawn, and in the process they were completely

63. *The Youth of Florida*. After Jacques Le Moyne, from T. de Bry, *America*, Part II, 1591

transformed. In place of Staden's haphazard drinking party [64] de Bry substituted a much more orderly scene, more like a classical feast of the gods with only a few exotic elements, such as *maracás* and feather headdresses and mantles, to provide some local color [65]. Staden's horrifying representation of cannibals preparing to cook a corpse [66] makes a still more striking contrast with de Bry's version which might almost be supposed to illustrate some account of

64. (ABOVE) *Brazilians*, 1557. Anonymous, after Hans Staden

65. (BELOW) *Brazilians*. Anonymous, after Hans Staden, from T. de Bry, *America*, Part III, 1592

66. (RIGHT) *Cannibal Scene*, 1557. Anonymous, after Hans Staden

the restoration and conservation of antique statues, so marmoreal are the well formed dead bodies [67]. De Bry's engravings have, moreover, a strange atmosphere of hushed tranquillity conspicuously absent from Staden's nervous and busy little illustrations. This vanishes from the next group of volumes devoted to Benzoni's *Historia* which was itself so sparsely illustrated that de Bry had to rely on imagination for most of the plates. On page after page the Spaniards appear in conflict with naked figures, and as the Indians are endowed with the physique and placed in the postures of antique heroes, their conquerors become the barbarians [68].

Like so many of his authors, de Bry was a Protestant and anti-Spanish and his collection of American travel literature, which includes nothing written by a Spaniard, gave vivid visual expression to the Black Legend. His idealization of the American Indians may therefore derive partly from a wish, conscious or subconscious, to point up the contrast between them and the cruel Spaniards. But artistic considerations must have played the dominant part. At a time when the only accepted models for the depiction of the nude were antique statues, de Bry and the artists he employed could not have conceived the nude figure of an Indian in any other way. Thus, the illustrations to this series of books, continued after the elder de Bry's death by his son who issued the tenth and final volume in 1618, and frequently reprinted, copied, and imitated during the next century and a half, very widely diffused the belief that America was peopled by a race barely distinguishable, physically, from the ancient Greeks. In the early eighteenth century, as we shall see, they were to be used as evidence to demonstrate the similarities between the religious rites of classical antiquity and the American Indian!

De Bry's approximation of the Indians to the ancient Greeks seems obvious enough today, but the extent to which it was intentional is open to question. There can be no doubt, however, about his intention in appending to the first volume of his *America* engravings of Picts, also after drawings by John White, for he stated it quite explicitly: "for to showe how the Inhabitants of the great Bretannie haue bin in times past as sauuage as those of Virginia." (White's drawings were adaptations from earlier representations of ancient Britons and not, as is sometimes claimed, from his own watercolors of the Indians.) The Picts were "barbarians" in both the classical and Christian sense of the

67. (ABOVE) *Cannibal Scene*. Anonymous, after Hans Staden, from T. de Bry, *America*, Part III, 1592

68. *Spanish Attack on Indians*, from T. de Bry, *America*, Part IV, 1594

THE NEW GOLDEN LAND

terms then in use and their inclusion for the reason so clearly stated would seem to prove that de Bry cannot have intended his classicizing images of the Indian to be understood as implying any meaningful parallel between them and the ancient Greeks and Romans. On the other hand, the engravings of Picts suggest that he was well aware of the interest which the discovery of America had aroused in the early history of Europe. Comparisons were inevitably being made; awkward questions were being asked. Might not the ancestors of modern Europeans have been like the inhabitants of America? They were "still in that first rude state which all other nations were in, before there was anyone to teach them," Las Casas had written. "We ought to consider what we, and all the other nations of the world were like, before Jesus Christ came to visit us."

The first attempt at ethnological classification was made in a book on missionary policy by the Spanish Jesuit José de Acosta, written in Peru in 1576–77 and published in 1589, and in his more widely read *Historia natural y moral de las Indias* (the word *moral* here signifying *mores* or customs rather than ethics), first issued in 1590, frequently reprinted in Spanish, and translated into Italian, French, Dutch, German, and English by 1604. According to Acosta there were three types of "barbarian," arranged hierarchically: first those who are literate, like the Chinese and Japanese; then those, like the Mexicans and Peruvians, who live in stable settlements with organized governments and religion; and finally the "savages," subdivided between those with the rudiments of organized life and those who live like wild beasts. With this scheme he adumbrated an evolutionary

69. *Tapuya War Dance*, c.1641–43. Albert Eckhout

[78]

xiv. *A Tapuya Brazilian*, 1641. Albert Eckhout

process from savagery through two degrees of barbarism to civilization—European, of course. Yet he was able to write of the Mexicans and Peruvians:

> If anyone should wonder at some of the rites and customs of the Indians and despise them as ignorant and stupid or detest them as inhuman and diabolical, let him observe that among the Greeks and Romans who formerly ruled the world, we find either the same customs or other similar ones, and sometimes worse....

Acosta's aim was to demonstrate that each of his three types of barbarian called for a different approach by the missionaries. But his book provided a convenient basic system of categorization which was to survive little altered until the development of scientific ethnography in the nineteenth century and indeed still persists to this day. It also suggested that all were worthy of study for the light they might shed on the ascent of man and the early development of civilized societies. And it was probably due to Acosta's influence that Europeans began in the early seventeenth century to study the primitive peoples of America more objectively and analytically than before. The most remarkable instance of this in the visual arts is Albert Eckhout's series of life-size portraits of Brazilians.

As we have seen, Eckhout was one of the artists employed by Maurits of Nassau in Brazil in the early 1640s. Accuracy was his aim and he depicted the Tapuya in exactly the same pains-

70. *Brazilian Woman*, 1641. Albert Eckhout

71. *Brazilian Man*, 1643. Albert Eckhout

taking way as he did the strange exotic plants among which they stand and the various indigenous animals and reptiles which appear in the foregrounds [XIV]. The weapons borne by the men and the baskets carried by the women are rendered with meticulous fidelity. And if the single figures stand in postures akin to those traditional in European portraiture, his enormous painting of a group of dancing warriors has no precedent of any kind [69]. In this truly extraordinary work he broke completely free from all formal and other conventions or stereotypes and succeeded in conveying a vivid and accurate impression of those gestures Léry had despaired of describing, as well as the frantic rhythm of the war dance. Cannibalism, relegated to its proper place, is indicated by Eckhout almost casually, as a mere incident in Brazilian life. Not until one looks closely at his picture of a woman crossing a stream does one notice that she is holding a severed forearm while a human foot sticks out of the neatly woven basket suspended from her head [70]. To his, or more probably to Count Maurits's, interest in racialism are due the paintings of people of mixed blood who were already very numerous in Brazil—a black woman with her mulatto son [72] and an elegant mestiza dressed in an ample silken gown and carrying a basket of flowers on her head, presumably the daughter of one of the many Portuguese settlers who took Indian wives.

72. *Black Woman with Mulatto Child*, 1641. Albert Eckhout

73. *Brazilian Woman and Child*, 1641. Albert Eckhout

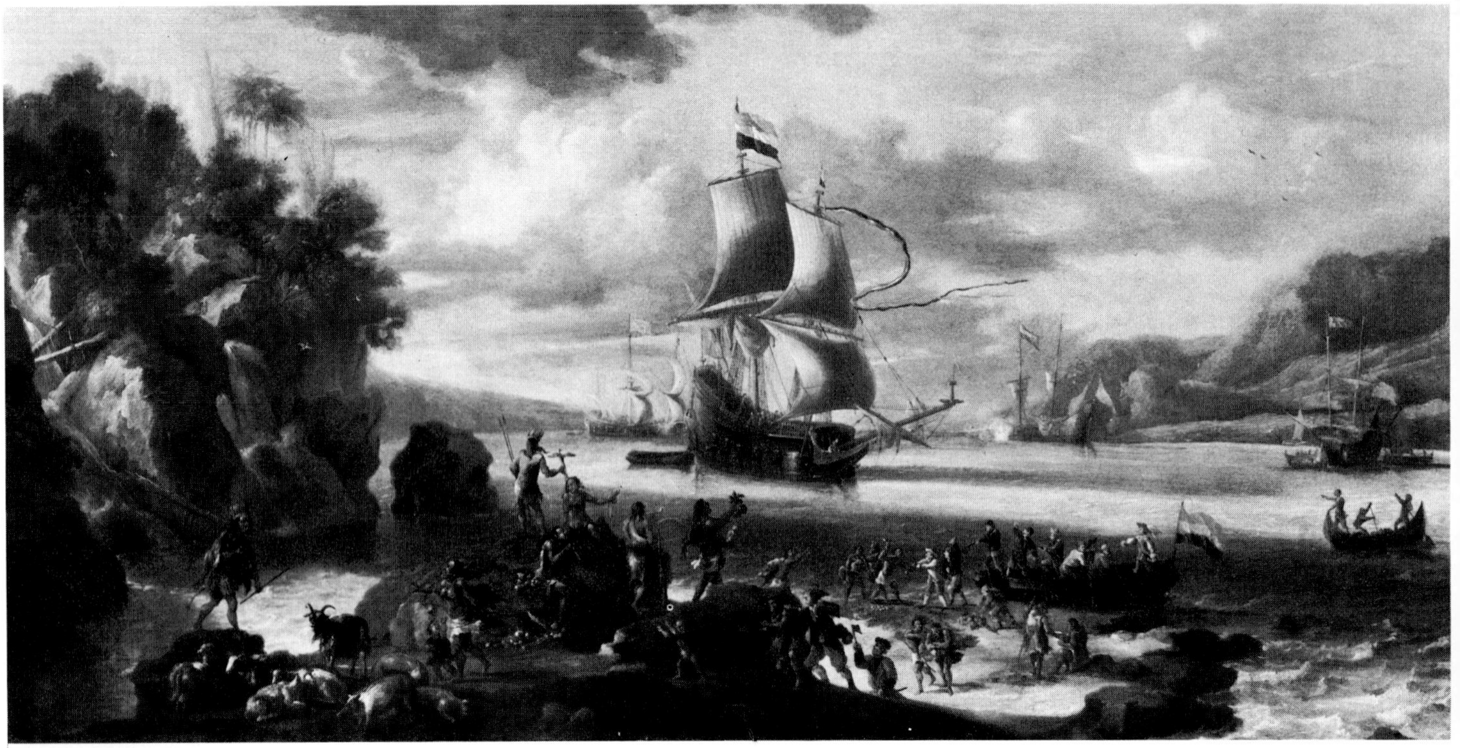

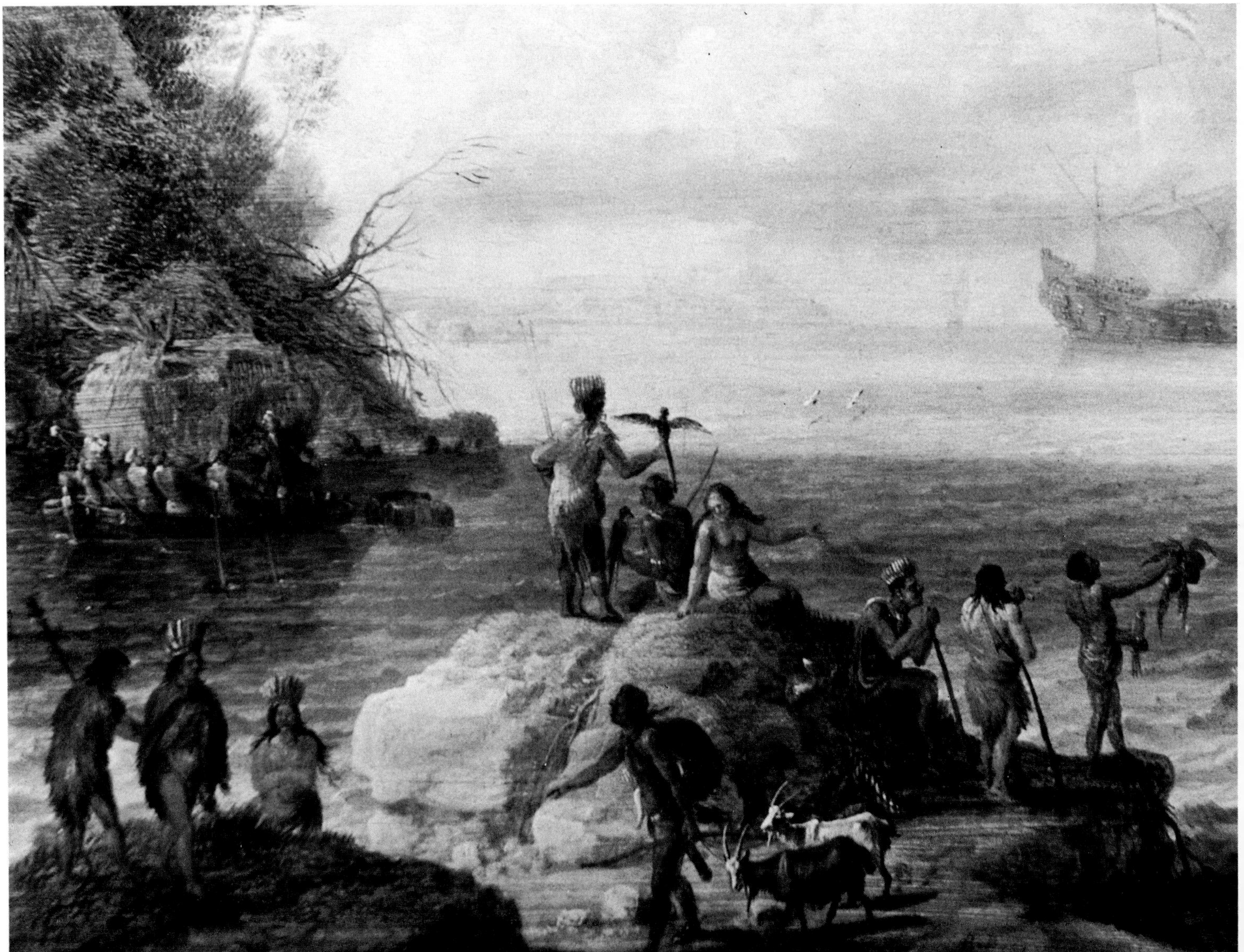

But these pictures were, perhaps, too frankly and disturbingly objective to have much success in Europe. When Eckhout's Brazilian paintings were used for the *Les Indes* tapestries woven at the Gobelins later in the century, not one of his Brazilian figures was included in them [97]. Despite the sudden growth of interest in ethnology, Europeans clung tenaciously to earlier conceptions of the Indian. Very shortly after Eckhout's Brazilian venture a marine painter, Bonaventura Peeters, began incorporating Indians with feather headdresses and skirts disporting themselves with parrots on the rocky coves and inlets of his imaginary America [74, 75]. They seem to have strayed out of some court masque — or to be welcoming newcomers to some exotic Cythera. Like contemporary allegories of America, these are purely conventional figures. But they corresponded more closely to the accepted European vision of the Indians than did Eckhout's unblinking glimpses of the reality.

74. (LEFT, ABOVE) *A West Indian Scene*, c.1650. Bonaventura Peeters

75. (LEFT) Detail from *A West Indian Scene*, 1648. Bonaventura Peeters

CHAPTER 4

A Land of Allegory

"IT IS A very striking fact that our classical authors had no knowledge of all this America which we call new lands," Étienne Pasquier, a Parisian lawyer, remarked in the early 1560s. To many Europeans it had also been a very disturbing fact, very difficult to assimilate. So the world continued to be described until late in the sixteenth century as if it were still the world known to the classical geographers Strabo and Ptolemy. Only the more clearsighted dared to admit that the old cosmography had been shattered and the hitherto unquestioned authority of Antiquity undermined. "The ancients were beguiled in many things touching the knowledge of the earth," wrote Geoffrey Fenton paraphrasing the great Florentine historian Guicciardini who, in the 1530s, had hinted at still more alarming consequences:

> Not only has this navigation confounded many affirmations of former writers about terrestrial things, but it has also given some anxiety to the interpreters of the Holy Scriptures.

In Protestant England, where the authority of the Bible was paramount, Fenton refrained from repeating Guicciardini's doubts on the interpretation which should now be put on Psalm XIX, Verse 4, and St. Paul's clear statement about the preaching of the Apostles—"their sound went into all the earth, and their words to the end of the world."

According to the old cosmography, the world consisted of three land masses. Ovid's term *triplex mundus*—the triple world—was so embedded in European literature that it continued in use long after the discovery of America, for example by Ben Jonson in 1609. This tripartite world had been represented diagrammatically by medieval artists as a circle divided into one half (for Asia) and two quarters (for Europe and Africa). In manuscript illuminations such an orb occasionally appears in the hand or beneath the feet of Christ. Personifications of the three continents are rare, the best known being those on the famous eleventh-century bronze candlestick in Hildesheim Cathedral. But the three Magi of the Epiphany had for long been associated with the descendants of the sons of Noah, who peopled the three parts of the world, and from the early fifteenth century they were often depicted as a European, an Asian, and an African. Despite superficial resemblances, however, such figures were not taken as prototypes for the allegories of the continents when they appear in the later sixteenth century.

Resistance to the notion of a four-part or even five-part world (an antipodean continent was postulated and named Australia two centuries before it was discovered) was gradually broken down in the course of the sixteenth century. Clerics began to welcome the missionary potentialities of the New World and to construe St. Paul's words as a prophecy, though some believed that St. Thomas had landed in America on his way to India (his footprints were even said to have been miraculously preserved on the Brazilian shore). Humanists who had previously been obsessed by the revival of classical letters, arts, and learning and valiantly tried to fit America into their scheme of things, began to take pride in the discoveries—itemized by a Portuguese as comprehending "new islands, new lands, new seas, new peoples; and what is

[84]

76. *America*, 1575. Etienne Delaune

more a new sky and new stars." For writers and Mannerist artists, bent on outdoing and not merely imitating their Antique models, the new cosmography was very convenient in as much as it proved that the ancients had in some ways already been surpassed. Christopher Marlowe made Tamburlaine boast:

> I will confute those blind geographers
> That make a triple region of the world,
> Excluding regions which I mean to trace.

The play was first printed in 1590 and in that same year Edmund Spenser wrote in *The Faerie Queene* (introduction to Book II):

> But let that man with better sense advize,
> That of the world least part to us is red;
> And daily how through hardy enterprize
> Many great regions are discovered,
> Which to late age were never mentioned.
> Who ever heard of th' Indian Peru?
> Or who in venturous vessell measured
> The Amazon huge river, now found trew?
> Or fruitfullest Virginia who did ever vew?
> Yet all these were, when no man did then know,
> Yet have from wisest ages hidden beene;
> And later times thinges more unknowne shall
>   show. . . .

Something of this new mood of self-confidence is reflected in the allegories of the four continents which began to appear in the 1570s. They figure on the title page of Abraham Ortelius's *Theatrum Orbis Terrarum* (Antwerp 1570) where America is a recumbent woman with bow and arrows and feathered hat, holding a severed head in her hand. In painting, the first, so far as is known, is in one of the outstanding masterpieces of Mannerist architecture and decoration, the palace at Caprarola, near Rome, built for Cardinal Alessandro Farnese, nephew of Pope Paul III who issued the bull proclaiming American Indians to be "true men." It was painted in 1574 by Giovanni de' Vecchi in a room decorated—probably under the Cardinal's supervision—with large frescoed maps and portraits of Columbus, Vespucci, Magellan, and Hernán Cortés. America is a somewhat dusky faced figure who is holding a cornucopia of abundance and is accompanied by a parrot. She is fully draped and, like the other three continents, seems to have been based on Roman prototypes for the allegorical representation of cities [XV]. A more distinctive personification of America was provided in 1575 by the Fontainebleau School Mannerist, Etienne Delaune, in one of a series of tiny engravings of the continents, perhaps recording a slightly earlier project for mural decoration. Here she is shown completely nude, save for a feather headdress, and holding a bow; on the ground beside her is a Brazilian type of club and a crouching long-necked animal, presumably a llama [76]. In 1577 the Swiss Jost Amman issued prints of the four

xv. Western Hemisphere of a world map with allegories of the continents, 1574. Giovanni de' Vecchi

A LAND OF ALLEGORY

continents characterized as landscapes with figures, that of America recalling the illustrations to Vespucci. Flemish print-makers were not far behind and two of them produced their versions of America in 1581. Philippe Galle depicted her as a stark naked Amazon with a human head dangling from her hand and a severed arm beneath her feet [77]. Jan Sadeler engraved a drawing by Dirk Barendsz of a naked woman holding an arrow, seated beneath a tree on which parrots perch and with a mountainous landscape behind with figures dredging gold dust in a river [78]. The main figure proved very popular and was copied on silver and pewter plates and tankards in the seventeenth century [79].

Several artists aimed at a composite image, combining as many characteristic American items as possible—naked figures, cannibals, gold seekers, exotic flora and fauna. Crispijn de Passe even contrived to work in the Aztec rite of

77. *America*, 1581–1600. Philippe Galle

78. *America*, 1581. Jan Sadeler, after Dirk Barendsz

79. Pewter tankard. Nuremberg, early seventeenth century

[87]

THE NEW GOLDEN LAND

80. (ABOVE) *America*, early seventeenth century. Crispijn de Passe

human sacrifice [80], while Stradanus presented the "discovery" by a well-dressed Vespucci, holding a banner with the Southern Cross in one hand and a mariner's astrolabe in the other, of a rather hefty America in a hammock while strange animals, including a tapir and sloth, prowl around the trees and a group of cannibals prepare their midday meal in the background [81]. To create a single image, comparable with that of Europa on her bull, was more difficult. But several artists attempted it. Maarten de Vos conceived America as a handsome nude girl with a very elaborate coiffure riding an outsize armadillo—sidesaddle of course [82]. She decorated part of the festival architecture set up for Archduke Ernst of Austria's ceremonial entry into Antwerp in 1594 and was immediately diffused in prints from which she was later copied on pottery stove tiles, silver tankards, and, in 1674, in plaster decorations on the façade of a house in Wernigerode, East Germany. The unsuitability of the armadillo as mount, especially for a bareback rider, may have persuaded Stefano della Bella to harness a pair to the chariot of his regal America on one of the playing cards he etched in 1644 to teach the young Louis XIV the rudiments of geography and history [83]. This design also was widely copied, for instance, on a massive silver dish made at Augsburg in 1689. The armadillo was sometimes confused, however, with the rhinoceros which it was said to resemble and is to be found snorting in many an allegory of America. Similar confusion about the size of the tapir seems to lie behind the choice of an elephant as the emblematic beast of Brazil. Usually the figure of America is accompanied by an alligator, as in Cesare Ripa's *Iconologia* of 1604, the handbook to which most baroque artists turned when they wanted to know how to represent an abstract idea.

Ripa's emblem served for both North and South America, but the different species of Amerindian—from the Eskimos to the Patagoni-

82. *America*, 1594. Maarten de Vos

83. *America*, 1644. Stafano della Bella

81. (LEFT) *Vespucci "Discovering" America*, late sixteenth century. Theodor Galle, after Stradanus (Jan van der Street)

84. *Allegory of America*, early seventeenth century. François van den Hoeye

ans—were also represented as single figures, on maps, in the illustrations and title pages to descriptions of the New World, and even in French and Italian costume books which nicely distinguished degrees of nudity and styles of featherwork. The main types appear, flanked by Columbus and Vespucci, in the clouds above an early seventeenth-century vision of Cuba, with natives smoking tobacco in the foreground and others trundling barrows of, presumably, gold ore across the beach [84]. Reading from left to right, there is a Canary Islander with sugar canes on his shoulder, a Floridian with bow and arrow and a snake, a Patagonian swallowing an arrow, a Chilean stark naked with club in hand, a Brazilian gnawing a human foot beside bundles of brazilwood, a Peruvian with gold mining implements, and an Eskimo with his fishing spear and kayak. In the center sits America herself dressed only in feathers, holding necklaces

[90]

in one hand and a bow in the other. This is the image which was to establish itself in the European imagination as "America." Derived initially from such early sources as the 1505 German woodcut of Brazilians [7], it persisted with only slight variations until well into the nineteenth century.

The sixteenth-century taste for allegory found expression not only in prints and paintings but also in elaborately devised spectacles. Indeed the four parts of the world were represented as *tableaux vivants* in the *Ommegang*—a popular festival—of 1564 in Antwerp, before any prints of them had been published. Allegorical allusions to America were also frequently incorporated in multimedia festival decorations. When Francesco de' Medici married Joanna of Austria (sister of Maximilian II) in 1565, a triumphal arch set up in Florence bore, as the official booklet records, a painting of an "uncivilised nymph little less than naked, in the midst of many new animals; and this represented the new land of Peru, with the other new West Indies, in large part discovered and ruled under the auspices of the most fortunate house of Austria." For the christening of their son three years later, paintings of the conversion of New Spain to Christianity and an allegory of the River Plate were commissioned, with others, to decorate the Florentine Baptistery. In 1598 the death of Philip II of Spain was marked by the Florentine court with a solemn requiem in San Lorenzo decorated with representations of the continents, including a feathered America holding a rattle, and a large grisaille painting originally executed for the funeral of Francesco I de' Medici and recording his reception of two Japanese princes but now refurbished to depict Philip II receiving emissaries from the New World. Among the magnificent spectacles put on for the marriage of the Grand Duke's son, Cosimo de' Medici, to Maria Maddalena of Austria ten years later, one of the several scenographically ingenious intermezzi showed the Florentine Vespucci discovering America [85].

An allusion to the New World was almost ob-

85. *The Ship of Amerigo Vespucci*, 1608. After Giulio Parigi

[91]

ligatory in any festival decorations erected in honor of the Hapsburgs at this period. Thus, when Rubens transformed the city of Antwerp for the state entry of the new Governor of the Netherlands, the Cardinal-Infante Ferdinand, in 1635 he designed an archway for the city mint in the form of the mountain of Potosí and its famous silver mines, derived from the frontispiece to the sixth volume of de Bry's books on America [86]. But most of his imagery was classical and one has to look hard at his sketches to spot the miners, monkeys, and parrots. For Rubens had assimilated America into an essentially Mediterranean view of the world. Already in his earlier allegory of the continents he had given pride of place to Europe with the Danube and Africa with the Nile and pushed to the side both Asia and America, representing the latter by a shadowy river god holding a coconut [87]. The discoveries and conquests of the sixteenth century had slowly established not only the idea of four continents but also that of European superiority to the other three. As an Italian, Giovanni Botero, put it most succinctly in 1591: Europe, though the smallest of the continents, "was born to rule over Africa, Asia and America."

In a painting of about 1636 Frans Francken II showed the Emperor Charles V enthroned while Europe kneels before him holding the imperial insignia and the other continents pay homage, together with representatives of his by then world-wide dominions [88]. It might easily be supposed to represent the climax of one of the many pageants and masques in which personifications of the world descended from their triumphal chariots or tripped across the stage and made obeisances to the sovereigns in whose honor they were organized. They presented their crowns to Louis XIII at a court ballet in Paris in 1643; they greeted Charles II after his coronation in London in 1661; they might even pay their respects to rulers of such limited domains as the Duke of Württemberg. America was characterized in all these shows by the riches in gold, silver, pearls, and precious stones which every European prince coveted, however remote his chance of obtaining them.

86. *Archway of the Mint*, 1635. Peter Paul Rubens

87. *The Four Continents*, c.1615. Peter Paul Rubens

A LAND OF ALLEGORY

Court masques and ballets sometimes made more specific allusions to America. *The Memorable Masque* performed before James I in London in 1613, with program and speeches by George Chapman and costumes by Inigo Jones, referred to the English colony at Jamestown. It was organized by the Gentlemen of the Inns of Court, many of whom had invested in the Virginia Company for which they hoped to obtain royal patronage. The piece began with rocks drawn aside to reveal "Virginian Princes" dressed in cloth of silver embroidered with suns, seated in a gold mine, and addressing a hymn to the setting sun, after which they turned to salute James as "Our dear Phoebus." The King is said to have been "exceedingly pleased" by the spectacle and especially by the dancers "all showfully garnished with several-hewed feathers"—but he declined to take the hint.

Some years later American colonies formed the subject of a ballet, *Le Temple de la Paix*, danced before Louis XIV at Fontainebleau on October 15, 1685. The "savages of the French provinces in America" who appeared in it represented not only the Canadian Indians but also the inhabitants of the vast area of Louisiana which La Salle had discovered, named after the King and claimed for France only three years

88. *Allegory on the Abdication of the Emperor Charles V at Brussels, October 25, 1555*, c.1636. Frans Francken II

[93]

THE NEW GOLDEN LAND

earlier. According to the synopsis, they "come to the temple of peace and make known by their songs and dances their pleasure in being under the rule of a powerful and glorious king who enables them to enjoy happy tranquility." One of them stepped forward to address Louis:

> We have crossed the vast bosom of the ocean to render homage to the most powerful of kings. He prefers to the happiness of being the conqueror of the world the glory of retaining in profound peace the enemies he has vanquished hundreds and hundreds of times. His name is revered by savage nations to the remotest shores. Everything echoes to the renown of his exploits. Ah! it is sweet to live under his laws.

The last two lines were repeated in chorus. It is an ironic coincidence that three days later, Louis signed the Revocation of the Edict of Nantes

89(a). (LEFT) *Indian Torchbearer*, 1613. Inigo Jones
89(b). (ABOVE) Costume design, early seventeenth century. Giulio Parigi

which drove so many of his subjects to seek refuge abroad, some in British America.

Although court masques and ballets of the seventeenth century were usually intended to instruct as well as to delight—like allegorical paintings—no very profound significance can be attributed to the American Indians who appeared in so many of them. Often they were no more than decoratively exotic, if not anachronistic, as in Giacomo Torelli's ballet of 1645, *La Finta Pazza*, which was ostensibly set in the Homeric world and concerned with the love of Achilles for Deidamia. *Il Tabacco*, conjured up by the Conte Filippo d'Aglié for the Savoy court in Turin on the last day of the carnival in 1650,

[94]

was a gay enchantment called by its author "un Balletto ridicolo," with dancers cavorting among exotic plants and parrots on the island of Tobago. Greater seriousness might have been expected of Davenant's *The Cruelty of the Spaniards in Peru. Exprest by Vocall Musick and by Art of Perspective in Scenes &c.* performed in the Commonwealth London of 1658. But despite its anti-Spanish and anti-Catholic message, it was a cheerful entertainment with "a Symphony being a wild Ayre suteable to the region," much singing, dancing, and acrobatics, cruelty limited to the penultimate scene, and all ending happily with the arrival of a British expeditionary force.

Drawings by Giulio Parigi, Daniel Rabel, Inigo Jones, and Borgonio show how "American Indians" were dressed—or partly dressed—in feathers for the European stage in the seventeenth century [89, 90, XVI]. Some of the elaborate baroque chariots or floats representing the New World in triumphal processions which passed through the streets of European cities are recorded in prints. And there are magnificent engravings of the costumes and fluttering panaches worn by the duc de Guise and his many attendants when he impersonated the "Roy Ameriquain" in the great *Carrousel* or tournament given by Louis XIV in the courtyard of the Louvre in 1662 [91]. But written descriptions of such festival occasions afford no less vivid glimpses of the diverse ways in which images of America were realized. In a masque given in London in 1613 with sets and costumes by Costantino de' Servi, America danced "in a skin coate of the colour of the juyce of Mulberies, on her head large round brims of many coloured feathers." A still richer outfit was provided for her appearance in a pageant put on by the Goldsmiths' Company in 1674. The commemorative booklet described her as:

> A strait stout Person, with a Tanned Face, Neck and Breast, with a triple chain of Diamonds about her Neck; sleak black Hair, a Coronet of Gold, with a great plume of Feathers, rich Jewels in her Ears, a short Vest of Gold, on short Bases of Silver; Sky-coloured Silk hose, and silver Buskins, lac'd with Gold Ribon in puffs, in one hand a Dart, in the other the banner of the Companies.

90. Ballet designs, 1626. Daniel Rabel

THE NEW GOLDEN LAND

91. American costumes worn at the Carrousel of 1662, 1671. François Chauveau

A LAND OF ALLEGORY

92. *America*, 1595. Paolo Farinati

Allegories of America occasionally served the Church as well as the State from the late sixteenth century onward. In lunettes of the continents painted in 1595 in a villa near Verona, America is represented as a half-naked (and atypically male) Indian holding in one hand a crucifix which rests on a large turtle and in the other a bow while his unregenerate fellows roast a joint of human flesh [92]. All four continents supported the Catholic Church in a complex allegory painted in the Munich Residenz shortly after 1611. But not until the mid-seventeenth century, and naturally enough in Rome, was the first truly memorable image binding the new cosmography to Catholicism created—Bernini's famous fountain in Piazza Navona. Ever since the day in 1651 when Bernini delighted his papal master Innocent X by turning the tap which set the waters roaring and sparkling from the rockwork, this fountain has exerted an almost irresistible popular appeal as the most exuberantly fantastic of all baroque extravaganzas. So it has become difficult to appreciate that it is based on a sophisticated *concetto*, of a type beloved in the seventeenth century, with several layers of meaning, as complex as a poem by John Donne and no less profoundly meditated.

The gigantic figures seated around the rocky base of the fountain represent the four great rivers and continents, the Danube for Europe, Nile for Africa, Ganges for Asia, and Plate for America, each accompanied by a characteristic animal. The River Plate, bald but surprisingly bearded, wears a jeweled band on his right leg, gold coins tumble out of the rock on which he sits, a prickly pear sprouts by his foot, and below an armadillo waddles out of a cavern [93]. He looks up at the obelisk, a symbol of divine light and

93. *The River Plate*, 1651. Gianlorenzo Bernini

eternity, crowned by a dove which signifies the Holy Ghost and was also the personal emblem of Innocent X. The central rock on which it stands is associated, however, with the hill of Calvary and the four rivers with those of Paradise. Thus, the idea of salvation under the Cross is interwoven with that of Catholic triumph over the four parts of the world.

Later in the century the continents began to play a symbolic part in the decoration of churches. Andrea Pozzo, as his first biographer remarked, "wishing to represent the great zeal of St. Ignatius in propagating the Catholic faith throughout the world," painted on the ceiling of S. Ignazio, Rome, a vast allegory in which a ray of light passes from Christ to the Saint whence it is refracted in four rays to the continents, each represented as a "bizarrely dressed Amazon." America is shown in the usual way, but the arrow she holds is an instrument of righteousness directed at the "fierce monster of impiety" falling beneath her feet [XVIII]. This was completed in 1694 and frequently imitated in allegories of the missions during the following decades. America might also appear alone as the representative of all the heathen peoples of the world, as in a pulpit in Bruges [94] and in a group by F. M. Brokoff carved for the Karlsbrücke in Prague in 1711, where she kneels beside St. Francis Xavier. But America is usually accompanied by the other three continents to signify the universality of the Church—gazing down on the baptismal font (as in St. Peter's, Rome), piously watching the altar from chancel walls, or listening to the words of a preacher on the pulpit [95].

Protestants were, of course, opposed to the Roman Church's claim of catholicity and its evangelizing zeal. (According to pious Italian historians, Calvinists encouraged Brazilians to eat Roman missionaries.) There is, perhaps a hint of this attitude in Frans Post's Brazilian landscapes in which deserted and half-ruined

94. *America*, c.1690. Anonymous, Netherlandish

95. *America*, c.1700. Hendrick Verbruggen

Jesuit churches make a striking contrast with the neat whitewashed houses and trim plantations of Dutch settlers. Another Dutch artist, Claes Berchem, made an allegorical drawing of America with a distinctly Protestant figure of Religion in the sky casting down a helmeted and mustachioed Iberian while an Indian holds his hands in an attitude of prayer. But as the Protestant churches made so little use of the figurative arts, the work of their missions in North America seems to have gone visually unrecorded.

In Catholic countries the theme of evangelization was sometimes carried over into secular paintings referring to America. The raising of the cross, for example, before which Indians fall in adoration, was the main incident in a highly imaginative evocation of the landing of Columbus painted in the Palazzo Ducale, Genoa, by Francesco Solimena (now destroyed). The religious mission of Columbus was later to be stressed in Mme du Boccage's epic poem *La Colombiade ou la Foi portée au Nouveau-Monde* (1757). Most painted allegories of America and the other continents seem, however, to have been secular and to have illustrated the expansion of human knowledge rather than the extension of the power of the Church. Outstanding among them is a series of paintings on copper executed by the Flemish painter Jan van Kessel between 1664 and 1666, in which each continent is represented by a group consisting of one large and sixteen smaller panels. That devoted to America is a treasury of geographical information—and misinformation—culled from a variety of illustrated books. The central panel depicts a kind of ideal *Wunderkammer* of American curiosities, such as any prince of the period would have been glad to possess, crammed with birds, beasts, fishes, reptiles, insects, shells, arms, and armor [XVII]. And as in nearly all such collections many of the exhibits are incorrectly classified. Here the two Indies have been confused. The woman and child dancing through the door, the two statues in niches, and the scene of suttee in the lowest of the three pictures on the right are not American but derived from a late sixteenth-century book of travels to the Portuguese East Indies by Jan Huygens. The armor in the corner seems to be Asian—a more easily understandable slip since such pieces were labeled "West Indian" in the Royal Armory in Madrid until late in the eighteenth century. The figure in the lower left corner, dark-skinned and wearing only a headdress, necklace, and skirt of feathers, holding one of the great weights of gold on the floor, and seated near a heap of pearls, coral, and coins spilled out of a big vase, personifies America. The large painted figures on the rear wall are recognizably Brazilian and were taken from prints in Wilhelm Piso's *Historia Naturalis Brasiliae* published in 1648 and based, in their turn, on Albert Eckhout's paintings.

Each of the smaller panels surrounding the central allegory represents a landscape with local wildlife and here van Kessel became still more fantastic [96]. According to him, there were unicorns near Buenos Aires, elephants at Vera Cruz, zebras at Porto Seguro, giraffes on Santo Domingo, and a hippopotamus outside Havana. In two panels he combined American fauna with Asian landscapes, showing toucans and Brazilian parrots perching near the Cabo pagoda in Ceylon and opossums on Amboyna. This would be less surprising if Van Kessel had made similar slips with the other continents or had not painted individual American birds with such meticulous accuracy. But if he fell short of modern standards of zoogeography, he did so in distinguished company. The notable zoologist Konrad von Gesner in his *Historia animalium* (1551) and the traveler Thevet had both described giraffes in South America. As we have already seen, elephants were often associated with Brazil (if not Mexico). And even as late as 1782 the Jesuit father Molina reported that a type of hippopotamus with webbed feet and a soft pelt, like that of a seal, had been seen wallowing in the lakes of Arauca.

The idea of the *Wunderkammer* or collection of natural and artificial curiosities also lies behind the magnificent series of tapestries, *Les Indes*, woven at the Gobelins factory in 1687. For they are based on paintings by Eckhout and Post which their patron, Prince Maurits of Nassau, gave to Louis XIV in 1678 together with examples of South American arms, utensils, animal skins and stuffed birds, fishes and reptiles. This

THE NEW GOLDEN LAND

96. (LEFT TO RIGHT) *Buenos Aires, Mexico City, Havana, Domingo, Porto Seguro, Vera Cruz*, 1664–66. Jan van Kessel

[100]

whole collection was put on show in the Louvre where it was a nine-days' wonder, transforming a room into something not unlike van Kessel's painting. The King saw it and expressed august approval; the Dauphin was so delighted by a hammock that he insisted on lying in it. But Prince Maurits's suggestion that the paintings might serve as models for tapestries—"to furnish one large room or gallery, which would be a very rare thing which can be found nowhere else in the world"—seems to have embarrassed those responsible for the artistic decoration of the royal palaces. They would hardly fit in with the classicizing style then in favor. So nothing was done for some years. But the French acquisition of Louisiana in 1682 and the departure of La Salle with settlers to colonize the region in 1684 gave a new significance to exotic American subject matter (also reflected in the ballet as we have already seen). In 1687 therefore three artists, including René-Antoine Houasse, author of many Olympian scenes, and the flower painter Jean-Baptiste Mannoyer, were commissioned to provide cartoons suitable for the Gobelins. This they interpreted rather freely. Not only did they omit Eckhout's Brazilian Indians, though they retained his black slaves; they also indiscriminately mixed the flora and fauna of Africa and America (some of Eckhout's paintings had been done in Angola on his way to Brazil), setting the zebra and the elephant beside the llama and anteater, and giving prominence to horses and camels imported into America by the Spaniards and Portuguese. Thus the idea of a tapestried cabinet of American natural history was submerged in a more generalized desire for exoticism and, perhaps, colonialism [97].

97. *Les Indes*, 1687. Gobelins

THE NEW GOLDEN LAND

Les Indes proved very popular and so many sets had been woven by 1737 that the original cartoons were worn out and Alexandre-François Desportes was commissioned to replace them. He designed an entirely new series, *Les Nouvelles Indes*, still further removed from the original paintings by Post and Eckhout, and presenting still more highly colored visions of the tropics with birds of paradise from the East Indies and tigers as well as American and African fauna. He also introduced figures which better conformed with eighteenth-century ideas about Indians than Eckhout's Tapuya [98, XIX]. They perfectly catch the spirit of Rameau's opera *Les Indes Galantes*, first performed in Paris in 1735, with its enchanting music and preposterous story.

Tapestries of the four continents were produced by nearly all the major factories of Europe. The most popular seem to have been those after cartoons by Ludwig van Schoor woven first at Brussels and widely imitated elsewhere. No fewer than fifty-eight of these extremely costly decorations (far more expensive than most paintings at this date) were sold between 1699 and 1709. The panel devoted to America shows a group of women seated among the riches of the New World and placidly waiting for a fleet of trading ships to sail in. And the

98. *Les Nouvelles Indes*, 1737–63. Gobelins

[102]

xvi. Ballet costume designs for *Peregrina Margherita*, 1660, and
Fenice Rinnovata, 1644. Tommaso Borgonio

XVII. *America*, 1664–66. Jan van Kessel

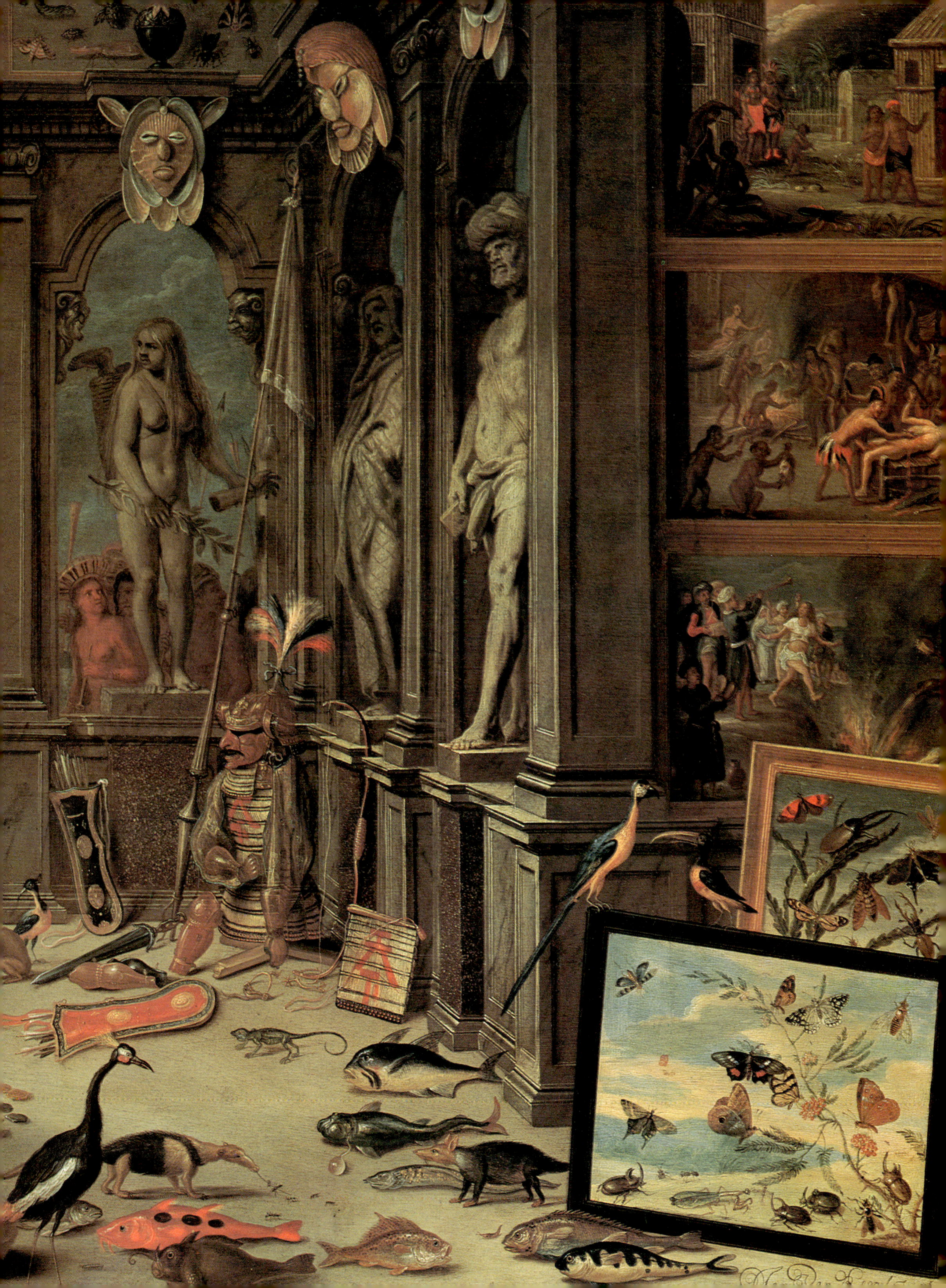

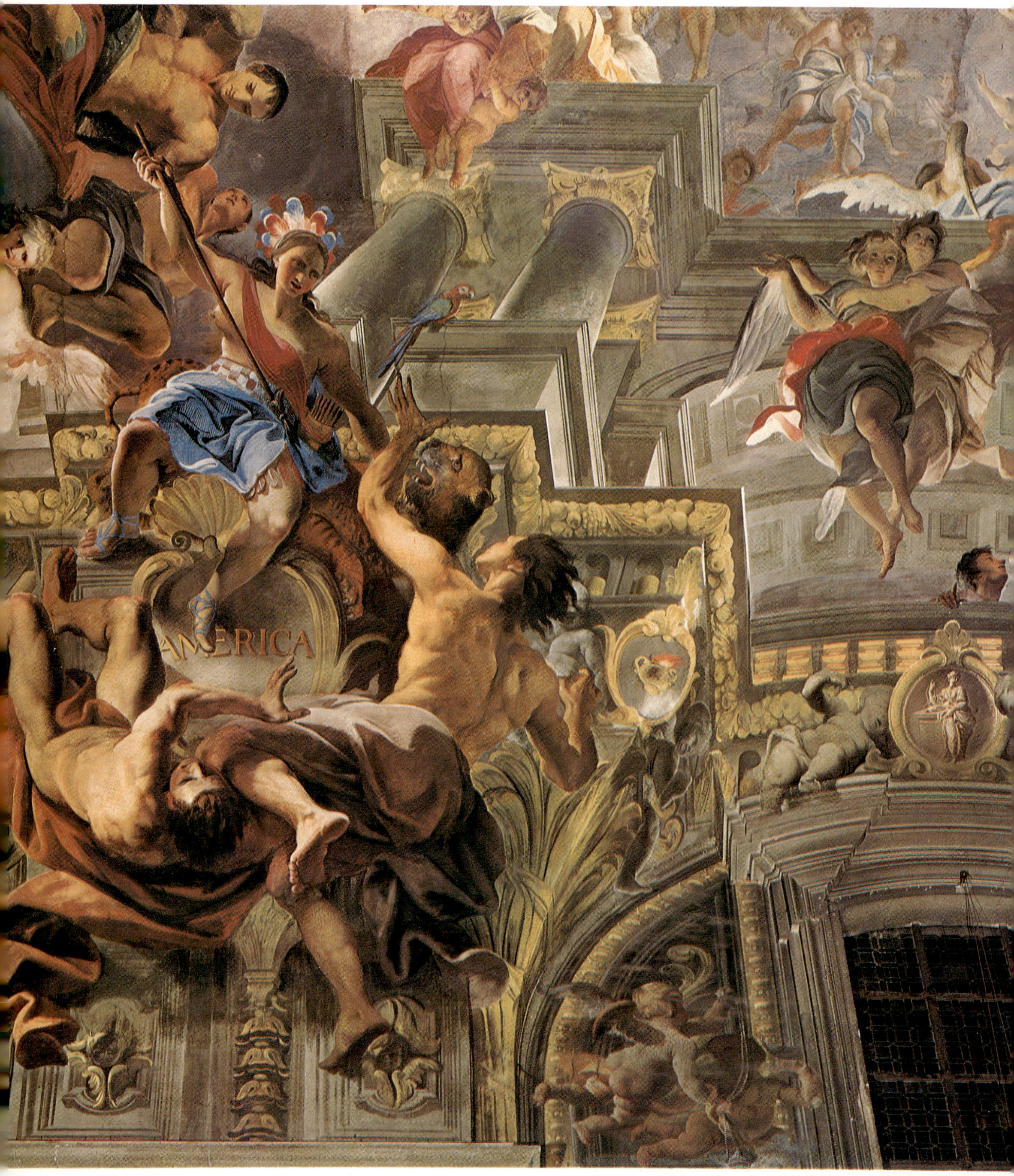
AMERICA

xix. *Les Nouvelles Indes*, 1737–63. Gobelins

xviii. *America*, 1694. Andrea Pozzo

[107]

THE NEW GOLDEN LAND

99. (LEFT) *America*, 1692. Lorenzo Vaccaro
100. (ABOVE) *America*, 1689–90. Luca Giordano
101. (BELOW) *America*, 1742. Jean Dumont

whole set seems to reflect a mercantile view of the world which had previously found expression in the carved Continents of 1656–58 on the west gable of Amsterdam town hall. For allegories of the continents often took their special meanings from their context. Thus, the statues in the gardens at Versailles might signify the world-wide power of the Sun King. Similarly, four massive silver groups made by the Neapolitan Lorenzo Vaccaro in 1692 for the Spanish viceroy easily acquired a religious meaning when they were presented to Toledo Cathedral in 1695 [99]. Here America, dressed in feathers and emeralds, holds the arrow which Pozzo endowed with such significance on the S. Ignazio ceiling, though to the sculptor it was probably no more than an emblem of savagery.

By the mid-eighteenth century images of America, as one of the four continents, were diffused throughout Europe in churches and palaces and private houses, painted on walls, ceiling, or canvases [100, 101], woven in tapestries, carved in marble, modeled in stucco or porcelain, embossed on silver, engraved on glass, painted on tablewares [102, XX], even carved on a sledge [103]. Almost invariably she continued to be represented naked or nearly so, with feathers in her hair and an arrow in her hand. But some of her attributes were slightly modified. The alligator, appropriate denizen of the watery continent, became her constant companion. Allusions to cannibalism were played down, if not omitted entirely, the severed limb being replaced by a head pierced with an arrow which, in a print after Gravelot, is juxtaposed with a church warden pipe almost as if to sug-

102. Tea-pot à *l'amérique*, c.1730. Meissen

xx. *America*, 1745. Meissen

A LAND OF ALLEGORY

gest that "smoking can damage your health." At the same time she acquired a more obviously erotic appeal [104].

The tendency away from solemnity in the arts of the early eighteenth century, so far from discouraging the production of allegories merely stimulated a demand for those with a strong sensual appeal, as we have already seen in the transformation of *Les Indes* into *Les Indes Galantes*. When the continents appeared at the wedding of the Duke of Württemberg in 1764 they figured, dressed by the Parisian master Bocquet, in a musical divertissement, *L'Art d'aimer* [105]. On this occasion America sang: "We love as long as we are loved; / We taste supreme happiness in the instinct which moves us; / Art seems to us an imposture, / And to find true pleasure we follow only Nature." The Indian girl who now symbolized the New World had all the sultry southern voluptuousness of such fictitious characters as Pereene from St. Kitts described by James Grainger:

103. (ABOVE, RIGHT) Sledge, c.1723. Georg Kaufmann
104. (BELOW) *America*, early eighteenth century. De Launay, after Gravelot
105. (BELOW, RIGHT) *Amériquain*, 1764. Nicolas Bocquet

XXI. *America*, 1753. Giovanni Battista Tiepolo

106. *America*, c.1750–60. Johann Wolfgang Baumgartner

> Such charms the old world never saw,
> Nor oft I ween the new.
>
> Her raven hair plays round her neck,
> Like tendrils of the vine;
> Her cheeks red dewy rosebuds deck,
> Her eyes like diamonds shine.

The erotic qualities suggested in the eighteenth century by the word "charms" were fully displayed in allegories of America by such artists as Francesco Solimena in Italy, Johann Wolfgang Baumgartner [106] in Germany, Edmé Bouchardon in France, and above all, by Giovanni Battista Tiepolo, the greatest European painter of his time.

Tiepolo's first conception of the American theme was realized on the great staircase ceiling of the Residenz in Würzburg, completed in 1753. His patron, the Prince-Bishop Carl Philipp von Greiffenklau, was probably influenced, in commissioning this vast fresco, by the staircase ceiling by Johann Rudolf Byss (1717) in nearby Schloss Pommersfelden, where the four continents pay homage to the Elector Lothar Franz von Schönborn and his little army. Similarly at Würzburg, the ostensible subject of the ceiling is the fame of the Prince-Bishop, trumpeted to the gods on Olympus and the inhabitants of the four corners of the earth. However, this rather unpromising program provided no more than a starting point for Tiepolo's sumptuously magnificent vision of the world which has more to do with "Enlightenment" than with the supposed fame of a petty Prince-Bishop. It is, of course, a completely Europocentric view. Africa, Asia, and America yield their treasures for the benefit of Europeans who alone practice the civilized arts of music, painting, sculpture, and architecture. America appears in her by now accepted guise, though slightly more robustly voluptuous than usual, with multicolored feathers in her hair, gold earrings and pendants, a bow strung across her shoulder, seated on a gigantic alligator with a brocade saddle [XXI]. There are stags

[113]

107. Detail of sketch for Throne Room ceiling, Royal Palace, Madrid, 1762. Giovanni Battista Tiepolo

and a parrot, a bundle of brazilwood, and a cornucopia with an abundance of exotic fruits. To the right a man turns a shapeless piece of meat on a spit—perhaps a discreet reference to the cannibal scene which had been usual in sixteenth-century allegories but would have introduced an incongruous note into this best of all possible worlds (though there are, nearby, some inconspicuous severed heads pierced by arrows). Two details deserve comment. One is the banner which seems to have been inspired by Mexican featherwork. The other is the outsize cup, presumably of chocolate—at that time one of the most highly prized of American products—which a pageboy is bringing to America herself. But Tiepolo was not, of course, attempting to provide a painted geography lesson and several elements in his picture of the New World belong properly to the Old. Of the figures on her left one is of a distinctly Mongolian cast, with a tall helmet; another wears a turban. The crescent of Islam mysteriously appears above a parasol near the featherwork banner. There are Italian cypresses and stone pines in the distance and the pageboy wears a sixteenth-century Venetian livery. Moreover, figures with Amerindian feathered headdresses peep out from behind the main groups

108. Detail of Throne Room ceiling, Royal Palace, Madrid, 1764. Giovanni Battista Tiepolo

XXII. Detail of Throne Room ceiling, Royal Palace, Madrid, 1764.
Giovanni Battista Tiepolo

representing Asia and Africa. For to Tiepolo at this date the whole world outside Europe—one might almost say outside Venice—appeared so colorfully exotic that he could hardly take it seriously.

After completing the Würzburg staircase ceiling fresco in 1753, Tiepolo returned to the theme of America in his vast ceiling fresco of the world paying homage to Spain above the throne room of the Royal Palace in Madrid, completed in 1764. As a visual image of America this is of much greater interest than that at Würzburg. The conventional allegorical figure of the continent is given a place of minor importance, the corner of the ceiling devoted to America being dominated, instead, by the ship of Columbus with the explorer on board [XXII]. In his preliminary sketch Tiepolo had shown Columbus standing on a disproportionately small ship with a high poop [107]. In the finished work he changed this completely—perhaps yielding to official Spanish pressure—showing him from the front, looking upward toward the personification of Spain in the center of the ceiling, standing on his long low ship which merges into a group of Neptune and his court (an emblem of Spanish rule over the seas) [108]. With both hands he indicates the cargo which he is bringing from the New World to the Old—mysterious bales and crates, a large catlike animal on a chain (perhaps a jaguar or puma), and the ubiquitous dead alligator. There are also savages, some merely conventional figures with feathers in their hair but also including the figure of a manacled slave who buries his head in his arms on the gunwhale in an attitude of despair—the very image of the noble, innocent, and defenseless but exploited Indian on whose behalf so many Spanish missionaries and government officials had striven against the colonists. Introducing an unexpected note of sensibility into the political apotheosis, he provides a poignant reminder of notions about American Indians contemporary with but very different from gaily elegant Rococo allegories.

CHAPTER 5

The Savage People of America

DISTINGUISHED VISITORS to Versailles in the later decades of the reign of Louis XIV were overawed on arrival by the magnificence of the Escalier des Ambassadeurs which conducted them up to the glittering splendors of the state apartments on the main floor. In the painted architectural decorations by Charles Le Brun above the expanse of highly polished and variously colored marbles, there were four simulated balconies filled with representatives of all the nations of the world—earlier arrivals, as it were, in the perpetual cortège of homage to the Sun King—and among them pride of place was given to an American Indian. The painting itself, together with the whole staircase, was later demolished but Le Brun's full-size cartoon survives to show how the Indian dominated the group of *les différentes nations de l'Amérique*—tall, with an expression of gravity and proud independence on his face, wearing only feathers on his head and a cloak thrown negligently over his shoulders, he displays a splendidly muscular physique which sets him apart from and above his fully dressed creole neighbors. Nudity alone would not have given him an heroic appearance: but he holds a club in his hand like Hercules and he has the well-proportioned beauty, "the dark quick lively eyes, the gentle soft expression of antique statues" which Giovanni da Verrazzano had noted in the Indians of Rhode Island a century and a half earlier. No figure more vividly exemplifies the notion of the "noble savage" [109].

The phrase "noble savage" was first used by John Dryden in his play of 1670, *The Conquest of Granada*:

> I am as free as nature first made man,
> Ere the base laws of servitude began,
> When wild in woods the noble savage ran.

Dryden was referring to the primitive inhabitants of Europe, of course, not to the American Indians, though the term "savage" was already, by this date, beginning to be used mainly for the latter. It would have been very unusual, however, to commend their way of life. In a celebrated passage in *Leviathan* (1651) Thomas Hobbes vividly described the "natural condition" of uncivilized mankind as one of perpetual war, "of everyone against everyone."

> In such condition, there is no place for industry; because the fruit therof is uncertain: and consequently no Culture of the Earth; no Navigation, nor use of commodities that may be imported by sea; no commodious buildings; no instruments of moving, and removing things as require much force; no knowledge of the face of the earth; no account of time; no arts; no letters; no society; and which is worst of all, continual fears, and danger of violent death; And the life of man, solitary, poore, nasty, brutish, and short.

And he went on to remark that "the savage people in many places of *America*" live "at this day in that brutish manner."

In his lengthy retort, *The Catching of Leviathan* (1658), Bishop Bramhall cited the Indians in an exactly contrary sense. He denied that there had ever been any place "where mankind was altogether without laws and without governors," even, he went on,

> amongst the most barbarous Americans who (except some few criminal habits which these poor degenerate people, deceived by national custom, do hold for noble) have more princi-

109. *The Peoples of America*, 1674–79. Charles Le Brun

ples of naturall piety and honesty and morality than are readily to be found in his [Hobbes's] writings.

These passages from Hobbes and Bramhall indicate clearly enough how Indians were used in polemical literature of the period. Time and again they were dragged into court to give evidence in theological, philosophical, and political disputes, few of which had any direct reference to them. They were cited simply because they were generally believed to preserve intact the most primitive state of human society. As Locke put it: "In the Beginning all the World was *America.*" He called on them to lend weight to his theories on the origin of property, the origin of kingship (with special reference to the justice of deposing James II), and the nonexistence of innate ideas, even about the deity. Though this did not prevent him from mentioning Peruvian cannibalism as an instance of how far "the busie mind of Man" can "carry him to a Brutality below the level of Beasts, when he quits his reason."

A century later Rousseau and Voltaire were each calling on the Indians in support of their, characteristically, opposed notions of the early stages of human life, the former picturing solitary hunters "forced, naked and unarmed, to defend themselves and their prey from other ferocious animals," the latter arguing that man

[119]

was from the start a social being. Diagnosing the social ills of Europe in his day, Rousseau cited "the state reached by most of the savage nations known to us" (i.e., the North American Indians) as "the state least subject to revolutions, the best state for man." This was the third stage in his scheme of social development, that in which man lived in a patriarchal communistic society before the discovery of iron and the development of agriculture.

> The example of the savages, who are nearly all found to be at this point, seems to afford further evidence that this state is the veritable youth of the world; and that all subsequent advances have been so many steps, in appearance towards the perfection of the individual, in reality towards the decrepitude of the species.

This was, of course, both attacked and misunderstood. Dr. Johnson dismissed it as "nonsense." "Sir, there can be nothing more false," he thundered at Boswell:

> The savages have no bodily advantages beyond those of civilised men. They have not better health; and as to care or mental uneasiness, they are not above but below it, like bears. No, Sir; you are not to talk such paradox: let me have no more on't. It cannot entertain, far less can it instruct.

For our present purpose, the main interest in these polemics lies in the pro-Indian literature to which may be traced the origin of the idea of the "noble savage." For when expatiating on the merits of the Indians, which they did at inordinate length, eighteenth-century writers drew largely on recent publications about them, most of which had been written by Jesuit and mendicant missionaries and presented an almost uniformly favorable view. The image of the good savage or *bon sauvage* (the more heavily loaded term "noble savage" does not seem to have been revived until the nineteenth century) was, however, one which took its form from Europe and only its coloring from the New World—like the vision of America itself. Classical figures were merely overlaid with "feathered cincture" and skin-deep tattooing; and sometimes even these distinguishing features were either reduced to a minimum or omitted altogether, as in Le Brun's cartoon or in such a print as that of a Canadian Indian funeral procession by Bernard Picart [110]. In literature, including travel literature, Indians tend to speak in the measured periods of classically educated orators, with no more than an occasional exotic metaphor.

As we have already seen, the Indians of Central and South America had often been associated with the Greeks of the Golden Age. For those living in the less clement climate of the North, however, different antique analogues had to be found. Marc Lescarbot, in his widely read *Histoire de la Nouvelle France* of 1609, had identified them with the austere Spartans. A Jesuit enthusing over the physique of the Canadian Indians in 1634—their strong, well-formed, agile bodies without any touch of effeminacy—declared them to be like the ancient Romans, with the handsome, powerful heads of a Julius Caesar, a Pompey, or an Augustus on their muscular shoulders. They were also likened to the more admirable barbarians in ancient history, and the great Dutch jurist Hugo Grotius developed a theory that they did not merely resemble but were actually descended from the *Germanii*. In 1634 he published a dissertation to demonstrate that they had the same gods, the same moral qualities (as described by Tacitus), and almost the same language. Other writers argued that they were the progeny either of the lost

110. *Canadian Indian Funeral Procession*, 1723. Bernard Picart

tribes of Israel or of Jews who had fled across the Atlantic after the destruction of Jerusalem. (In the early nineteenth century Lord Kingsborough squandered an entire fortune trying to prove this theory.)

The parallels drawn between the Indians and ancient Greeks or Romans were, in origin, mainly physical. As Columbus was the first to note, the inhabitants of Hispaniola were quite unlike the Africans. This differentiation was often stressed in later times, most notably perhaps by Defoe who was at pains to show that Man Friday had no Negroid features.

> He was a comely, handsome fellow, perfectly well made, with straight strong limbs, not too large, tall and well shaped. . . . He had a very good countenance, not a fierce and surly aspect, but seemed to have something very manly in his face; and yet he had all the sweetness and softness of an European in his countenance, too, especially when he smiled. His hair was long and black, not curled like wool; his forehead very high and large; and a great vivacity and sparkling sharpness in his eyes. The colour of his skin was not quite black, but very tawny, as the Brazilians and Virginians, and other natives of America are, but of a bright kind of dun olive colour, that had in it something very agreeable, though not very easy to describe. His face was round and plump; his nose small, but not flat like the negroes; a very good mouth, thin lips, and his teeth well set, and white as ivory.

By this time the Africans were generally regarded as being an inferior race, readily associated with Aristotle's definition of born slaves. Their features were against them. Significantly, the one conspicuously noble African in seventeenth- and eighteenth-century European literature is the hero of Aphra Behn's *Oroonoko, or the Royal Slave* (1678) who, however, is endowed with the pride, love of liberty, and bravery usually ascribed to the Indians and the physical features which they share with Europeans—long hair, a Roman nose, and a shapely mouth "far from those great turn'd tips, which are so natural to the rest of the Negroes."

The Indians benefited as much as the Africans suffered from classical ideals of beauty and the neo-Platonic belief that the naked human body manifested the qualities of the soul. Thus, very soon after the discovery of America, the simple virtues which had been ascribed by medieval preachers to the mythical "good African" were not merely transferred to the Indians but considerably heightened in the process (with lamentable consequences for the Africans who had very few European champions until late in the eighteenth century). In the seventeenth century it became quite customary for the missionaries who enthused over the finely built, athletic bodies of the nearly naked Indians to describe in hardly less glowing terms their grave dignity, the respect they showed their elders, their hospitality, their scorn for worldly possessions, their courage and ability to undergo pains and privations without complaint. "The Indians exercise the obedience, patience and poverty which the Franciscans profess," wrote Juan de Palafox de Mendoza, Bishop of Pueblo de Los Ángeles in Mexico, in a treatise which accused the missionaries of corrupting them (printed in Spain in 1650 and brought out in France at Jansenist instigation in 1672).

The most influential seventeenth-century accounts of the Indians were, however, those in the annual *Relations* sent by Jesuits from Canada to Paris where they were heavily edited, printed, and circulated throughout France in order to raise funds. They were slanted in such a way as to suggest that the work of evangelization, though superhumanly difficult, might be achieved—with God's grace and the financial assistance of the faithful. While no attempt was made to disguise the atrociously ingenious cruelty with which Jesuits had been tortured and put to death, the natural virtues of the Indians were stressed. "We see in the savages the fine remains of human nature which are entirely corrupted among civilized people," wrote Père Chauchetière in the *Relation* of 1694:

> Of all the eleven passions they have only two, anger is the greater: and yet they seldom show it excessively except in war. To live in common without quarrels: to content themselves with little without avarice; to be assiduous in work; one can imagine no people more patient, more hospitable; they are affable, liberal, moderate in their speech. Indeed, all our Fathers and the French who lived among the savages reckon that life is passed more sweetly among them than among us.

Though intended to show that the Indian lacked only Christianity to become a paragon of virtue, the Jesuit reports had the very opposite effect on some skeptical European readers—suggesting that he could manage very well without. This was the interpretation put on them by the baron Louis Armand de Lahontan (or La Hontan), a *libertin* in every sense of the word, in three volumes published in 1703 in The Hague for protection from French censorship, the last of which purports to record his conversations with a Huron chief named Adario. As so much of Lahontan's information seems to have been silently lifted from the Jesuits' *Relations*, which he vociferously attacked, it is more than a little difficult to assess the extent of his personal acquaintance with the Indians. But his experiences, aided by a fertile imagination, enabled him to add many significant and picturesque touches to the vision of Indian life—an account of courtship for instance. The young gallant would, he said, take a burning torch to the bed of his beloved who would blow it out if she felt inclined to accept his advances. Not content with this delicate sketch of *amours sauvages* which particularly charmed French readers (Chateaubriand was to allude to it a century later), Lahontan went on to praise the Indians for their advanced views on divorce. They thought it monstrous, he said, to bind themselves to one another without any possibility of breaking the marriage bond. Europeans who submitted to such a custom were born slaves deserving nothing but servitude. The Indians regarded the liberty of the heart as the most precious of all treasures. Their attitude to religion was similarly free and admirable, according to Lahontan, for they believed that "man ought never to relinquish the privileges of reason which is the noblest faculty with which God has enriched him."

Their views on politics, as voiced by the sage Adario, were no less subversive. "Nature knows neither distinctions nor pre-eminemce in individuals of the same species, thus we are all equals," he declared. Among the Indians, the poor man's right to the superfluity of the rich was so well established that no laws were needed to secure it.

> This willing respect for Natural law is the unique wealth of our society, it is what we have in place of regulations, usages and customs. We consult solely the Light of Nature and reconcile with it our sentiments and our wills.

He had been to France and prophesied that at some future date the masses would rise

> to restore the rights of the nation, destroy the property of individuals, make an equal and just distribution of wealth, in a word establish a form of government so equable and humane that all members of society would participate in it, each deriving his fortune from the common happiness.

The frontispiece to the volume shows a naked Indian trampling underfoot a crown, scepter, and book of laws. One may wonder how seriously these revolutionary ideas were taken in early eighteenth-century Europe. They are extremely unusual. Nothing quite like them—or rather nothing quite so explicit—was expressed by any other writer at the time, or for many years to come, apart from the author of a popular, lighthearted comedy, *Arlequin Sauvage*, based partly on Lahontan and first performed in Paris in 1721, who gave some of Adario's remarks to one of the characters, largely in jest. Lahontan had, nonetheless, succeeded in portraying the state of nature, without law, king, or religion, in a new and entirely favorable light. He had also reinforced the links between the savage people of America and the republicans of antiquity.

Many passages from Lahontan were quoted and illustrated by Bernard Picart in his book on idolatrous ceremonies and customs (Amsterdam 1723). Here the courtship ceremony is depicted almost as if it were the story of Cupid and Psyche [111]. Similarly classical figures dance around the pyre on which Indians of the Hudson Bay area sacrifice to the Great Spirit Quitchi-Manitou the goods they obtained by trading with the French [112]. Other plates are simply copied from de Bry and perpetuate his late sixteenth-century vision of the Indians, but the book as a whole expresses that new interest in comparative religion which was just then being taken up, for various reasons—by orthodox churchmen who studied the vagaries into which the devil had drawn the heathen, by deists who yearned to find a single basic faith underlying all creeds (*Christianity as old as Creation*), and by skeptics who sought to prove that all religions were equally false.

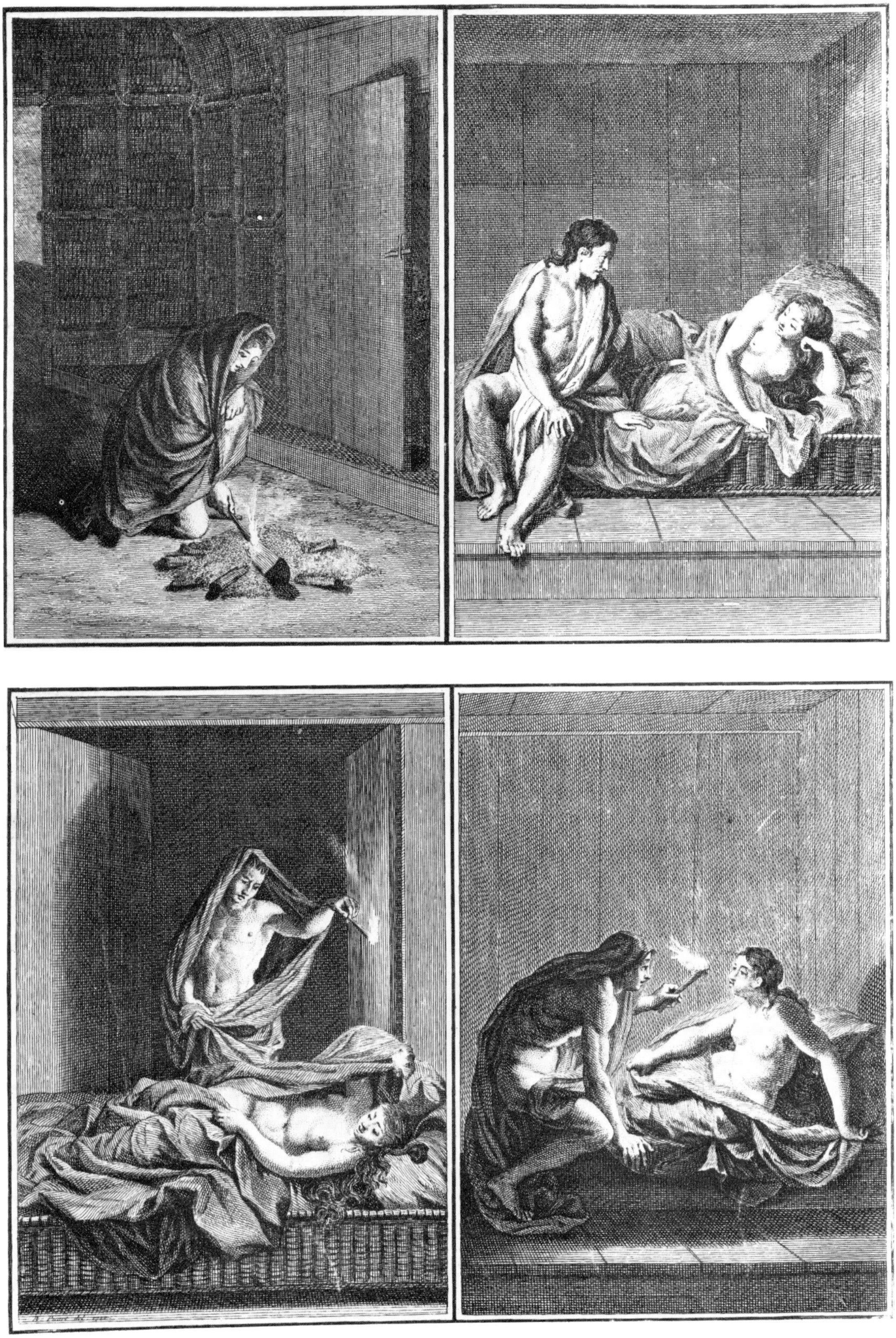

111. *Indian Courtship*, 1723. After Bernard Picart

The whole question of the Indians' religion—if any—had fascinated Europe from the beginning. As the significance of fetishism was not understood and the rites of the Aztecs and Incas were construed as devil worship, it was often stated that they had no religion. The dangerous inferences to be drawn from this notion, which was widely diffused by the missionaries, seem to have passed unnoticed until the early eighteenth century when theologians found themselves obliged to counter the spread of disbelief by proposing logical arguments for the existence of God. As the Jesuit father Joseph François Lafitau pointed out, the supposition that the Indians had no idea of God

> gave the atheist reason to conclude that there is an almost complete world of nations which have no religion, and that the religion found elsewhere is the work of human prudence and an artifice of politicians who have invented it to rule people by a belief which is mother of superstition.

It was partly to "destroy this false idea" that he published his two-volume work on the customs of the American Indian compared with those of Antiquity in 1724—a remarkable book which contains a precocious essay in comparative ethnology.

Lafitau gave an entirely new meaning to the comparisons which had so often been drawn between the Indians and the ancient Greeks. Having worked among the Iroquois as a missionary, he found that his knowledge of Antiquity helped to explain their customs just as their initiation rites, funeral ceremonies, and marriages illuminated what he had read in the ancient authors. For instance, Herodotus's account of how the Lycians had taken their names from their mothers, and not their fathers, might be explained by the same custom which still prevailed among the Hurons and Iroquois. The way in which the Indians wore the skins and horns of animals revealed the origin of the European myth of the satyr—and the point was illustrated by two Greco-Roman satyrs standing between an ancient German and an Indian [113]. Beneath these he placed medieval knights and their

112. *Sacrifice to the Great Spirit Quitchi-Manitou*, 1723. After Bernard Picart

113. Illustration to P. Joseph François Lafitau, *Moeurs des sauvages amériquains comparées aux moeurs des premiers temps*, 1724

helms to show how the symbolism of the horn had persisted. As much concerned with the "premier temps" of Europe as with the savage people of America and far from wishing to ennoble the latter, Lafitau sought to provide logical explanations for the origin of all pagan cults which would not conflict with the teaching of the Church. He argued, in fact, that pre-Christian Europeans were just as savage as the Indians. But he was widely misunderstood. And his illustrator, by basing his Indians mainly on de Bry's engravings, merely gave new life to the belief that they were barely distinguishable from the ancient Greeks.

While such images were in circulation it is hardly surprising that an English writer, John Shebbeare, should have invoked the most famous of all antique statues to describe Canassatego, the Indian hero of his novel *Lydia* (1753):

> The air, attitude, and expression of the beauteous statue of Apollo, which adorns the Belvidera palace [sic] at Rome, were seen animated in this American the instant he had discharged his deadly shaft. And though the fair complexion of the European natives was not to be found in this warrior, yet his face and countenance precluded the perceiving of that defficiency, the perfection of his form and expression of his visage were such that the Grecian sculptors of the famed statue of Laocoon, or the fighting gladiator, might have studied him with instruction and delight.

Needless to say, this body betokens a just and virtuous soul. His beloved Yarico is no less beautiful, with a "bosom hard as wax, and formed like the statue of a Grecian sculptor, where no unnatural restraint has spoiled their shape and situation." And that bosom harbors only natural emotions. These two paragons are juxtaposed with the corrupt and perfidious English in a comparison between the natural and artificial which was soon to become a cliché of the sentimental novelist. Twenty years later, in Henry Mackenzie's widely read and wept-over *Man of the World*, a character contrasts life in England with that of an Indian tribe of whose cruelty he was well aware:

> My imagination drew, on this side, fraud, hypocrisy, and sordid baseness; while on that seemed to preside honesty, truth, and savage nobleness of soul.

Although eighteenth-century Europeans derived their visual impressions of Indians mainly from book illustrations, such as those we have already mentioned—and there were many more of the same kind—they had several opportunities to see them in the flesh as well, especially in England. In 1710 a group of colonists carefully stage-managed the presentation of four Iroquois to Queen Anne in order to impress them with British might and obtain their alliance in war against the French in Canada and also to impress their own needs on the British court. The French in Louisiana organized a similar visit of four Osages to Paris in 1725. Creek Indians were taken to London in 1734 and parties of Cherokees in 1730, 1762, 1765, and 1766. From 1766 to 1768 the Methodist minister Sampson Occom, known as "the pious Mohegan," toured England preaching in dissenting chapels and raising funds for a mission school. The more famous Joseph Brant, grandson of one of the Iroquois presented to Queen Anne, visited England in 1775–76 and again in 1785.

The "state visits" of sachems, usually called "Indian kings," to England were fully reported in the press. That of 1710, the first, naturally aroused the most interest and led to several pamphlets, poems, and periodical articles including an essay by Addison printed in the *Spectator* which carried their fame around Europe (though it was, in fact, no more than a satire on English manners in the tradition of Cicero's letter from a Scythian). John Verelst painted their portraits, from which prints were published in which they cut a rather odd figure. For while he made no attempt to disguise the strange markings on their faces he placed them in the poses held by bewigged English squires, gun in hand and surveying their broad acres [114]. Twenty years later seven Cherokee chiefs on a visit to London were depicted in European dress, standing in a landscaped park, just as if they were members of the English nobility or at least the landed gentry. Even when the exotic hair styles and garb of these visitors were emphasized, as in a print of the Cherokee warrior Ostenaco, they retained the well-bred poise and elegant gestures of "nature's gentlemen" [115].

[125]

114(a). *Ho Nee Yeath Taw No Row, King of the Genereth-garich*, 1710. Jean Simon, after John Verelst

114(b). *Sa Ga Yeath Qua Pieth Tow, King of the Maquas*, 1710. Jean Simon, after John Verelst

114(c). *Tee Yee Neen Ho Ga Row, Emperor of the Six Nations*, 1710. Jean Simon, after John Verelst

115. *Austenaco, Commander in Chief of the Cherokee Nation*, 1762. Anonymous

THE SAVAGE PEOPLE OF AMERICA

During these same years a few artists who had lived among the Indians depicted them in their natural habitat—with strikingly different results. The *farouche* figures with tousled hair and bold streaks of warpaint in the anonymous *Codex canadensis* of about 1700 could hardly be mistaken for English gentry, let alone Grecian statues [116]. Nor could the Indians drawn in Louisiana by Alexandre de Batz in the 1730s. As the inscription reveals, one of his watercolors shows the widow and son of a chief killed by the Natchez with his grim successor brandishing a pole on which three scalps are displayed [117]. De Batz clearly had no illusions about the realities of life and sudden death among the savage people of America. Gustavus Hesselius, a Swedish artist working in Philadelphia, succeeded in preserving a detached view when recording the features of two chiefs of the Lenni-Lenâpé tribe in portraits he painted for John Penn in 1735. One feels convinced that to an impartial observer, the grave sad-eyed Lapowinsa looked much as he does in Hesselius's portrait [118]. But such impartial views of the Indians were rare at this period and were to become still rarer later in the century.

116. *Indian*, from the *Codex canadensis*, c.1700

117. (LEFT) *Indians, New Orleans*, 1732. Alexandre de Batz
118. (ABOVE) *Chief Lapowinsa*, 1735. Gustavus Hesselius

[127]

In forming these views and attitudes the wars in North America doubtless played a part—quite as important a part as abstract philosophical discussions on the state of nature, especially in England. They certainly brought individual Englishmen into closer contact with the Iroquois than ever before. One of them was George (later 4th Viscount and 1st Marquis) Townshend, who succeeded to the command of the British army after Wolfe's death at Quebec in 1759. He was an amateur artist, already notorious for the caricatures in which he had guyed his acquaintances, and in a series of drawings he recorded his visual impressions of the Indians. Making no attempt to conceal the unattractive appearance and bloodthirsty ferocity of these strange but useful allies, he depicted "an Indian who has wounded his enemy & pursues with his tomahawk to scalp him," a "War chief completely equipped with a scalp in his hand," and a brave going to war with his squaw, baby, and small son who has already taken to smoking [119]. The picture they present of Indian life is certainly not a pretty one, yet Townshend was clearly fascinated by the Indians. When he returned to England he took with him specimens of their clothes and weapons and also a live boy intended as a present for Lord George Sackville, who prudently declined to accept him. Thomas Gray saw him one day in January 1760 at Townshend's house. He was brought into the drawing room to entertain the guests, along with Townshend's collection of "scalps & some Indian arms & utensils." However, Gray wrote:

> When they were gone, the Boy got to the box & found a scalp which he knew by the hair belong'd to one of his own nation. He grew into a sudden fury (tho' but eleven years old) & catching up one of the scalping-knives made at his master with intention to murther him, who in his surprise hardly knew how to avoid him, & by laying open his breast, making signs, & with a few words of French Jargon, that the boy understood, at last with much difficulty pacified him. The first rejoicing night [i.e., victory celebration] he was terribly frighted, and thought the bonfire was made for him, & that they were going to torture & devour him. He is mighty fond of venison blood-raw; & once they caught him flourishing his knife over a dog that lay asleep by the fire, because (he said) it was *bon manger*.

119. *Outewas Indians,* 1759. George Townshend

THE SAVAGE PEOPLE OF AMERICA

The facial features of this boy and the relics of the Canadian campaign seem to have been used later in the same year by Robert Adam in designs for a monument to Townshend's brother Roger (killed at Ticonderoga) which show the Indian in a rather different light [120]. Adam's first idea for the monument had been to have a sarcophagus with a relief of Roger Townshend's death, translated into classical language, carried by nude youths wearing nothing but loincloths. But he replaced these supporters by Indian braves in moccasins and leggings with scalping knives, tomahawks, and powder horns, probably justifying this exoticism by the ancient Roman practice of incorporating barbarian prisoners, sometimes as telamones, in monumental sculpture. Thus, though the figures carved on the monument—erected in Westminster Abbey in 1761—may now seem to embody the eighteenth-century ideal of the noble savage, they were probably intended to represent barbarians subdued by civilization.

The Indians in Benjamin West's paintings are similarly ambiguous. An American by birth though long resident in England, West can have had few illusions about their true character. In 1766 he had provided illustrations for William Smith's *Historical Account of the Expedition against the Ohio Indians*, which described Colonel Henry Bourquet's battle with and pacification of the Indians after Pontiac's conspiracy. His painting of *William Penn's Treaty with the Indians* shows how savage breasts had been subdued not by force of arms but by Quaker justice and kindness—exemplifying the benefits of wise colonization rather than the merits of savagery. The pensive figure of the Indian in his most famous work, *The Death of Wolfe*, seems to have the sensibility of noble Indians in contemporary fiction though in fact he may have been

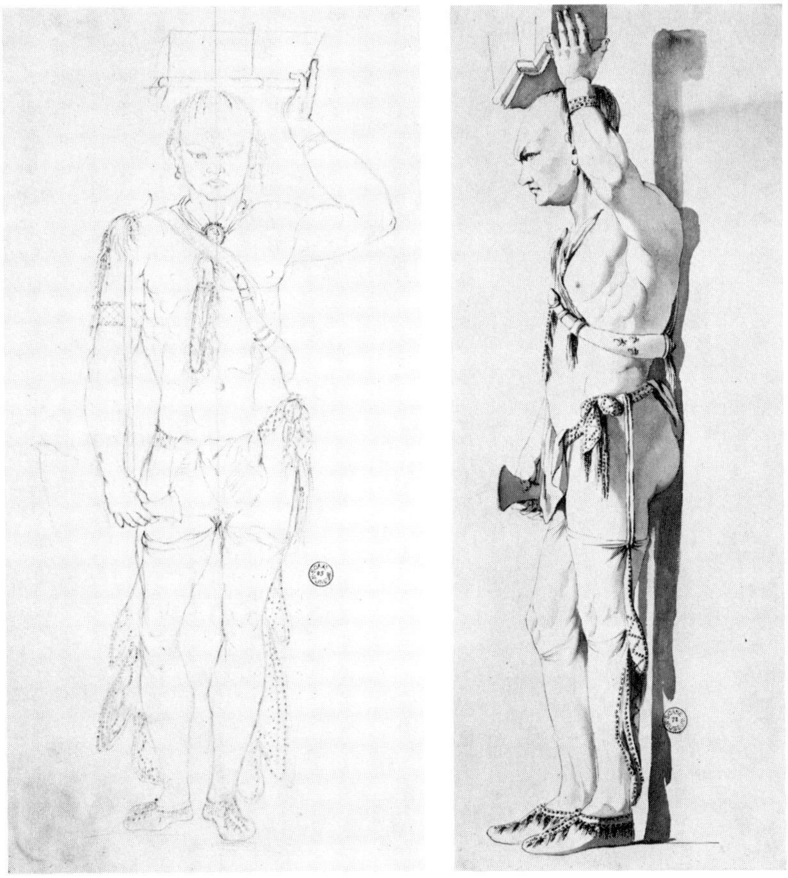

120(a). Designs for the Townshend Monument, 1760. Robert Adam

120(b). The Townshend Monument in Westminster Abbey, 1761

[129]

included only to commemorate the part played by the Five Nations in the war against the French [121]. A different problem is raised by the portrait in which he showed Colonel Guy Johnson, the Superintendant of Indian Affairs in the Northern Colonies, with Thayendanegea, better known as Joseph Brant, behind him. This has been interpreted as showing a loyalist and his Mohawk ally "darkly plotting" the overthrow of the colonies; and indeed the picture was probably painted when Johnson took Brant to London in 1775–76 to secure his support for the Crown. But the rather wraithlike figure of Brant might equally well be interpreted as the genius of the place — an emanation of the distant

121. (ABOVE) Detail from *The Death of Wolfe*, 1770. Benjamin West

122. (ABOVE, RIGHT) *Thayeadanegea, Joseph Brant, The Mohawk Chief*, 1775–76. George Romney

123. (RIGHT) *Joseph Brant*, c.1800. Wilhelm von Moll Berczy

vision of an encampment by Niagara—in silent communion with his white protector. To Europeans like James Boswell, who, as we have seen, had come under Rousseau's spell, Brant seemed to personify the virtues of natural man. And it was in this role that he was painted, resplendant in his feather headdress, with a look of proud independence on his face, by both the American Gilbert Stuart and the English George Romney [122]. Brant seems to have fascinated artists and many years later a German, Wilhelm von Moll Berczy, was to depict him as an old man [123]—pointing as if to the "humbler heav'n" of Alexander Pope's "poor Indian" and believing that

>admitted to that equal sky
>His faithful dog shall bear him company.

While the image of the noble savage was gradually crystalizing, a fierce dispute about other aspects of America and its inhabitants was raging on both sides of the Atlantic. Buffon began it with his "greatest fact" that all the mammals of the New World were smaller and the indigenous people weaker in every way than those of the other continents. This was soon taken up by Voltaire, though he made no more than a passing reference to it. Neither he nor Buffon was primarily concerned with America. But a young Dutchman, Cornelius de Pauw, a follower of both, concerned himself exclusively with the denigration of America in his fashionably entitled "Philosophical researches on the Americans or memoranda for a history of the human race," published in Berlin in 1768–69. His motives in writing this extraordinary tirade—whose influence was to be no less extraordinary—are obscure. But Frederick the Great's attempts at this time to prevent his subjects from emigrating to America must certainly be taken into account. No one could have depicted the New World in a more luridly depressing light than de Pauw.

"It is without doubt a terrible spectacle to see one half of the globe so disfavoured by nature that everything there is degenerate or monstrous," he wrote. Fishes, amphibians, reptiles, and insects flourished in the humid, unwholesome climate of the American continent, but all other creatures degenerated, not excepting Europeans who settled there. The Indians were stupid, weak, undersized, the women unfecund, and the men hairless and thus unvirile—like eunuchs—though given to homosexuality and the "secret vice." They did not represent the hopeful youth of humanity but its degenerate, sick old age. Needless to say, de Pauw had never been to America. He relied on other books, mostly sixteenth-century books, for his information. From Vespucci and Oviedo he gathered his salacious tidbits on sexual malpractices. But, ironically, he seems also to have resorted to the writings of Las Casas and others who had tended to exaggerate the feebleness of the Indians to prove that they were not born slaves, and thus to protect them from exploitation. The more recent writings of the Jesuit missionaries he dismissed as attempts to glorify themselves by representing their converts in as favorable a light as possible.

This preposterous rigmarole provoked an immediate contradiction from Antoine-Joseph Pernety who had accompanied Bougainville to the Falkland Islands in 1763 and was now working as a librarian for Frederick the Great. The Indians were all fine, well-made figures of men, he declared, and there were giants in Patagonia. They were not naturally hairless but very particular in shaving themselves. If they lived simply, that was because these "philosophes rustiques" spurned worldly cares and ambitions. De Pauw replied in a much longer *Défence* based on rather wider reading. To this Pernety responded in an ill-organized work of nearly a thousand pages which defeated its own end. Thus de Pauw, despite the fact that he had never crossed the Atlantic, became the accepted "authority" on America in eighteenth-century Europe and was commissioned to write the article on it for the supplement to the great *Encyclopédie*, published in 1776.

In the meantime, in 1770, a minor *philosophe*, the Abbé Raynal, had published his long philosophical history of the two Indies (owing something to de Pauw but more to Buffon and Voltaire), in which he assembled all the picturesque and scabrous details he could unearth on the subject of the American Indians. The work was frequently reprinted (thirty-seven editions before 1820) and soon became one of the most frequently consulted sources for information about non-European peoples. There can therefore be little doubt that the image of the Indian not as a noble savage but as a weak, backward, or degenerate creature was that which prevailed among the "enlightened" in Europe as a result of this eighteenth-century continuation of "the great debate" about America. Such figures appear in the drawings made by Alexandre-Jean Noël who went to California in 1769 with the French astronomer, the Abbé Chappe d'Auteroche, to observe the transit of Venus. So puny are these ill-favored specimens of the Indian race that one may wonder whether some of them are children or undersized adults [124]. Noël also depicted the drab squalor in which they lived under the rule of the clergy.

Buffon, Voltaire, de Pauw, and Raynal had all been outspokenly hostile to the Indians. A more judicious account of them emerged from William Robertson's *History of America* which was first published in 1777 and held its place as the standard history of the discovery and conquest of the New World until the 1840s. In it the views of sixteenth-century and later writers are synthesized clearly and cautiously, with due allowance for bias. Robertson was well aware of the differences between the inhabitants of the tropical and other zones, as between the Mexicans and Peruvians and the tribes of Brazil and North America. But when he came "to form a general estimate of their character, compared with that of more polished nations," the picture he painted of the Indians was anything but favorable. Their intellectual powers were narrow: in politics they had "neither foresight nor temper to form complicated arrangements with respect to their future conduct"; and in personal relationships they showed little natural affection. "Hardness of heart," "insensibility," "taciturnity," and "cunning" were their outstanding characteristics. Three paragraphs were enough to summarize their virtues, which Robertson listed as "fortitude," "attachment to their community," and an "independent spirit." But even these were hardly redeeming qualities:

> The bonds of society sit so loose upon the members of the more rude American tribes, that they hardly feel any restraint. Hence the spirit of independence, which is the pride of a savage, and which he considers as the unalienable prerogative of man. Incapable of control, and disdaining to acknowledge any superior, his mind, though limited in its powers, and erring in many of its pursuits, acquires such elevation by the consciousness of its own freedom, that he acts on some occasions with astonishing force, and perseverance, and dignity.

But this association of the spirit of independence with savagery (with all the terms of praise carefully qualified) makes one wonder if Robertson was not thinking also of the Colonists who had signed the Declaration of Independence the previous year.

The Revolution focused fresh attention on North America. After the British had suffered several defeats Raynal felt bound to retract his comments on the degeneracy which overtook Europeans who settled in America. Other statements of the *philosophes* were also questioned—

124. *Californian Indians*, 1769. Alexandre-Jean Noël

THE SAVAGE PEOPLE OF AMERICA

though by no means quashed—and the Indians were seen in a more favorable light once again. In 1781 Jean-Jacques-François Le Barbier chose a passage in Raynal's history as the subject for a painting to be submitted to the Paris Salon: Indian parents mourning over the grave of their dead child which the mother sprinkles with her milk. This strange picture seems to have been rather popular (an engraving was published of it [125] and some years later J.-C. Marin modeled the two figures in terra cotta) probably because of the sentiment and overtones, for it clearly reflects two of Rousseau's preoccupations—the virtue of breastfeeding and the superior sensibility of simple people living in the bosom of nature. A few years later Crèvecoeur's *Letters from an American Farmer* (published in England in 1782) appeared in a French edition with the addition of several passages which included, as a reviewer remarked, "comments on the way of life and character of the savages which would have transported J.-J. Rousseau." And it was from one of these additional passages that Antoine Borel took the subject for two drawings illustrating how an Indian restores the peace of a farmer's family by finding a lost child [126]. Ideas about nature in general, not only about America, were changing in these years.

125. *Indian Parents Mourning over the Grave of Their Deceased Child*, 1786. P.–C. Ingouf, after Jean-Jacques-François Le Barbier

126. *L'Enfant Perdu*, c. 1785. Antoine Borel

caricatures, damaged but did not dispel notions of noble savagery. In Charlotte Smith's once popular novel *The Old Manor House* (1793), the treachery and brutality of the Iroquois is described, but the English officer hero is saved by an honest Indian—true to a vow of friendship. In real life too, bonds were forged between the Redcoats and their Indian allies. Sir John Caldwell clearly treasured the memory of the time he spent with a detachment of Ojibwa who elected him their chief with the Indian name Apatto. He had this happy moment commemorated in a portrait which shows him with a tomahawk and wampum belt in his hands, dressed in the feathers and moccasins which his descendants have preserved as relics to the present day [127]. It is an unforgettable image of the savage baronet as noble savage.

Another soldier who served with the British army—though an American by birth—William Augustus Bowles, threw in his lot with the Creek Indians among whom he lived for some twenty years. In 1790–91 he led a delegation of Creeks and Cherokees to London to propose a madcap scheme for the conquest of Mexico. So glamorous a figure could hardly fail to catch public attention. His dictated memoirs were published and his portrait was exhibited at the Royal Academy in 1791 suggesting that he had gone native in the most elegant manner [128]. A newspaper report described him as "a gentleman of fortune born in America, and educated in all the refinements and luxuries of Great Britain" who had "attached himself to a female savage . . . and adopted the manners of the virtuous though uncultivated Indian." At the same time the great surgeon, John Hunter, seems to have commissioned William Hodges to paint the likenesses of two of the Cherokees for his collection of portraits of racial types [129], which already included a woman from Labrador, a Malay woman, a Chinaman, and the famous Polynesian Omai. Although these were all executed as scientific anthropological records, those of the Indians and of Omai in no wise contradict fanciful belletristic notions of savage nobility.

Preconceived ideas might also be confirmed by the several late eighteenth-century books

127. *Sir John Caldwell as an Ojibwa Chief*, c.1782. Anonymous, English

English attitudes to the Indians were modified in different ways by the American Revolution. Their behavior as auxiliaries to the British army, which shocked supporters of the Colonists' cause and was gruesomely depicted in

128. *William Augustus Bowles*, 1791. Thomas Hardy

129. *Cherokee Indian*, 1791. William Hodges

which described life among the Indians, whatever the intentions of their authors may have been. *The History of the American Indians* (1775) by James Adair, who had passed many years as a trader with the Chickasaw and Cherokee, was written to prove their descent from the lost tribes of Israel. However, it also included a great deal of detailed and accurate information about their languages, beliefs, and customs. Apart from commenting on the baneful influence of French traders and missionaries, Adair drew no philosophical comparisons between savage and civilized society; and he neither idealized nor denigrated the Indians. It was from this work, nevertheless, that Joseph Wright of Derby took the subject for his picture of an Indian widow lamenting her warrior husband beneath the tree on which his weapons are displayed—perhaps the most poignant image of what Henry Mackenzie had called "savage nobleness of soul" [130]. But whereas Adair had described this mourning ceremony simply as a custom which kept squaws "obliging to their husbands, by anticipating the visible sharp difficulties which they must undergo for so great a loss," Wright depicted the widow as a moral exemplar of universal significance, on a par with the noblest Roman matrons. She sits in an attitude of frozen grief exposed to the elements whose fury seems to express the violence of passion raging in her bosom. In everything apart from the feathers in her hair she is identical with the figures carved on Neoclassical tombs at the same period.

[135]

130. *The Indian Widow*, 1783–85. Joseph Wright of Derby

Adair's book, which was not reprinted in England though translated into German in 1782, was soon overshadowed by Jonathan Carver's *Travels through the Interior Parts of North America* (1778)—an immediate best-seller. Carver also had spent many years among the Indians and did his best to provide a dispassionate, objective account of their life and customs. But the London publisher to whom he sold his manuscript had it entirely rewritten and embellished with wholly imaginary passages which probably secured its success throughout Europe. On one of these additions Schiller in 1798 based his dirge for an Indian warrior—*Nadowessische Todtenklage*—which Goethe greatly admired.

This poem sums up the late eighteenth-century ideal of the Indian living according to nature's law. "Where are the hawk-eyes which tracked the reindeer over the billowing grass?" the mourners ask. "These are the limbs that bounded through the snow like the stag, these are the arms which bent the strong tense bow. . . .

Bringet her die letzten Gaben,	With the parting gifts provide him!
Stimmt die Todtenklag!	Sing his death-lament!
Alles sey mit ihm begraben,	All things be entombed beside him
Was ihn freuen mag.	That may yield content!

The objects buried with him included his tomahawk, the knife with which he had taken so

[136]

many scalps, and the red body paint that would enable him to shine in the land of souls. The more violent aspects of the state of nature are here accepted without comment. Similar laments, redolent of the seemingly limitless prairies and the wide open spaces of North America, could be found in other travel books of the period, such as Samuel Hearne's *A Journey from Prince of Wales Fort in Hudson's Bay to the Northern Ocean* (1795) which inspired Wordsworth's "Complaint of a Forsaken Indian Woman":

> Before I see another day,
> Oh let my body die away!
> In sleep I heard the northern gleams;
> The stars they were among my dreams;
> In sleep did I behold the skies,
> I saw the crackling flashes drive;
> And yet they are upon my eyes,
> And yet I am alive.
> Before I see another day,
> Oh let my body die away!

But Wordsworth adopted a different attitude to the Indian in *The Excursion* (1814). Here the Wanderer visits the United States and, disappointed by "this unknit Republic," sets off in search of "Primeval Nature's child," the noble savage,

> More dignified, and stronger in himself;
> Whether to act, judge, suffer or enjoy.

A still greater disappointment awaits him. And in a few lines he marvelously evokes the two antithetical views of the Indian:

> So, westward, tow'rd the unviolated woods
> I bent my way; and, roaming far and wide,
> Failed not to greet the merry Mocking-bird;
> And, while the melancholy Muccawiss
> (The sportive bird's companion in the grove)
> Repeated, o'er and o'er, his plaintive cry,
> I sympathised at leisure with the sound;
> But that pure archetype of human greatness,
> I found him not. There, in his stead, appeared
> A creature, squalid, vengeful, and impure;
> Remorseless, and submissive to no law
> But superstitious fear, and abject sloth.

CHAPTER 6

The Land of Liberty

In 1785, two years after the Independence of the United States had been recognized by the Treaty of Paris, the Abbé Raynal sponsored a competition for the best essay on the topic "Has the discovery of America been beneficial or harmful to the human race?" Events had forced the debate on the supposed inferiority of America to take a new turn. *Philosophes* like Raynal, who had accepted de Pauw's contention that mankind deteriorated in the New World, were obliged to think again when they saw the thirteen colonies defeat France's old enemy England and at the same time realize so many enlightened ideals of justice and liberty in the constitution of the new nation. Was it still possible to agree with de Pauw that the discovery of America had been the greatest calamity in human history, they asked themselves. Of the eight essays which survive, four argued that it was, and four that it was not. No prize was awarded.

One of the more enthusiastic of the pro-American essays was that by a Physiocrat, the Marquis de Chastellux, who had been interested in America for some years and had served under Rochambeau in the War of Independence. He had already asked in his treatise *De la félicité publique* (1772):

> Who could not experience a thrill of pleasure in thinking that an area of more than a hundred thousand square leagues is now being peopled under the auspices of liberty and reason, by men who make equality the principle of their conduct and agriculture the principle of their economy?

Economic factors were given prominence in the essay he wrote for Raynal's competition. The discovery of America had stimulated commerce, increasing riches and wages and turning the attention of European nations from military despotism to the "equilibrium of wealth," he maintained. But America had also opened up a vast asylum to "persecuted virtue, frustrated ambition and crime hesitating between despair and repentance," thus providing for the maintenance of the good, the exile of the unfortunate, and the reformation of the vicious. He concluded with an oratorical address to the United States which sums up the attitudes of the *Américanistes* at this period:

> Worthy allies of our King, worthy friends of our nation, you have regenerated the whole continent of which you inhabit but a part; by your virtues you have expiated three centuries of crimes and horrors. . . . Oh, fatherland of Franklin, of Washington, of Hancock, of Adams, who could wish that you had not existed for their sake and for ours? What Frenchman can fail to bless this country where the first auspices of a very happy reign have been manifested and which has produced the first laurels to grace the revered brow of our young monarch?

It would be interesting to know if Jean-Jacques-François Le Barbier was aware of this essay competition when he painted, a year after it was announced, a series of allegories of the continents for the French national tapestry factory at Beauvais. He seems to have had a special interest in America and had already drawn on Raynal's history for his picture of Canadian Indians which he exhibited in the Paris Salon in 1781 [125]. His allegories of Europe and America might almost illustrate Chastellux's essay. In the allegory of Europe Minerva is enthroned alongside personifications of the arts and of Europe (with shields of the sovereign states): bales signify the benefits of commerce and above them a child, naked but for a tricolor panache, hovers in the sky with the standards of victory—alluding to the war in America. The tapestry of America is more explicit. Fame hangs a portrait of George Washington on a Tuscan column (emblem of simplicity, strength, and martial prowess); Minerva, with a thunderbolt and a shield bearing the Bourbon lilies, menaces a cowering Britannia and a couple of snarling jaguars. Up in the clouds Peace and Plenty recline beside the traditional emblem of America—a feather-crowned Indian girl with bow and arrows—while a buxom figure holds up a new symbol, a flagpole from which the Stars and Stripes flutters beneath a cap of liberty [XXIII]. Louis XVI was to have sent a set of these tapestries together with a matching set of seat covers to George Washington, but the weaving was not completed until March 1791, when the time for such royal gifts was quickly passing, and it was never sent. By this date, too, the cap of liberty had acquired a new Jacobin significance. Five years later the tapestries intended for George Washington were sold by the Revolutionary authorities because they bore the emblems of *féodalité* (the Bourbon lilies) which made them unsuitable for the decoration of a public building.

Although a very ancient symbol, the cap of liberty was relatively unfamiliar in France before the American Revolution. When the Abbé de Saint Non made an aquatint after Fragonard's drawing of *Liberty Crowning Franklin* [131] in 1778 he found it necessary to tell a print collector:

> If you know something of iconology, you will recall that a cap held up on a pole or baton is the emblem of Liberty, as a lamp is of Knowledge or the scales of Justice: thus it would be impossible to characterise it otherwise.

In the following years it came to form an almost indispensable part of any allegory of the United States—in paintings and prints [132], on medals,

131. *Liberty Crowning Franklin*, 1778. Abbé de Saint Non, after Jean-Honoré Fragonard

132. *Independence of the United States*, 1786. L. Roger, after Duplessis Bertaux

THE NEW GOLDEN LAND

133. *American Independence*, c.1782. Toile de Jouy

[140]

and even on *toiles de Jouy* made to decorate fashionable boudoirs [133]. But the idea behind the symbol is by no means easy to define. The word liberty has many different and sometimes contradictory meanings. As Isaiah Berlin has remarked, it is "a term so porous that there is little interpretation that it seems able to resist."

One type of liberty had been associated from the very beginning with the American Indians, supposedly living without laws, kings, or religion. The imitation of this state of nature was rarely advocated before the eighteenth century, however, though its merits were often discussed. "It might at first be believed that they are without any form of government and that, living in complete independence, their conduct is ruled only by chance and the wildest caprices," wrote the Jesuit P.-F.-X. de Charlevoix of the Iroquois in 1744.

> Nevertheless they enjoy nearly all the advantages that well regulated authority can obtain from the most civilized [policée] nations. Born free and independent they have a horror of the very shadow of despotic power yet they rarely stray from certain customs and principles founded on good sense, which hold the place of laws and which in some way do duty for legitimate authority.

This spirit of independence and hatred of despotism soon came to be ascribed to all the peoples of North America. When William Robertson wrote of the "Americans" in 1777 that "all are freemen, all feel themselves to be such, and assert with firmness the rights which belong to that condition," he was still referring to the Indians. But it was of the Colonists that Edmund Burke spoke when he told the House of Commons two years earlier that

> a love of freedom is the predominating feature which marks and distinguishes the whole: and as an ardent is always a jealous affection, your colonies become suspicious, reactive, and untractable, whenever they see the least attempt to wrest from them by force, or shuffle from them by chicane, what they think the only advantage worth living for.

The similarities between these two passages are mainly verbal—more apparent than real. Burke was careful to clarify his meaning later in his speech. "The people of the colonies" were, he said, "not only devoted to liberty but to liberty according to English ideas and on English principles." Nevertheless, the feathered Indian holding a cap of liberty on a pole was widely regarded as an appropriate symbol for the independence of the thirteen colonies.

Another type of freedom—liberty of conscience—had been associated with white settlers in America since the sixteenth century. Coligny had attempted to establish French colonies, first in Brazil and then in Florida, partly to provide a haven for his fellow Huguenots, more than half a century before the Pilgrim Fathers landed on Cape Cod. "Safe from the Storms and Prelat's rage," Puritans found in the Bermudas an "isle so long unknown, and yet far kinder" than their own, as Andrew Marvell recorded. A little later Dutch Labardists (a Quietist sect which seceded from the Roman Church) took refuge in Surinam. After 1681 Dissenters from all parts of Northern Europe settled in Pennsylvania where they were guaranteed complete religious freedom.

The freedom from coercion which these emigrants sought had, of course, political implications as well. These people were Protestants, as Burke remarked, "and of that kind which is most adverse of all implicit submission of mind and opinion. This is a persuasion not only favourable to liberty, but built upon it." The dissenting churches had sprung up in direct opposition "to all the ordinary powers of the world" which they justified by a strong claim to natural liberty. All Protestantism is "a sort of dissent," he said.

> But the religion most prevalent in our northern colonies is a refinement on the principle of resistance; it is the dissidence of dissent; and the protestantism of the protestant religion.

The famous Mayflower Compact, by which the Pilgrim Fathers bound themselves to obey whatever laws their elected governor should make, is generally and rightly regarded as the first statement of American political democracy. But their aim was to establish a theocratic rather than a democratic community; and their elective system was a simple application to practical affairs of the process by which they chose their pastors and elders. The idea that North America was a land of political and religious liberty derives less from them than from the much more widely publicized constitution of Pennsylvania. Pamphlets published from 1681 in French, Dutch, and German by William Penn's agent, Benjamin Furly, described both the liberty of conscience enjoyed there and the system by which laws were made and taxes levied only by a representative government elected by secret ballot.

Pennsylvania soon came to be regarded as an ideal state, especially by the French. A glowing account of it was published in one of the most widely read intellectual periodicals of the day, Jean Le Clerc's *Bibliothèque choisie* (1712). Voltaire spread its fame more widely still. Penn had, he said, succeeded in bringing down on earth "the so much boasted golden age, which in all probability never existed but in Pennsylvania." There every man was "in truth a king, for he is free and he is a citizen. He cannot harm anyone, and no one can harm him; he thinks what he pleases without being persecuted." Montesquieu in *De l'esprit des lois* (1748) also paid tribute to William Penn, that "veritable Lycurgus." Penn was, indeed, soon ranked among the great lawgivers, as James Barry was to depict him in the lecture hall of the Royal Society of Art in London, standing between Alfred the Great and Lycurgus to whom he shows the constitution of Pennsylvania [134].

Voltaire was also largely responsible for diffusing the legend of "the good Quaker" as a kind of noble savage of Christianity, which found expression in a curious mid-eighteenth-century print of *L'Assemblée des Couacres* [135]. "These Quakers have a most extraordinary way of living," the inscription states. "No one has more of anything than the others, all goods being held in common. . . ." But the lines beneath attribute to them another type of liberty which was more generally associated with the American Indians: sexual license.

134. *William Penn with Lycurgus and Alfred the Great*, 1777–83. James Barry

135. *Quaker Meeting*, mid-eighteenth century. Anonymous, French

All that we forbid seems ridiculous to them; nothing is excessive in their view; they taste all the pleasures, and lovers satisfy their desires without penalty; so long as the spirit speaks they do so without scruple. Among us all lovers would like to be Quakers. . . .

This was, however, no more than a popular *libertin* misconception of the Quaker way of love. To men of the Enlightenment, Pennsylvania was a living confutation of the conservative belief that a strong church was necessary to preserve morality or that freedom inevitably led to anarchy. Hence the prominence given to articles on Pennsylvania, Philadelphia, and the Quakers in the *Encylopédie* (1765).

It was with well-prepared interest, therefore, that enlightened Europeans watched the struggle of the American Colonists for "life, liberty and the pursuit of happiness." In the late summer of 1776 the internationally fashionable European watering place, Spa in Flanders, was electrified by the news that the "courageous audacity" of the insurgents had forced the British to evacuate Boston, so the Comte de Ségur later wrote.

> I was particularly struck to see burst forth in everyone so keen and universal a sympathy for the revolt of a people against their king. The serious English card-game "whist" was suddenly replaced in all the salons by a no less sober game which was christened "Boston."

That winter *Les Insurgents* became the rage of Paris. A letter writer told the story of a woman so smitten by enthusiasm for them that her lover could gain her attention only by disguising himself as an American Quaker "burning with love for Liberty—and Madame." In Germany in 1776 Friedrich Maximilian von Klinger chose a highly topical American Revolutionary setting for his tragedy, *Sturm und Drang*—soon to give its name to a whole literary movement which advocated the freedom of the passions. There can be no doubt that the shot fired at Lexington was very soon heard round the world. But reactions to it were—and to this day remain—as varied as the meanings given to the word liberty.

The cause of the Colonists was espoused no less fervently in England than in France, though for somewhat different reasons. It is a very remarkable fact that of the several hundred satirical caricatures on American affairs published in London between 1765 and 1782 only three are strongly anti-American—a fact which cannot be explained simply by the natural tendency of satirists to be "agin the government." (They had reacted quite differently to the recent war

136. English caricature, 1765. Anonymous

THE NEW GOLDEN LAND

137. *Lord Chatham and America*, c.1766. Derby porcelain

against the French in Canada.) These "impolitical prints" do, however, suggest that English support for the Colonists was rarely disinterested. Many of them are little more than attacks on Bute's unpopular administration. One of the first, issued immediately after the passing of the Stamp Act in March 1765, is entitled: *The Deplorable State of America or Sc[otc]h Government* [136]. Here Liberty lies down saying, "It is all over with me," and Mercury, patron of commerce, remarks, "It is with reluctance I leave ye." The damage done to British trade by the mismanagement of American affairs is the subject of another print of the same year showing an Indian woman bowed under the yoke of the Stamp Act, holding a bag of money and surrounded by bales of goods and idle merchantmen on the sea behind her. The repeal of the act, effected by Lord Chatham the next year, was often depicted by caricaturists simply as a triumph for trade. At about the same time a Derby porcelain group was showing Chatham with an unaccountably dark-skinned America who kneels before him in gratitude [137].

The Stamp Act also raised a constitutional issue which acquired increasing prominence in

138. *The Phoenix or Resurrection of Freedom*, 1776. James Barry

139. *The Tea Tax Tempest*, 1778. Carl Gutenberg

parliamentary debates in which the main theme of opposition speakers was the liberties of British subjects as established by the Glorious Revolution of 1688 and given a theoretical basis by John Locke. "Our fellow-subjects in America" were descended from those who fled there "rather than submit to the slavish and tyrannical principles, which prevailed at that period in their native land," Lord Chatham reminded the House of Lords in 1774. "And shall we wonder," he asked,

> if the descendants of such illustrious characters spurn, with contempt, the hand of unconstitutional power, that would snatch from them such dear-bought privileges as they now contend for?

The Declaration of Independence, so strongly influenced by the writings of Locke, confirmed the identification of the Colonists' cause with the Whig ideal. Thus, in December 1776, Burke's friend and protégé James Barry issued a print, *The Phoenix or Resurrection of Freedom* [138], in which a group of men standing by a monument "to the Memory of British Freedom"—a recumbent figure mourned by Locke—turn to a pastoral landscape where a man is ploughing and figures dance near a trim classical temple bearing the words LIBERT. AMERIC. and crowned by a phoenix from whose wings Liberty arises. Time scatters flowers on fragments of sculpture labeled "Athens," "Rome," "Florence" in memory of earlier republics. Two years later American Independence was set in the context of modern European republics by a German engraver who reissued an English print, *The Tea Tax Tempest*, with the addition of two roundels, one showing William Tell, inscribed *Switzerland 1269*, the other an auto-da-fé inscribed *Holland 1560* [139].

[145]

At this time it was widely, if erroneously, believed in England that George III, abetted by Bute, was plotting to seize absolute power. Defeats suffered by the British army in America could therefore be interpreted as victories for the constitution. In this way a caricaturist gleefully recorded the retreat from Concord to Lexington while an opposition group styled the Constututional Society voted a hundred pounds for the relief of the widows, orphans, and parents of their "BELOVED American Fellow Subjects who FAITHFUL to the Character of Englishmen, preferring Death to Slavery, were for that Reason only inhumanly murdered by the KINGS Troops." The use of German mercenaries in the war was particularly objectionable to the opposition. "Alas! that I should live to see Brunswickers, formerly defenders of Liberty [of Prussia against France in the Seven Years War] now employed to subjugate the Colonies and destroy the constitutional rights of America", said the Duke of Cumberland, alienated brother of the King. But the employment of Indian auxiliaries was still worse. Chatham denounced the government for letting "the savages of America loose" on "innocent unoffending" Colonists,

> loose upon the weak, the aged, and defenceless; on old men, women and children; upon the very babes upon the breast, to be cut, mangled, sacrificed, burned, roasted, nay to be literally ate.

This gruesome theme attracted several caricaturists, one of whom showed George III joining his Indian allies in a cannibal picnic while a porter staggers under a case of scalping knives, tomahawks, and crucifixes (an allusion to the King's supposed Roman Catholic leanings) labeled "presents to Indians £96,000" [140].

Apart from the constitutional issue, the American war was unpopular in England partly—perhaps mainly—because of increased taxes to pay the army and the decline in trade. Hence the wide diffusion of a caricature entitled *A Picturesque View of the State of the Nation for February 1778* which was even copied on pottery plates. It represented "the commerce of Great Britain" as a cow, with the American Congress sawing off her horns, a Dutchman milking her, and a Frenchman and Spaniard "each catching at their respective shares." The freedom of the merchant to trade was as dear to the English as the freedom to determine how they should be taxed—without which, according to Burke, "no shadow of liberty could subsist."

In France too, commercial interests played an important part in determining attitudes to the American Revolution. This is clearly brought out in several prints, one of which shows Admiral d'Estaing leading muzzled animals "representing the people of Great Britain" and giving a palm to America who is enthroned among crates and barrels labeled "rice for France," "tobacco for Holland," "tobacco for Russia," "indigo for France," and "tobacco for France 1780" [141]. As patron of trade, Mercury often appears

140. English caricature, 1780. Anonymous

141. French caricature, 1780. Anonymous

same reason, no doubt, allegories of American Independence figure prominently among the carvings on an obelisk in the French west coast dockyards at Port-Vendres.

To the French court the freedom of the seas was an issue of far greater importance than the liberties of American citizens. But American Independence was also seen as a victory over England and thus a revenge for the humiliations France had suffered in the Seven Years War. As Chastellux remarked, America yielded the first laurels to deck the brow of Louis XVI. Hence the juxtaposition of the Bourbon lilies with the cap of liberty—as on Le Barbier's tapestry—which was soon to look so strange. In the same way, Louis-Nicolas van Blarenberghe was commissioned by the Crown to execute paintings of the siege and battle of Yorktown together with those of French victories in the War of Austrian Succession. Several other French artists depicted the battles of the American Revolution, appar-

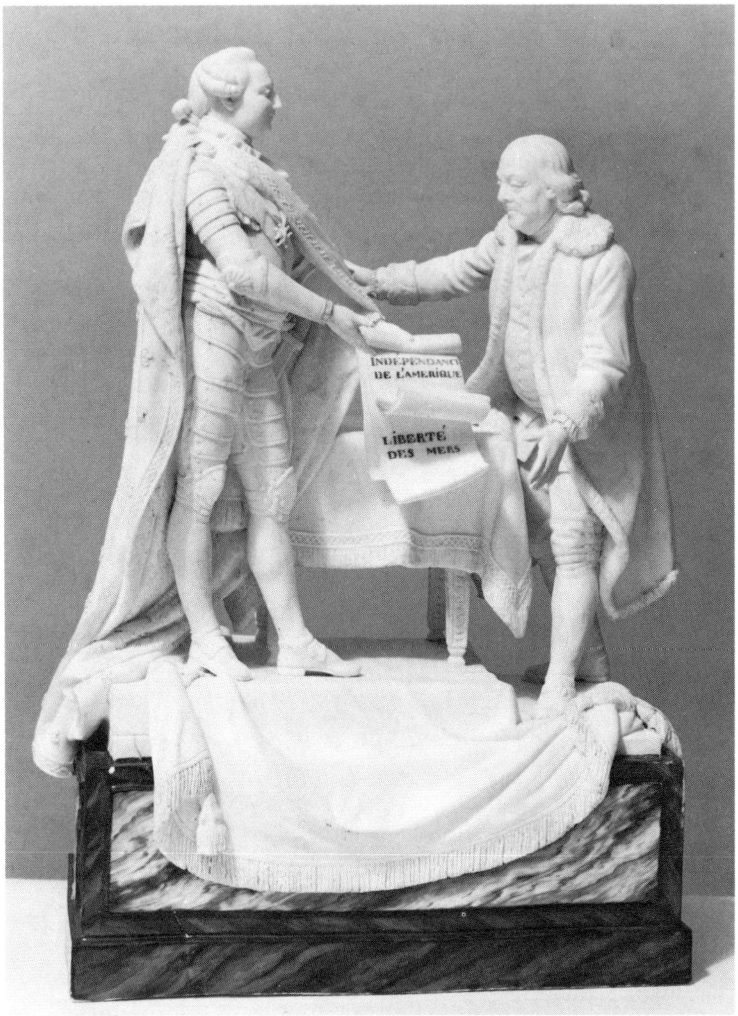

142. *L'Amérique indépendante*, 1778. Jean-Charles Le Vasseur, after Antoine Borel

in French allegories of American Independence. In that by Antoine Borel he sits beside the figure of Liberty [142]. But here greater prominence is given to Courage attacking Britannia who, in her fall, overthrows Neptune with a broken trident and smashed rudder bearing the English coat of arms. It is a reminder that the desire to assert the freedom of the seas encouraged the French (later joined by the Spaniards and the Dutch) to support the United States against England. *Indépendance de l'Amérique* and *Liberté des Mers* are inscribed on the documents which Louis XVI hands to Franklin in a delicate porcelain group made at the Niderviller factory, the proprietor of which, Adam Philippe Custine, fought in the American war [143]. For the

143. *Louis XVI and Franklin*, 1782–85. Niderviller porcelain

ently on their own account. Engravers of the Royal Mint were free to provide models for medals ordered by Americans—one shows Washington and the taking of Boston; another, John Paul Jones and his battle with the English frigate *Serapis* [144]. The Académie des Inscriptions provided the Latin legends for other medals including that (commissioned by Franklin) which has on the obverse the head of Liberty and on the reverse Minerva with the Bourbon shield attacking the British lion while America as the infant Hercules strangles serpents representing the British armies.

The French soldiers who fought in the American campaign were later to be described as "jeunes philosophes à talons rouges," who returned thirsting to establish a similar republic in France. To what extent, if at all, this is true is likely to tease historians of both revolutions for a very long time. Some of the returning French soldiers were, of course, to play a part in the French Revolution, and—perhaps wise after this event—to record how their hearts "palpitated at the sound of the growing awakening of liberty, seeking to shake off arbitrary power." But an accurate view of their reactions at the time is hard to find. Many of those who sailed with Lafayette on the *Victoire* in 1777 went back to France immediately, disgruntled that they had not received the welcome (and the army commissions) they expected. Not all the soldiers in Rochambeau's army were impressed by the new nation. Quakers, for instance, did not live up to the picture Voltaire had painted: one disappointed Frenchman found them "just as selfish, hypocritical, and vicious as the rest of humanity." The egalitarian society which showed no deference to birth was thought to place too great an importance on wealth. Claude Blanchard admired the way of life of the farmers working their own land and thought it would suit him well. "This way of living, this sweet equality has charms for thinking men." But, he added, "Americans love money, and *hard* money." Was this materialism any better than that of the British, he wondered. What appealed most were the civil liberties enjoyed by Americans—freedom of thought, religious toleration, equality under the law, and the

144(a). (ABOVE) Medal of Washington, c.1776–82. Benjamin Duvivier
144(b). (BELOW) Medal of John Paul Jones, c.1776–82. Augustin Dupré

rights of private property which, of course, the *philosophes* had been championing in France for many years. Surprisingly few showed any interest whatever in the democratic systems of government adopted by the thirteen states.

The almost unqualified enthusiasm in Paris for the Americans was inspired largely by Benjamin Franklin, who seemed to epitomize the new nation. "Everything in him announced the simplicity and innocence of primitive morals," wrote Michel René Hilliard d'Auberteuil:

> Franklin had laid aside the wig which formerly in England hid the nudity of his forehead. . . . He showed to the astonished multitude a head worthy of the brush of Guido [Reni] on an erect and vigorous body clad in the simplest garments. His eyes were shadowed by large glasses and in his hand he carried a white cane.

With his battered fur hat, long white hair, homespun coat, and sparkling white linen he looked the very image of "le bon Quaker." But he was much more besides—writer, scientist, and *philosophe*. At a time when science was a fashionable pastime, his experiments with electricity won him special renown. Turgot linked them with his political ideals in a famous epigram, illustrated by Fragonard [145]—"He snatched the lightning from heaven and the sceptre from tyranny."

There was an enormous demand for portraits of Franklin, especially in France, engraved, etched, painted on porcelain and canvas, modeled in terra cotta or wax, carved in marble. Greuze was said to have caught "all the nobility of a free soul, all the wisdom of a well organized head, all the sagacity of a statesman" in his portrait of this "bienfaiteur de l'Humanité." But the most admired and talked about was that by Joseph Siffred Duplessis, exhibited at the Salon in 1779 with the one word *Vir* on the frame [146]. Commenting on it in a letter to the Margravine of Baden, Pierre-Samuel Dupont wrote:

> It is not enough to say that Franklin is handsome: one must say that he has been one of the world's most handsome men. . . . His large forehead suggests strength of mind and his robust neck the firmness of his character. Evenness of temper is in his eyes and the smile of an unshakable serenity on his lips. Work seems never to fray his nerves. His wrinkles are gay; they are tender and proud, not one of them careworn. One can see that he has imagined more

145. *The Genius of Franklin*, 1778. Marguerite Gérard, after Jean-Honoré Fragonard

146. *Benjamin Franklin*, 1778. Joseph Siffred Duplessis

than he has studied, that he has played with the sciences, man and affairs. And it is still almost as a game that in his declining years he labours to found the greatest republic. They have put under his portrait this laconic inscription *Vir*. There is not one trait in his appearance or his life to belie it.

Franklin became a kind of symbol of enlightened man, the representative of his compatriots who could be seen as the chosen people of the Enlightenment. "They are the hope of the human race," Turgot remarked in 1778, "they may well become its model."

Washington, who never crossed the Atlantic, was a much less vivid personality to Europeans, and most portraits of him were perforce derived from paintings and drawings by American artists. Very few European artists had the chance to see him face to face. But Houdon went to Mount Vernon in 1785 to model his bust from life for the statue he had been commissioned to carve by the Virginia Assembly, on the advice of Franklin and Jefferson. In the bust Washington is an antique hero with Roman drapery on his shoulders. In the statue, which was not completed until 1796, he is dressed in the uniform of Commander-in-Chief, standing beside a plow — emblem of agriculture — and the fasces which symbolize the unity of the thirteen states [147]. Here he appears as a new type of hero, the man of his own time, instinct with human dignity but without the *hauteur* and the trappings of European princes, the wise leader rather than the ruler of his people — the "new man who acts upon new principles" of Crèvecoeur's definition. Houdon was no less successful with other American sitters — the genial countenance of Franklin, the sharply intelligent face of Jefferson (a personal friend), the dashing John Paul Jones, the handsome Robert Fulton, and the rough, uncompromising, nineteenth- rather than eighteenth-century features of Joel Barlow — but the statue of Washington is

147. *George Washington*, 1785–96. Jean-Antoine Houdon

XXIII. *America*, tapestry panel, and two chairs with tapestry covers, 1786–91. Beauvais, after Jean-Jacques-François Le Barbier

more than a portrait, however penetrating: it is the image of American democracy.

"The spectacle of a great nation where the rights of man are respected demonstrates that these rights are universal to all peoples," Condorcet wrote in 1786. To him the United States proved

> the influence which the enjoyment of these rights has upon the general welfare, by showing that the man who has never feared outrage against his person acquires a nobler and finer soul; that he whose property is always safeguarded finds probity easy; that the citizen who is subject only to law has truer patriotism and greater courage.

This free atmosphere was, he believed, conducive to the advance of Enlightenment, the only means of ameliorating the lot of mankind. With as many men engaged in the pursuit of knowledge as there were in Europe, the rate of progress would be twice as rapid — and "this progress will include both the useful arts and the speculative sciences." These optimistic views were widely held by the *philosophes* in the years immediately after the American Revolution. There was some divergence of opinion, however, as to the desirability of cultivating the arts equally with the sciences. A visit to the United States convinced Brissot de Warville that "the ability to encourage the agreeable arts is a symbol of national calamity." The Americans had done well to prefer material progress, good housing, street lighting, and bridge building, not to mention sanitation (he wrote a lyrical account of the privies which he contrasted with those in the most aristocratic *hôtels* of Paris).

In the picture of American liberty projected on the screen of the European imagination in the last two decades of the eighteenth century there was, however, one black spot which sometimes grew and spread so that at times it all but came to dominate the whole picture. When the American fever was at its height in 1788 a writer in the *Mercure de France* acidly commented:

> The friends of justice and humanity will perhaps be astonished to learn that in the United States, in that asylum of peace, happiness and liberty, which has so often re-echoed to those sacred words "all men are created equal," there are still today nearly seven hundred thousand slaves.

148. *Homage to Franklin*, c.1779–82. Christian August Lorentzen

This was an uncomfortable fact that few Americanists could overlook. Franklin's presidency of the Philadelphia Abolition Society did him credit, but the need for such a body drew attention to this blemish on the American system. And it is perhaps significant that in the many portraits and allegorical representations of Franklin very few so much as allude to his work for the slaves [148]. Some years later Mme de Staël told Jefferson (a slave owner, albeit a reluctant one) that if only the United States would abolish slavery "there would be at least one government in the world as perfect as human reason can conceive."

Opposition to slavery in the eighteenth century was due in the first place to thinkers of the Enlightenment, especially Montesquieu whose eloquent arguments were echoed by Voltaire and the *Encyclopédistes*. All the *philosophes* who supported the American Revolution held slavery to be an offense against natural law and humanity. In England, Hume presented the philosophical and Adam Smith the economic objections to it. But there the slaves also found advocates of a very different type among churchmen and dissenters who were wholly out of sympathy with rationalism, deism, or atheism and, in some instances, with the American Colonists as well. "How is it that we hear the loudest *yelps* for liberty among the drivers of negroes?" Dr. Johnson asked in *Taxation No Tyranny* (1775). All the narrow bigotry of his character came out in his denunciation of the Colonists and all its warm humanity in his attack on slavery.

The Society for the Abolition of the Slave Trade, founded in London in 1787, had a distinctly religious tone which it took from the Quakers and from the evangelical William Wilberforce. It included gentle, pious, humane William Cowper who inveighed against slavery as "human nature's broadest, foulest blot," yet saw the independence of the United States not as the triumph of liberty but merely as another example of the "perfidy of France." He seems almost to have regarded America as a land of slavery. In his popular ballad, *The Negroe's Complaint*, which was set to music and is said to have been sung in the streets of London, he ascribed its climatic and other peculiarities to God, as a judgment on the slave owners. Had slavery been ordained by "One who reigns on high?" he asked.

> Hark! he answers—Wild tornadoes
> Strewing yonder sea with wrecks;
> Wasting towns, plantations, meadows,
> Are the voice with which he speaks.
> He, forseeing what vexations
> Afric's sons should undergo,
> Fix'd their tyrants' habitations
> Where his whirlwinds answer—No.

The propaganda issued by the Abolitionists was directed mainly against the British slave traders who supplied Brazil and the West Indies as well as the United States. And the visual image they diffused most widely (apart from the Society's somewhat sentimental emblem) was the engraved plan and section of a slaver showing in what appalling conditions the Africans were stowed on their transatlantic voyage. Two antislavery paintings exhibited by George Morland at the Royal Academy in 1789 contrasted the humane hospitality offered by Africans to shipwrecked sailors with the cruelty of the slave traders on the same coast. An engraving of the latter was published in Paris in 1794 with the proud inscription that "this vile trade" had been abolished by the National Convention [149]. The numerous prints of black figures inscribed "moi libre" which appeared at the same time presumably refer to the liberated inhabitants of the French islands [150]. But abolitionist literature and images could hardly fail to reflect also on the United States. It is perhaps significant that Fuseli in 1808, a year after the Act of Parliament abolishing the slave trade had been passed and also at the moment when Anglo-American relations were rapidly deteriorat-

149. *The Slave Trade*, 1794. John Pettit, after George Morland

150. *Moi Libre*, c.1794. Anonymous

THE NEW GOLDEN LAND

ing, should have painted Cowper's Negro as an heroic example of human dignity calling down the wrath of heaven on the American coast. Here the Negro has inherited the qualities formerly ascribed to the Indian. Similarly, and very strikingly, Robinson Crusoe's Indian Man Friday now becomes an African [151]—and has remained so ever since.

William Blake was unusual among Englishmen in his support for both slaves and the American Revolution—and the French Revolution as well. He seems to have been brought face to face with the horrors of slavery in 1791 or slightly earlier when he was commissioned to engrave illustrations to J. G. Stedman's *A Narrative of a five Years' expedition against the Revolted Negroes of Surinam* [152a]. His sympathy is obvious, especially in the plates depicting the slaves' endurance in suffering. This might be

151. French clock with Robinson Crusoe and Man Friday, c.1810. Anonymous

152(a). (ABOVE) Illustration to J. G. Stedman, *Revolted Negroes of Surinam*, 1796. William Blake

152(b). (RIGHT) Page from *America*, 1793. William Blake

thought simply an expression of outrage at the abuses of slavery (like many other eighteenth-century comments in art and literature including Voltaire's Surinam episode in *Candide*) rather than a denunciation of the institution itself. But in the "Little Black Boy" of *Songs of Innocence* he went beyond the arguments of the Abolitionists to denounce the color prejudice itself on which belief in black inferiority and slavery was based. At about the same time he wrote his *Visions of the Daughters of Albion* (published in 1793), a deeply complex allegory of freedom, love, and slavery, based on Stedman's *Narrative,* and also his panegyrics of the American and French Revolutions.

In *America* [152b] Blake told how:

Red rose the clouds from the Atlantic in vast wheels of blood,
And in the red clouds rose a Wonder o'er the Atlantic sea,
Intense! naked! a Human fire, fierce glowing, as the wedge
Of iron heated in the furnace: his terrible limbs were fire
With myriads of cloudy terrors, banners dark and towers
Surrounded: heat but not light went thro' the murky atmosphere.
The King of England looking westward trembles at the vision.

His celebration of the Revolutions was, however, the expression of a desire for liberties more radical than those envisaged by either the signers of the Declaration of Independence or even the makers of the first French Republican constitution. He demanded absolute liberty of the body and soul in both physical and mystical senses. Toward the end of *America* he described one of the happy results of the Revolution:

The doors of marriage are open, and the Priests in rustling scales
Rush into reptile coverts, hiding from the fires of Orc,
That play around the golden roofs in wreaths of fierce desire
Leaving the females naked and glowing with the lusts of youth.

It was a vision which might well discomfort the Puritan daughters of the American Revolution — just as his allegory of sex and slavery would surely have appalled Wilberforce.

"The American Revolution gave birth to the French Revolution," Brissot de Warville told his fellow Jacobins on July 10, 1791. He was among those who attempted to form a French constitution which owed much to the American model. But by the time he met his unlamented death on the guillotine in October 1793, the child (if it can be considered as such) bore very little resemblance to the parent. The French espoused a new concept of liberty no longer based on the sanctity of property: a liberty, moreover, which could be achieved only by a total abjuration of the old regime — of king, law, and faith. To some it looked more like tyranny.

Immediately after the War of Independence, hopes of America had run so high in France and so many Frenchmen were tempted to emigrate that Benjamin Franklin felt bound to publish a pamphlet correcting "ambitious ideas and expectations." The United States was a land of labor where only industrious and skillful workmen would be welcomed, he wrote, it was no *pays de Cocagne*. But the vision of pastoral tranquillity which Crèvecoeur had conjured up was enhanced in many eyes by the outbreak of political disturbance at home. A few months after the fall of the Bastille some thousand emigrants — dupes of the notorious Scioto Company — set sail for, they hoped, an easier and quieter life in southern Ohio. In the following years a number of aristocrats took refuge from the Terror in the United States. Mme de La Tour du Pin found happiness on a farm near Albany though most of her refugee compatriots spent their time complaining of the manners and the food and hoping for the restoration of the *ancien régime* — including those "abuses" which they considered to have been the best part of it.

The United States was rapidly becoming a land of royalist *émigrés* and Jacobins regarded it with increasing suspicion and hostility. In 1795 the publication of Jay's Anglo-American trade treaty opened the floodgates to a torrent of abuse in the French press. One writer declared that the tyranny of Russia was preferable to the so-called liberty of the United States. Washington himself was denounced as a traitor and a dupe of the British. His rehabilitation was, however, brought about by Napoleon who seized on his death in 1799 as an opportunity to link the Consulate with the orderly ideals of the American Revolution. "Washington is dead,"

Napoleon wrote in the Order of the Day which decreed official mourning:

> That great man fought against tyranny; he consolidated the liberty of his country. His memory will forever be dear to the French people, as to all free men of the two worlds, and especially to the soldiers of France who, like him and the soldiers of America, are fighting the battle for liberty and equality.

Ceremonies were held, orations were delivered, and eulogies printed. With an ambiguity which may have been intentional one writer remarked:

> It often happens that after great political crises there arises an extraordinary man who by the sheer power of his character restrains the excesses of all parties and brings order out of chaos.

But the comparison backfired on Napoleon after he had made himself Emperor. Carlo Botta tacitly but very obviously contrasted the first President with the first Emperor, much to the detriment of the latter, in his history of the American War of Independence, first published in Paris in 1809 and frequently reprinted after 1814. This was the book Antonio Canova read while working on the statue of Washington he carved for the state capitol of North Carolina at Raleigh between 1817 and 1820 (it was destroyed by fire in 1831). Canova showed Washington as an antique hero dressed in Roman costume, holding in his hand a tablet inscribed: "Giorgio Washington al popolo degli Stati Uniti 1796. Amici e concittadini" (George Washington to the people of the United States 1796. Friends and fellow citizens) [153]. Commemorating Washington's retirement from politics at the end of his second presidency, Canova celebrated the act of noble renunciation of power which most sharply distinguished him from Napoleon. In Italy the statue was given a more topical significance. Pietro Giordani, an opponent of the reactionary regime imposed by the Congress of Vienna, congratulated Canova on representing Washington as "the pacific legislator and governor of his country which is also unique in its peace and prosperity." The statue had made "the most fervent thoughts boil" in his head. Italy, afflicted by the malignity of foreigners and the cowardice of its own people,

153(a). Model for statue of George Washington, 1818. Antonio Canova

153(b). *Lafayette in 1825 Viewing Canova's Statue of Washington*, 1840. Albert Newsam, after J. Weisman and E. Leutze

would, he wrote, be vindicated when it had earned a statue by Canova of Carlo Alberto of Savoy, then the white hope of Italian liberals.

In these years political idealists in several countries of Europe were turning their eyes toward America. There, in the great undeveloped spaces, they could project their dreams for an ideal community. As early as 1794 Coleridge and others in England were seriously planning to establish a Pantisocratic republic on the banks of the Susquehanna. "Twelve gentlemen of good education and liberal principles" accompanied by as many ladies were to embark next year for "a delightful part of the new back settlements" where two or three hours of work a day would be enough to provision the colony and the rest of their time could be given wholly to reading, discussion, and the education of their children in complete freedom of political and religious opinions. This came to nothing, but after the Restoration a number of Bonapartists with less lofty aspirations were lured to Texas by what Balzac was to call "one of the most terrible confidence tricks ever to have been disguised as a 'national appeal.'" Contemporary prints record the mirage of pastoral bliss which was conjured up for their encouragement [154]. Only a little later Charles Fourier presented his blueprint for a new society to the Ambassador of the United States in Paris. And some ideal communities of a socialist cast were founded, by Robert Owen at New Harmony, Indiana, in 1825 [155]; by Étienne Cabet at Icaria, Iowa, in 1848; and by Victor Considérant (Fourier's chief disciple) at Reunion, Texas, in 1855. The United States not only provided cheap land but also a democratic system which could embrace such commonwealths.

154. *Champ d'Asile, Texas*, c.1818. Anonymous, French

155. Robert Owen's project (1825) for a communal settlement at New Harmony, Indiana

It was, however, with reference to their own affairs that most Europeans looked to America in the early nineteenth century. "I may be wrong, but when I view America at first hand I feel something unknown stirring in the future," wrote Baron Hyde de Neuville, a French royalist as bitterly opposed to Napoleon as to the Jacobins, who went to the United States in 1807.

> I sense that the tyranny which weighs down our unhappy country is not the last word of the new century, and that a new wind is blowing across the world, at once the cause and product of our Revolution. The precise consequences are difficult to predict and will be slow in developing, but I am beginning to think that America has discovered the secret and anticipated the hour.

The United States had enabled him to see that liberty need not be represented by a blood-stained bonnet. Back in France he praised—to Louis XVIII—its "fine and wise constitution which protected every liberty and infringed upon none." The American conception of liberty which had seemed insufficiently radical to the Jacobins appeared increasingly attractive to moderates, whether royalist or republican. Thus the officials of the July Monarchy commissioned Auguste Couder to paint for Versailles a huge *Surrender at Yorktown* to commemorate the part played by France in establishing American independence [156]. An evocation of Washington by the republican Ary Scheffer probably dates from the same period [157].

Alexis de Tocqueville's *Democracy in America* (1835–40) was conceived and read as a study of the implications which the American social system had for Europe. "I wished to show what a democratic people really was in our day," he told a correspondent shortly after the first part appeared. While reducing, he hoped, the "ardour of the republican party . . . without disheartening them," he also "endeavoured to abate the claims of the aristocrats and persuade them to bend to an irresistible future" by demonstrating that "under a democratic government the fortunes and the rights of society may be respected, liberty preserved, and religion honoured." This wise and judicious work soon became a textbook for politicians and theorists who sought a way out of the vicious cycle of

[158]

156. *Surrender at Yorktown*, 1837. Auguste Couder

157. *George Washington on Horseback*, c.1830–40. Ary Scheffer

revolution and repression into which continental Europe had been swept.

Under the Second Empire those who feared a recurrence of 1848 while resenting the despotism of Napoleon III, turned still more frequently to the example of the United States, especially after 1865 when the most conspicuous blot was expunged from the picture of American liberty. The assassination of Lincoln in the same year provided an occasion for a demonstration of Franco-American republican solidarity. Despite the opposition of the Imperial authorities, a large number of Frenchmen subscribed for a gold medal to be sent to the President's widow. On one side it was inscribed: "Dedicated by the French Democracy to Lincoln," and on the other: "Liberty, Equality, Fraternity." Together with it went a letter signed by twenty-six leading republicans including Jules Michelet, Louis Blanc, and Victor Hugo.

Also in 1865, at a dinner party given by Edouard-René Lefebvre de Laboulaye, the idea of erecting a Franco-American monument to the independence of the United States was first mooted. De Tocqueville's successor as the leading *Américaniste*, Laboulaye was the author of numerous pamphlets on the American Civil War as well as a monumental three-volume *Histoire des États Unis* (1855–66) in which, like Botta before him, he tacitly compared America with France. But he obtained a wider diffusion for his idea through an entertaining satire, *Paris en Amérique* (published in 1863 and reprinted nineteen times in four years), in which he poked fun at all those who deplored the "Americanization" of Europe for political, social, religious, or (like the Goncourt brothers) aesthetic reasons. In the later 1860s he collaborated with the Napoleonic regime in the hope of liberalizing it, but after 1870 he emerged as a leading moderate Republican and played a part in shaping the constitution of the Third Republic. It was in connection with the promotion of this republican ideal that he and a group of like-minded Frenchmen commissioned Bartholdi to execute the statue of *Liberty Enlightening the World* [158] eventually erected in New York harbor at the joint expense of private subscribers in America and France—the most prominent monument to the French vision of America as the land of liberty and one which was to stand as a symbol of hope when freedom was jeopardized in Europe.

158. *The Statue of Liberty under Construction in Paris,* 1883. Victor Dargaud

CHAPTER 7

The Exotic South

THE LAND OF LIBERTY was visualized in the late eighteenth century as an extension and idealization of Europe. In popular prints the events of the American Revolution were depicted against backgrounds indistinguishable from it. One of them, engraved at Augsburg, which purports to show the destruction of a royal statue in New York, might easily be supposed to record an uprising in some small German principality were it not for the inscription and the presence of a few black men tugging at ropes to pull down a splendid baroque monument. To this artist, evidently, European and North American scenes were interchangeable. But Central and South America, which had previously dominated the picture of the whole continent and provided the scantily feather-clad figure as its allegorical symbol, remained a strangely exotic terrain—a still inaccessible and still almost entirely unexplored land where the two mysterious empires overthrown by the Spaniards had flourished among vast primeval forests populated by cannibals, venomous reptiles, and birds as gaudily colored as the flowers which hung from the branches of every tree. Thus, in addition to liberating the United States from British rule, the Revolution decisively cut them off from the rest of the continent in the European mind.

In 1777 at the very moment when the French were becoming engrossed by the "great and sublime spectacle" of the American Revolution, they were reminded of the very different sultry southern world by Marmontel's two-volume novel *Les Incas*. This book (begun in the later 1760s) had a topical anticolonial message, but its main purpose was to denounce religious fanaticism. The villain of the work is Pizarro's chaplain Valverde, the hero Las Casas (who speaks more like a deist of the eighteenth century than a Dominican of the sixteenth), and the victims the defenseless Peruvians. "There are few works," a reviewer (Diderot?) remarked, "whose object is more essentially moral, more worthy of the philosopher and citizen." Yet one may wonder if it was not read mainly for the exotic local color which Marmontel had so skillfully drawn from the writings of Herrera and the half-Peruvian Inca Garcilaso de la Vega. Artists certainly seized on this aspect of the book, particularly relishing the combination of exoticism and eroticism in the scene where a cacique's wife cures the sick Las Casas by breast-feeding [159a]. In Italy Pietro Benvenuti selected

159(a). *The Sublime Loyalty of the Cacique Henri*, 1810.
Jean-Jacques-François Le Barbier

159(b). (ABOVE) *Orozimbo Saving Amazili*, c.1820. Pietro Benvenuti

160. *Les Incas*, 1826. Dufour & Leroy scenic wallpaper

one of the more dramatic scenes for one of his great *machines* (later misinterpreted and retitled *America Saving Europe*) [159b]. And if some faint Rousseauist moral purpose may be discerned in such illustrations, none whatever remains in the boldly composed and brilliantly colored but purely decorative *papiers peints* printed at the Dufour factory in 1826 [160].

The Incas had made their bow in imaginative literature before Marmontel. They figured in a long section of Martin Le Roy de Gomberville's five-volume episodic novel *Polexandre* (1626–37), which also brings in the Aztecs. As the victims of the Conquistadors they appeared on the stage in Davenant's strange piece *The Cruelty of the Spaniards in Peru* (1658) and in Voltaire's *Alzire* (1736). A French playwright, Le Blanc, found in the story of the first Inca, Manco Capac, the theme for a tragedy in which he could expound ideas about natural and civilized man picked up from Rousseau (1763). And after Marmontel the conflict between Spaniards and Peruvians once again attracted the attention of dramatists, notably in August von Kotzebue's *Die Spanier in Peru* (1795) from which Richard Brinsley Sheridan drew the plot for his last and least successful play, *Pizarro* (1799).

The wise government of the Incas had been celebrated in European political literature from the time of Bacon onward, and their worship of the sun was often represented as a highly rational religion. Montesquieu thought differently, however, seeing in the downfall of the Incas the fate of all absolutist monarchies built on superstition. But Count Algarotti—protégé of Frederick the Great—found in the Inca empire a model of enlightened despotism which united the "perfect obedience and complete contentment of the people." According to him, it fell only because Atahualpa, an American Caligula, failed to maintain the equilibrium.

Yet Manco Capac, Atahualpa, and the Incas never engaged European attention as did Montezuma and the Aztecs. The Aztec religion might be difficult to defend, but it was far more vividly, titillatingly colorful: their political system, interpreted by Europeans as an aristocracy with an elective monarchy, was intriguingly complex;

and the combination of nobility and human weakness in the personality of Montezuma himself was the very stuff of tragedy, especially when confronted by Cortés. In Dryden's *The Indian Emperor* (1665) he ends by committing suicide like a good Roman. An imaginary conversation between Montezuma and Cortés in Fontenelle's *Dialogues des Morts* (1684) contrasts nobility masked by Aztec barbarity with savagery thinly veiled under European manners. "Civility measures all your steps," Montezuma remarks, "dictates all you say, encumbers all your conversation and cramps all your actions, but does not enter your hearts; and all the justice which should be in your intentions, is found only in your pretexts." Frederick the Great made the conflict the subject of an opera for which he wrote the libretto and Carl Heinrich Graun the music in 1755. "You will appreciate that I have taken the side of Montezuma," the philosopher-king wrote to Algarotti in Italy; "Cortés will be the tyrant."

> Thus it will be possible also in music to direct some jibes against the Catholic King. But I am forgetting that you are in a land of the Inquisition; I apologise and hope to see you soon in an heretical country where even the opera may serve to reform manners and destroy superstition.

The diametrically opposed pro-Catholic and pro-Spanish line was taken by Alexis Piron in a tragedy *Fernand Cortez* (1744) and by a minor writer named Boesnier in a curious "heroic poem" in prose, *Le Mexique conquis* (1752). But the simple confrontation of characters in an exotic setting generally sufficed for Mexican operas. They ranged from Vivaldi's *Montezuma*, first performed in Venice in 1733, to Spontini's *Fernand Cortez* (1809), which enjoyed steady popularity in the early nineteenth century, being praised by both Berlioz and Wagner. For a Berlin performance the sets were designed by Schinkel [161].

Throughout this long period, from the sixteenth to the early nineteenth century, the visual image of Montezuma remained surprisingly unchanged. A life-size full-length portrait of him, accurate in details of costume, had been painted by an unknown European in Mexico, probably in the late sixteenth century and sent to Florence [162]. This provided the source for

161. Stage design for Spontini's *Fernand Cortez*, 1820. Karl Friedrich Schinkel

162. *Montezuma*, late sixteenth century. Anonymous

xxiv. *View of Jalapa and Pico de Orizaba* and *Distant View of Orizaba*, 1831. Johann Moritz Rugendas

an engraving in the 1699 Italian edition of Solís's pro-Spanish history of the conquest of Mexico and seems also to have inspired, if only indirectly, the Montezuma which a Viennese artist included in a series of portraits of "the most famous men of all periods" in 1807 [163]. There is only one major difference: where the original painter had shown Montezuma in an architectural setting, Gindl placed him where every noble savage ought to stand—out of doors and in the bosom of nature. In such a guise he may be imagined declaiming Dryden's heroic couplets, arguing in the exquisitely modulated French of Fontenelle, singing the elegant cavatinas composed by Graun for Frederick the Great, or booming the romantic arias of Spontini.

Despite interest in the political institutions of the Incas and Aztecs and in the personality of Montezuma, the arts of both Mexico and Peru attracted surprisingly little European attention in the quarter-millennium after the conquest. Mexican featherwork and hard-stone carvings were prized, as we have seen, but as natural rather than artistic curiosities. Codices aroused rather more interest, especially for the light they shed on the religious beliefs of the Mexicans and the supposed similarities, or even connections, with those of the Ancient Egyptians. Such esoteric subjects were much discussed at a time when pagan cults were being earnestly studied by orthodox Catholics, mystagogues, and probably the elusive silent minority of skeptics. Thus woodcuts of Mexican gods (derived from an Italian copy of a Mexican codex) figured prominently in an appendix by Lorenzo Pignoria to the 1615 edition of Vincenzo Cartari's work on the images of ancient gods [164]. At about this date too, Samual Purchas acquired the post-conquest Codex Mendoza (now in the Bodleian

163. *Montezuma*, 1807. Karl Lorenz Gindl

164(a). Copy of Mexican codex, 1566–89. Pedro del Ríos

164(b). Page from Lorenzo Pignoria's appendix, "Imagini degli del indiani," to V. Cartari, *Le vere e nuove imagini de gli dei delli antichi*, 1615

THE NEW GOLDEN LAND

xxv. *Tropical Landscape—An American Indian Struggling with an Ape,*
1910. Henri Rousseau le Douanier

Library, Oxford), which he described as the "choicest" of his jewels—

> a Historie, yea a Politicke, Ethike, Ecclesiastike, Oeconomike History, with just distinctions of times, places, acts and arts . . . which our light and slight apprehensions terme not barbarous alone, but wilde and savage.

He included reproductions of nearly all its pages in the third volume of his great collection of travel literature published in 1625. An earlier Mixtec codex (now in the Austrian National Library) came under the eye of the Danish naturalist Ole Worm who had a copy made of part of it in 1650 [165], and from this an engraving was published in the catalogue of his museum. It was from such copies, sometimes at third or fourth hand and so lamentably lacking in the firm draftmanship as well as the brilliant color of the originals, that most Europeans were obliged to derive their impressions of Mexican art. It is hardly surprising that the more skeptical supposed the codices to be no more than meaningless pattern books for jewelers.

As we have already seen, most of the goldsmiths' work sent from Mexico and Peru to Europe in the early sixteenth century was promptly

[166]

converted into bullion. One gold vessel, however, known as the "cup of Montezuma," escaped and was picked up by the first Lord Orford in Cadiz in the 1690s. At a meeting of the Society of Antiquaries in London in 1738 a drawing of it was shown and copied into the minute book, with the comment that the workmanship was "very mean" [166]. Fortunately the piece itself was shown in 1765 when the Society was given a watercolor of it by Paul or Thomas Sandby from which it is clear that it must in fact have been a fine Peruvian gold effigy beaker, probably of the Chimu culture [167]. Nevertheless, William Robertson, the historian of America, was not at all impressed. "The features are gross, but represented with some degree of art," he wrote, allowing its authenticity because it was "certainly too rude for Spanish workmanship." He was equally contemptuous of Mexican codices in which

> every figure of men, of quadrupeds, or birds, as well as every representation of inanimated nature, is extremely rude and awkward. The hardest Egyptian style, stiff and imperfect as it was, is more elegant. The scrawls of children delineate objects almost as accurately.

As for some terra-cotta masks brought back from the Musquito coast and published in *Archaeologia* where they were likened to "the scenic masques of the ancient Romans," they merely provided "an additional proof of the imperfect state of the arts among the Americans." In 1778, another English antiquary de-

165. Copy of a Mixtec codex, 1650. J. Ludolph

166. Lord Orford's "Cup of Montezuma," 1738. Anonymous

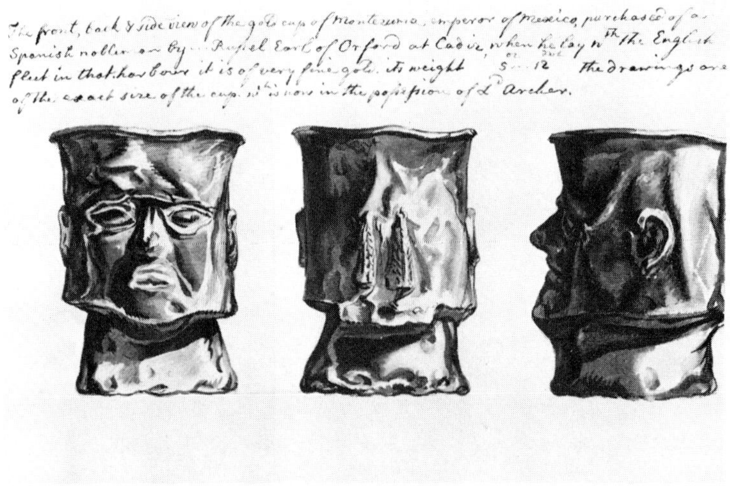

167. Lord Orford's "Cup of Montezuma," 1765. Paul or Thomas Sandby

scribed some handsome carved stone vessels from the same district as "the produce of that middle stage of civilisation which has just left nature, and not arrived at taste in art."

Although eighteenth-century Europeans delighted in Far Eastern art, however strange and bizarre, and had begun to admire their own medieval antiquities, however rude and Gothic, they seem to have been unable to respond to pre-Columbian artifacts except as interesting curiosities. Few indeed are the instances of anything further, and those few are rather equivocal. In about 1720, for instance, a Mexican greenstone mask was given a body, or half a body, and an exquisite jeweled metalwork setting which transformed it into an exotic fantasy [168]. This, and one earlier example already mentioned [19], seem to have been almost the only instances of according to pre-Columbian art the treatment so often given to Chinese, though a pair of giant seventeenth-century pottery vases (themselves decorated in the European style) made at Guadalajara in Mexico were embellished with carved and gilt American Indian supporters for the Florentine Marchese Ginori (founder of the Doccia porcelain factory) in the early eighteenth century [169], and two coarser red pottery vases from Paraguay were set in silver mounts by Johannes Schlatter in 1747 for the Imperial court at Vienna (now in the Kunsthistorisches Museum). Such artistic mestizos are, however, conspicuous by their rarity.

It was perhaps only natural that the arts should have played a small part in the European vision of America at a time when its inhabitants tended to be condemned or, by the followers of Rousseau, commended for their lack of the refinements or artifices of civilization. Information about the "savage" way of life of the Indians in the North colored attitudes to the ancient civilizations of the center and the South. Thus de Pauw represented the vaunted grandeur of Tenochtitlán as a myth put about by the Conquistadors to aggrandize their own achievement. "The so-called palace occupied by the Mexican kings was a hut!" he declared, and the Inca capital Cuzco no more than a huddle of "little shacks without chimneys and without windows." And his opponent Pernety was equally dogmatic and equally ill-informed.

Neither de Pauw nor Pernety had been to Mexico or Peru: they relied on the wildly contradictory reports of earlier writers. In fact, ever since the early sixteenth century access to the Spanish colonies had been made very difficult even for Spaniards. The Dutch and Portuguese colonies could be more easily visited, but they had no relics of the higher cultures and the travel literature about them gives the impression that the whole southern continent was of interest only to naturalists (America as a whole was often said to have geography but no history). Hence the importance of an Italian, Lorenzo Boturini Benaduci, who was allowed to go to Mexico in 1736 as agent of a Spanish condesa. He soon began to investigate Mexican history and

168. Mexican greenstone mask in a European mount, c.1720

[168]

169. Guadalajara vase on a carved and gilded wood stand, early eighteenth-century Florentine

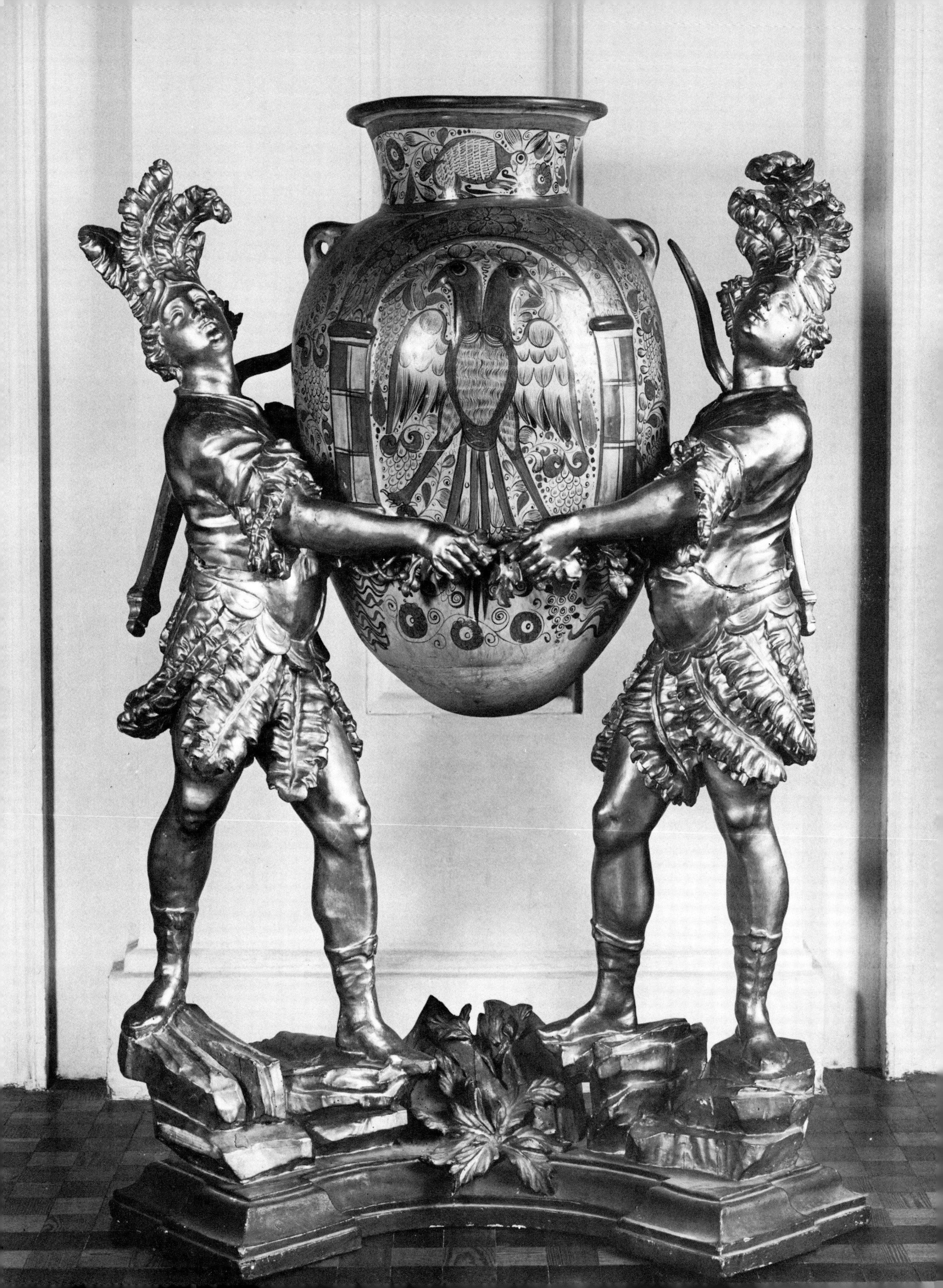

despite mishaps and worse—the Viceregal authorities eventually confiscated the large collection of codices he had assembled and expelled him in 1744—he was able to write his *Idea de una nuova historia general de la América septentrional* (Madrid 1746). This is no more than the prospectus for a much longer work, which he never lived to complete, but in it Boturini gave a new look to Mexican civilization by examining it in the light of the great Neapolitan philosopher, Giovanni Battista Vico's ideas on the early history of mankind. Boturini also provided the first accurate assessment of the Mexican achievement in astronomy. But his book made little impact and its significance went unrecognized until the late nineteenth century.

A far greater contemporary success was the voluminous *Storia Antica del Messico* (1780–81), written by a Jesuit, Francisco Javier Clavigero, who had been expelled from Mexico with other members of his order in 1767. Clavigero set out to contradict the erroneous notions (not least about the degeneracy of Creoles) diffused by de Pauw, Raynal, and Robertson. And in the process he painted a very alluring picture of the Mexican landscape and of the wise government and also the arts of the Aztecs. If he could not go quite so far as to commend Aztec religion, with its human sacrifices and cannibalism, he yet found it "less superstitious, less obscene, less childish and less unreasonable than that of the most cultivated nations of ancient Europe." There were several other widely read publications of the same period which rehabilitated the pre-Columbian civilizations. Gian Rinaldo Carli, an administrator of the enlightened despotism of the Emperor Joseph II, sang the praises of both Inca and Aztec institutions. In 1804 another Jesuit, Pedro José Márquez, published in Rome an account of the recently discovered buildings at Tajín and Xochicalco, the first work on Mexican archaeology to appear in Europe. The next year the King of Spain commissioned Guillermo Dupaix and an artist, Luciano Castañeda, to make a record of the surviving Aztec monuments. But old ideas die hard, and the 1808 edition of Robertson's history still included a categorical declaration that "at this day there does not remain even the smallest vestige of the existence of any ancient Indian building public or private, either in Mexico or in any province of New Spain.... The large mound of earth at Cholula, which the Spaniards dignified with the name of temple, still remains, but without any steps by which to ascend or any facing of stone. It appears now like a natural mount covered with grass and shrubs, and possibly it was never anything more."

All these late eighteenth-century writers had axes to grind. When they were not thinking of European affairs they were almost invariably intent on proving or disproving some theory of American inferiority. The contributions they made to a greater understanding of the ancient civilizations of America were undermined by their polemics. But European ideas were changing. Herder in *Outlines of a Philosophy of the History of Man* (1784) pleads for all civilizations to be judged according to their own merits—not by the European classical touchstone—and it was this as much as his chapter on American Indians that influenced Alexander von Humboldt, that remarkable *uomo universale* of the nineteenth century, who was to play a major part in reshaping the European vision of the South. Alluding to Raynal and Robertson, Humboldt remarked:

> These writers regard as barbarian every state of humanity outside the type of culture which they have created according to their systematic ideas. We should not admit these clear cut distinctions between barbarous and civilized nations.

A few scientists had been allowed to visit the Spanish colonies in the eighteenth century, notably La Condamine in 1735, but Humboldt and his botanist companion Aimé Bonpland were the first Europeans with the equipment (intellectual as well as scientific) to profit fully from extensive exploration in South America [170]. They were amazed by what they found there. Everything seemed new; nothing was familiar. "What a fabulous and extravagant country we're in!" Humboldt wrote to his brother shortly after landing in New Andalusia in July 1799.

> Fantastic plants, electric eels, armadillos, monkeys, parrots: and many, many, real, half-savage Indians.

What trees! Coconut palms, 50 to 60 feet high; *Poinciana pulcherrima* with a big bouquet of wonderful crimson flowers; pisang and a whole host of trees with enormous leaves and sweet smelling flowers as big as your hand, all utterly new to us. As for the colours of the birds and fishes—even the crabs are sky-blue and yellow!

Up till now we've been running around like a couple of mad things; for the first three days we couldn't settle to anything; we'd find one thing, only to abandon it for the next. Bonpland keeps telling me he'll go out of his mind if the wonders don't cease soon.

The fact that they eventually discovered more than three thousand new species of plants (not to mention varieties) indicates not only their industry but how little the regions through which they traveled had ever before been investigated by competent naturalists. Thirty volumes were needed to publish their observations—botanical, entomological, zoological, geological, astronomical, meteorological, historical, and artistic.

Trained as a geologist and mining engineer, Humboldt had obtained a passport giving him free access to the Spanish colonies probably because the King of Spain hoped he might discover new mineral deposits. America was still the land of gold in Spanish eyes. And Humboldt was to investigate, from a detached and enlightened point of view, the old legend of El Dorado. Occasional remarks in his writings, especially the popular *Personal Narrative of Travels to the Equinoctial Regions of America*, allude to the conventional eighteenth-century view of America. "When we speak in Europe of a native of Guiana," he wrote,

we figure to ourselves a man whose head and waist are decorated with the fine feathers of the macaw, the toucan and the humming-bird. Our painters and sculptors have long since regarded these ornaments as the characteristic marks of an American.

Stories of cannibalism clearly fascinated him although he thought them much exaggerated. But he had an uncomfortable moment when, on the Orinoco, far from the nearest white settlement, a mild and intelligent Indian who helped to hold the astronomical instruments, casually remarked that marimonde monkeys, though dark, had much the taste of human flesh.

He told us that his relations (that is, the people of his tribe) preferred the inside of the hands in man, as in bears. This assertion was accompanied with gestures of savage gratification. We inquired of this young man, so calm and so affectionate in the little services he had rendered us, whether he still felt sometimes a desire to eat of a Cheruvichahena. He answered, without discomposure, that, living in the mission, he would eat only what he saw eaten by the Padres.

To Humboldt, with his cool objectivity, the South American reality was far more interesting than the myth. With him the absurd "dispute," initiated by Buffon, now passed out of the realms of science and pseudoscience (even if it was still to haunt other writers, as we shall see). He showed that the relative sizes of animals and plants in the Old and New Worlds was

170. *Humboldt and Bonpland on the Orinoco.* Anonymous, after Keller

wholly irrelevant to any serious study of natural history. At the same time he demonstrated that South America was stranger, richer, more exotically mysterious than the most imaginative of artists or writers had ever dreamed. The many volumes published under his close and detailed supervision contain the first accurate, illustrated conspectus of the landscape, people, plants, birds, animals, fishes, and shells of tropical America [171]. He also reproduced Aztec codices in color for the first time. But his interest in the New World was not exclusively scientific and historical. In his *Essai politique sur le Royaume de la Nouvelle Espagne* (1811) he showed how the mineral resources, especially the silver mines, of Mexico might be exploited. As this appeared very shortly after Mexico had achieved independence (it was published in Paris and translated into English within a year) it was probably responsible for bringing the Mexican mines under English control—with financially disastrous results twenty years later.

While Humboldt's publications were coming out, Central and South America gradually became more easily accessible to Europeans and shortly after the end of the Napoleonic wars several French artists went to Rio de Janeiro to teach in the academy founded by the Regent Dom Pedro, soon to constitute himself Emperor of Brazil. The most notable were Nicolas-Antoine Taunay, who occasionally sent Brazilian landscapes to be exhibited in the Paris Salon, and Jean-Baptiste Debret, who made numerous studies of daily life between 1816 and 1831, using lithographs after some of them to illustrate his *Voyage pittoresque et historique du Brésil* (Paris 1834–39). An Austrian, Thomas Ender, went to Brazil in 1817 with the group of scientists who accompanied the Archduchess Leopoldina (wife of Dom Pedro) and during the next twelve months made some seven hundred delicate drawings and watercolors, recording with great fidelity the vast landscapes, the banana plantations, trim villas with paved terraces, and street scenes of low whitewashed houses [172, 173]. The boat which took Ender to Brazil also carried two Bavarian naturalist explorers, Carl Friedrich Philipp von Martius and Johann Baptist von Spix who did for the Amazon what Humboldt had done for the Orinoco. Their su-

171. *Chimborazo,* 1810. Bouquet, after Thibault

172. *Maranhao Island, Brazil*, 1817. Thomas Ender

173. *Brazilian Landscape*, 1817. Thomas Ender

174. *Spix and Martius in the Amazonian Forest*, 1819. From C. F. P. von Martius, *Flora brasiliensis*, 1840–46

175. *Prince Maximilian of Wied-Neuwied in Brazil*, 1820. From Prince Maximilian of Wied-Neuwied, *Travels in Brazil*, 1820

perbly illustrated books brought the hothouse darkness of the jungle, its pullulating immensity, its labyrinthine malevolence, into placid European drawing-rooms [174]. The primeval forests of South America, with their vast masses of swarming and malignantly tangled vegetation, inimical to intruding man, were vividly described and illustrated in several other works of nineteenth-century travel, notably in Prince Maximilian of Wied-Neuwied's *Travels in Brazil* (London 1820) and, much later and more widely diffused, in Paul Marcoy's *Journey across South America* (1869) with wood engravings by E. Riou [175, 176]. All these conveyed to Europe powerful and disturbing images of a vast, stifling, hostile continent of vegetable flux.

176. *The Sageota Canal, Peru*, 1869. E. Riou, from P. Marcoy, *Journey across South America*, 1869

Humboldt had not been able to take an artist on his expedition—representations of him in South America are imaginary evocations—and his books had to be illustrated by artists working from his own rather rudimentary sketches, dried specimens of plants and dead animals and birds. But no one was better aware than he of the need for painters to represent them in their natural habitat. In *Views of Nature* (1808), his least specialized and probably his most read book, he remarked that it would be worth a great artist's while to study the various species of plants, not in hothouses or from descriptions of botanists, but in the "grand theatre of tropical nature."

> How interesting and instructive to the landscape painter would be a work that should present to the eye accurate delineations of the sixteen principal forms enumerated, both individually and in collective contrast! What can be more picturesque than the arborescent Ferns, which spread their tender foliage above the Mexican laurel oak! what more charming than the aspect of banana-groves, shaded by those lofty grasses, the Guadua and Bamboo! It is peculiarly the privilege of the artist to separate these into groups, and thus the beautiful images of nature, if we may be permitted the simile, resolve themselves beneath his touch, like the written works of man, into a few simple elements.

Such a work would, he believed, be a service not merely to science but also to the arts. Half a century later he was able to say that what Hodges (the artist on Captain Cook's first expedition) had done for the islands of the South Seas, had been done for tropical America "in a much grander style and with greater mastery" by Rugendas, Bellermann, and Hildebrandt. William Hodges had, in fact, painted the Polynesian islands according to the classical tradition of landscape painting, and some of his pictures might at first sight almost be mistaken for views of the Roman Campagna or the Bay of Naples. Like so many artists of his time he seems to have looked at nature through a Claude-glass in order to fit it into the scheme of things. But Rugendas and Bellermann were Romantics. They rejected the old conventions, paid greater attention to the face of nature than to any ideal that might be discerned beneath it, were keenly sensitive to the peculiarities of light and color and form in the landscape, and sought, above all, to convey an impression of the emotions it had aroused in them.

Johann Moritz Rugendas first went to South America at the age of nineteen in 1821 as draftsman on an expedition which the Russian Consul-General, Baron von Langsdorff, planned to lead to the interior of Brazil. He stayed for four years, making on his own account a large number of drawings with which he returned to Europe. Wishing to publish some of them he naturally got in touch with Humboldt who warmly responded to his work and commissioned some drawings of plants. Lithographs after a hundred of his Brazilian views were published with a brief text translated into French as *Voyage pittoresque dans le Brésil* (issued in four parts, Paris 1827–35). On the proceeds he was able to travel to Italy, still the mecca for German landscape painters. But, much encouraged by Humboldt, he again crossed the Atlantic in 1831 and spent the next sixteen years traveling from Mexico to Chile, Peru, Bolivia, Argentina, Uruguay, and Brazil. He painted the jungle steaming with torrid humidity, the bare rocky landscapes of the Andes, a religious *fiesta* with gaudily colored statues carried unsteadily through throngs of kneeling Creoles and Indians and Mestizos, huge sun-baked plazas almost deserted in the midday heat—and always he conveyed something of the thrill of travel. For these impetuously bold sketches of subjects glimpsed, rather than studied, are instinct with wanderlust—as if he had barely had time to record the scenes that struck his fancy before passing restlessly on to find what lay on the other side of the forest or beyond the next steep mountain range [XXIV].

Ferdinand Bellermann, who was sent to Venezuela in 1842 with a travel grant which Humboldt obtained for him from the King of Prussia, was an artist of a different stamp. His sketches are precise and delicate, sometimes almost pernickety. But his drawings of matted, airless forests in which every leaf of every plant is sharply delineated, of trees stifled by lianas which creep into their branches and create webs of tortured lines [177], of stony places where only the fiercely armed cactus and steely leaved agave can

177. *Primeval Forest, Venezuela*, 1843–47. Ferdinand Bellermann

thrive, such an oil sketch as that of a great echoing empty gorge or another of the entrance to a dark cave in a mountainside reveals the beauty, the mystery, and the terror of a landscape untouched and seldom visited by man [178]. Every plant is as accurately depicted as Humboldt could have wished, yet the drawings have a nightmarish quality akin to that of the etchings of Rodolphe Bresdin. Bellermann recorded the fierce struggle for survival in the natural world of tropical America as effectively as Rugendas depicted the brilliance of its color and light and life.

In addition to describing the natural history of tropical America, Humboldt included in his *Vues des cordillères et monuments des peuples indigènes de l'Amérique* (Paris 1810) a few en-

178. *Near Mérida, Venezuela*, 1843–47. Ferdinand Bellermann

gravings of Aztec carvings—the first to be widely seen in Europe—as well as buildings. Europeans had no opportunity to see any large-scale Aztec sculpture until 1824 when William Bullock staged a Mexican exhibition in the Egyptian Hall in London. Casts of the famous Calendar Stone (found under the Cathedral of Mexico City in 1790), the Stone of Tizoc usually known as the "sacrificial stone," and the terrifying statue of Coatlicue together with a few original carvings were shown among the botanical specimens, stuffed birds, and modern artifacts [179]. A real live Mexican in his national costume was brought over to act as guide—though he could speak no English. Comments on this exhibition are so remarkably few that it is difficult to assess what impression it made. The carvings were acquired by the British Mu-

179. *The Mexican Exhibition, London*, 1825. A. Aglio

seum, however, which presumably indicates some serious interest in them. They formed the basis of a pre-Columbian collection which was gradually and somewhat haphazardly augmented in the course of the century, the most notable accessions being those brought back from Mexico by Henry Christy in 1857.

In the early nineteenth century if pre-Columbian antiquities were studied in Europe at all, it was for the evidence they provided of the early history of civilizations about which some very strange theories were propounded. Only in order to prove that Mexico had been colonized by the Jews did Lord Kingsborough commission copies of all the Mexican codices in Europe and publish them in lavish folio volumes from 1831 onward. And it was only in the process of assembling materials for a history of calligraphy that that most voracious of manuscript collectors, Robert Curzon, later Baron Zouche, acquired from the Convent of San Marco in Florence a codex which had probably been sent to Europe by Cortés. His attitude is vividly expressed in a letter in which he described this "very fine" Aztec manscript to a crony:

It is about 30 feet long, and covered on both sides with frightful figures of horrible Americans, beautifully done, tho' in a strange style, in bright colours. I have been after this tome for many years . . . the most curious, and certainly the most entirely incomprehensible wollum that I have got.

Many years were to pass and a revolution in European aesthetics was to take place before an artist who saw it in the British Museum in the early 1920s could list it among the "superb pictorial achievements that every art student ought to investigate." But that is to anticipate.

The buildings of Central America with their intricately carved decorations seem to have excited greater and more widespread interest, perhaps partly because of their exotic settings. For whether they stood in arid wastes with cactuses and agaves thornily triumphing over their tumbled stones, or lurked among the rank vegetation of dark green jungles, they could always be represented in an advanced state of that picturesque decay so much admired by Europeans at this time. These memorials of savage rites and beliefs in boodthirsty gods who might still haunt their precincts came to occupy a prominent position in the vision of tropical America. Drawings of those in Mexico by Luciano Castañeda (1805–8) were used to illustrate one of Lord Kingsborough's volumes in 1831 and also J.-H. Baradère's *Antiquitées mexicaines* published in Paris in 1834. These are still in the eighteenth-century tradition of topographical draftsmanship, neat, objective, and a little dull. Executed in much the same style as those of Egyptian monuments, they may even have given some specious support to the theory that both cultures had the same origin. There is more feeling for atmosphere in the series of lithographs after drawings by a German architect, Carlos Nebel, published in Paris in 1836 (with an introduction by Humboldt) as *Voyage pittoresque et archéologique dans la partie la plus intéressante du Mexique*. Here the vision of the cruel tropical jungle is for the first time visually integrated with that of the darkly mysterious civilization of the Aztecs. Maya carvings were carefully reproduced in Juan Galindo's *Description of the Ruins of Copán* (1836), and the ruins picturesquely represented in their settings by Jean Frédéric Maximilien de Waldeck in his *Voyage pittoresque et archéologique dans la province de Yucatan* (Paris 1839) — an engaging eccentric who later depicted himself being carried over the Chiapas from Palenque to Ocotzinco [180].

While this new interest in Central America was at its height, John Lloyd Stephens and Frederick Catherwood — an English architect with some experience of archaeological draftsmanship gained in the Middle East before he went to New York — set off for Yucatan. Catherwood's drawings, the lithographs after them in *Incidents of Travel in Central America* (1841), and the wonderfully colored aquatints in *Incidents of Travel in Yucatan* (1843) are the most famous of all depictions of the Maya ruins, thanks partly to Prescott who praised them highly in his *History of the Conquest of Mexico*. As responsive to the architecture as he was sensitive to the general atmosphere, Catherwood went far beyond any of his predecessors — or, for that matter, any of his successors — in capturing the *genius loci*. Indeed he almost rivals Piranesi. Sometimes he shows us strange buildings entangled and sink-

180. *Jean Frédéric Maximilien de Waldeck Being Carried over the Chiapas*, 1870. J. F. M. de Waldeck

ing, almost visibly, into the primeval slime [181]; sometimes he brings us suffocatingly close to some intricately carved panel, allowing us to see just enough of the surroundings to realize that this is no safely housed museum piece. At any moment, one feels, a snake may slither out of the undergrowth: and half-demented priests bent on sacrifice may still lurk in the dark green forests where the fallen Maya idols retain, even after so many centuries, the primitive vigor of their carving [182, 183]. Many later artists were to draw and paint and more erudite archaeologists to describe the ancient monuments of Central America, but none more effectively stamped on the European imagination the image of these strange civilizations which seem, in Catherwood's drawings, to emerge like natu-

181. *Maya Stele (C) at Copán*, 1843. Frederick Catherwood

ral forces out of the dark jungle that will once again reclaim them.

While travel books such as those by Nebel, Waldeck, and Stephens and Catherwood were revealing how extraordinary and impressive Central American monuments were, European interest in the history of the Aztecs and Incas continued to grow. Prescott's two histories were almost as widely read in England as in the United States, and even before they had appeared Macaulay remarked that "every schoolboy knows who imprisoned Montezuma and who strangled Atahualpa." In 1845, indeed, John Everett Millais, still of schoolboy age, made his precocious debut at the Royal Academy in London with a large painting of *Pizarro Seizing the Inca of Peru*. And a few years earlier a less gifted English painter, Henry Perronet Briggs,

182. *The Mouth of the Wells of Itzá*, 1843. Frederick Catherwood

THE EXOTIC SOUTH

183. *Archway, Casa del Gobernador, Chichén Itzá*, 1843. Frederick Catherwood

184. *The First Conference between the Spaniards and Peruvians*, c.1840. Henry Perronet Briggs

had depicted *The First Conference between the Spaniards and Peruvians* [184]. Nevertheless, pre-Conquest American subjects ranked fairly low among painters and writers in nineteenth-century England. Southey's long poem of 1805 about exploits of the Welsh prince Madoc in America in the twelfth century was, in every sense, a "sport" though it seems to have been widely read and was frequently quoted by Prescott. A more reliable guide to general trends in these matters is the enormously popular schoolboy story writer G. A. Henty. He set his stirring yarns in all parts of the world and in all periods of history, writing an average of three a year from 1876 onward, yet he did not turn to Central America until 1891 when he published *By Right of Conquest; or, With Cortez in Mexico*. This is the story of a handsome, clean-limbed English lad who is shipwrecked in Campeche, be-

[182]

friended by a slave girl, narrowly escapes human sacrifice, fights alongside the Spaniards, marries an Aztec princess, and returns to England where all good Henty stories have their happy ending. The narrative contains a good deal lifted from Prescott and also some self-righteous reflections on the fall of the Aztec empire which, Henty said, "enslaved and tyrannized over the nations they subdued, extending them no rights or privileges, but using them simply as a means of supplying the pomp and luxury of the capital and providing men for its wars" — so unlike the empire ruled over by his own dear Queen. Rider Haggard used a somewhat similar plot in *Montezuma's Daughter* (1893), but the Aztec heroine commits suicide and thus enables the hero to return home, marry a fair English rose, and write his memoirs at the order of Queen Elizabeth.

Nature, rather than history or art, continued to dominate the visual image of Central and South America. At the great international exhibitions which so clearly reflect the European view of the world in the mid-nineteenth century, the Latin American states were initially represented almost exclusively by natural products. In London in 1851, for example, Chile showed only a lump of gold ore weighing 3 cwt., New Granada, emeralds and a bag of cocoa, Mexico, wax models of fruits, flowers, and reptiles, landscapes in relief, and a collection of woods which, to quote the catalogue, "may prove of value to the naturalist." From Brazil came some examples of leather-work made by "the less civilized of the inhabitants" and a bouquet of flowers composed of feathers and beetles' wings presumably by the more sophisticated. At the Paris exhibition of 1867 a glade in a virgin forest was constructed around a very strange monument apparently made from pieces of brazilwood [185]. For the same show the Mexicans

185. Brazilian forest, Exposition Universelle, Paris, 1867

186. Replica of the temple of Xochicalco, Exposition Universelle, Paris, 1867

187. Peruvian section of the Central and South American Pavilion, Exposition Universelle, Paris, 1878

erected a replica of the temple of Xochicalco, complete with a row of skulls hanging from the cornice and a cast of the Mother of the Gods Coatlicue standing in the central portal [186].

The arts of Latin America were more fully represented in the Paris exhibition of 1878 [187, 188] and it was probably here that Christopher Dresser saw the Peruvian vessels which inspired his designs for ornamental vases made at the Linthorpe Pottery in Yorkshire immediately afterward. Dresser was one of the first European artists to submit to American influence. In Naxca pottery vases, with their twin spouts, and Mochica stirrup-shaped flasks he saw new possibilities for what he called "intelligent and imaginative eclecticism." Naturally, he toned

188. Central and South American and other exhibits, Ethnographical Gallery, Exposition Universelle, Paris, 1878

down their strange and vibrantly colored decorations to make them suitable for appearance alongside Chinese blue and white porcelain and Japanese fans in an aesthete's home. The savagery of Peruvian pottery made a very different, very positive appeal to Gauguin who had been familiar with it since his childhood, when he spent four years in Peru, and it markedly influenced the vases he began to make in 1888.

In the meantime Gauguin had returned to America for a brief visit—though not in search of pottery. His aim was *pour vivre en sauvage*. "I am taking my brushes and paints and will find new strength in a place far removed from civilized man," he wrote as he was setting off for Panama in April 1887. He was bitterly disappointed and obliged to work as a laborer on the canal, then under construction, to earn enough money to move on to Martinique. Here he found "Nature at its most exuberant" and painted it with a new vigor, reveling in its brilliant contrasts of color. In a score of tapestrylike pictures he left a vivid and accurate impression of Martinique [189]; but to live as a savage he had to find a home still further away from civilization.

As visions of tropical America—rather than just views—Gauguin's West Indian scenes are far surpassed by the jungle pictures of Henri Rousseau "le Douanier." In the first, painted in 1891 (now in the National Gallery, London), there is nothing demonstrably American—indeed it includes an Asiatic tiger. But Rousseau let it be believed that he had done seven years' military service as a bandsman in Mexico, in the French detachment sent to support the Emperor Maximilian between 1861 and 1867, and many of his friends supposed his exotic landscapes to be Mexican. Apollinaire certainly thought they were. He stated that Rousseau had been there, while admitting that when questioned, Rousseau remembered only the exotic fruits the soldiers had been forbidden to eat! At the famous banquet given in Rousseau's honor by Picasso in 1908, he proposed the toast to him with these words:

189. *Fruit Pickers, Martinique*, 1887. Paul Gauguin

Tu te souviens, Rousseau, du paysage astèque.
Des forêts où poussaient la mangue et l'ananas,
Des singes répandant tout le sang des pastèques
Et du blond empereur qu'on fusilla là-bas.
Les tableaux que tu peins, tu les vis au Mexique.

There is, of course, no reason to believe that Rousseau ever left France. His jungle scenes are pure fantasies—some of the most extraordinary and powerful ever created, beautiful and sinister evocations of violence and terror, and perhaps his supreme masterpieces [190]. For in them, as in no other works, he was able to fuse his "primitive" visions and obsessions with an equally "primitive" subject matter, releasing all his pent-up poetic powers in an extraordinary feat of sustained imaginative transformation. Apollinaire wrote that while painting his jungle pictures, Rousseau felt their imaginative reality so intensely that he often had to throw open the windows to escape from his self-induced spells! Whether or not he intended them to be American jungles it is impossible to tell, but several have specifically American features—Mexican cactuses, which he presumably knew from potted specimens in the Jardin des Plantes in Paris, Brazilian jaguars, one of which he adapted from a press photograph, and, most explicitly of all and significantly enough in the culminating landscape of the whole series, painted in the last year of his life, an American Indian complete with the traditional feathered headdress and skirt [XXV].

The ferocity of Mexico is felt again very sharply in the poems which D. H. Lawrence wrote at Taos in 1922. In "Eagle in New Mexico" he associated the bird with the religion of the Aztecs:

Why do you front the sun so obstinately,
American eagle?
As if you owed him an old, old grudge, great sun: or
 an old, old allegiance.
When you pick the red smoky heart from a rabbit or
 a light-blooded bird
Do you lift it to the sun, as the Aztec priests used
 to lift red hearts of men?
Does the sun need steam of blood do you think
In America, still,
Old eagle?
Does the sun in New Mexico sail like a fiery bird
 of prey in the sky
Hovering?
Does he shriek for blood?
Does he fan great wings above the prairie, like
 a hovering, blood-thirsty bird?
And are you his priest, big eagle
Whom the Indians aspire to?
Is there a bond of bloodshed between you?

Beneath the surface of modern Mexico he saw with horrified fascination the relics of a past at once sensuous and morbid, repellent and alluring, terrifying and beautiful. In the National Museum there were "snakes coiled like excrement, snakes fanged and feathered beyond all dreams of dread." And at Mitla "under its hills, in the parched valley where a wind blows the dust and the dead souls of the vanished race in terrible gusts," there were carved courts with

> a hard, sharp-angled, intricate fascination, but the fascination of fear and repellence. Hard, four-square, sharp-edged, cutting, zigzagging Mitla, like continual blows of a stone axe. Without gentleness or grace or charm.

And the ponderous pyramids of San Juan Teotihuacán:

> The house of Quetzalcoatl wreathed with the snake of all snakes, his huge fangs white and pure today as in the lost centuries when his makers were alive. He has not died. He is not so dead as the Spanish churches, this all-enwreathing dragon of the horror of Mexico.

South of Mexico a whole vast continent remained a largely uncharted world. Hiram Bingham's astonishing discovery of the lost city of the Incas, Vilacampa, in 1910 showed how much there still remained unknown, how much secrets were still unbroken. And the mysterious disappearance of Colonel Fawcett in Brazil in 1925 reminded the adventurous of the impenetrability and deep malevolence of the Amazonian forests. Both ideas, as old as European knowledge of the New World, were combined by Evelyn Waugh in *A Handful of Dust* (1934) when Tony Last sets off to find a lost city on the undemarcated frontier between Brazil and Surinam and ends up as the prisoner of a white planter gone native to whom he is obliged to read Dickens, day after day, week after week, endlessly. The account of his exploration is an hilarious parody of all the travel books about South America since its discovery, with echoes of Martius and Spix, of Humboldt and even perhaps of Hans Staden's sixteenth-century story of his life

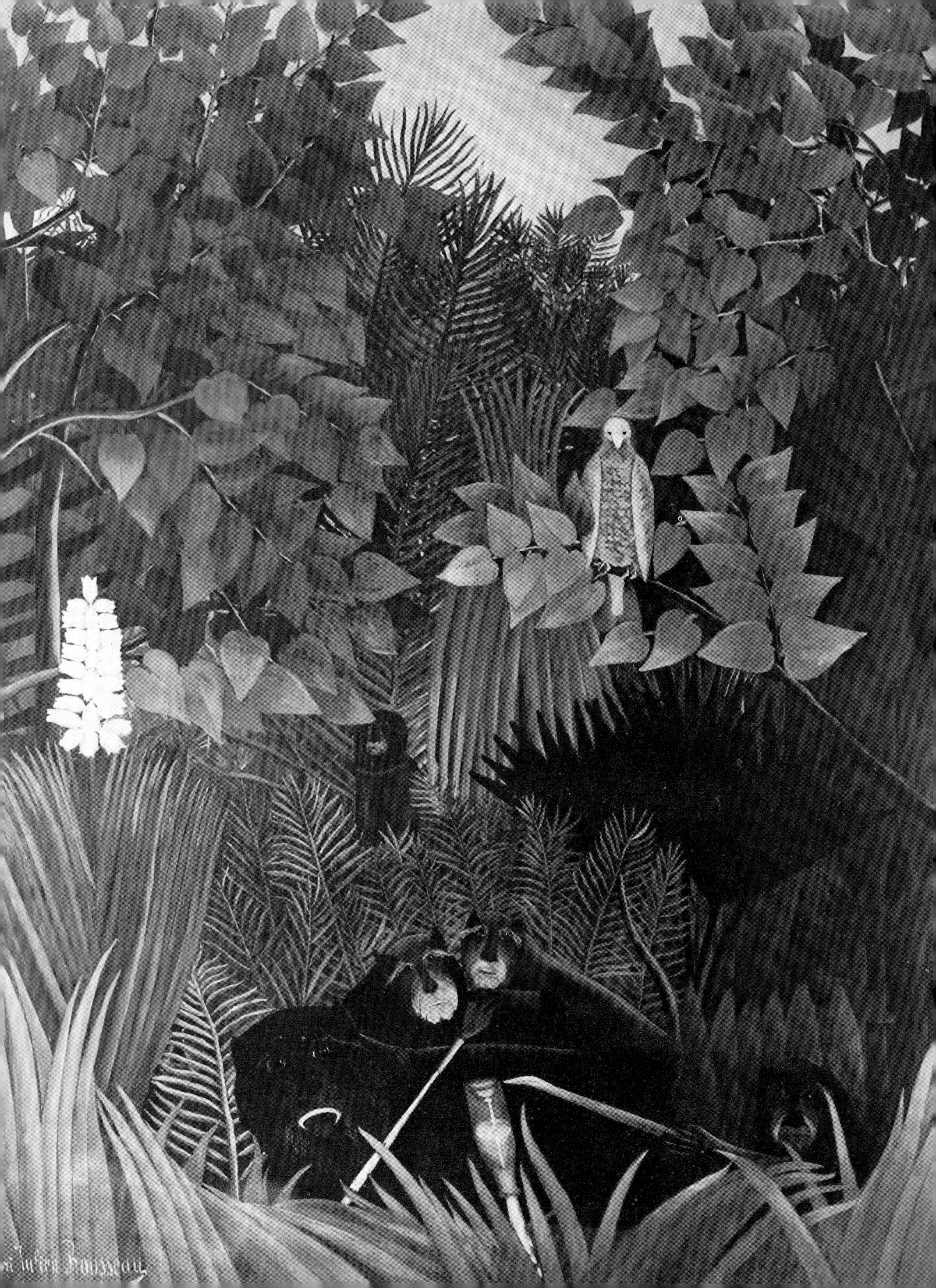
Julien Rousseau

among the cannibals. In the European mind South America had changed very little during four hundred years. In the cities there are even now struggles for political power, as in the days of Pizarro. It has not yet ceased to be a land of adventure. It is still covered with rank primeval vegetation, beautiful and cruel, which hints that the waters of the flood may still linger in its insect-infested swamps and rivers alive with reptiles.

190. *Joyeux Farceurs*, 1906. Henri Rousseau le Douanier

CHAPTER 8

The Prejudged Land

Where shall I learn to get my peace again?
To banish thoughts of that most hateful land,
Dungeoner of my friends, that wicked strand
Where they were wreck'd and live a wretched life;
That monstrous region, whose dull rivers pour,
Ever from their sordid urns unto the shore,
Unown'd of any weedy-haired gods;
Whose winds, all zephyrless, hold scourging rods,
Iced in the great lakes, to afflict mankind;
Whose rank-grown forests, frosted, black, and blind,
Would fright a Dryad; whose harsh herbag'd meads
Make lean and lank the starv'd ox while he feeds;
There bad flowers have no scent, birds no sweet
   song,
And great unerring Nature once seems wrong.

THE "MOST HATEFUL LAND" is the United States, the writer John Keats, and the date October 1819. Some eighteen months earlier Keats had told a friend about his brother George's "resolution to emigrate to the back Settlements of America, become a farmer and work with his own hands after purchasing 1400 hundred [sic] Acres of the American Government." The plan had met with his "entire consent," he said, because George was "of too independant and liberal a Mind to get on in trade in this Country." The brothers had apparently read Morris Birkbeck's recently published *Notes of a Journey in America* which gave an account of agricultural prospects in the New World no less enticing if more prosaic than Crèvecoeur's a generation earlier. But after George had left, Keats reread Robertson's *History of America* and the fears aroused by this very different account were soon to be amply confirmed. For George, instead of joining Birkbeck's farming settlement in Illinois literally sunk his capital in a Mississippi trading enterprise at Louisville, Kentucky.

Abruptly, the bright vision of America as the land of liberty and freedom of opportunity dissolved into that of the wet and inhospitable continent. The lines Keats wrote on "that most hateful land" derive from Buffon and de Pauw, as well as Robertson, with echoes of the most famous poetic account of the fate of British emigrants in America—that in Goldsmith's *Deserted Village* describing the former inhabitants of Auburn on "that horrid shore" with its "matted woods where birds forget to sing," its "poisonous fields with rank luxuriance crown'd."

> While oft in whirls the mad tornado flies,
> Mingling the ravag'd landscape with the skies.

That Keats should have passed from one purely literary image of America to another is hardly surprising: he had no direct experience of the country. But many writers who had, were equally prejudiced. They set off from Europe with clear preconceptions of the promised land—derived from a long tradition to which the poems of Marvell, Drayton, and Waller belong, as well as more recent pro-emigration and pro-republican literature—and when their too high hopes proved to be dupes they promptly turned to an equally old and familiar anti-American tradition. Thus, the Irish poet Thomas Moore, traveling through the United States and Canada in 1803-4, declared:

> I went to America with prepossessions by no means unfavourable, and indeed rather indulged in many of those illusive ideas, with respect to the purity of the government and the primitive happiness of the people, which I had early imbibed in my native country, where, unfortunately, discontent at home enhances a very

distant temptation, and the western world has long been looked to as a retreat from real or imaginary oppression; as, in short, the elysian Atlantis, where persecuted patriots might find their visions realised, and be welcomed by kindred spirits to liberty and repose. In all these flattering expectations I found myself completely disappointed. . . .

His first American poems, written on Bermuda, express the old Elysian view of the Caribbean—indeed they allude to both *The Tempest* and Edmund Waller—but on the mainland he abandoned this mellifluous note, citing, like French anti-Republican critics, the persistence of slavery as evidence that American talk of liberty was mere hypocrisy. "Oh! Freedom, Freedom, how I hate thy cant," he declaimed, and, from Washington, wrote:

'Tis evening now; beneath the western star
Soft sighs the lover through his sweet segar,
And fills the ears of some consenting she
With puffs and vows, and smoke and constancy.
The patriot, fresh from Freedom's councils come,
Now pleas'd retires to lash his slaves at home;
Or woo, perhaps, some black Aspasia's charms,
And dream of freedom in his bondsmaid's arms.

(Lest there be any doubt, a footnote indicates that the last lines refer to Jefferson.)

Moore's American poems ranked fairly low but they were not without influence in England where his songs were warbled in innumerable drawing rooms by eligible young maidens. The slanderous reference to Jefferson's "black Aspasia" was to be taken up by Mrs. Trollope and, more notably, by Dickens in *Martin Chuzzlewit*, where Moore's description of Columbia was also quoted:

Her bloom is poison'd and her heart decays.
Even now, in dawn of life, her sickly breath
Burns with the taint of empires near their death.

Indeed it was from Moore rather than de Pauw that Dickens seems to have derived his notion of America's humid and unhealthy climate which gradually overshadowed his favorable first impressions and was to be given such prominence in his *American Notes for General Circulation* as well as in the American chapters of *Martin Chuzzlewit*.

The same violent shift from one view of America to another appears in the writings of the German poet, Lenau. Disaffected with Metternich's Europe, he set off in 1832 for the United States which he had already hailed as:

Du neue Welt, du freie Welt,
An deren blütenreichem Strand
Die Flut der Tyrannei zerschellt,
Ich grüsse dich, mein Vaterland!

He expected to find in America not only freedom but also nature more beautiful and powerful than in Europe. Disillusion set in soon after he reached Baltimore in October, though it did not prevent him from buying four hundred acres of land in central Ohio some six weeks later. A single American winter was enough, however, to send him scurrying back to Europe. "Buffon is right when he says that in America men and animals deteriorate from generation to generation," he wrote. "I have not seen here a brave dog, a spirited horse, a man full of passion. Nature is terribly languid. There are no nightingales nor any other true song-birds." Although this psalmist of *Weltschmerz* was by no means averse to a melancholy scene, the vast American forests, where death seemed to triumph over life and no birds sang, proved altogether too much of a bad thing. The whole country was one huge bath of mist. "Polluted air and creeping death" were all he found. These were the "swinish" not the "united" (*verschweinte, nicht vereinte*) States, which could be recommended only as a school of privation. His poems express his longing for the homeland whither he soon returned. His more violent denunciations of America, in his letters, long remained unprinted. But wide publicity was given to his dismal view in a popular German novel by Ferdinand Kürnberger, *Der Amerika-Müde* (1855), supposedly based on his misadventures.

Dickens and Lenau are but two—albeit the most distinguished from a literary point of view—of the many European writers who recorded their personal impressions of the United States in the first half of the nineteenth century. The successful outcome of the American Revolution precipitated a flood of literature on the new nation—travel books, histories, treatises, guides for immigrants. In English alone some eighty books on travels in North America were published between 1785 and 1835, and the numbers continued to grow during the next two decades. The idea of going to America in order to write a book was well established by the time *Pickwick Papers* appeared in 1836–37. Tony Weller, mooting a scheme for rescuing Mr. Pickwick from the Fleet prison and smuggling him across the Atlantic, remarks: "And then let him come back and write a book about the 'Merrikens as'll pay all his expenses and more, if he blows 'em up enough." Of all these volumes, the vast majority seem to have been favorable to the United States, indeed some are little more than propaganda for emigrants. But as the vocabulary of invective is richer than that of praise, the books that "blew up" the United States tend to be the more memorable. Thus, while publications which painted a not inaccurate picture of the United States as a land of plenty and opportunity encouraged nearly two million Englishmen, Scotsmen, and Irishmen to forsake poverty and their homeland for a new life in the New World, it was the less appealing accounts which shaped the vision of America in the minds of stay-at-homes in Europe. The favorable comments in Dickens's *American Notes*, for instance, were completely overshadowed by his strictures on manners, institutions (especially prisons), and the climate. Similarly, the disgruntled Mrs. Trollope appears to have been accorded more attention than the amiable Harriet Martineau except—and it is a big "except"—when she inveighed against slavery.

Mrs. Trollope's account of America and those of several others—notably H. B. Fearon (1819), William Faux (1823), Basil Hall (1830), the Rev. Isaac Fidler (1833), and Captain Marryat (1839)—were read as warnings by their conservative-minded middle-class readers. For these were years of political upheaval in England, with the Reform movement, the Corn Laws troubles, and Chartism; and bleak accounts of how things had gone even further in America confirmed their belief that Democracy should be restrained, if not halted. Armchair travelers generally like to be reminded of their wisdom in staying at home.

The least prejudiced of these travelers was probably Henry Fearon who went to "determine whether America and what part of it was eligible for a person like myself with a small fortune and a large family to settle in." He was by no means unfavorably impressed but, he believed, America was essentially "the poor man's country" where only the lower orders fared better than in England. Although he admired the simple-living, high-thinking tone of ex-President John Adams's household, he was dismayed by manners elsewhere. "On the surface of society," he found "a carelessness, a laziness, which freezes the blood and disgusts the judgment." Dirty side streets with pigs rootling in the muck, the untidy dress of even the more affluent Americans, the way in which they bolted their food in unsociable silence, the abominable habit of tobacco chewing and spitting, addiction to drink and gambling, distressed him. He was shocked by the way in which slaves were treated in the South, where he saw a black boy of fourteen brutally flogged. And he detected corruption in politics. That "the principle of at least liberty is acknowledged, and the fact of a free government exists" was commendable—he could not say the same for Great Britain—but he declared that "American theory is at least two centuries ahead of American practice."

Whereas Fearon and others, such as William Faux and Basil Hall, went to America solely in order to investigate conditions there, the more notorious Frances Trollope went as an emigrant in the hope of restoring the fortune her husband had incompetently lost. But the bazaar for the sale of fancy goods which she opened in Cincinnati was a disastrous failure and it was only as a last resort that she turned to authorship. In her book she kept the true purpose of her visit disingenuously dark. She inveighed against the effect of democracy on manners—without of course explaining that it was her "trade" which debarred her from "polite" society—and all but a very few Americans fell under her condemnation. "I do not like them," she declared. "I do not like their principles, I do not like their manners, I do not like their opinions." As her son Anthony later remarked,

> No observer was certainly ever less qualified to judge of the prospects or even of the happiness of a young people. No one could have been worse adapted by nature for the task of learning whether a nation was in a way to thrive.... Her volumes were very bitter; but they were very clever, and they saved the family from ruin.

The domestic manners of which Mrs. Trollope painted so disagreeably vivid a picture, the impertinence of strangers, the difficulty of obtaining domestic servants (and the custom of calling them "help" which still grates on English ears) would hardly have deterred a single emigrant from crossing the Atlantic. To the ragged and half-starved, warm clothes are of greater importance than the care with which they are worn and wholesome meals than the speed with which they are consumed. The emigrants came from low down the social scale, lower even than the poor crofting family of Thomas Carlyle who remonstrated with one of his brothers: "Nor shall you ever seriously meditate crossing the great Salt Pool to plant yourself in the Yankeeland. That is a miserable fate for anyone, at best; never dream of it. Could you banish yourself from all that is interesting to your mind, forget the history, the glorious institutions, the noble principles of old Scotland, that you might eat a better dinner perhaps?" The difference between the visions of America presented in the travel books written for a middle-class public and that conveyed in literature addressed to those who might wish to emigrate and seek a better life for themselves and their children is very striking indeed—nowhere more so than when the travel writers come across emigrants in Ameria.

Fearon described the arrival of a boatload of Dutch "redemptioners" (those who bound themselves to pay their fare from the wages they received on arrival):

> As we ascended the side of this hulk, a most revolting scene of want and misery presented itself. The eye involuntarily turned for some relief from the horrible picture of human suffering which this living sepulchre afforded.

From his heart, he said, he "execrated the European cause of their removal, which is thus daily compelling men to quit the land of their fathers to become voluntary exiles in a foreign clime." The fate of the Irish emigrants working on the Chesapeake and Ohio canal touched the heart even of Mrs. Trollope who knew nothing of the conditions from which they had escaped. Characteristically she drew some large general conclusions from the "situation of these poor strangers" working "in the broiling heat of the

191. *Emigrants on the St. Lawrence*, 1872. Gustave Doré

THE NEW GOLDEN LAND

sun in a most noxious climate . . . close to the romantic but unwholesome Potomac." Yet she doubted "if the labouring poor of our country mend their conditions by emigrating to the United States." Emigrants should go to Canada, she thought, with its fertility, its fine climate, and, of course, its British way of life. Dickens, who had no illusions about the condition of the poor in England, felt rather differently when he encountered a group of emigrants from Gloucestershire on their way to Montreal, "far from home, houseless, indigent, wandering, weary with travel and hard living. . . ." Some thirty years later W. F. Ainsworth described a group of German emigrants on the same waterway:

. . . how much to occupy the understanding and interest the heart is offered by the sight of 300 people leaving Europe for America! They all looked deplorable enough, poor things! and seemed to have suffered much from the hardships of the voyage; they were very poorly clad too, and a few rather tastefully costumed Indian women, whom we had on board, were gazed at so respectfully by our German peasant lads, that if they had had to speak to them, I am convinced they would have addressed them as "Madame" or "Mademoiselle."

The passage was illustrated with an imaginative evocation of the scene by Gustave Doré [191].

Emigration was so familar an aspect of the life of nineteenth-century Europe that it inevitably attracted the attention of artists—often satirically. A German print contrasts a scene of hopeful departure with a depiction of life in a swampy forest [192]. Others, published in both Germany and England, are sometimes in the form of strip-cartoons. But none, perhaps, is as effective as the views of Eden by Phiz in *Martin Chuzzlewit* [193].

The most famous of all emigrant images—*The Last of England*—was painted by Ford Madox Brown in 1852–53. The subject is said to have been suggested to him by the departure of the Pre-Raphaelite sculptor Thomas Woolner for Australia. But in the picture there is no suggestion as to where the young couple are bound.

192. *The European Dream; The American Reality*, c.1830. Anonymous, German

193. *The Thriving City of Eden as It Appeared on Paper* (ABOVE) and *The Thriving City of Eden as It Appeared in Fact* (RIGHT), 1844. "Phiz." From C. Dickens, *Martin Chuzzlewit*

All that matters is that they are leaving England. In other emigrant paintings, such as that by Richard Redgrave [194] in which a young family take leave of a smiling English pastoral landscape, there is no doubt that America was the destination—indeed Redgrave accompanied it with four lines of verse echoing the sentiment of Goldsmith's *Deserted Village*:

> Have we not seen, round Britain's peopled shore
> Her useful sons exchanged for useless ore?
> Forced from their homes, a melancholy train,
> To traverse climes beyond the western main.

In 1856 the Danish artist Christen Dalsgaard depicted a Mormon evangelist visiting a carpenter's family [195] and, presumably, persuading them to emigrate to Salt Lake City, as several thousand Europeans had done in the previous few years (2,700 went from England alone in 1853). At the Paris Salon of 1861 Théophile Schuler showed a painting of emigrants from Alsace disconsolately seated on an American quay—human flotsam, washed up and, apparently, abandoned [196]. And shortly before the end of the century Angelo Tommasi depicted a

194. (ABOVE, RIGHT) *The Emigrants' Last Sight of Home*, 1858–59. Richard Redgrave

195. (RIGHT) *A Mormon Evangelist Visiting a Danish Carpenter's Family*, 1856. Christen Dalsgaard

196. *The Emigrants*, 1861. After Théophile Schuler

197. *Emigrants Waiting to Embark*, 1896. Angelo Tommasi

sad group of Italian peasant emigrants with their baskets and battered baggage waiting to depart [197].

However, all these striking—and convincing—visual images are totally misleading. In reality, emigrants left Europe and especially England in a singularly joyful mood. Not a wet eye was to be seen as the ships floated out of Liverpool docks—and this despite the fact that steerage accommodation was often worse than that of the slave ships, for captains had no financial interest in the welfare of their human cargo once the redemptioner system had been abandoned, and deaths on the voyage or shortly after arrival in America were by no means uncommon. But the vast majority survived and, so far as one can tell, found if not the land of their dreams at least one which provided a better livelihood than they had ever known previously.

The happy outcome of emigration found no reflection in European art, however, apart from propagandist prints such as those which advertised the delusory delights of Champ d'Asile. To the European artist and the predominantly middle- and upper-class public for which he worked, emigration to America was simply the last desperate resort of the destitute—the destitute but for the £3.10s which bought him a transatlantic steerage passage.

The United States itself did not seem to have much to offer the nineteenth-century European artist. Little patronage was to be found there: still less in Europe for paintings of North American subjects. A relatively few engravings were enough to satisfy European curiosity about the topography of the country. Significantly, two of the most notable sets of them, though by English artists, were published in the United

States—William G. Wall's *Hudson River Portfolio* (New York 1820) and a series of views by William Henry Bartlett illustrating the American N. P. Willis's *American Scenery* (1840) and *Canadian Scenery* (1842). Many of these prints were copied onto English earthenware dinner services but these also were made mainly, perhaps exclusively, for the American market [198]. Similarly, the great French manufacturer of *papiers peints*, Jean Zuber, issued in the 1830s panels of scenic wallpaper representing scenes from the history of the American Revolution and also views of Niagara, West Point, Boston, and other places grouped under the general title "Picturesque America." They too were made mainly for export to America.

It may at first sight seem surprising that visual images of North America should have enjoyed so little popularity in Europe at a time when travel books were so phenomenally successful. But the books themselves provide the reason. Although the American landscape is often praised in general terms it is consistently described as scenery without history or sentiment. As Mrs. Trollope remarked, the Ohio River "would be perfect" if only its banks were adorned occasionally with "a ruined abbey, or feudal castle, to mix the romance of real life with that of nature." Some fifty years later Matthew Arnold made a similar point with greater subtlety when he complained that America lacked "the *interesting*" which derived from distinction and beauty.

> The charm of beauty which comes from ancientness and permanence of rural life the country could not yet have in a high degree, but it has it in an even less degree than might be expected. . . . If we in England were without the cathedrals, parish churches, and castles of the catholic and feudal age, and without the houses of the Elizabethan age, but had only the towns and buildings which the rise of our middle class had created in the modern age, we should be in much the same case as the Americans. We should be living with much the same absence of beauty through the eye, from the aspect of outward things.

He asked a German portrait painter whom he found painting and prospering in America how he liked the country. "How *can* an artist like it?" was his answer.

It was not merely that the United States was

198. *Niagara Falls*, Staffordshire pottery dish, c.1830

deficient in castles and monasteries. From the European point of view there were no accepted "beauty spots"—with one outstanding exception, of course: Niagara. The very name of this natural wonder was poetry to Lenau—before he crossed the Atlantic. "How beautiful it is, the simple name Niagara! Niagara! Niagara!" he wrote in 1832. The iciest critics of the American scene melted before it. Mrs. Trollope was completely overwhelmed by the "wonder, terror and delight. . . . I wept with a strange mixture of pleasure and pain." And Dickens, who devoted ten days to its contemplation, wrote the by then almost obligatory purple passage about it. Niagara recurs in books about North America as regularly as the Leaning Tower and Pompeii in Italian travel books. Other North American features which caught the travel writers' eyes were of a different kind—tobacco chewing and spitting, for instance. Mrs. Trollope devoted several pages to this distasteful subject, so did Dickens and many others down to the present century when Rupert Brooke (who picked up many of his predecessors' themes) called the United States *El Cuspidorado*. The rapidity with which meals were consumed at the table d'hôte called for a description from nearly all European visitors. They also remarked on the American fondness for iced drinks and hot rooms. (Dickens began the long line of complaints about American central heating.) Even the conversations they recorded with chance acquaintances seem to have changed astonishingly little in the course of a hundred years. There is a no less remarkable sameness about the extracts they quote from the newspapers. In fact American travel literature has a monotonous uniformity to be attributed not so much to a lack of observation, perhaps, as to the tendency of travel writers to focus, often unconsciously, on what their predecessors had noticed and pointed out.

If the salient features of life in the United States were indeed those presented by the travel writers, it is hardly surprising that most European artists should have found North America barren terrain. The landscape lacked the exotic abundance of the southern continent. It was a Europe without historical associations. No cozy genre scenes could be derived from the domestic manners of the inhabitants. Nor had the raw life in the Wild West as yet acquired any picturesque appeal. Slavery might have provided stimulating subject matter for a socially conscious artist, but few such artists went to America. Eyre Crowe's strikingly cool and realistic painting of a slave market in Richmond, Virginia — done from drawings made on the spot until he was thrown out by the angry slave dealer and his clients — is in every way exceptional [199]. Collectors, whether American or European, preferred pictures and statues of dazzlingly white Greek slave girls in the remote past — ideal images of captive femininity — to painful reminders of a present evil. Ruskin, who owned for a time and deeply admired Turner's masterly and terrifying *Slavers Throwing Overboard the Dead and Dying* (1840), found the subject too

199. *Slave Market at Richmond, Virginia*, 1852. Eyre Crowe

disturbing and sold it. Even the final abolition of slavery inspired relatively few large-scale works. The "peculiar institution" seems to have been regarded as a subject best left to the makers of prints. Hundreds of engravings and lithographs about slavery were issued, ranging from sentimental illustrations to *Uncle Tom's Cabin* by way of straightforward *reportage* to bitterly satirical cuts in *Punch* [200]. Many anti-abolitionist prints were also published, including one prompted by the 1839 riots which followed emancipation in Jamaica—with a centerpiece of a ship jettisoning a cargo of slaves as it is pursued by a British man-of-war which may perhaps have inspired Turner's great picture [201].

Illustrated periodicals also provided thousands of Europeans with visual images of other aspects of life in the United States, of the fast-growing, populous, and prosperous cities—a bird's-eye view of New York was widely diffused—of the modern mechanical inventions so closely associated with America and also of current events. Some of these prints were made

LIBERTY, EQUALITY, FRATERNITY.
DEDICATED TO THE SMARTEST NATION IN ALL CREATION.

200. *Punch* cartoon, 1848. John Leech

201. Anti-Abolitionist flyleaf, c.1839. Anonymous, French

[199]

202. Gold Rush flyleaf, c.1850. Dembour et Gangel

ONE GOOD TURN DESERVES ANOTHER.

Old Abe. "WHY I DU DECLARE IT'S MY DEAR OLD FRIEND SAMBO! COURSE YOU'LL FIGHT FOR US, SAMBO. LEND US A HAND, OLD HOSS, DU!"

203. *Punch* cartoon, August 9, 1862. John Tenniel

from American drawings or, after the midcentury, photographs, but their selection was determined strictly by European interests and preconceptions. The California Gold Rush, for example, which began in 1848, attracted great attention in Europe and the adventures of prospectors were frequently illustrated both from drawings done on the spot and from imaginative evocations. A French flyleaf has a view of gold seekers at work, very reminiscent of de Bry, accompanied by a poetic text declaring that in this country corn grows without being sown, the winter is as warm as our summer, there are eight harvests a year, and a tree flowers the day it is planted [202]. Evidently, in some recesses of the European mind, the image of America had changed surprisingly little in three centuries. Better informed artists employed by the *Illustrated London News* reflected only a more sophisticated *plus ça change* attitude.

The United States citizen, "this new man," was a more recent phenomenon whose visual image was created for the English mainly in the pages of *Punch*. He began his career as Brother Jonathan (a name originated by Americans during the Revolution), clad partly in the Stars and Stripes and with the uncouth manners of a country bumpkin. By dressing Abraham Lincoln in this costume Tenniel created the figure of Uncle Sam (a name first used in the War of 1812 when the initials U. S. still had no immediate connotation for the American troops) — tall, lean, goateed, with outsize hands and feet, wearing striped trousers and a broad-brimmed hat. During the Civil War — when *Punch*, like many Englishmen, favored the Confederates despite hostility to slavery — this figure of Lincoln was made to utter the kind of remarks, about liberty for example, which travel writers had cited as instances of American hypocrisy. In one of the most memorable of Tenniel's cartoons a craftily unctuous Lincoln solicits the support of an unusually dignifed black man, saying: "Why I du declare it's my dear old friend Sambo! Course you'll fight for us, Sambo. Lend us a hand old hoss, du" [203].

European artists who traveled in the United States in the first half of the nineteenth century chose subjects by a mental process akin to that of the newspaper editors and caricaturists, isolating features which they supposed to be typical. They thus tend to reflect current European views of America without adding much to them. There is a close connection between their work and the travel books of the same period. Indeed some of the more vivid pictures of American life were drawn by the travel writers. In 1811–12 Pavel Petrovich Svinin, secretary to the Russian Consul General in Philadelphia, while gathering notes for periodical articles and a volume entitled *A Picturesque Voyage in North America* (St. Petersburg 1815) made a whole series of charming bright watercolors of scenes from daily, and night, life in the streets of the city with its spruce new buildings which he greatly admired [204]. Svinin also recorded strange religious ceremonies, rustic diversions, some landscapes (including Niagara by moonlight), a group of Indians performing a dance in a theater, and so on [205]. Captain Basil Hall,

205. *A Philadelphia Anabaptist Immersion During A Storm*, 1812. Pavel Petrovich Svinin

206. *At the Theatre*, c.1830. August Hervieu

204. *"Worldlyfolk" with Chimney Sweeps Before Christ Church, Philadelphia*, 1812. Pavel Petrovich Svinin

another writer who drew his own illustrations, worked with the aid of a camera lucida (immediate forerunner of photographic apparatus) so that there could be no doubt of their fidelity. But naturally he depicted only those subjects he described in his text—the village of Rochester, still no more than a shanty town, an uninviting log cabin, villainous frontiersmen, and black slave drivers. A French artist, August Hervieu, accompanied Mrs. Trollope and provided her with illustrations of the domestic unmannerliness of the Americans—at home, in the law courts, at religious meetings, at the theater [206]. They both looked at American life through the same pair of jaundiced lorgnettes. The splendors of the Capitol he represented by a member of Congress blowing his nose in his hand, a spittoon on the floor beside him; the scenic grandeur of the Mississippi by a fog-bound steamer; and the romance of the West by the bleak desolation of Nashoba surrounded by dead trees. If he had intended to deter other French artists from crossing the Atlantic he could hardly have done better.

Several of the Europeans who made visual records of ordinary life in the United States in these years were amateurs—Peter Petersen Tofft, a Danish gold prospector, Edward Fanshawe, a British naval officer. The latter sketched a street scene in Sacramento, illustrating that American passion for newspapers on which so many writers had commented. Professionals also went to America, usually in the hope of picking up commissions though they found little demand for any painting other than portraits. Some painted Indian subjects for which, as we shall see, there was a market in Europe. As the possibilities for landscape painting were supposedly limited, they looked to the towns, only to be confronted with greater difficulties. Eduard Hildebrandt, sent to America in 1843 by that *voyageur manqué* and artist Friedrich Wilhelm IV of Prussia, was able to paint such already famous views in Brazil as sunset over Rio de Janeiro. In Boston he found a vantage point from which the city could be "composed" around the Massachusetts State House. But a town like Buffalo, which had neither distinc-

207. *Buffalo, New York*, 1844. Eduard Hildebrandt

208. *Broadway, New York*, c.1855. Hippolyte Sebron

tion of site nor prominent monuments, posed a problem. He solved it by emphasizing the ramshackle "picturesque" squalor of recent buildings on which travelers had often remarked and which seemed to suggest that the city was old in youth and "blasted ere her prime" [207]. A French artist, Hippolyte Sebron, exhibited at the Paris Salon of 1855 a large view of Broadway, New York, under snow with horse-drawn passenger sledge, up-to-date fire engine, and its tall plain buildings, so different from those in the main thoroughfares of European cities [208]. But he seems to have received no encouragement to repeat this enterprising experiment and devoted the rest of his time in the United States to landscapes—Niagara, inevitably, and the exotic swamps of Louisiana. Half a century was to pass before the American city was to appeal to European artists again—for its modernity.

In May 1866 an artist of far greater ability than any who had been to the United States earlier in the century—the Swiss painter Frank Buchser—landed in New York. That he arrived with preconceived ideas there can be no doubt, but his paintings and drawings show how he modified them during the next five years while the country itself was changing. Politically he was a radical who had fought under Garibaldi in Italy in 1849, and his visit to the United States had a political motive. A group of his friends, who wished to liberalize the Swiss constitution, had been much encouraged by the victory of the Union in America. A plan was mooted in 1865 to commemorate the end of the Civil War with a large painting in the parliament house at Berne as a tribute from the only European republic to the United States, which could now be called, without any equivocation, a land of freedom.

[203]

XXVI. *William H. Seward in His Garden*, 1869. Frank Buchser

Buchser was the obvious choice for such a work. No official commission was given to him, however, and he traveled on his own account.

From New York, Buchser went straight to Washington where the letters of introduction with which he was armed opened every door, enabling him to meet within a few days President Johnson, the Secretary of War (Stanton), the Secretary of the Treasury, and General Banks. He was even provided with a temporary studio in the Capitol. Very soon he came to know the powerful Secretary of State, William H. Seward, [XXVI] and the brothers General William and Senator John Sherman. His first American painting was of a fellow-countryman, however, Johann August Sutter, who had opened up the Sacramento valley in California and owned the mill race in which gold was found in 1848 — to his own impoverishment, as his lands and herds were ruined by the prospectors. Buchser portrayed him with his twinkling eyes and wide-brimmed straw hat as the very image of the genial adventurous Far Western buccaneer [209].

In the late summer of 1866 Buchser joined the Sherman brothers on a journey across the great plains west of Omaha — and here his talents blossomed. Traveling by train as far as Fort Kearney, he immediately responded to the poetry of the "Eternal Plains" and to the romance of the railroad, though he was soon to lament its destructive effect [210]. For the next six weeks his hand seems never to have been idle. He was indefatigable in recording what he saw, filling

209. *Johann August Sutter*, 1866. Frank Buchser

210. *Eternal Plains, August 22, 1866*. Frank Buchser

211. *Crossing the River Platte*, 1866. Frank Buchser

several notebooks with pencil drawings and whenever he had a chance dashing off oil sketches as well, while waiting for the rest of the party to ford the Platte, or after they had struck camp for the night [211]. The landscape of western Kansas and Colorado, so seldom visited by Europeans and never before painted, impressed him not only by its sheer size, by the vast and stupendous views, but also by its extraordinary and strange richness of color in the early fall. "The hills are covered with trees of yellow, red and green-mellon [sic] — the whole is submerged in a flood of light," he wrote in his slightly faulty English on one drawing. And then, there were the Indians whose encampments he also drew and painted.

After returning to Washington, Buchser put some of his sketches on show in his studio together with a large finished picture of *Sunset on the Plains* and soon began to be noticed in the press. An enthusiastic review appeared in the *National Intelligencer* on November 10, another in the *Sunday Chronicle* the next month.

And in the following April a writer in the Baltimore *Catholic Mirror* commented:

> How little idea have most of us of the magnificence and beauty of our land! We read in the dailies of the Plains, Forts Kearney, Laramie, &c., names inappropriate it is true and much better replaced by poetic Indian ones, and we associate them with such dreary dismal scenes; yet with what a charm to the eye of a foreigner have these glimpses of true nature. A spirit of enterprise too will soon work changes. "There is to be a railroad there," says the artist by our side, recalling us from our reverie, "and that will spoil all."

Most Americans painters were still, at this date, looking at their native landscape through Claude glasses or Salvator Rosa spectacles. Buchser was perhaps the first to appreciate and respond to its own strongly individual character; and as his work was fairly widely exhibited in America it may well have had some influence on the younger generation of American artists.

But Buchser was interested in life as much as in landscape. Shortly after he reached Washington he had painted a group of young Negro bootblacks which was exhibited in a store under

212. *The Volunteer's Return*, 1867. Frank Buchser

the title *Blacklegs* and caused something of a stir. The picture itself has vanished, but the press comments survive and are of great interest. The *Morning Chronicle* on August 8 compared it not unfavorably with the work of Murillo, then so much admired for his paintings of Spanish street boys, while the *National Intelligencer* commented the following day:

> Few supposed that a really great artist would go into the very streets of Washington, among the dusky hued ragged and vagabond *gamins* to find fitting materials for his pencil. Scarcely one of our own artists but would have considered this too great a condescension. With them it is to go abroad rather than work the gold mine at our feet.
>
> Mr. Buchser simply went into the streets of Washington, and there he found material in all its variety and richness, waiting only the hand of genius to grasp and divulge it with success: and with this material he has produced a picture which, for boldness of conception, strength of color, correctness of anatomy, and exquisite delineation of character has never been excelled in this country, and places the artist in the highest rank of his profession. . . .

Thus encouraged, Buchser quickly went on to exploit the vein he had opened. Early in 1867 he completed a painting of black boys playing marbles, which was exhibited in the rotunda of the Capitol, and another called *The Volunteer's Return*, which was hung in the spring show of the National Academy of Design [212]. Both were highly praised. One writer pertinently remarked that Buchser had succeeded where so many American painters had failed because he had "studied the negro character" in Africa. Buchser thus "caught to the very life the spirit and character, the dress and carriage of these people, and portrays them in no spirit of ridi-

213. *Woodstock, Virginia*, 1867. Frank Buchser

cule but with the most genuine sympathy and comprehension of them." However, the main reason for the great interest aroused by these pictures was pointed out by the *Evening Post*:

> The African seems just beginning to assume a prominent place in our art, as he has for some time in our politics; and it is the natural consequence of the late war that the characteristics of the negro race in America should become a subject for the study of the artist as well as the political philosopher. Still our artists have been slow in turning the new subjects offered them to account; so that it has been a common remark that but few works of any value as illustrating the war have yet been produced, and only a small number of them relate to the part taken by negroes.

These reviews expressed, of course, educated Yankee opinion: Buchser had yet to encounter the racial prejudice of the defeated South. In the summer of 1867 he spent some months in Woodstock, Virginia, where the suspicions of the local populations were soon aroused and he was denounced in the local paper, *The Shenandoah Herald*, for disturbing the "equanimity" of "our usually quiet little village." In his work there Buchser had by no means neglected the sunnier side of Virginian life, as his wonderfully evocative street scene reveals [213], but he had also found subjects among the recently freed black population and was accused of having made squalid images of their living conditions in order to stir up further hatred against the Virginians. Had they seen the nobility and proud independent spirit with which he endowed one of his black models they would doubtless have been still more shocked [214]. Although stoutly defended by the Washington press, Buchser felt it prudent to leave Woodstock.

The grand historical picture which Buchser had gone to America to paint and for which he had made some sketches immediately after his arrival, seems to have been more or less forgotten as he found the reality of the United States in transition far more interesting than the myth of the land of liberty. He painted memorable portraits of the two great Civil War generals, Lee and Sherman [215]. A stay on Staten Island

214. *A Black Man*, c.1867. Frank Buchser

215. *General Sherman*, 1869. Frank Buchser

216. *New York Bay*, 1867–68. Frank Buchser

217. *William Cullen Bryant*, 1867–68. Frank Buchser

yielded a charming, indeed idyllic view of New York Bay [216] as well as a few portraits, including one of W. C. Bryant [217]. In the summer of 1868 he went in search of Indians around the Great Lakes—but he was sadly disappointed. On Lake Superior he noted in a sketchbook:

> All the storys of Indians in these quarters are when seen close nothing at all. The full blood if found is utterly spoiled by the imitation of the whites. These costumes are more like the tasteless maskerade of a beggar than an Indian, they can only be used as staffage in a landskip therefore let us make for the south.

Only occasionally therefore do Indians appear in his finished landscapes, though he made a number of oil sketches and drawings of them and their encampments, valuable for their freshness of observation and lack of any sentimentality or "romance" [218].

For centuries the free and noble Indian had been compared favorably with the black slave. Buchser, like de Tocqueville, recognized that the

Red Men belonged to America's past and that the future lay with the blacks and whites. So he returned to the South where their relationship could best be studied. At Charlottesville he painted *An August Morning in Virginia* [219]—an enchanted view of a plantation house with a trim white fence separating the garden from a field of corn, the white family with its horses and black servants—while in other paintings he depicted the filth and decrepitude of the shacks in which the black people lived. But the subject of his most important picture, The *Ballad of Mary Blane*—which he regarded as the masterpiece of his American years—is miscegenation [220]. The ballad told the story of a slave whose wife was taken from him by a white man, and the picture shows a black man singing it to a colored group which includes a mulatto girl. Monticello is in the background—perhaps as a reminder of Jefferson and his "black Aspasia" (shades of Tom Moore and Mrs. Trollope!). When this work was shown at Tiffany's in New York in 1871 the *Tribune* fully appreciated its meaning and significance:

> Buchser's negro paintings are progressive. He seems to have been impressed at first with the grotesque or the merely picturesque in the negro character, but he was not slow to penetrate to the poetical and to do justice to the sympathetic nature and grave earnestness underlying that levity which Slavery superinduced upon cheerfulness. But his latest advance is the most important. He had discerned the ambition, the hope and the aspiration that mark the great transition which the negro race in this country is now undergoing—a transition, perhaps, the most rapid, gigantic, and beneficent which the history of the human race has yet witnessed. For him who possesses the genius to become the historian upon canvas of this grand progress—this sudden leap from Slavery and concomitant barbarism to freedom and civilization—there is here one of the most fruitful fields which art has ever attempted to cultivate.

But perhaps the picture went too near the bone: Buchser failed to find an American buyer and

218. *Indian Encampment*, 1868. Frank Buchser

219. *An August Morning in Virginia*, 1869. Frank Buchser

220. *The Ballad of Mary Blane*, 1870. Frank Buchser

xxvii. *The Cotton Office, New Orleans*, 1872–73. Edgar Degas

XXVIII. *Indiens Peaux-Rouges*, 1891. Pellerin & Cie

returned with it to Europe. It was shown in London where it was completely misunderstood by a writer in *The Era* who placed it in the "humorous class of work" while finding "real downright fun" in another picture to which he refers as the "Nigger Volunteer."

Buchser's paintings, exhibited in Washington, New York, and Boston and as we have seen, highly praised in the American press, may well have had some influence on American artists, notably Winslow Homer who began to paint Southern Negro life in a somewhat similar manner in 1875, but Buchser's refreshingly unprejudiced view of the United States remained a personal one. What he saw was a country in the throes of momentous transition—the Midwest on the point of being transformed by the railroad, Indians rapidly losing their racial integrity, white society in the South just beginning to recover from defeat, a black population freed from slavery but barely emerging from destitution. His image of America corresponded to none of the stereotypes and, perhaps for that very reason, he failed to find many buyers for his American paintings either in the United States or Europe. The few he sold were, significantly, portraits, landscapes, and "picturesque" Negro subjects. The works which now seem most interesting and valuable were still in his studio when he died.

In October 1872, eighteen months after Buchser returned to Europe, a very much greater painter, Edgar Degas, sailed for the United States. He had been unwell and needed a change of scene, so took the opportunity of going to visit his relations in New Orleans where his mother had been born and his uncle, Michel Musson, was a prosperous cotton merchant. Two of his brothers, René (who had married Musson's daughter) and Achille, were also in business there, and Edgar Degas traveled with the latter who had been on a trip to France. With this family connection, he must have crossed the Atlantic unusually well prepared for what he would find, and his letters reveal that he was not disappointed. He was impressed by the traffic in New York harbor, "where steamers from Europe arrive like buses at a station," and—unlike most Europeans—by the sleeping cars on the railroad which took him south. In colorful New Orleans "everything attracts me," he wrote—the orange gardens and the painted houses, beautiful dark-skinned women behind their half-open green shutters, "old women in their ample Madras peignoirs going to the market," "children all in white and so snow white when cradled in black arms," "Negresses either in white mansions with fluted columns or in orange gardens; ladies in muslin in front of their little houses, steamboats with two funnels as high as factory chimneys; and the fruit dealers with their shops chock-full; and the contrast between the busy, so well arranged offices and this immense black animal force, etc., etc.—And the pretty purebred women, the charming quadroons, and the well built Negresses!" But, as an artist, such subjects were not for him and he said he would "leave them all without regret." They might serve such a specialist in exoticism as Biard, he wrote, and "Manet would see lovely things here, even more than I do," but even "he would not make any more of them. One loves and gives art only to those things to which one is accustomed. New things capture your fancy and bore you by turns." Nevertheless, the few paintings he did in New Orleans are by far the most beautiful and memorable ever made of life in the United States—albeit they are of a limited and perhaps rather special view, that of the enclosed and still predominantly French society in New Orleans.

221. *Mme René de Gas, New Orleans*, 1872. Edgar Degas

THE NEW GOLDEN LAND

"One does nothing here," he wrote soon after he arrived; "it lies in the climate." And a somewhat sultry atmosphere of Southern gentility hangs over his New Orleans portraits. Nothing stirs in the lethargic noontide as his blind cousin and sister-in-law Mme René de Gas with her full-blown figure sits pensively on a wide soft sofa [221]. A family friend, dark-haired and sleepy-eyed, lolls behind a table, her limp glove lying by a vase which holds the lank drooping leaves and heavy voluptuous flowers of an exotic plant [222]. In an enclosed Southern garden, hot and dusty even in the late fall, children play idly and quietly in the doorway to the house [223]. Life seems to be pleasantly easygoing even in Michel Musson's business premises

222. *Femme à la Potiche*, 1872. Edgar Degas

223. *Children in New Orleans*, 1872–73. Edgar Degas

224(a). Sketch for *The Cotton Office, New Orleans*, 1872–73. Edgar Degas

where he examines a specimen of cotton with an abstracted air [XXVII]. Achille de Gas is shown in the center, absorbed in the local newspaper while René leans against a window in the outer office. Here there is no suggestion of the frantic bustle popularly associated with commercial life in America, nor is there any hint of the problems confronting the cotton industry in those difficult post-bellum years. This apparently inconsequential composition (which was, in fact, most carefully devised, with several preliminary sketches [224]) gives an impression of comfortable, even lackadaisical, prosperity—a society cushioned on bales of white cotton.

After he returned to Europe in the spring of 1873, Degas is said to have remarked that his voyage had been almost useless, though he showed two of his New Orleans pictures in the second Impressionist exhibition of 1876—*The Cotton Office*, which was bought by the Museum of Pau, and *The Courtyard of a House*, which can no longer be traced. He was never to make a

224(b). *M. H. de Clermont, New Orleans*, 1872–73. Edgar Degas

225. *Strike on the Baltimore-Ohio Railroad*, 1877. Anonymous, French

226. *Aux Etats-Unis—Lynching Negroes*, c.1890. After L. Carrey

second visit. Nor did any other European artist of comparable ability go to the United States in the nineteenth century. This may seem surprising in view of the important part that American collectors had already begun to play as patrons of European and especially French art. But their attention was directed to London and Paris by the same cultural currents which drove Whistler and Sargent across the Atlantic. Generally, those who wanted paintings of their homeland were those who also wished to encourage the American school: admirers of European artists were usually enamored of the European scene. And among Europeans, the belief still prevailed that the United States offered little subject matter for the artist. In the late nineteenth century their vision continued to be fed mainly by the prints in periodicals which illustrated whatever was topically newsworthy, presenting America as a land of swift material progress, the Golden Land still of opportunity but rent with the violence of strikes, robberies, and lynchings [225, 226].

CHAPTER 9

Good Indians

However hostile they might be to the citizens of the United States, most nineteenth-century European visitors had a word of sympathy for the indigenous population—decimated, dispossessed, and apparently doomed to extinction. Captain Basil Hall found himself "amongst the Oneida tribe of Indians, living on a strip of land called a reservation, from being appropriated exclusively to these poor remains of the former absolute masters of the territory—the native burghers of the forest!" Mrs. Trollope naturally espoused the cause of "this most unhappy and ill-used people." When she was in Washington, "the measures for chasing the last of several tribes of Indians from their forest homes, was canvassed in Congress, and finally decided upon by the *fiat* of the President." It was with special interest, therefore, that she scrutinized the portraits of some Indian chiefs by Charles Bird King. "They have but two sorts of expression," she wrote,

> the one is that of very noble and warlike daring, the other of a gentle and *naive* simplicity, that has no mixture of folly in it, but which is inexpressibly engaging, and the more touching, perhaps, because at the moment we were looking at them, those very hearts which lent the eyes such meek and friendly softness, were wrung by a base, cruel, and most oppressive act of their *great father.*

A few years later Harriet Martineau attended a debate in the Senate "on the sad subject of the injuries of the Indians," noting with pity the presence of some Cherokee chiefs.

De Tocqueville, too, gave a sympathetic chapter to them in the first volume of *Democracy in America* (1835), attributing their plight mainly to the retreat from civilization of the animals on which they lived but also remarking, ironically, on the "treaties" by which they were being gradually displaced. The Americans "kindly take them by the hand and transport them to a grave far from the land of their fathers," he wrote and, comparing the modern Americans with sixteenth-century Spaniards, concluded:

> The Spaniards were unable to exterminate the Indian race by those unparalleled atrocities which brand them with indelible shame, nor did they even succeed in depriving it of its rights; but the Americans of the United States have accomplished this twofold purpose with singular felicity, tranquilly, legally, philanthropically, without shedding blood, and without violating a single great principle of morality in the eyes of the world. It is impossible to destroy men with more respect for the laws of humanity.

The calamities of the Indians seemed to him irremediable.

No such subject could escape the compassionate eye and pen of Charles Dickens. On the boat from Cincinnati to Louisville he was lucky enough to run into a Choctaw chief,

> dressed in our ordinary every-day costume, which hung about his fine figure loosely, and with indifferent grace. On my telling him that I regretted not to see him in his own attire, he threw up his right arm, for a moment, as though he were brandishing some heavy weapon, and answered, as he let it fall again, that his race was losing many things beside their dress, and would soon be seen on the earth no more: but he wore it at home, he added proudly. . . .
> . . . He was a remarkably handsome man; some years past forty, I should judge; with long black hair, an aquiline nose, broad cheek-bones, a sunburnt complexion, and a very bright, keen, dark and piercing eye. There were but twenty thousand of the Choctaws left, he said, and their number was decreasing every day. . . .
> He took his leave; as stately and complete a gentleman of Nature's making, as I ever beheld; and he moved among the people in the boat another kind of being.

The Indians who emerge from these accounts still possess many of the distinguishing traits described by eighteenth-century and earlier travelers and writers: but attitudes toward them have changed. No longer do they stand apart from the benefits and stresses of the white man's world. They are, rather, the hapless victims of the supposedly irresistible march of material progress. Fortitude and gravity had for long been ascribed to them; but now they have acquired the fatalism and melancholy of the Romantic hero swept along by circumstances over which he has no control. Poor, unhappy, forlorn, are the words now used to describe the people who had previously been admired for their proud independence or condemned for their inhuman viciousness.

The melancholy Indian made his bow on the European scene in the very first year of the nineteenth century in Chateaubriand's *Atala*. In the preface to the first edition, Chateaubriand claimed that this work had been written "dans le désert et sous les huttes des Sauvages." But this is less than probable. Beneath the webs of mystification which he later wove around his five-month visit to America in 1791 few hard facts can be discerned. He seems to have crossed the Atlantic, like so many others of his class, to escape the revolutionary troubles in Europe—though he later claimed that his aim was to find the Northwest Passage! He is known to have called with a letter of introduction on George Washington who was indisposed and unable to see him—though he later wrote a vivid account of his meeting with the "soldier citizen, liberator of a world." There can be no doubt, however, that he visited Niagara, which provided him with material for no less than three descriptions in poetic prose; and his account of his first sight of Indians, in *Mémoires d'outre-tombe*, has the ring of truth:

> There were a score of them, men and women, all daubed with paint like sorcerers, half naked, with slit ears, crows' feathers on their heads and rings in their noses. A little Frenchman, his hair frizzed and powdered, wearing an apple-green coat, a drugget jacket and a muslin jabot and ruffles, was scraping a pocket fiddle and making those Iroquois dance *Madelon Friquet*. M. Violet (that was his name) was the savages' dancing master. They paid him for their lessons in beaver skins and bears' hams. He had been a scullion in General Rochambeau's service during the American war. . . . In speaking to me of the Indians, he always said: "Ses messieurs sauvages et ses dames sauvagesses." He took great pride in the nimbleness of his pupils; and, indeed, I have never seen such capers. Holding the little fiddle between his chin and chest, M. Violet would tune the magic instrument; he would cry out to the Iroquois: "Take your places!" And the whole troop would leap like a band of demons.
>
> Was it not a terrible experience for a disciple of Rousseau, this introduction to savage life through a dancing lesson given to some Iroquois by General Rochambeau's former scullion? I was strongly tempted to laugh, but I felt cruelly humiliated.

Chateaubriand's other accounts of Indian life in the wilderness could easily have been derived from eighteenth-century travel literature, albeit written with far deeper appreciation of the natural surroundings—from sultry, steaming subtropical forests, irridescent with clouds of fluttering butterflies, tremulous with humming-birds, and raucous with parakeets and blue jays, to bat- and serpent-infested swamps and the vast primordial expanses of the savannahs with their slow-moving rivers and awe-inspiring solitudes.

In his memoirs Chateaubriand remarks that he returned to France in 1792 with "two savages of an unknown species: Chactas and Atala." And he may well have sketched out a story which corresponded to the subtitle of his novel—*Les amours de deux sauvages dans le désert*. But the book that appeared in 1801 and was intended to form part of the *Génie du Christianisme* must have been written not only after Chateaubriand had returned to the Catholic faith, while serving with the Royalist counterrevolutionary army in 1792, but also after he had experienced the misery of exile in England. It was not in the forests of America but in Kensington Gardens, London, that—as he stated in another passage in his memoirs—"re-reading the diary of my travels overseas, I drew from them the loves of *Atala*."

The hero of this story is Chactas, member of the Natchez tribe, who had been fostered and educated by a Spaniard named Lopez but returns to the wilds. Falling into the hands of fierce Indian tribes, he is condemned to be tortured to death, only to be rescued by Atala, a half-Indian girl who is a Christian and a daughter of Lopez. They escape together and after traveling through an exotic landscape find their way to the Mission of Père Aubry. Here Atala reveals that in fulfillment of her mother's dying wish she took a vow of virginity and poisons herself in order to escape further temptation. All this took place in the late seventeenth century, but in the epilogue the narrator relates how by Niagara he met an Indian couple, the last of the Natchez, lamenting the death of their newborn baby. The woman tells him that Père Aubry was martyred by the Cherokees and that Chactas, after being taken prisoner by the French and sent to Europe, eventually returned to the Natchez, never married, but adopted a melancholic young Frenchman named René — her grandfather!

The Indians in the background of this strange tale of sacred and profane love owe much to earlier literature. The cruelty of the slow death, from which Chactas is rescued but which Père Aubry suffers, had often been described by missionaries. From the anti-clerical Lahontan, Chateaubriand took his charming description of a young Indian glimpsed through the trees as he goes, torch in hand, to discover his fate in the cabin of his mistress, resembling "the Spirit of Spring, traversing the forests to reanimate Nature." The first sentences of the lament of the last of the Natchez for her dead child are translated word for word from Jonathan Carver. Atala and Chactas, however, are truly savages of a new species. Both are partly Europeanized, she by birth and he by education. They are endowed with tender sensibility and, though passionate,

227. *The Burial of Atala*, 1808. Anne-Louis Girodet-Trioson

their love affair is conducted with a moral decorousness wholly lacking in previous accounts of *amours sauvages*. Above all, she is a Christian while he has come under Christian influence and is converted through her death. Atala and Chactas thus have the best of both worlds, uniting the spontaneous feelings ascribed to children of nature with the higher emotions which, Chateaubriand believed, were brought into the world by Christ.

Published at the very moment when France was returning to the arms of Mother Church, *Atala* scored an immediate success, mainly no doubt for its Christian message but also because of its moving story of young love and its descriptions of exotic nature—the most beautiful and vivid that had yet been inspired by America. It was printed and reprinted, adapted for the stage, set to music, imitated, parodied, and, of course, illustrated—in small engravings and large oil paintings, in sculpture, on clocks, even on cheap pottery plates. In 1802, the year after publication, Gautherot—a pupil of David—exhibited in the Paris Salon a painting with life-size figures of Chactas carrying the dead Atala to her grave, preceded by Père Aubry. This work was followed in 1806 by Hersent's *Atala Taking Poison*, in 1808 by Lordon's *Atala's Last Communion* and Girodet's famous *Entombment of Atala*, in 1810 by Grenier Saint-Martin's *Death of Atala*—and many more were to be painted in later years.

Significantly, all these Empire period paintings represented the death of Atala and the grief of Chactas. True to Neo-classical precepts, the artists strove to emphasize not the picturesque, local peculiarities but the eternal verities expressed in Chateaubriand's story. Exoticism was therefore played down. Girodet, for instance, had begun by representing Chactas with strongly Indian features and his hair tied up in a scalp-lock, but in the finished painting he left only an earring and a few inconspicuous plaited strands in his abundant mop of black hair to indicate his race [227]. With his magnificently muscular physique, Chactas is depicted as the

228. *The Death of Atala*, 1830. Cesare Mussini

personification of strength subdued by frail virginity, of the passions of the body overcome by the purity of the soul. But Chateaubriand's book is more than a moral diatribe: hence its success. And Girodet seized upon its mélange of religious sentiment and erotic impulse and its exaltation of unconsummated passion—which haunted the Romantic imagination—to create an unforgettable image of love and death.

The Chactas of Girodet's picture is a prototype for the melancholy star-crossed European Romantic hero as much as for the nineteenth-century Indian. Artists of later generations increased his exotic appearance. In popular prints he was often shown with feathers in his hair—to Chateaubriand's horror. An Italian, Cesare Mussini, painted him in 1830 with conspicuous Indian accouterments [228]. The French sculptor François-Joseph Duret showed him not only in Indian attire but squatting in a characteristic posture, grieving for Atala [229]. In Gustave Doré's engravings—made for the most memorable of the illustrated editions of the story—the human figures are dwarfed, or rather, overwhelmed by and lost in the immensity and grandeur of the wild, untamed landscape [230]. But in whatever guise Chactas appears and whatever the incident from the story, he is always a soulful, melancholy figure.

Delacroix, however, broke away from the scenes previously illustrated and chose an episode from the epilogue to *Atala,* depicting the last of the Natchez mourning their dead child [231]. This great painting, with its exquisitely tender figures by a wide expanse of river inexorably flowing past them, even goes beyond Chateaubriand to become a poignant lament for the passing of a whole race. Perhaps Delacroix's imagination had been fired by the plaintive words which the mother addresses to her son: "If you had remained among us, dear child, with what grace would your hand have bent the bow! Your arm would have subdued the furious bear, and on the summit of the mountain your footsteps would have challenged the running deer." Some of these phrases also occur in Victor Hugo's elegy *La Canadienne* (written in 1819 and published in *Annales Romantiques* in 1825), in which an Indian mother sings a dirge for her

229. *Chactas,* 1836. François-Joseph Duret

dead child suspended in the branches of a tree. It is unlikely that either Delacroix or Hugo was aware of the lines which Chateaubriand had omitted, tactfully, from his source in Jonathan Carver's *Travels:* "How fatal would thy arrows have proved to the enemies of our bands. Thou wouldst have drunk their blood, and eaten their flesh, and numerous slaves would have rewarded thy toils."

230. Illustration to *Atala*, 1860. Gustave Doré

231. *Les Natchez*, 1824–35. Eugène Delacroix

Yet the image of the bloodthirsty savage survived alongside that of the poor, gentle, dispossessed, and melancholy Indian. Both types appear, of course, in *Atala* where the difference between them is ascribed to the benign influence of Christianity. They are also present in Thomas Campbell's once popular if now seldom read poem about an incident in the Revolution, *Gertrude of Wyoming* (1809), though the Indian he inaccurately cast as villain of this piece was, in fact, a Christian—

>   the Monster Brandt,
> With all his howling desolating band . . .
> Red is the cup they drink but not with wine.

As we have already seen, wide publicity had been given to the atrocities committed by the Indians during the Revolutionary War, and especially by those fighting for the British, who were rewarded with a new rifle for every sixteen scalps, and such incidents revived memories of the cruelty ascribed to Indians by writers of earlier periods. Stories of how missionaries had been martyred, as described in the Jesuit *Relations* which Chateaubriand used for *Atala,* may well have been in Goya's mind when he made a drawing of a group of Red Indians hustling a captive monk or friar into a cave [232]. This

232. *American Indians Capture a Monk*, c.1812. Francisco Goya

233. *Scenes of Cannibalism*, c.1812. Francisco Goya

strange work may be associated with four paintings of stark naked cannibals, two of which have been identified as depicting the deaths of the Jesuits Gabriel Lallement and Jean de Brébeuf who were tortured and killed (but not eaten) by the Iroquois in 1649 [233]. The paintings have always been associated with martyrdoms near Quebec, though Goya's source of inspiration is unknown. A print of the Jesuit Mission's martyrdom by the Indians was issued in Paris in 1690 but it bears no pictorial relationship to Goya's paintings which, indeed, have no specifically Indian details—the cannibals even have hair on their faces and bodies, unlike Indians.

In the Revolution and again in the War of 1812 the Indians fought mainly on the side of the British, latterly in direct response to the steady erosion of their territories by the United States. Their behavior could thus be blamed on the British. But American settlers had from early times distrusted and feared them—and not simply because the tribes of the hinterland represented an ever present threat to their precarious existence. The Puritan, who believed as firmly in the gospel of work as in Holy Writ, looked with suspicion on a people who devoted their entire lives to what were generally regarded as the "sports" of hunting and fishing. They were as bad as the godless lords of the manor in England from whom he had escaped. Indians were also part of the unfriendly wilderness which it was their mission to redeem. It was to be cleared, cleansed, and brought under cultivation. If the Indians proved recalcitrant and refused to be converted and live like good Christians tilling the soil and trading, they must be outwitted or subdued by force. Only when American life became more urban and industrial, and the wilderness acquired positive merits, could the Indian be seen in a more favorable light. Even so, the pioneer blazing the trail of civilization toward the West has remained, for most Americans, a nobler figure—and, ironically, it was to recapture his way of life rather than that of the Indians that the great movement for wilderness preservation gathered force in the mid-nineteenth century.

In Daniel Boone, the Kentucky frontiersman who battled against both nature and the Indian tribes, the Americans found one of their first national heroes, quickly elevated to almost mythical status, and made the subject of numerous books and paintings. He was first mentioned by John Filson in *The Discovery, Settlement and Present State of Kentucke* (1784), evicting the Indians by the treaty of Sycamore Shoals, founding Boonesborough, settling vast tracts of virgin land, and dreaming of its future opulence. In 1813 his own nephew devoted to the same theme an epic poem in which an angelic Spirit of Enterprise selects Boone as the bringer of commerce, wealth, and the arts to the trans-Allegheny wilderness. An enormously popular biography published by Timothy Flint in 1833 told of Boone's delight in the thought that "the rich and boundless valleys of the great west—the garden of the earth—and the paradise of hunters, had been won from the dominion of savage tribes, and opened as an asylum for the oppressed, the enterprising, and the free of every land."

Beside this official version of the Boone story there arose another which recounted his love of the backwoods life for its own sake, of his retreat from the advance of civilization, and his complaint, on one occasion, that he had been obliged to move on because "I had not been two years at the licks before a d——d Yankee came, and settled down *within a hundred miles of me!!*" This was the legend which Byron took up and diffused throughout the English reading world in the eighth canto of *Don Juan* (1823):

> The General Boon, back-woodsman of Kentucky,
> Was happiest among mortals anywhere;
> For killing nothing but a bear or buck, he
> Enjoyed the lonely, vigorous, harmless days
> Of his old age in wilds of deepest maze.

There is, of course, a reflection of Byron himself in this characterization:

> 'Tis true he shrank from men of his own nation,
> When they built up unto his darling trees,—
> He moved some hundred miles off to a station
> Where there were fewer houses and more ease;
> The inconvenience of civilization
> Is, that you neither can be pleased or please;
> But where he met the individual man,
> He shewed himself as kind as mortal can.

Yet, despite Byron, the legend of Daniel Boone never caught on in Europe. Nor did that of Davy Crockett, a still more popular folk hero in the United States. A couple of English comments reveal the reason clearly enough. "Democracy and the 'far-west' made Colonel Crockett," a contributor to the *London and Westminster Review* wrote in 1839. "He is a product of forests, freedom, universal suffrage, and bear-hunts." That same year an English visitor to Louisville, R. G. A. Levinge, noted with more outspoken distaste:

> Everything here is Davy Crockett. He was a member of Congress. His voice was so rough it could not be described—it was obliged to be drawn as a picture. He took hailstones for "Life Pills" when he was unwell—he picked his teeth with a pitchfork—combed his hair with a rake—fanned himself with a hurricane, wore a cast-iron shirt, and drank nothing but creosote and aquafortis. . . . He could whip his weight in wildcats—drink the Mississippi dry—shoot six cord of bear in one day—and, as his countrymen say of themselves, he could jump higher, dive deeper, and come up dryer than anyone else.

On the whole, the English preferred the Indians who not only devoted themselves to the gentlemanly exercise of hunting but had the manners and reserve of "nature's gentlemen."

To the European artist, the uncouth frontiersman seemed poor material though he did occasionally put in an appearance in illustrated papers, generally in conflict with Indians. In 1850 an American publisher commissioned a series of drawings of frontier life but was dissatisfied with the four that were executed—by Jean-François Millet—and abandoned the project. A small edition of lithographs after them was later published in France. Two represent the capture and rescue of the daughters of Daniel Boone and Richard Calloway from the Indians [234], the others *The Leap of Major McCullough* and *Simon Kenton alias Butler Tortured by the Indians*. But Millet was unable to transfer his extraordinary sympathy for the French peasant to the American backwoodsman. Indians dominate the first two scenes and lurk like spirits of the wilderness in the last, where the central figure

234. *The Rescue of the Daughters of Daniel Boone and Richard Calloway*, 1850. Jean-François Millet

tied to the back of a horse is a repetition of the Mazeppa image, beloved of the Romantics but a well-worn cliché by the mid-century. Millet had never crossed the Atlantic and relied for details on Karl Bodmer—and Bodmer, as we shall see, had devoted his time in America to the depiction of the red men, not the whites.

In this context European attitudes to James Fenimore Cooper's Leatherstocking Tales are revealing. They enjoyed great success not only in England but also in France where translations appeared very soon after, sometimes the same year as, the original editions. The hero of this first great American epic is, of course, the backwoodsman, Leatherstocking himself, an Odysseus of the forest and prairie. An unlettered philosopher and undogmatic moralist whose character owes something to Daniel Boone, but much more to Cooper's creative imagination, he has a profound significance for Americans. Almost paradoxically, he was, and is, a symbol of an old, simple way of life, already passing away by the 1820s, and of a new appreciation of and desire for harmony with nature. A recent critic has called Natty Bumppo "a kind of tutelary spirit of the American land." But all this passed over the heads of Cooper's European readers. They were more interested in the Indians who conformed to the stereotypes set by, mainly European, travel writers of the eighteenth century—the brave, wise, sentimental Uncas and the devious, cruel, mercenary Magua. Thus, Henry Crabb Robinson (friend of Blake and Wordsworth and a sensitive critic) in 1827:

> I was employed nearly all the day in reading *The Last of the Mohicans,* the first of Cooper's novels which I have read with pleasure. He has skillfully availed himself of the poetical features of the Indian character and drawn several highly finished characters of semi-barbarous life. The perils arising out of the ferocity of national habits and qualities excite strong sympathy, but the civilised personages are made perhaps too uninteresting. They properly enough hold a subordinate rank and are an illustration of Rousseau's remark of the superiority of the savage over the unarmed civilised man. The mixture of Indian life and character is the only poetical element in North American romance.

European artists who illustrated the Leatherstocking tales reacted to them in the same way. The most notable were the brothers Alfred and Tony Johannot, who seized on the Indian scenes [235]. So also did most of the now forgotten painters and sculptors who exhibited scenes and subjects from Fenimore Cooper in the annual Paris Salons. In the theater this partiality had, of course, to be limited. In *Les Mohicans*— an operatic travesty rather than an adaptation, put on at the Opéra in 1837—the Indians outnumber the frontiersmen who are augmented by an English colonel, his daughter, and her lover, and a dancing master called Jonathas, but are not allowed to steal the show. The whites all fall into the hands of the Mohicans who prepare to eat them, but (shades of Chateaubriand) Jonathas charms them with the music of his fiddle and keeps them dancing until English troops arrive to save the situation.

The costumes for *Les Mohicans* were designed by one P. Lormier (otherwise unknown), who followed Cooper's description of the frontiers-

235. Illustration to *The Last of the Mohicans,* 1827. Tony Johannot

236. Costume designs for *Les Mohicans*, 1837. P. Lormier

[230]

man's clothes and provided him with an almost excessively *longue carabine* [236]. He appears to have made use of fairly accurate representations of an Indian blanket and calumet, or perhaps the objects themselves, for the accouterments of the Mohican chief. For a Brave and a Medicine Man, however, he reverted to the stock images established by de Bry two and a half centuries earlier. This is the more surprising as several parties of Indians had recently visited Europe and one had caused something of a stir in Paris.

A Seneca chief and six braves were taken in 1817 to England where they appeared in the theatres in Liverpool, Manchester, Leeds, and London, performing their tribal dances to delighted audiences. "This unique and novel Entertainment meets general Approbation," an advertisement in the *Leeds Intelligencer* declared:

> It is a natural and simple illustration of the Native Manners and Customs of a Nation totally uncivilized, but who from pure and unsophisticated Dictates of Nature, look up with Confidence to the Great Spirit for Protection here, and immortal Felicity *hereafter.*

In 1819 a group of Oneidas was taken to France [237]. But far greater interest was aroused by the six Osages who arrived at Le Havre in July 1827 — a few months after the French translation of *The Last of the Mohicans* appeared.

They were at first treated like the "State visitors" of the eighteenth century — presented to Charles X, entertained by the *noblesse,* and when they visited the theater seated in a box from which they addressed the audience. The Chief even made a balloon ascent. For a short while they were the rage of Paris: booklets were published about them and their portraits were engraved [238]. But once the novelty had worn off they were regarded as little more than fairground exhibits, and after being dragged around Belgium and Germany they fell on very hard times. In 1830 a public subscription had to be raised for their repatriation.

Meantime, several European artists had found their way into the wilds of North America and sketched the Indians they encountered. Some were amateurs like George Heriot, who became the Postmaster General of British North America and made watercolors of Indian ceremonies as well as landscapes in the English topographical tradition, or Charles-Alexandre Lesueur, who went to the United States as a naturalist in 1815 and spent ten years at Robert Owen's utopian New Harmony in Indiana from 1825 onward, or Peter Rindisbacher, who emigrated from Switzerland in 1821 to the colony established by Thomas Douglas, 5th Earl of Selkirk, on the Red River in Western Canada. Rindisbacher is per-

237. *The Oneidas in Paris,* 1819. Anonymous

238. *The Osages in Paris,* 1827. H. V. (Horace Vernet?)

haps the most interesting, for he was a frontiersman himself and all his best work was done during his early years there, before he settled in St. Louis as a professional artist. In one of his first American drawings he showed a white youth in long jacket and tight trousers (presumably himself) smoking a pipe of peace with an Indian family in their wigwam. It vividly calls to mind the many later nineteenth-century stories for boys which recount the exploits of a young Paleface among the Redskins. An ebullient sense of boyish excitement and adventure animates his work [239]. Nor was it unappreciated—indeed his drawings were much in demand at Fort Garry and some were sent to England—and engravings after a few were later published in America. He played an important part in directing American artists to Indian subjects including, significantly enough, the much more famous George Catlin, who never ventured into the wilds in winter and seems to have used one of Rindisbacher's paintings of buffalo hunting in the snow as a model—though not without introducing picturesque but incorrect details (war paint and gala outfits of feathers).

Another Swiss artist, Karl Bodmer—much more accomplished than Rindisbacher—arrived in the United States in 1832 as draftsman to Maximilian, Prince zu Wied-Neuwied, then touring the North American interior in order to prepare a sequel to his book of travels in Brazil. After wintering at New Harmony, they traveled far up the Missouri and then went South to spend a second winter with the Mandan Indians. As they traveled Bodmer made numerous watercolors—of the prairies with browsing bison, of individual Indians, their encampments, and the corpses of their dead rotting in trees [240]. These provided the basis for the atlas of lithographs published to illustrate the Prince's *Reise in das Innere Nord-Amerika* (Coblenz 1839–41). But there is a striking difference between the surviving drawings made on the spot and the published prints after them [241, 242]. The former have an elegiac atmosphere of almost uncanny tranquillity—the silence of the great empty spaces—while the prints include several scenes of violent movement, such as a bloody battle between the Assiniboins and Piegans with the central figure brandishing a scalp he has just

239. *Indian Hunters Pursuing the Buffalo in the Spring*, c.1825. Peter Rindisbacher

240. *Leather Tents of the Assiniboins, near Fort Union*, 1833. Karl Bodmer

taken, or a Mandan dance with buffalo masks and much stamping, leaping, bending, and gyrating in a wild frenzy. Reflecting and, no doubt, appealing to the late Romantics' taste for violence, these prints illustrate the spontaneous, uninhibited vitality of nature which civilized men had lost. At the same time, echoes of the Homeric world are subtly introduced, quite appropriately, for the Homeric Greeks were as much admired in the 1830s as earlier, though for their primitive vigor rather than their noble simplicity and calm grandeur. The set of preconceptions which enabled Lafitau, in the early eighteenth century, to compare Indians with ancient Greeks had been replaced by another derived from new attitudes to both types of "primitive."

The European tendency to look at Indians through classical spectacles is also evident in Ferdinand Pettrich's sculptures. He went to the United States in 1835 in the hope of obtaining a commission for work on the Capitol. As none was immediately forthcoming he turned to carv-

241. *Mandan Indian Buffalo Dancer*, 1833. Karl Bodmer

242. *Bison Dance of the Mandan Indians,* 1833. Alexander Manceau, after Karl Bodmer

ing funerary monuments but also modeled busts and full-length statues of Indians, even a relief of the bison dance, which found their way to the Ethnological-Missionary Museum in the Vatican. Eventually, he was commissioned to carve a statue of an Indian, the dying Tecumseh [243]. The choice of subject is significant.

In the early years of the century Tecumseh emerged as the most notable leader the Indians had ever had. As chief after chief was persuaded, often with the aid of alcohol, to surrender his hunting grounds to the Americans and move ever farther west—in 1808 the Osages gave up 48,000,000 acres in return for an annual $1,000— he realized that the Indians could survive only if they preserved their racial integrity and united against their depredators. With his brother Tenskewata, a half-blind medicine man known as The Prophet, he initiated a remarkably successful movement for moral regeneration, banned all contact with the whites except for trade, and prohibited the consumption of strong drink. He also formed a defensive confederation of the Northwest tribes. But it was too late, by a century or more. The frontiersmen took fright and William Henry Harrison, Governor of the Indiana territory, advanced and sacked his village of Tippecanoe in 1811. Tecumseh was thus driven to ally himself with the British in Canada, became involved in the War of 1812, and was killed at the Battle of the Thames the next year. This was a decisive victory for the whites, and one long remembered. In 1836 when Richard M. Johnson, who claimed to have shot him, was campaigning for the office of Vice President, his supporters chanted:

> Rumpsey-dumpsey, rumpsey-dumpsey
> Colonel Johnson killed Tecumseh.

His unsuccessful Democratic opponent on that occasion was Harrison, elected President five years later as "the Hero of Tippecanoe." Safely dead, Tecumseh could be regarded as a "good Indian" by all parties: hence the commission for a statue of him. But that carved by Pettrich, showing him as an antique hero in all but costume, won less than enthusiastic approval when it was finally delivered in 1856. Perhaps it was too heroic. The portraits which Charles Bird King was commissioned to paint of the Indian chiefs who complaisantly signed treaties with the United States government provided more acceptable images of Indians for the politicians in Washington.

It would of course be untrue to suggest that Indians were admired only by those who were divided from them by some three thousand miles of water, though distance did lend enchantment. Many Americans were saddened, though backwoodsmen might rejoice, by the frequently repeated statement that the Indians as a race "were about to become extinct"—first made in 1824 by the Secretary for War. Nor should it be supposed that the European image of the Indian was still a purely homegrown product. Transatlantic interchange blurred, if it did not eradicate, the old distinction between European and American views of the subject. Fenimore Cooper blended ideas (as well as misinformation) derived from French and English books with those of his compatriots to present a picture of the Indian character which was accepted in Europe as authentic. Though they had less influence, more authoritative works were available, notably *The History of the Indian Tribes of North America* published in 1836 by Thomas L. McKenney, who was head of the United States War Department's Bureau of Indian Affairs. To Americans, however, the Indians remained a problem after they had ceased to be a menace. Europeans were in a better position to lament their fate.

The careers of two American artists, Alfred

243. *The Dying Tecumseh*, 1856. Ferdinand Pettrich

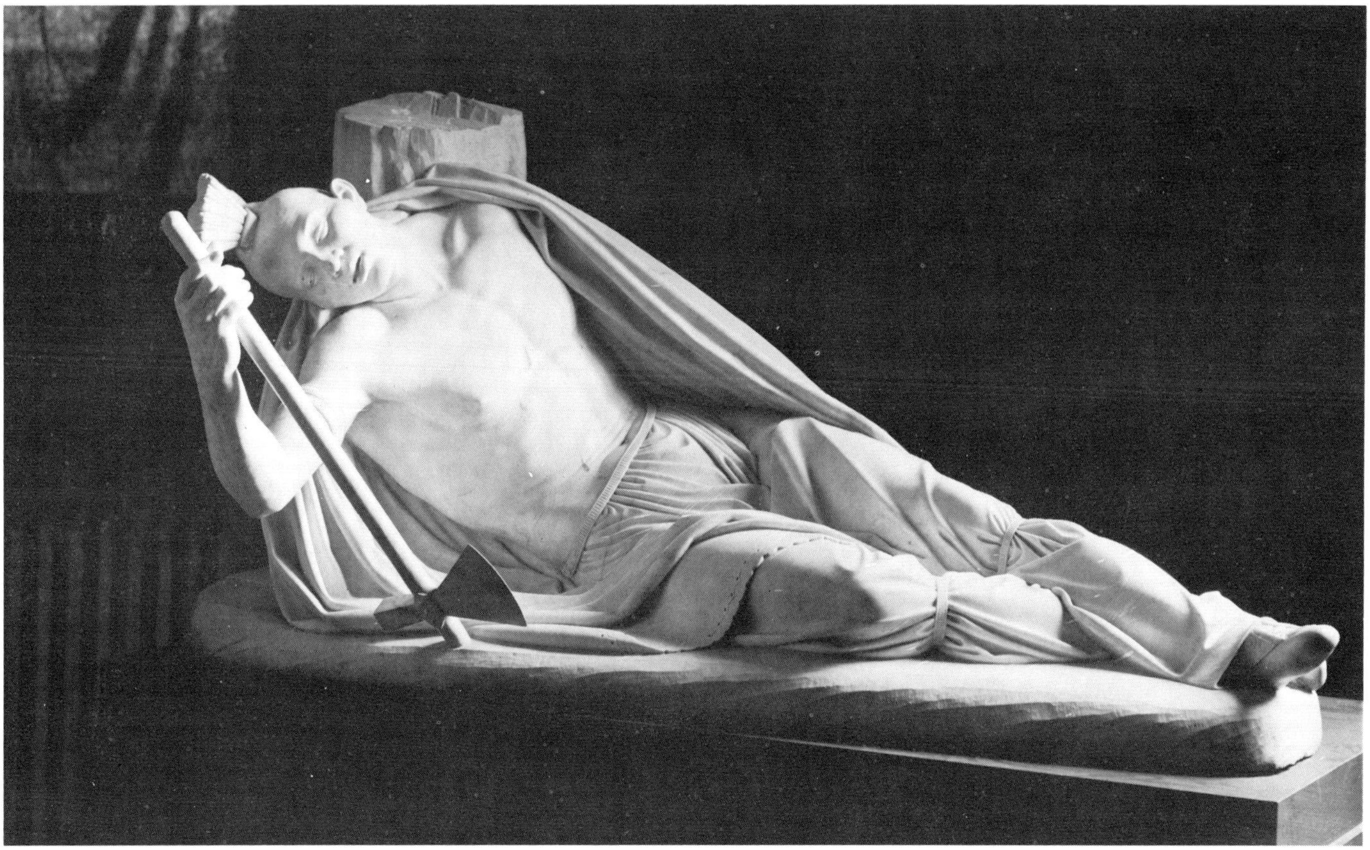

Jacob Miller and George Catlin, reveal very clearly the difference in attitude prevailing on either side of the Atlantic. In 1837 Miller was commissioned by an eccentric baronet, William Drummond Stewart, who had spent some years roaming the wilds in search of adventure, to accompany him on a final tour and execute a series of paintings for his castle in Scotland. A more than competent draftsman (trained in Paris), Miller made hundreds of watercolors and drawings of landscapes and animals and trappers as well as Indians which he later worked up into finished oil paintings. Complaining bitterly of the discomforts of the trek, he never again ventured into the West. He sold a few Indian scenes, such as *Beating a Retreat* (Boston Museum of Fine Arts) and a strangely bloodless *Running Fight—Sioux and Crows*, but the brilliantly fresh sketches in which he captured the strangeness and beauty of the unspoilt West remained unknown until the present century.

George Catlin went West on his own account. The sight of some Indians in Philadelphia in 1824 fired him with a desire to paint them not, as previous American artists had done, in the city but in their own surroundings. It was not until 1832, however, that he was able to travel up the Missouri (just ahead of Bodmer) on the first steamship of the American Fur Company and begin his wanderings in the wilderness. During the next few years he spent as much time as he could among the Indians, traveling with numerous rolls of canvas on which he recorded their appearance, in order, he said, "to snatch from hasty oblivion . . . a truly lofty and noble race." The Indians, he wrote, were "knights of the forest, whose lives are lives of chivalry and whose daily feats, with their naked limbs, must vie with the Grecian youths in the beautiful rivalry of the Olympic games." In his paintings, however, he made no attempt to idealize the Indians: he shows them as neither the bloodthirsty enemies nor the pathetic victims of the march of progress. And this may well account for their lack of success. After showing his "Indian Gallery" of some five hundred works in the United States, he set out with them for Europe in 1839, and did not return for another thirty years.

In London his collection was shown at the Egyptian Hall in Piccadilly. Dickens was among the many visitors and Catlin even secured Royal attention. Queen Victoria's name heads the list of subscribers to the first of his many books. To augment interest in his gallery he then devised a kind of Wild West show, employing a number of Cockneys, dressed in blankets and feathers and with their skin suitably colored, to execute simple Indian dances until he was able to secure the services of nine genuine Ojibwa Indians who were soon succeeded by a dozen Iowas. Having exhausted the interest of the English public by 1845, he crossed over with his Indians and his paintings to France where still greater success awaited him.

Although several earlier troupes of Indians had appeared in Paris, Catlin's aroused greater attention than any of them, thanks probably to his superior showmanship. Louis-Philippe was delighted, put the *grande salle des séances* of the Louvre at his disposal, ordered a command performance, and commissioned replicas of fifteen pictures including a portrait of one of the Iowa braves, Little Wolf (though only a painting of the Indian Ball Game, now at Blérancourt, was in fact delivered). A print by Henry Emy gives some idea of their performance [244]. And to George Sand we owe a wonderfully vivid account of the impact made by the sudden and carefully stage-managed entrance of the Indians

244. *Catlin's Ioway Indians*, 1845. Henry Emy

245. *Catlin's Ojibway Indians*, 1845. Eugène Delacroix

in their feathers and war paint. She saw them off-stage as well and the tenderness displayed by Little Wolf to his dying squaw inevitably reminded her of Chactas and Atala. But for Delacroix, who attended the performance with her, the Indians had different connotations. Some years earlier he had had his idea of antiquity revitalized by the Arabs of North Africa and now he found similar qualities in the Indians. "The chief brandishing his lance is Ajax defying the gods," he wrote. "In the scalp-dance, the women leaping on their toes with such noble and mysterious poise, and holding the lance with the scalp on top, recall the Panathenaic virgins of Phidias." Later he made some drawings of another party of Ojibwas, who came to Catlin's aid when the Iowas returned home, showing them, perhaps unconsciously, in the attitudes of the ancient Greeks he had recently painted on the Luxembourg ceiling [245].

Catlin's paintings seem to have attracted attention mainly for their subject matter, representing, as George Sand remarked with characteristic exaggeration, "hideous scenes of initiations into mysteries, of agony, torture, of Homeric chases, of deadly combat; in sum, all the testimony and all the fearfully dramatic scenes of savage life." (In fact, Catlin steered clear of the more gruesome subjects.) Humboldt, who happened to be in Paris, admired them as ethnographic records and a decade later persuaded the King of Prussia to buy from Catlin 104 drawings (destroyed in the last war) and ten oil paintings which still survive. The artistic merits of the works were little appreciated. In the consensus of Paris opinion Catlin was an "intrepid traveller" and "mediocre painter." Only Baudelaire, very much less highly regarded as an art critic by his contemporaries than he is by posterity, delivered a dissenting verdict.

THE NEW GOLDEN LAND

> When M. Catlin came to Paris, with his Museum and his Ioways, the word went round that he was a good fellow who could neither paint nor draw, and that if he has produced some tolerable studies, it was thanks only to his courage and his patience. Was this an innocent trick of M. Catlin's, or a blunder on the part of the journalists? For today it is established that M. Catlin can paint and draw very well indeed. . . . M. Catlin has captured the proud, free character and the noble expression of these splendid fellows in a masterly way.

Catlin seems to have gone to Europe partly in the hope of selling his "Indian Gallery" en bloc, probably to Queen Victoria or Louis-Philippe. Disappointed, he shipped it back to America. Daniel Webster and a group of Northern senators urged the United States government to buy it, but were defeated by Southerners who felt it might arouse sympathy for the Indians whose lands they coveted. Shortly afterward Catlin went bankrupt and his paintings were sold to a Philadelphia boilermaker who stored them in a cellar. Not until 1879, seven years after Catlin's death, were the pictures finally given to the Smithsonian Insitution by a private donor. The Indians still remained a problem at this time but they had been recently decreased by famine, sickness, and the efforts of Colonel George Custer, until he bit the dust at the Little Bighorn in 1876. The handsome blond Custer became the hero of millions of American schoolboys who took up his attitude of respectful hostility toward the Redskins, akin to that of English country gentlemen to foxes.

Shortly after the mid-century, European artists began increasingly to paint Indian subjects for their own sake and not merely as illustrations to travel books and novels. Theodor Kaufmann, a German who found political asylum in the United States after 1848, made a specialty of such pictures, the most notable showing a group of Indians stealthily wrecking a railroad by night—with a train puffing toward them and its doom. A young French painter, Jules-Emile Saintin spent some ten years in the Wild West from about 1855 making sensitive drawings of Indians, many of which he used later for two Salon pictures, *Pony Express* [246] and *Femme de Colon enlevée par les Indiens Peaux Rouges,* which showed a very white naked girl borne away by an Indian on horseback, an example of that near-pornographic genre so popular during the Second Empire. At the same time, as we have already seen, Frank Buchser was traveling across the plains and around the Great Lakes on the lookout for Indian subjects, and some years later a Dane, Carl Rohl-Smith, modeled a handsome portrait bust of a chief named Kicking Bear [247] as well as a monument to the American soldiers who had been massacred at Fort Dearborn by Indians in the War of 1812.

Rosa Bonheur, that doughty painter of virile beasts, had no need to cross the Atlantic for Wild Western specimens—they came to her at Fontainebleau. An American admirer in Wyo-

247. *Chief Kicking Bear*, 1892. Carl Rohl-Smith

246. Study for *Pony Express*, c.1860. Jules-Emile Saintin

GOOD INDIANS

248. *Buffalo Bill on His White Horse*, 1889. Rosa Bonheur

249. The Buffalo Hunt, 1889. Rosa Bonheur

ming provided her with mustangs, authentically Western but so wild that even she was unable to master them. Fortunately Buffalo Bill [248] — a man after her own heart — was able to relieve her of a couple. Members of his troupe, some of whom are said to have come from no farther away than Southern Italy, served as models for her several paintings and drawings of Indians as svelte and muscular as the horses they ride [249]. But she also depicted, from imagination perhaps aided by photographs, such scenes as bison fleeing from a prairie fire and an Indian encampment with squatting squaws and brooding braves among the wigwams [250]. It is interesting to compare her carefully detailed pictures of the 1890s with a wonderfully spirited painting of the same period by Pierre Bonnard, showing two Indians apparently galloping into the twentieth century [251].

The late nineteenth-century European's image of the Indian was derived, however, not so much from works of art of this quality as from the illustrations in periodicals and books. Fenimore Cooper's novels had fathered a vast progeny of adventure stories. Gabriel Ferry's *Coureur des Bois* (1853), with a French hero who allies himself with the Comanches against the dreaded Apaches (enemies to other Redskins as well as Palefaces), despite its seven-volume length, enjoyed enormous popularity, ran into a dozen editions, and was translated into German, Spanish, Danish, and English. Writing mainly for the young, Gustave Aimard turned out some fifty novels with such enticing titles as *Les Trappeurs de l'Arkansas* (1858), *La Forêt vierge* (1870), *L'Aigle Noir des Dakotahs* (1878). His heros were also French, their allies Indians, and the villains invariably Anglo-Saxons. "I hate the English and the Americans of the North who are, if possible, still worse than John Bull," he remarked in *Les Outlaws du Missouri*. Things are very different, naturally enough, in the novels of

250. *Indian Encampment*, c.1890. Rosa Bonheur

251. *Peaux Rouges*, c.1895. Pierre Bonnard

[241]

THE NEW GOLDEN LAND

Mayne Reid. Generally set in Mexico, abundantly populated with villainous Roman Catholic Spaniards, his heros are exclusively WASP. And, no less naturally, a Teuton as blond and fearless and clean-limbed as Siegfried made his bow in 1875 in the stories of Karl May, Hitler's favorite author. He finds friends among Indians who have preserved their racial purity and enemies among those corrupted by Americans of British or French descent who are his villains. Of all these post-Fenimore Cooper stories of life among the Indians published in Europe—and there were many more lower down the literary scale, corresponding to American "dime novels"—only those of Karl May have stood the test of time and are indeed as widely read today as in the author's lifetime. More than two and a half million copies of his first Indian novel, *Winnetou*, have been printed in Germany alone: the total number of his books published in Germany now tops twenty-four million copies and they are still being printed.

Among Karl May's admirers was George Grosz, himself to contribute notably to the European image of America, as we shall see. He even made a pilgrimage to visit his boyhood hero and was dismayed to find him living a cozy *gemütlich* life in the suburbs of Dresden, far, far different from that of his manly heroes in the Wild West. For, as Grosz wrote in his autobiography:

> The reading of these books awakened in the youngster a yearning—that secretly exists in practically every German—for distant lands and exotic adventures. (These books could well have been the result of the ardent propaganda of the time for German colonial expansion.) Yes, indeed, we certainly had a warm place in our hearts for our great, blond German-American hero, Old Shatterhand, who with one blow of a clenched fist could lay low a horse, not to mention a contemptible betrayer. . . .

The narrator-hero was accompanied by an unusually handsome and virtuous Apache Indian, Winnetou. Next to the strong white Old Shatterhand, Grosz remarks,

> he was one of the ideals of the German youth of my day. He actually became a national figure, even more famous than his renowned colleagues, Uncas and Chingachgook, because there was something "German" about him.

252(a). Covers of Karl May's *Winnetou*, 1893 and c.1900 editions

252(b). Designs for covers of Karl May's *Winnetou* and *Am Rio de la Plata*, 1904–5. Sascha Schneider

These novels owed their success not only to their nationalistic message and cult of racial purity. Karl May was an expert storyteller. Although he had never been to the Wild West when he began to write about it, he was well up in literature on the Indians and his accounts of their way of life are extraordinarily vivid and convincing. Endearingly comic characters like Sam Hawkens (a German of course) are carefully introduced to relieve what would otherwise be a monotonous conflict between deadly serious paragons of virtue and demons of vice. And he had the wit to ingratiate himself with bookish boys who admired the exploits of a superman they could never hope to emulate: Old Shatterhand knows more about the Indians on arrival in the West than those who have spent their lives there because, like Karl May and his *liebe Leser*, he had read about them in Germany. Even Winnetou, the Apache, has read *Hiawatha*. As very few women appear and there is never any sentimental "spooning," these novels were supposed by parents, in the innocence of their hearts, to provide healthy reading for young Hermann and little Hans. But to the modern reader the homosexual overtones are obvious enough. The narrator's account of his first meeting with Winnetou, his fine physique, his velvety eyes, and his beautiful black hair, might almost come from *The Song of the Loon*—without, however, the least suggestion of anything "below the belt," the tone being intensely moral throughout, in a muscularly Protestant way.

Most novels about Indians are set in the past, though seldom more than a generation back: Cooper's are just before the Revolution, Mayne Reid's and Gustave Aimard's in the late eighteenth century, Karl May's in the 1860s when the railroads were being laid across the prairies. They also depict the Indians as a race nobly drawing to its end. "Like the lustre of the dying lamp, their glory shone the brightest as they were about to become extinct," wrote Cooper of the Mohicans. Seventy years later Karl May commented:

> Yes, the red race is dying. From Tierra del Fuego to well beyond the lakes of North America, the sick giant lies stretched out, knocked down, crushed by a remorseless destiny that knows no pity. It has fought with all its might against fate, but in vain. Its strength is gradually ebbing. It has only a few last gasps to breathe and the spasms which shake its naked body announce the nearness of death.

By then the Wild West itself was dying; the trappers and cowboys were soon to become figures from a colorful past. The heroes and heroines of the dime novels—Deadwood Dick, Kit Carson, Calamity Jane—seem to have reached Europe relatively late in the day. Buffalo Bill did not arrive in person until the late 1880s, making his English debut in honor of Queen Victoria's golden jubilee. Unlike the Indians they were never absorbed into European mythology. Thus, the most famous of all European operas set in America, Puccini's *La Fanciulla del West*—first performed in New York in 1910—was derived from a play by the American David Belasco [253]. Significantly, the only Indian in it has a very

253. Advertisement for Puccini's *La Fanciulla del West*, first performance in Italy at La Scala, Milan, 1910–11. Giuseppe Palanti

minor part, Minnie's attendant Wowkle. But the action takes place in the California of a half-century earlier. The makers of Western films have honored the same time conventions, however topical their themes may be. Nostalgia for days when men and women rode horses, dressed in more fanciful clothes, lived more passionate and exciting lives, closer to nature, gives the genre much of its appeal. And Europeans who have imitated them, most notably Sergio Leone, the master of the "spaghetti Western," have prudently followed suit, differing from their models only by making the West still wilder, more violent, and more primitive.

Cowboys, ranchers, sheriffs, and Indians are figures of the past also in another, psychological sense. Since stories about them tended to be written increasingly for a young audience, they gradually became part of the European's childhood memories. An adult watching a Western is able not only to see a mythological section of American history but also to relive a part of his own past. For before these films were first shipped across the Atlantic, European children had for a generation or more been playing at cowboys and Indians. In the mid-nineteenth century the firm of Pellerin at Épinal in France printed penny-plain-two-pence-colored sheets of *Sauvages de l'Amérique*, some of which could be cut out and made into puppets, still conforming to the generalized eighteenth-century image of the Indian as a figure dressed only in feathers. These could hardly satisfy children who had read the novels of Gustave Aimard and were well informed about the costumes and customs of the different tribes. In 1891 Pellerin began to publish sheets of *Indiens Peaux-Rouges* which fairly accurately rendered Sioux, Comanches, Apaches, and so on derived from illustrations to books and periodicals [XXVIII], as, for instance, in the case of the Indian with a scalp [254]. One sheet which has both Redskins on horseback and the men in blue of the United States army was indeed inspired by the Indian rising of 1891 and entitled *Les Derniers Peaux-Rouges*. At about the same time little tin or lead figures of American soldiers and Indians made their way into European nurseries which were

254. *Indian Scalping an Enemy*, c.1860. Anonymous, French

soon echoing with shrill war-whoops [255]. Out of doors, in gardens and suburban copses, wigwams appeared and children with chicken feathers in their hair were to be found stealthily stalking one another or solemnly and silently pursuing an enemy in Indian file. Further impetus was, of course, given to this childhood cult of life on the frontier by the Boy Scout Movement (founded in 1908), partly inspired by the plan of a popular American nature writer, Ernest Thompson Seton, for a boys' organization to be called Woodcraft Indians.

As the Indians were believed to be dying out, though the report was somewhat exaggerated, their image burned ever brighter in the European imagination. And in the London of 1935 tumultuous success greeted the arrival of a tall, gaunt, hook-nosed figure, dressed in moccasins and elaborately fringed buckskin and wearing a

255. Red Indians and U.S. soldiers, painted lead or tin figures, c.1900

single feather in his long braided black hair—all the more so as he had come to plead for the expiring race not of Indians but of beavers [256]. Raising his hand and slowly pronouncing the words, "I am Wa-Sha-guon-Asin, Grey Owl, I come in peace," he won every heart. The moment could hardly have been more opportune. As Europe lurched toward war, trappers seemed less dangerous than Fascists and Nazis, beavers easier to save than Jews. His books, which sold in the thousands, his lectures, and the films of his life in the great forests and wilds of Canada showed how man might still live in perfect harmony with nature. His second visit, in 1937, culminated in a command performance at Buckingham Palace before the King, Queen, Queen Mother, and the two Princesses Elizabeth and Margaret Rose. Defying protocol, he insisted that the Royal Family should be seated in the great glittering drawing room before the double doors were thrown open and he, not the Royal Family, made his entrée. He addressed George VI in the Ojibwa tongue, adding: "which, being interpreted, means 'I come in peace, brother.'" His talk was so well received that he had to speak for an extra ten minutes at the special request of Princess Elizabeth. Finally he took his leave, holding out one hand to the King and tapping him on the shoulder with the other, in which he held his highly ornamented gloves—"Good-bye, brother. I'll be seeing you."

Grey Owl claimed to be no more than a half-caste, the son of a Scotsman and an Apache Indian who had formed part of Buffalo Bill's troupe. He certainly looked the part. Lloyd Roberts, who visited him in Canada, found him

the first Indian that really looked like an Indian—an Indian from those thrilling Wild West days of covered wagons, buffalos, and Sitting Bulls. The stamp of his fierce Apache ancestors showed in his tall, gaunt physique, his angular features, his keen eyes, even in his two braids dangling down his fringed buckskin shirt.

In fact, he had no Indian ancestry whatsoever. His name was Archie Belaney, he was born in Hastings, an English south coast resort, brought up by two genteel maiden aunts, and educated at the local grammar school. Though he went to Canada in 1906, at the age of eighteen, he adopted neither the name nor the persona of Grey Owl until 1930 when he began to write and devote himself to the cause of the beavers. But as a child he had played at being a Redskin, he had devoured countless books about the Indians, and he knew exactly how the English thought one of them ought to look, speak, and act. A charlatan he certainly was, but also an artist. He created an almost perfect European image of the Red Indian, and it is impossible to doubt his genuine love of the Indians, the beaver, and the wilds.

256. *Grey Owl*, 1931

CHAPTER 10

Land of the Future

"AMERICA, you are better off than our old continent," Goethe wrote in a poem of 1827 addressed *To the United States:*

> Amerika, du hast es besser
> Als unser Kontinent, das alte. . . .

In twelve densely packed and allusive lines a new vision of the New World is opened up. Its deficiencies are seen to have been advantages. With no ruined castles (*keine verfallene Schlösser*) to keep memories of feudalism and dissension alive, as they did in Europe, American poets would be immune from picturesque stories of "knights, robbers and ghosts." But the central message of the poem had a wider significance. Take advantage of the present moment, he urged the Americans—

> Benutz die Gegenwart mit Glück!

Goethe's phrases—so memorable in German, so weighted with overtones and undertones that defy translation—echo down through the nineteenth and into the twentieth century, outlining the vision of America as the land of the future though the phrase itself seems to have been coined by Hegel, in a typically inverted manner. In his philosophy of history (1830–31), Hegel called America *das Land der Zukunft*—

> the land of the future where, in the ages that lie before us, the burden of the world's history shall reveal itself—perhaps in a contest between North and South America. It is a land of desire for all those who are weary of the historical lumber-room of old Europe.

World history moved from East to West, he believed: Asia was the beginning and Europe "absolutely the end of history." But as neither philosophy nor history was concerned with the future, "America has no interest for us here," he blandly concluded. Two decades later Heine saluted America in a poem more strongly reminiscent of Goethe. "This is America! This is the New World!" he wrote:

> This is no graveyard of Romance,
> This is no pile of ruins,
> Of fossilized wigs and symbols,
> Of stale and musty tradition.

From his Paris exile he thought of going there, but was put off by the domestic manners of "the great freedom-stable inhabited by egalitarian boors, where men chew tobacco and spit without spittoons."

In 1887 Engels wrote of the "more favoured soil of America, where no mediaeval castles bar the way, where history begins with the elements of modern bourgeois society as evolved in the seventeenth century." That same year the Socialist Wilhelm Liebknecht, founder of the German Social Democratic Party, remarked in an account of his recent travels through the United States that no relics of feudalism weighed down Americans. "No traditions, no handed-down prejudices" prevented them from taking part in a "fresh, pulsating present." A writer of a very different complexion who had also recently been to America, Oscar Wilde, included the following dialogue in *A Woman of No Importance* (1893):

> LADY CAROLINE PONTEFRACT: There are a great many things you haven't got in America, I am told, Miss Worsley. They say you have no ruins, and no curiosities.

HESTER WORSLEY: The English aristocracy supply us with our curiosities, Lady Caroline. They are sent over to us every summer regularly, in the steamers, and propose to us the day after they land. As for ruins, we are trying to build up something that will last longer than brick or stone.

The idea of America, and especially the United States, as a land without a past was interpreted in a wide variety of ways by Europeans, as was the picture it summoned up of what Europe might be like in the future, the latter being viewed often with some despondency. Attitudes were seldom clearcut, however, and those of the Socialists display their full complexity. In the 1850s Marx and Engels studied with alarm what the latter called "the necessarily rapid and rapidly growing prosperity of the country, which makes bourgeois conditions look like a *beau idéal*." For it drew off so many of the more enterprising European workers who were "easily Americanised" and promptly lost their fighting spirit. The Civil War gave Marx hope not so much on account of the abolition of slavery (welcome though that was) but because he foresaw that the victory of the Union would stimulate Northern industry, favor the development of capitalism, and rapidly create, he thought, social conditions as deplorable as those of Europe. America would thus lose its appeal to emigrants. In the preface to the 1867 edition of *Das Kapital* he wrote:

> As in the eighteenth century the American War of Independence sounded the tocsin for the European middle class, so in the nineteenth century, the American Civil War sounded it for the European working class.

European, not American. But when big business boomed still more than he had predicted during America's gilded age, he began to wonder whether it might not be creating favorable conditions for revolution. In the United States, "capitalist economy and the corresponding enslavement of the working class have developed *more rapidly* and *more shamelessly* than in any other country," he noted with satisfaction in 1881.

The violence of American strikes, the open, pitched battles between the police and workers of Pittsburgh and elsewhere, and such incidents as the Chicago Haymarket affair, widely publicized and often illustrated in the European press [257], seemed to confirm Marx's belief. The United States was approaching the "greatest and most universal revolution, whose end will be the abolition of wage-slavery," H. M. Hyndman wrote in 1886. "America is directly on the verge of a revolution," another English Socialist, Charles Lawrin, proclaimed in 1906 and the following year August Bebel told his comrades in the United States: "You Americans will be the first to usher in a Socialist republic; you are now in the darkness before dawn."

These are, of course, extreme statements of views which were seldom held outside Marxist circles. H. G. Wells, for example, who was famil-

257(a). *American Strikes*, from *Illustrazione Italiana*, May 23, 1886

257(b). *Chicago "Haymarket" Executions*, from *Illustrazione Italiana*, December 4, 1887

iar with and sympathetic toward current Socialist literature, summed up the situation rather differently after visiting the United States in 1906.

> The European reader must dismiss from his mind any conception of the general American population as a mass of people undergoing impoverishment through the enrichment of the few. He must substitute for that figure a mass of people, very busy, roughly prosperous, generally self-satisfied.

Nevertheless, Marxists went on believing in America as the land of their particular future right up to the outbreak of the Russian Revolution. Shortly after that began, Lenin stood the whole idea of America as the land of Socialism's future on its head, citing the United States— "the freest and most civilized country"—as proof that a democratic republic was anything but beneficial to the workers. "What do we find there?" he asked in 1918. "The brazen rule of a handful, not even of millionaires but multi-millionaires, while the people are in slavery and servitude." But Trotsky, as late as 1940, was once again looking to America for the dawn of "the new epoch of an independent class movement of the proletariat and at the same time of—genuine Marxism."

While Marxists scanned the American scene for signs of imminent revolution, other Europeans watched the astonishingly rapid growth of general prosperity and the accumulation of vast private fortunes on the other side of the Atlantic with different hopes and fears. Conservatives had long seen in the United States, especially after the Civil War, a distasteful glimpse of what Europe would be like should parvenu industrialists take over from the old landed aristocracy. The purse-proud, cigar-smoking American millionaire now barged his way to the forefront of the European vision of America, assessing everything by size and commercial value, demanding breakneck progress and modernity—yet strangely susceptible to old world charm, even of feudal titles and ruined castles. In caricatures Brother Jonathan lost his rusticity as he acquired a plutocratic air, and the traditional relationship between him and John Bull was reversed—as in a cartoon of 1902 by Max Beerbohm where the former is the arrogant rich man of the world and the latter a simple countryman begging assistance [258].

In the wake of the millionaire came the millionairess with her ropes of pearls and sparkling diamonds. When the Austrian painter Hans Makart decorated the ceiling of a Viennese palace in the 1870s with an allegory of the four continents, the old image of America had long since fallen out of use and he represented her in a low-cut evening dress, sipping champagne [259]. A name was found for this new personification in an operetta put on in Vienna in 1907—*Die Dollarprinzessin*. In the meantime, George Du Maurier had enabled readers of *Punch* to see American millionairesses studying Burke's *Peerage* before setting out for Europe, and traveling without their fathers. "Pa's much too vulgar!"

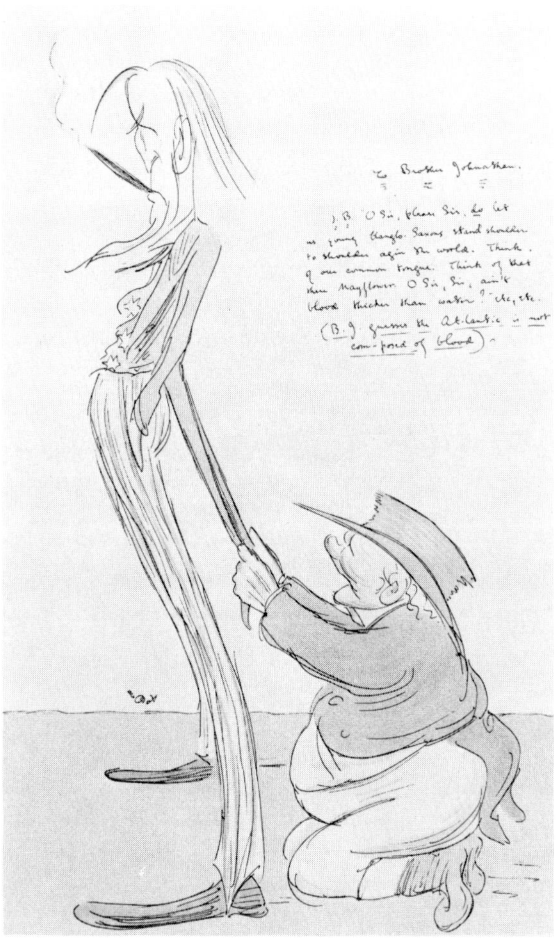

258. *To Brother Jonathan*, 1902. Max Beerbohm

[250]

259. *America*, detail of ceiling, c.1870. Hans Makart

one of them explains. "It's as much as we can do to stand Ma!" But Boldini succeeded in capturing something of the tireless vivacity, elegance, and charm of these invaders in his portrait of Consuelo (Vanderbilt), Duchess of Marlborough, very much at home amid the splendors of Blenheim [260].

American money—and the notion that Americans were exclusively occupied in amassing it—led to the belief that they had little time or opportunity for culture. Europeans generally assumed that the arts did not flourish in the United States. The only American painters and sculptors at all widely known were those who had settled in Europe, from Benjamin West to Whistler, Sargent, and Mary Cassatt. Only the useful arts could be practiced there. As the official catalogue of the Great Exhibition of 1851 put it:

The expenditure of months or years of labour upon a single article, not to increase its intrinsic value, but solely to augment its cost or its estimation as an object of *virtù*, is not common in the United States. On the contrary, both manual and mechanical labour are applied with direct reference to increasing the number or the quality of articles suited to the wants of a whole people, and adapted to promote the enjoyment of that moderate competency which prevails among them.

The merits of this American approach did not pass unnoticed by discerning visitors to the 1851 Exhibition, which gave Europeans their first opportunity to see a wide range of American products. A German, Lothar Bucher, singled out simple American furniture for its "freedom from that gingerbread carving which tears at our hands and clothing, and the absence of the right angles of those currently popular Gothic chairs which are hunching everyone's shoul-

[251]

260. *Consuelo, Duchess of Marlborough and Lord Ivor Spencer-Churchill,* 1906. Giovanni Boldini

ders." He thought that "American domestic equipment breathes the spirit of comfort and fitness for purpose"—an astonishingly forward-looking comment for 1851, anticipating, in fact, the most advanced European attitudes of two or more decades later.

The official French report on the Centennial Exhibition at Philadelphia in 1876 commended what it called the "Pullman car style" of furniture with simple moldings, very little carving, manufactured in separate parts which were easily assembled. And Europeans were no less appreciative of American tools and machines. The head of the German delegation to Philadelphia in 1876 described the axes, hoes, hunting knives, and hammers "executed with such variety and beauty as cannot but excite admiration." Two years later Julius Lessing, director of the Berlin Museum of Industrial Arts, was similarly impressed by the aesthetic qualities of tools shown in the United States Pavilion at the World's Fair in Paris.

American inventions, from industrial equipment to electric light bulbs and patent furniture, were increasingly exhibited and illustrated in the European press and the United States gradually came to be regarded as the land of the machine, the labor-saving device, and mechanized living, especially, of course, the bathroom with constant hot water which figured prominently in every book about America from Laboulaye's *Paris en Amérique* onward. But already in the 1860s there were European aesthetes complaining about the spread of this technological progress, of "l'américanisation de la France," as the Goncourts called it. However, the quite exceptional gifts of several nineteenth-century American architects were recognized in Europe much earlier than is often supposed. Henry Hobson Richardson was widely influential in Finland, Sweden, Germany, and England, by the 1890s when enterprising European architects such as Adolf Loos began going to America to study the "skyscrapers" and other new buildings there. Sullivan was less directly influential but perhaps even more admired in Europe, being praised, together with Richardson and Richard Morris Hunt, as "an innovator of new formulas," by Samuel Bing, the German-born French-naturalized entrepreneur of Art Nouveau and, indeed, the inventor of the term.

In a book published in 1895 Bing remarked that in America "*yesterday* no longer counts while *today* exists only as a preparation for *tomorrow*." He was unusual in his appreciation of the bursting, energetic vitality beneath the frenzy of American life. Few if any earlier Europeans seem to have been so positively responsive to the visual excitement of New York, where "that infinity of space, water, and land merged in a chaos of throbbing life" is spread before the visitor. Here skyscrapers, which would look monstrous in Europe, were in perfect keeping. New York "cries out for domination by that silhouette of dense masses," he wrote. This new American architecture was imbued "with the dominant spirit of the race, a spirit that delights in undertakings of powerful scope, conceived at the opportune moment and boldly pushed to the extreme." In the decorative arts also America had suddenly shown "singular powers of initiative and youthful vigour, in sharp contrast with the thinning blood" of Europe. Louis Comfort Tiffany's glass with irridescent abstract patterns (marketed by Bing in France) was a truly "new art" and typically American. "Tiffany dreamed a dream of Art for the Future," Bing wrote. And elsewhere he argued that America "has a marked advantage over us, in that her brain is not haunted by phantoms of memory; her young imagination can allow itself a free career." She has a "special destiny," not having the perennial European burden of "the *cult*, the *religion* of . . . traditions." It is hardly surprising to find him quoting the first eight lines of Goethe's poem.

Just as Tiffany freed himself from the bondage of historical styles, the American dancer Loïe Fuller broke away from all the time-worn conventions of the traditional Romantic ballet. When she appeared at the Folies Bergères in 1892 she made a sensation "playing strangely with her veils and electric light," as Edmond Goncourt remarked. She was no less enthusiastically received in London. And years later W. B. Yeats was to recall how she "enwound a shining web, a floating ribbon of cloth." Her serpentine dances—"The Butterfly," "The Orchid," "The Fire," "The Lily"—were doubly novel, in the swirling, billowing, floating forms of her veils of chiffon and in the constantly changing shot-silk effects of the colored lights which illuminated them from every side, for she appeared suspended in air as she danced on a glass platform. The latest developments in electric lighting (itself an emblem of America) were employed by her to create a newly liberated art of the dance. She gradually assembled a staff of some fifty electricians. The fluid, cloudlike forms which she, as it were, released now seem to epitomize Art Nouveau. But the extraordinary beauty of her performance was captured only by Toulouse Lautrec in his famous lithographs—each print differently colored—in which she seems almost to anticipate the abstract art of Arp and Miró [XXIX].

The evanescent beauty of the forms created by Loïe Fuller in her dances and the fragile delicacy of Tiffany's glass captivated the addicts of Art Nouveau. But for many Europeans the vision of the future presented by the United States was still a rather nightmarish one. The word *cauchemar* reverberates through French accounts of America—by Paul Bourget in 1895, by Pierre Loti in 1913, and by Georges Duhamel in his *Scènes de la vie future* of 1930. All of them discourse on the monstrosity of skyscrapers, the dehumanized activity of the cities, and the vulgarities of the rich. Most English writers gave the same impression. And, of course, in the one great European novel set in America in this period—Kafka's unfinished *Amerika*—this malign, *angst*-ridden aspect is immortalized.

It might be supposed that the Italian Futurists would have found their promised land of dynamic technology in the United States. The first of their declared aims was "to destroy the cult of the past, the obsession with Antiquity, pedantry and academic idealism," and another, "to represent and glorify everyday life, incessantly and tumultuously transformed by victorious science." But their attitude to America was oddly ambivalent. In the early days of the movement Marinetti extolled Walt Whitman as the antiacademic hero of antiliterature and much of their architectural manifesto published above the name of Antonio Sant' Elia in 1913 (though a joint composition) reads like a description of an American city and must surely have been inspired by one:

We no longer feel ourselves to be the men of the cathedrals and the ancient moot halls, but men of the Grand Hotels, railway stations, giant roads, colossal harbours, covered markets, glittering arcades, reconstruction areas and salutary slum clearances.

We must invent and rebuild *ex novo* our modern city like an immense and tumultuous shipyard, active, mobile and everywhere dynamic, and the modern buildings like a gigantic machine. Lifts must no longer hide away like solitary worms in the stairwells, but the stairs—now useless—must be abolished, and the lifts must swarm up the facades like serpents of glass and iron. . . .

Sant' Elia's designs for a *Nuova Città* with bold, clean-lined skyscraper towers also owe an obvious debt to New York and Chicago—there were no skyscrapers in Europe as yet [261]. One fourteen-story apartment house even has illuminated advertising on the skyline. Yet American influence was explicitly rejected in the second and more widely diffused version of the manifesto, probably written in collaboration with Marinetti.

261. Designs for *Nuova Città*, 1913. Antonio Sant' Elia

262. *Buffalo Bill*, 1905. Maximilien Luce

In the minds of progressive European architects a firm distinction was drawn between the engineering and "architectural" abilities of their opposite numbers in the United States (except for Frank Lloyd Wright). Factories and other utilitarian and industrial buildings seen in America between 1893 and 1896 by the young Viennese architect Adolf Loos — later to coin the phrase "ornament is crime" — aroused his keen admiration and inspired his own astringent style which was to play an important part in the modern movement in Europe. Similarly, it was only the plainest buildings that appealed to Walter Gropius, who remarked in 1911 that "the newest work halls of the North American trusts can bear comparison, in their overwhelming monumental power, with the buildings of ancient Egypt." Le Corbusier in *Vers une Architecture* (1923) warned his *confrères*: "Let us listen to the counsels of American engineers. But let us beware of American architects." His book is illustrated with six factories and eight grain elevators in the United States, against one of the former and none of the latter in Europe. Engineers "not in pursuit of an architectural idea, but guided simply by the necessities of an imperative demand," he explained, "show us the way to create plastic facts, clear and limpid, giving rest to our eyes and to the mind the pleasures of geometric forms." He seems to have believed that art belonged to the Old World, only nature and technology to the New and — as Reyner Banham puts it — saw the American engineer as a kind of noble savage.

The Wild West coexisted, if somewhat uncomfortably, with the mechanized, chromium-plated city of the future in the European vision of America. Buffalo Bill's troupe provided subjects for the neo-Impressionist Maximilien Luce, better known for his industrial landscapes [262].

[255]

THE NEW GOLDEN LAND

And Buffalo Bill himself seems to be the subject of a Cubist picture painted by Picasso in the spring of 1911, perhaps in preparation for his first New York show the same year [263]. Flowing blond hair and a suggestion of a cowboy hat may be discerned but there is some doubt as to whether the title may not have been merely a *blague*. In any event, America seems to have fascinated Picasso during these early Cubist years. Gertrude Stein recalled in the *Autobiography of Alice B. Toklas* how he loved American comic strips—especially *The Katzenjammer Kids*—and how she had to save up her American newspapers and magazines for him. But he was well aware of urban America as well and his typically ambivalent vision of the New World later crystallized in the costume he designed for the New York Manager in *Parade*—cowboy boots, red pleated shirt-front, stove-pipe hat, and a huge superstructure like a skyscraper [264]. With a "story" by Cocteau, choreogaphy by Massine, music by Satie, costumes and set by Picasso, and production by Diaghilev, *Parade* represented all that was most modern and up-to-date in the arts at the time of its first performance in 1917—and for several decades after-

263. *Buffalo Bill*, 1911. Pablo Picasso

LAND OF THE FUTURE

264. The New York Manager in *Parade*, 1917. Pablo Picasso

"I have been profoundly impressed by the vast mechanical development of America," the Cuban-born but cosmopolitan Francis Picabia told a reporter from the New York *Tribune* in 1915.

> The machine has become more than an adjunct of life. It is really a part of human life—perhaps the very soul. In seeking forms through which to interpret ideas or by which to expose human characteristics I have come at length upon the form which appears most brilliantly plastic and fraught with symbolism. I have enlisted the machinery of the modern world and introduced it into my studio.

Two years later he illustrated in his periodical *291* (published in Barcelona) an electric light bulb reflecting the words "flirt divorce" and entitled *Américaine*. On another page he reproduced a mechanical drawing of a spark plug inscribed "For-Ever" and entitled *Portrait of a Young American Girl in a State of Nudity*. In New York Picabia and Marcel Duchamp were the leading lights in the circle which developed most of the ideas soon to be associated with Dada (though the name was invented independently in Zurich in 1916). For the 1917 exhibition of the New York Society of Independent Artists—a rather stuffy organization—Duchamp submitted the famous urinal, "signed" *R. Mutt*. The truculent choice of subject might seem to reflect current European notions about the supposed American tendency to equate plumbing with civilization. Some of his other "readymades" were American products, like the snow shovel entitled *In Advance of the Broken Arm*. His aim was, of course, to overturn traditional artistic values and the cult of the handmade in both Europe and America. But his work in New York may well have helped to confirm the belief that America was destined to produce the art of the future, as Bing had prophesied.

ward. America therefore plays an important part in it. A teenage American girl who looked, according to Cocteau, "capable of going down on the *Titanic*," was dressed in a sailor jacket, danced ragtime, and quivered like a film image. Cocteau originally intended her entry to be accompanied by the noise of typewriters and a voice from a megaphone: "Cube tic tic tic tic on the hundredth floor." The New York Manager was to shout through a megaphone: "Titanic, toctoc tic tedelboc tadeltac. . . . Come in, learn the American way, the tremors, the short circuits, the detectives of the Hudson, Ragtime, factories, railroads. . . ." This is a burlesque figure, but the mechanized way of American life was beginning to interest artists from a wider point of view as well.

While Picabia and Duchamp were in New York, an artist who had certain affinities with them, George Grosz, was dreaming of America in his Berlin tenement. As we have already seen, he had been a childhood admirer of Karl May's Wild West stories. Probably to take his mind off the war, which he hated, he painted a self-portrait in cowboy outfit entitled *The Ad-*

[257]

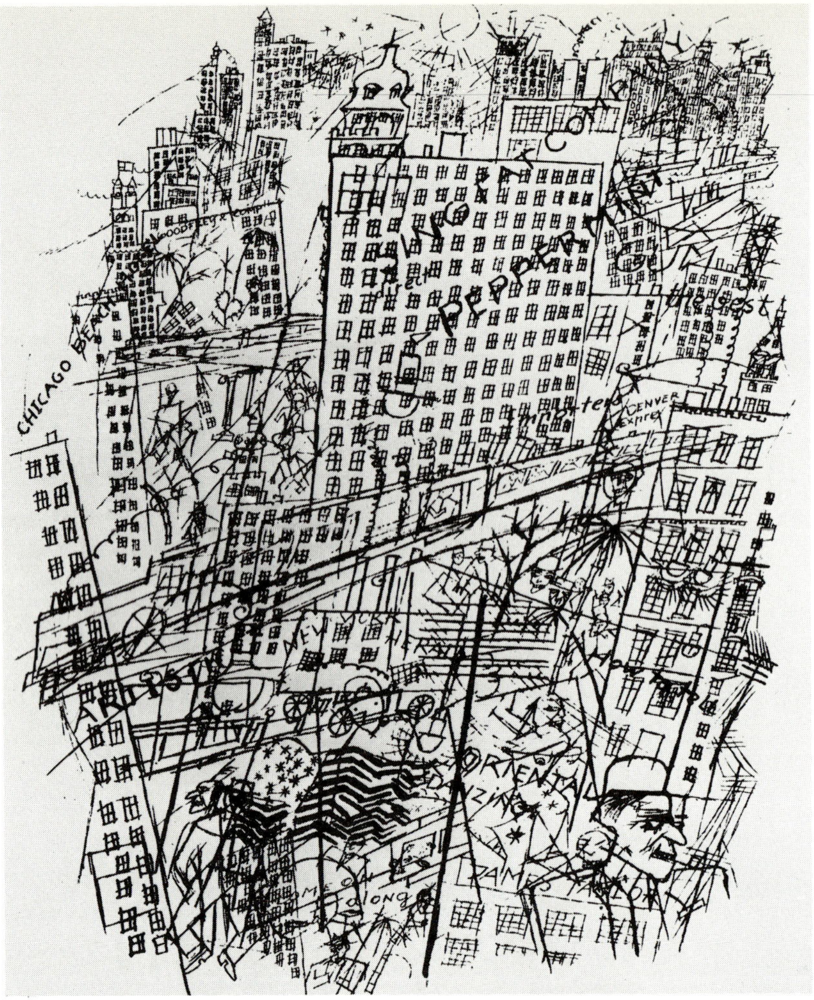

265. *Memory of New York*, 1916. George Grosz

266. Stills from *Metropolis*, 1926. UFA, sets by Otto Hanke

venturer—a work strongly influenced by the Italian Futurists. But he also made such drawings of the contemporary American scene as *Old Jimmy*, the interior of a sleazy bar, and *Memory of New York*, with skyscrapers, elevated railways, and a great deal of advertising [265]—all of them quite imaginary, of course.

In Germany the new vision of the United States as the land of the future had been summoned up in 1913 in Berhard Kellermann's *Tunnel*, an enormously popular science fiction novel about life in the mechanized America of steel and concrete linked with Europe by a tunnel under the Atlantic. In 1926, when the producers of the German film *Metropolis* wanted to represent the Berlin of the future, they provided it with New York's elevated railroad and clustered skyscrapers [266]. Ten years later the English film of H. G. Wells novel *The Shape of Things to Come* had sets—devised in consultation with Fernand Léger—similarly inspired by the American cityscape [267].

Art Nouveau was the first European style in which America figured prominently and to which American artists made a significant and individual contribution. They played a still more important part in the brighter, brisker, and sometimes brasher Art Deco style which originated in France in the early 1920s but reached its climax in Radio City Music Hall and the Chrysler Building in New York. By this date European designers hankering after streamlined up-to-the-minute modernity naturally turned to America—their new chromium-plated land. Some even looked beyond the cities to the immemorial America of the Indians, drawing inspiration from their brilliantly colored, simply patterned artifacts that were still being made, or to the stepped pyramids of the Aztecs which were adapted—with sublime inconsequence—to chests of drawers, clocks, and even radio sets.

In England Art Deco was often called "jazz modern" and thanks to the development of the gramophone and the radio, jazz swept rapidly across Europe in the 1920s and '30s, providing a soundtrack to the visual image of America, especially black America which now began to loom large in European minds. Ragtime, origi-

267. Still from *Things to Come*, 1936. Alexander Korda

nated by black pianists in the Middle West, was heard in Europe before 1908 when Debussy wrote "Golliwogg's Cake-walk," the first of several piano pieces influenced by it. In 1917–18 Stravinsky wrote "Ragtime for Eleven Solo Instruments." But the music made by the black people of New Orleans was first heard elsewhere—and for the first time called jass, jaz, or jazz—in Chicago in 1914 and in New York early in 1917. The first gramophone records, issued by RCA Victor in 1917, reached Europe almost immediately, soon to be followed by a jazz band playing at the Casino de Paris in November 1918. "I recall the shock, the sudden awakening this staggering rhythm, this new sonority brought," Darius Milhaud wrote a few years later. Coming immediately after the war, it seemed to typify the spirit of the new era which was opening. Its success was mainly with the young who danced the fox-trot, rushed to see such groups as The Blackbirds [268], and eagerly

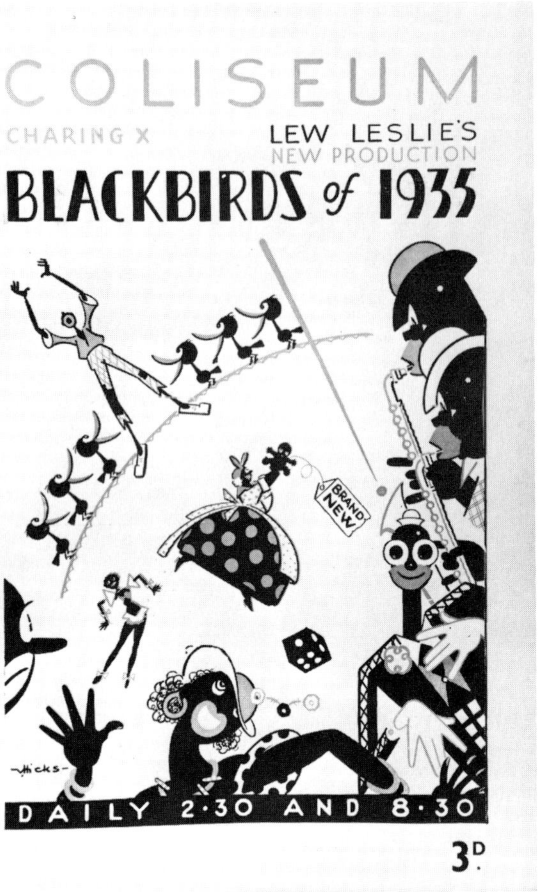

268. Theater program, 1935. "Hicks"

bought recordings of Louis Armstrong and "Jelly Roll" Morton. The American black musician emerged as a new type of popular hero—the central figure in the jazz opera by Ernst Křenek, *Jonny spielt auf* (first performed in Leipzig in 1927). In these years, however, jazz came to be regarded not only as musically modern but as politically subversive, especially after the first performance in 1927 of the Kurt Weil/Bertolt Brecht anticapitalist jazz opera *Mahagonny*, which is set in America. In 1933 the Nazis banned the broadcasting of jazz altogether—which of course had the effect of transposing it into a symbol of America as a land of liberty as well as the land of the future.

Musical expression of a different kind was given to the idea of transatlantic modernity in the avant-garde orchestral piece *Amériques* which Edgard Varèse, who eventually settled in the United States, wrote in 1925. "It describes no definite place but should be considered a symbol of the discoveries of new worlds on earth, in space, and also in the human mind," he stated. Yet its disturbing sonorities (which make a strange contrast with Dvorak's rather sentimental symphony *From the New World* of thirty years earlier, not to mention Wagner's march for the first Centennial in Philadelphia in 1876) bring vividly to mind the sights and sounds of New York—echoes of police-car sirens screaming through empty downtown streets at night, the muffled bass of traffic pouring down the great canyonlike avenues, and the shrill wind howling around the skyscrapers. Not that *Amériques* could be described as "program music," to which it bears about the same relationship as do Mondrian's abstractions to topographical painting.

Piet Mondrian, in fact, also responded enthusiastically to jazz and took from it the titles for his last two great pictures, painted in the United States—*Broadway Boogie-Woogie* [XXX] and *Victory Boogie-Woogie*. "True Boogie-Woogie I conceive as homogenous in intention with mine in painting," he wrote: "destruction of melody which is the equivalent of destruction of actual appearance: and construction through the continuous opposition of pure means—dynamic rhythm." Although he was nearly seventy, his move from blacked-out London, where his studio had been destroyed in an air raid, to neon-lit New York had an extraordinary, tonic, and invigorating effect on him. His work began, almost immediately, to acquire new life, to develop once more in new directions. Black lines were eliminated and his paintings began to vibrate with juxtaposed color like flashing lights.

The night lights of New York made a no less strong impression on another refugee from Nazi-occupied Europe, Fernand Léger, who wrote:

> I was struck by the illuminated advertisements that swept the streets. You were there, talking to someone, and suddenly he became blue. Then the colour disappeared and another came, and he became red, yellow. That kind of projected colour is free, it is in space. I wanted to do the same thing in my canvases.

269. *Adieu New York*, 1945. Fernand Léger

Modern urban life fascinated him and he commemorated his years of wartime exile in *Adieu New York* [269]. He was stimulated by the "increased sense of movement and violence" in America, strong colors, "girls in sweaters" (like his beefy *Grande Julie* in the Museum of Modern Art), and above all, by "bad taste . . . one of the valuable raw materials for the country." The American countryside, however, afforded him a more perplexing glimpse into the future. Spending his summers near Lake Champlain he was much struck

> by the broken down farm machines I would come across abandoned in the fields. For me it became a typical feature of the American landscape, this carelessness and waste and blind and ruthless disregard of anything worn or aged.

Sigfried Giedion described how he scrutinized the rusting machinery on an abandoned farm with Léger, who remarked: "Ce spectacle ne se voit pas en Europe." It heightened Léger's awareness of the struggle between organic nature and mechanization in the modern world. "For me the contrast in the United States between the mechanical and the natural is one of great anti-melodic intensity," he wrote shortly before returning to Europe.

[261]

But old ideas die hard. The surrealist André Masson declared that his vision of America had been and, even after four years there during the war, perhaps still was "rooted in Chateaubriand." The savagery of the New World, "the feeling that nature may one day recover its strength and turn all back to chaos" struck him even in Central Park, New York. Max Ernst had to go farther afield, to Arizona, for similar intimations and for landscapes as weird in color and form as any product of his subconscious. He recorded them in several memorable paintings, perhaps best of all in the minute illustrations reproduced with his poems as *Seven Miracles*. The cities of America might represent the world of the future, but he infinitely preferred this miraculously preserved segment of an elemental primitive past where the Hopi Indians still retained their ancient traditions, stubbornly resisting the advance of material civilization.

The American way of life from which Ernst sought refuge was just what appealed to a younger generation of English artists who were reaching their maturity at this same moment—the blatant advertising, processed food and plastic gadgets, streamlined motorcars and super-streamlined blondes, the jukebox, TV, and the musical. At the Institute of Contemporary Arts in London in 1952 Edouardo Paolozzi gave an epidiascope projection of images from American magazines (still rarities in England) for an appreciative audience of young artists, architects, and critics including Richard Hamilton, John McHale, the Smithsons, Lawrence Alloway, and Reyner Banham. Four years later Hamilton and McHale, with the architect John Voelcker, devised a section of an exhibition, *This is Tomorrow*, in which the profusion of images mainly from American popular sources struck most visitors as a deliberate flaunting of the worst aspects of American culture. It was summed up in Hamilton's collage, reproduced on the poster and in the catalogue, *Just what is it that makes today's homes so different, so appealing?* [270]. Several more collages, paintings, and prints derived from similar sources were made

270. *Just what is it that makes today's homes so different, so appealing?* 1956. Richard Hamilton

xxix. *Loïe Fuller,* 1892. Henri de Toulouse Lautrec

xxx. *Broadway Boogie Woogie*, 1942–43. Piet Mondrian

271. *The Solomon R. Guggenheim*, 1965.
Richard Hamilton

by Hamilton in the next few years [271]. But his work was misconstrued as an attack either on art or on the consumer society associated with America. He was, in fact, aiming at a new art which should be, according to his definition of 1957, "popular, transient, expendable, low cost, mass produced, young, witty, sexy, gimmicky, glamorous and big business." He denied any satirical intention. His paintings were not "a sardonic comment on our society," he wrote. "I should like to think of my purpose as a search for what is epic in everyday subjects and everyday attitudes. Irony has no place in it except in so far as irony is part of the ad man's repertoire." He did, however, reveal a new attitude to the United States.

It was in the 1920s that the United States first became familiar, visually, to Europeans through the cinema, and since the 1940s it has become increasingly so through the media, just as it has been brought physically closer by jet aircraft. Most Europeans have, perhaps, a clearer image of it today than of foreign countries in their own continent. Clearer, but not necessarily more objective. Through the cinema America exported its own vision of itself as a land of clashing contrasts between opulence and squalor, idealism and corruption, city gangsterism and small-town peace and plenty, all laced with the recurrent theme of violence "as American as cherry pie." Yet Italian and German films are enough to remind one that the European vision of America remains distinct—very much so in such outsanding films as Franco Rossi's *Smog* and Antonioni's *Zabriskie Point*. And that extraordinary phenomenon, the "spaghetti Western" and its German counterpart, is, among other things, a comment on the (quite natural) inability of American producers to grasp the European vision of the Wild West. The German Westerns, indeed, derived initially from stories by Karl May written long before he had any direct experience of America. Here the "good" European Old Shatterhand and the noble Winnetou—*der rote Gentleman*—still lead their adventurous lives in a primeval landscape instantly recognizable as American even though the films are shot in Europe. It might even be claimed that in them the sixteenth-century vision of America as a terrestrial paradise of innocent and noble savages still tangentially survives.

The lawns of the California Garden of Eden are now kept green with automatic sprinklers, the rivers have been diverted into sky-blue swimming pools, the inhabitants still bask naked in the sun without thought of toil, and perpetual spring still reigns there—at any rate in David Hockney's paintings. In 1961 he made his first visit to the United States, before he had been to any country on the European continent. The result was a series of etchings, *A Rake's Progress*, which wryly charts the American career of an English artist who loses his friends as soon as he has spent his money and ends by joining the "mindless mass." Two years later he decamped to California on an intuition which, he told an interviewer on one of his several return visits, proved right.

> I came because I thought it would be very sexy. One of the things that prompted me to come here was a magazine called *Physique Pictorial*. I noticed that it was published in Los Angeles, so I assumed that's what life was like here. The photographs portrayed what a certain life was like in Los Angeles and, in a way, it was true.

272. *Savings and Loan Building*, 1967. David Hockney
273. *Rocky Mountains and Tired Indians*, 1965. David Hockney

XXXI. *A Bigger Splash*, 1968. David Hockney

They were accurate if you looked for it. So I thought the place would turn me on in many ways, in all kinds of ways. And it did.

Hockney was entranced with the whole ambience, including the architecture which he was soon painting [272]. But he did not lose all his preconceptions immediately. An Indian subject was traditionally obligatory for a European artist in America and in 1965 he completed his imaginary and fantastic *Rocky Mountains and Tired Indians* which includes all the right ingredients, deserted landscape, cactus, totem eagle, and for good measure, a plastic Eames chair [273]. But at about the same time, he began, he says, "to paint California as it really appeared to me."

His is a vision of an almost insistently brand-new world where all is bright and clean and

274. *A Lawn Sprinkler*, 1967. David Hockney

sparkling. The houses and their furnishings and even the grass, the flowers, and palm trees seem to have been only just delivered, factory-sealed [274]. Everything is artificial, and so abundant that it can be immediately thrown away and discarded after use, as if with the prodigality of Nature, so that the images of America as an earthly paradise and as the land of the future are now completely fused. Yet, for all the confident lucidity and the easy, unobtrusively compact designs these strangely compelling pictures are slightly enigmatic. The judicious and meticulous coolness of the handling hints at something else—is it emptiness and despair?—lurking just behind. The relaxed poses of the figures all but conceal nervous tension: an appearance of outward plenty all but masks a void within. A bigger splash echoes rather unnervingly in the preternatural calm of an urban garden in which the only other sign of human presence is an empty chair [XXXI].

* * *

In a story written by the Italian novelist Ignazio Silone in 1930, a mysterious impresario visits a small village in the Abruzzi and gradually accumulates what little wealth it has. The way in which he enriches himself reminds the local population of the success stories of emigrants who had effortlessly made their fortunes in the United States. "The peasants have to cross the sea to find America but this robber has found it here," they say.

"America?" the others answered. "America is far away and doesn't look like this."

"America is everywhere," the Impresario told those who referred the argument to him. "It's everywhere, you just have to know how to look for it."

Many Europeans have spent years searching for this promised land of everlasting youth and sunshine and gold. Some have found it almost accidentally, even in that great continent which lies beyond the Western Sea and blocks the route to Cathay.

Notes

General

There are no books which deal generally with the European visual image of America, but several exhibition catalogues are relevant: *The French in America*, Detroit Institute of Arts, 1951; *The Painter and the New World*, Montreal Museum of Fine Arts, 1967; Roy Strong: *A Pageant of Canada*, The National Gallery of Canada, Ottawa, 1967; and Hugh Honour: *The European Vision of America*, The National Gallery, Washington, D.C., The Cleveland Museum of Arts, and the Grand Palais, Paris, 1975–76. Lynn Glaser: *Engraved America*, Philadelphia 1970, provides an anthology of woodcuts and engravings from the late sixteenth to the early nineteenth century with a minimum of information. Very useful, on the other hand, are two amply illustrated and documented volumes published by Paul Elek—W. P. Cumming, R. A. Skelton, and D. B. Quinn: *The Discovery of North America*, London 1971, and W. P. Cumming, S. Hillier, D. B. Quinn, and G. Williams: *The Exploration of North America*, London 1974.

The following, which deal generally with the European literary image of America, are indispensable—first and foremost Antonello Gerbi: *La Disputa del Nuovo Mondo: Storia di una polemica 1750–1900*, Milan-Naples 1955, now available in a slightly expanded English translation (by Jeremy Moyle) as *The Dispute of the New World*, Pittsburgh 1973; J. H. Elliott: *The Old World and the New, 1492–1650*, Cambridge 1970; and, though nationally limited in scope, two older books by Gilbert Chinard which remain unsuperseded: *L'Exotisme Américain dans la Littérature Française au XVIe Siècle*, Paris 1913, and *L'Amérique et le Rêve Exotique dans la Littérature Française au XVIIe et au XVIIIe Siècle*, Paris 1913, now available in a photographic reprint, Geneva 1970. Also essential are R. R. Cawley: *Unpathed Waters*, Princeton 1940 (dealing with the impact on English literature of sixteenth-centure exploration); M. Kraus: *The Atlantic Civilization*, New York 1949; Howard Mumford Jones: *O Strange New World* (1952), London 1965; Rosario Romeo: *Le scoperte americane nella coscienza italiana del Cinquecento* (1954), Milan-Naples 1971; Henri Baudet: *Het Paradijs op Aarde* (1959), translated by E. Wentholt as *Paradise on Earth*, New Haven 1965; Edmundo O'Gorman: *The Invention of America*, Bloomington 1961, and S. Skard: *The American Myth and the European Mind*, Philadelphia 1961.

There are two outstanding bibliographies of "Americana"—Henry Harrisse: *Biblioteca Americana Vetustissima. A Description of Works Relating to America published Between the Years 1492 and 1551*, New York 1865 (reprinted Madrid 1958), and Joseph Sabin: *A Dictionary of Books Relating to America, from its discovery to the present time*, London 1868–1936, twenty-nine volumes listing 150,756 items (reprinted Amsterdam 1961–62).

As this book was going to press, transcripts reached me of some of the papers read at a congress held at the University of California, Los Angeles, in February 1975—*International Conference on First Images of America: The Impact of the New World on the Old*. The complete papers will, I understand, be published.

Chapter 1

In the vast literature on the discovery of America the works of Samuel Eliot Morison are outstanding—*Admiral of the Ocean Sea: A Life of Christopher Columbus*, Boston 1942; *The European Discovery of America: The Northern Voyages*, New York 1971; *The European Discovery of America: The Southern Voyages 1492–1616*, New York 1974. His edition of *Journals and Other Documents of the Life and Voyages of Christopher Columbus*, New York 1963, is indispensable. There is also the Penguin *The Four Voyages of Christopher Columbus*, edited and translated by J. M. Cohen, Harmondsworth 1969. Several facsimiles have been published of the various editions of Columbus's first letter, notably *The Letter of Columbus on the Discovery of America: A facsimile of the Pictorial Edition*, New York 1892, with an introduction by Wilberforce Eames listing extant copies of the first sixteen editions. But for a collection of Columbus documents in their original languages the student must still go to the fourteen volumes of Cesare de Lollis (ed.): *Raccolta di documenti e studi pubblicati della R. Commissione Columbiana*, Rome 1892–94. Two very useful volumes in the *Nouvelle Clio* series clearly state the historical problems connected with the discovery and conquest of the New World and have extensive bibliographies—Pierre Chaunu: *L'Expansion européenne du XIIIe au XVe siècle* and *Conquête et exploitation des nouveaux mondes*, both Paris 1969. See also C. R. Crone: *The Discovery of America*, London 1969. For general accounts and discussions of discovery in the late fifteenth and sixteenth centuries see Georg Friederici: *Der Charakter der Entdeckung und Eroberung Amerikas durch die Europäer*, Stuttgart-Gotha 1925, Boies Penrose: *Travel and Discovery in the Renaissance 1420–1620*, Cambridge, Mass., 1960, and John Hale: "A World Elsewhere" in Denys Hays

NOTES

(ed.): *The Age of the Renaissance*, London 1967, pp. 317–43.

For the first visual images of America see Götz Pochat: *Der Exotismus während des Mittelalters und der Renaissance*, Stockholm 1970. S. Lorant: *The New World: The First Pictures of America*, New York 1946, has a misleading title: it deals with the first two volumes of de Bry's *America* (see below).

López de Gómara's famous remark appeared in the dedication to Charles V of his *Historia de las Indias*, Saragossa 1552.

Medieval beliefs about Atlantic islands are fully described in William H. Babcock: *Legendary Islands of the Atlantic*, New York 1922, which attempts to prove that each of them represents a real place. For a corrective to this thesis and several later theories about pre-Columbian voyages see Morison: *Northern Voyages*, pp. 81–111, see also Loren Baritz: "The Idea of the West" in *American Historical Review* LXVI (1961), pp. 616–40. For the Norse voyages to North America there are Joseph Fischer: *The Discoveries of the Norsemen in America*, London 1903, and two books by Gwyn Jones: *The Norse Atlantic Saga*, London 1964, and *A History of the Vikings*, London 1968. The best modern translation of *The Vinland Sagas* is by Magnus Magnussen and Herman Pálsson, Harmondsworth 1965.

The standard edition of *Mandeville's Travels* is that of M. C. Seymour, Oxford 1967. For an account of the relationship between Columbus's writings, medieval travel books, and the realities of the New World see Leonardo Olschki: *Storia letteraria delle scoperte geografiche*, Florence 1937, and "What Columbus Saw on Landing in the West Indies" in *Proceedings of the American Philosophical Society* LXXXIV (1941), pp. 633–59. As late as 1596 Walter Raleigh in *The Discoverie of the Large, Rich and Bewtiful Empyre of Guiana* remarked apropos of headless men with eyes in their shoulders: "Such a nation was writen of by Mandeville, whose reports were held fables for many years, and yet since the East Indies were discovered, we find his relations true of such things as heretofore were held incredible." They were, so Raleigh had been told, to be found in the Ewaipanoma tribe on the Caura River in Venezuela and are illustrated in the Latin edition of his book (Nuremberg 1599). For a discussion of this type of monstrosity, known to Europeans as Blemmyae and associated with India, see R. Wittkower: "Marvels of the East: A Study in the History of Monsters" in *Journal of the Warburg and Courtauld Institutes* V (1942), pp. 159–97.

On America and the idea of Paradise see A. B. Giamatti: *The Earhly Paradise and the Renaissance Epic*, Princeton 1966, and Harry Levin: *The Myth of the Golden Age in the Renaissance*, Bloomington and London 1969.

A recent account of Pietro Martire d'Anghiera—known in England and the U.S.A. as Peter Martyr—with bibliography is by R. Almagià in *Dizionario biografico degli Italiani*, vol. III, Rome 1961, pp. 257–60. The first complete edition of *De Orbe Novo . . . Decades Octo* was published at Alcalà in 1530, reprinted under the guidance of Richard Hakluyt, Paris 1587: the standard modern edition is that issued at Madrid, 1892. The first three books were translated into English by Richard Eden in 1555 and the whole work by M. Lok in 1612. The only modern English translation (which leaves much to be desired) is by F. A. McNutt, New York-London 1912. Martyr's *Epistolario* was published in a faulty edition in 1530 and in full at Amsterdam, 1570. The standard modern edition is that of José Lopez de Toro in *Documentos Inéditos para la Historia de España*, vols. IX–XII, Madrid 1953–57. These letters include five which are frequently quoted as evidence of the impact of Columbus's first voyage. One of them begins, "*Levantad el espiritu, mis dos sabios ancianos, escuchad el nuevo descubrimiento!*" But their dates are puzzling, ranging from May 14 to November 1, 1493, so they can hardly represent his immediate reactions to the arrival of Columbus at the Spanish court early in April. Their authenticity has been questioned (cf. I. Bernays: *Petrus Martyr Anglerius und sein Opus Epistolarum*, Strassburg 1891). If they are in fact by Martyr it seems possible that they were written some years after the event. Comments on Columbus's first voyage are very few, but the earliest reference in literature appears to be that in Sebastian Brandt's *Narrenschiff*, Basel, 1494: "*Auch hat man sydt in Portegal/Und in Hyspanien uberal/Golt-inseln funden, und nacket lüt/Von den man for wust sagen nüt,*" Englished by Wynkyn de Worde, 1509: "There was one that knewe that in yles of Spayne was enhabitents. Wherefore he asked men of Kynge Ferdynandus & wente & foude them, the which lyved as beestes."

The only copy of the illustrated Latin edition of Columbus's letter published in Basel is in the New York Public Library. For the woodcut frontispiece to Dati's poem see Max Sander: *Le livre à figures italien depuis 1467 jusqu'à 1530*, Milan 1942, nos. 2352–55.

The description of the first Indians in London comes from Robert Fabyan: *The Concordance of Histories*, London 1516. The full text of Cantino's letters is in H. P. Biggar: "Précurseurs de Jacques Cartier 1497–1534" in *Canadian Archives Publications*, no. 5, Ottawa 1911, pp. 61–66.

For the parrots on the Cantino map and also the accuracy with which cartographers of this period represented fauna see Wilma George: *Animals and Maps*, London 1969. For the map in Munich see Friedrich Kunstmann: *Atlas zur Endeckungsgeschichte Americas*, Munich 1859.

For Vespucci see the catalogue of the *Mostra Vespucciana*, Florence 1954–55. For the many editions of the *Mundus Novus* see Roberto Levillier in *Boletín del Instituto de Historia Argentina "Doctor Emiliano Ravignani,"* 2nd series, I (1956), pp. 1–83 (with comparative texts printed side by side). Facsimiles of some editions were issued by Princeton University Library in 1916, also in Uribe White: *Edición Facsimilar de las Cartas de Vespucio*, Bogotá 1942. R. Romeo: *Le scoperte americane*, provides the best account of the implications of Vespucci's letters.

The Doesborch broadsheet was published by M. E. Kronenberg: *De Novo Mondo, Antwerp . . .* , The Hague 1927. See also Walter Oakeshott: *Some Woodcuts by Hans Burgkmair*, Oxford 1960, for it and for Burgkmair's plates in *The Triumph of Maximilian*. For the German print [7] see W. Eames: "Description of a wood engraving illustrating the South American Indians in 1505" in *Bulletin of the New York Public Library* XXVI (1922), pp. 755–60; Georg Leidinger, "Die älteste bekannte Abbildung Sudamerikanischer Indianer" in *Gutenberg Festschrift*, Mainz 1925, pp. 179–81; Rudolf Sculler: "The Oldest Known Woodcut Illustrations of South American Indians" in *Indian Notes* (Museum of the American Indian) VII (1930), pp. 484–96. Another print of about the same date attributed to G. Stuchs of Nuremberg shows Vespucci's ship sailing into an estuary populated with giants (reproduced in Glaser: *Engraved*

America, p. 16, from the James Ford Bell collection).

For the Waldseemüller map of which the only surviving example is in the collection of Prince von Waldburg zu Wolfegg und Waldsee, Schloss Wolfegg, see J. Fisher and F. R. von Wieser: *The Oldest Map with the Name of America of the Year 1507*, Innsbruck 1903, reprinted Amsterdam 1968.

It is significant that the great Portuguese epic, Luis de Camoes: *Os Lusiades* (1572), is devoted to eastward exploration though he does remark almost casually of Portugal, "Dominions in America she has;/And, were there more *Worlds*, Thither she would pass" (Canto VII in Richard Fanshawe's translation, 1.14).

The Triumph of Maximilian (Albertina, Vienna) was ascribed to Altdorfer by Frans Winzinger: "Albrecht Altdorfer und die Miniaturen des Triumphzuges Kaiser Maximilians I" in *Jahrbuch der Kunsthistorischen Sammlungen in Wien* LXII (1966), pp. 157–72, who connects the Indians in it with a rather shadowy background figure in Altdorfer's *Crowning with Thorns* in the abbey church of St. Florian, Austria. For the woodcut version of the *Triumph of Maximilian* see Franz Schestag: "Kaiser Maximilian I. Triumph" in *Jahrbuch der Kunsthistorischen Sammlungen des Allerhöchsten Kaiserhauses I* (1883), pp. 154–81. There is a modern reprint with a most useful introduction, Stanley Appelbaum: *The Triumph of Maximilian I*, New York 1964. The Brazilian origin of the feather cap and scepter in Dürer's drawing was identified by William C. Sturtevant in "First Visual Images of America," to be published in *Proceedings of the International Conference on First Images of America: The Impact of the New World on the Old*. The two drawings of Indians in the British Museum were described as "Eingeborenen" and attributed to Burgkmair by Peter Halm: "Hans Burgkmair als Zeichner" in *Münchner Jahrbuch der bildenden Kunst* 3 F. XIII (1962), pp. 125–29.

Between the publication of Vespucci's letter and the conquest of Mexico references to America are infrequent. In about 1508 an Augsburg printer issued *Copia der Neuen Zeitung aus Brasilien* (unique copy in Staatsbibliothek, Augsburg) but its woodcut illustrates Funchal in Madeira. John Rastell, in *An Interlude of the Four Elements* [c. 1517, printed in Percy Society XXII (1848)], refers to the discoveries and remarks, "O what a thynge had been than,/Yf that they that be Englyshmen/Myght have ben the furst of all/That there shulde have taken possessyon,/And made furst buyldynge and habytacion,/A memory perpetyall!" News of the circumnavigation was first spread in an anonymous pamphlet, *Eine schöne Newe zeytung*, Augsburg 1522, and in the letter of Maximilianus Transylvanus, who interviewed survivors, *Epistola de admirabili & novissima Hispanorum in Orienttius navigationi...*, Cologne 1523.

The first edition of Pigafetta's narrative was in French, *Le voyage et navigation faict par les Espagnols es isles de Mollucques*, Paris (1525); the first English translation was by Richard Eden in *Decades of the Newe Worlde or West India*, London 1555; the standard modern edition and English translation is James A. Robertson: *Magellan's Voyage Around the World*, Cleveland 1906.

Giovanni da Verrazzano described his voyage in a letter to Francis I first printed in G. B. Ramusio: *Terzo Volume delle navigatione et viaggi*, Venice 1556, translated into English by Hakluyt 1582. The fullest accounts of him are by R. Almagià: *L'Importanza geografica delle navigazioni di Giovanni da Verrazzano*, Florence 1962, and in Lawrence C. Wroth: *The Voyages of Giovanni da Verrazzano 1524–1528*, New Haven 1970. Cartier's account of his first voyage was also first printed by Ramusio: *Terzo Volume*, translated into English 1580, and included in Hakluyt's second edition 1600. The standard modern edition is that of H. P. Biggar: "The Voyages of Jacques Cartier" in *Canadian Archives Publications*, no. 11, Ottawa 1924—for further bibliography see Morison: *Northern Voyages*, 1971, pp. 381–82.

For Ponce de León see Leonardo Olschki: "Ponce de León's Fountain of Youth: History of a Geographical Myth" in *The Hispanic American Historical Review* XXI (1941), pp. 361–85—but for a corrective as regards Ponce's age see Morison: *Southern Voyages*, p. 503, who also reproduces a woodcut of a European vision of the fountain by Hans Sebald Beham, including parrots, possibly to suggest an American location.

On G. B. Ramusio's collection of travel literature *Delle navigationi et viaggi*, Venice 1550–56 (frequently reprinted), see George B. Parks: *The Contents and Sources of Ramusio's Navigationi*, New York 1955. Richard Hakluyt began with *Divers Voyages touching the Discovery of America...*, London 1582 (reprinted by Hakluyt Society, London 1850); then *The Principall Navigations, Voiages and Discoveries of the English Nation...*, London 1589 (reprinted Hakluyt Society, 1965); and finally a three-volume edition, *Discoveries &c of the English...*, London 1598, *The Second Volume of the principall Navigations...*, London 1599, and *The Third and Last Volume of the Voyages, Navigations, Traffiques and Discoveries...*, London 1600. The standard modern edition, i.e., *The Principal Navigations...*, 12 volumes, Glasgow 1903–5. A selection is available in paperback—R. Hakluyt (ed. Jack Beeching): *Voyages and Discoveries*, Harmondsworth 1972.

For the French publications see Geoffrey Atkinson: *Les nouveaux horizons de la renaissance française*, Paris 1935.

On the economic question see Earl J. Hamilton: "American Treasure and the rise of Capitalism" in *Economica* IX (1929), pp. 338–57; Walter Prescott Webb: *The Great Frontier*, London 1953; H. and P. Chaunu: *Séville et l'Atlantique*, 8 vols., Paris 1955–59; and the balanced summary of their various theories and much other material by J. H. Elliott: *Old World and New*, pp. 54–78.

The standard edition of Cortés's dispatches is that by Mario Hernandez Sanchez-Barba, *Cartas y Documentos*, Mexico 1963. For the many early editions see José Toribio Medina: *Ensayo bio-bibliográphico sobre Hernan Cortés*, Santiago de Chile 1952. For pamphlets describing the conquest of Mexico see Henry W. Wagner: "Three Accounts of the Expedition of Fernando Cortés, printed in Germany between 1520 and 1522" in *Hispanic American Historical Review* IX (1929), pp. 176–212. For Bernal Diaz: *Historia verdadera de la conquista de la nueva España*, Madrid 1632, there is a standard modern edition by Joaquín Ramirez Cabañas, Mexico 1944, and English translation by H. P. Maudsley, Hakluyt Society, London 1908–16, and a readable but sadly abridged and truncated translation by J. M. Cohen, Harmondsworth 1963.

On the tendency to describe the conquest of the New World in terms of the medieval romance see Luis Weckmann: "The Middle Ages in the Conquest of America" in *Speculum* XXVI (1951), pp. 130–41. The possible American significance of the scene in the background of

NOTES

the *Virgin of the Palm* was suggested by Jacques Foucart in *Le XVIe Siècle Européen* (exhibition catalogue, Petit Palais), Paris 1956–66, no. 191. For the apocalyptic interpretation of the conquest see John Leddy Phelan: *The Millennial Kingdom of the Franciscans*, Berkeley 1956. For the various interpretations of and extensive literature on Jan Mostaert's painting see Hugh Honour: *European Vision of America*, no. 6.

The writings of Las Casas are listed in the critical bibliography by Lewis Hanke (*Bartolomé de Las Casas*, Santiago de Chile 1954) who is also the editor of the standard edition of the *Historia de las Indias*, Mexico 1965. The *Historia*, which was not printed until the nineteenth century, may have circulated in manuscript in the sixteenth. But the ideas of Las Casas were diffused mainly by the *Brevissima relación*, Seville 1552. See also the notes to Chapter 3 below. There is a biography of Girolamo Benzoni by A. Codazzi in *Dizionario biografico degli Italiani*, vol. VIII, Rome 1966, pp. 732–33; an English translation of his *Historia* by W. H. Smyth is in Hakluyt Society, London, 1st series, vol. XXI 1857. Apart from library catalogues (British Library, etc.) and bibliographies (notably J. Sabin), the main source for de Bry is still Armand Gaston Camus: *Mémoirs sur la collection des "Grands et Petits Voyages,"* Paris 1802.

For another Spanish view of the retaking of Bahia, probably painted on the spot and making a strange contrast with Maino's picture, see Enrique Marco Dorta: *La recuperación de Bahia por Don Fadrique de Toledo (1625). Un cuadro español de la época*, Seville 1959.

Chapter 2

For early importations of Mexican art into Europe see F. Anders and D. Heikamp, "Mexikanische Altertümer aus suddeutschen Kunstkammern" in *Pantheon* XXVIII (1970), pp. 205–20; D. Heikamp: *Mexico and the Medici*, Florence 1972; and D. Heikamp: "American Objects in Italian Collections of the Renaissance and Baroque," International Conference on First Images of America: The Impact of the New World on the Old, University of California, Los Angeles, 1975. For reactions to the Aztecs in European literature see Benjamin Keen: *The Aztec Image*, New Brunswick 1971.

The German text of Dürer's remarks is in A. Dürer: *Schriftlicher Nachlass*, ed. H. Rupprich, Berlin 1956, vol. I, p. 155.

For the inventories of objects sent to Spain by Cortés see L. Torres de Mendoza: *Colección de documentos inéditos relativos al descubrimiento, conquista y organización de las antiguas posesiones Españoles . . .* , Madrid 1869, vol. XII, pp. 318 ff. For other comments see Henry R. Wagner: "Three Accounts of the Expedition of Cortés." The hard-stone carvings are dispersed; three examples of featherwork are in the Museum für Volkerkunde, Vienna, two shields are in the Württembergisches Landesmuseum, Stuttgart, and another shield formerly in Vienna was taken back to Mexico in the nineteenth century by the Emperor Maximilian and is now in the Museo Nacional de Historia, Castillo de Chapultapec (see K. A. Nowotny: *Mexikanische Kostbarkeiten aus Kunstkammern der Renaissance*, Vienna 1960, and F. A. Anders: "Der Federkasten der Ambraser Kunstkammer" in *Jahrbuch der Kunsthistorischen Sammlungen in Wien*, LXI (1965), pp. 119–32). For the Peruvian gold-work see Antonio de Herrera: *Historia General de los hechos de los Castellanos en las yslas y en tierre del Mar Oceano (1492–1553)* Madrid, 1601–15, dec. 5, lib. 6, cap. 13, quoted by William H. Prescott: *History of the Conquest of Peru*, chapter IX. For the American objects in the 1561 inventory of Charles V's possessions see R. Beer in *Jahrbuch der Kunsthistorischen Sammlungen des Allerhöchsten Kaiserhauses* XII (1891), p. clxx. For *Wunderkammer* see J. von Schlosser: *Die Kunst- und Wunderkammer der Spätrenaissance*, Leipzig 1908. Hammocks seem to have excited particular curiosity and to have been the first American artifacts illustrated in European books, e.g., G. Fernandez de Oviedo y Valdes: *De la natural hystoria de las Indias*, Toledo 1526, f. xvii verso.

For Aldrovandi see M. Cermenati: *Ulisse Aldrovandi e l'America*, Rome 1906, and G. Montalenti in *Dizionario biografico degli Italiani*, vol. ii, Rome 1960, pp. 118–24. John Dee's obsidian mirror is described by Hugh Tait: "The Devil's Looking Glass: The Magical Speculum of Dr. John Dee" in W. H. Smith (ed.): *Horace Walpole, Writer, Politician, and Connoisseur*, New Haven and London 1967, pp. 195–212. For Walter Cope's collection see Clare Williams: *Thomas Platter's Travels in England 1599*, London 1937, pp. 171–73.

The Mexican quails and hummingbirds in the Vatican Loggie (now more clearly seen in eighteenth-century engravings than on the walls) were first spotted by N. Dacos: "Présents américains à la renaissance, l'assimilation de l'exotisme" in *Gazette des Beaux Arts* 6, LXXIII (1969), pp. 57–64. For ornithological illustrations see E. G. Allen: "The History of American Ornithology before Audubon" in *Transactions of the American Philosophical Society* NS., XLI, pt. 3 (1951), pp. 386–590. Ligozzi's drawings in the Uffizi were rather summarily catalogued by M. Bacci and A. Forlani: *Mostra di disegni di Jacopo Ligozzi*, Florence 1951. His less highly finished drawings for Aldrovandi belong to the University of Bologna and are as yet unpublished. For American animals in the sixteenth century see Paul Delaunay: *La zoologie au seizième siècle*, Paris 1962; for their appearance on maps, Wilma George: *Animals and Maps*. The verses on the armadillo (with others on the iguana and hummingbird) are among the papers of Sir Hans Sloane, British Library MSS Sloane 4020, f. 218. The llama was first illustrated in Pedro Cieza de León: *Parte Primera de la Chronica del Peru*, Seville 1553, p. cxxiiii verso. For Poggini's medal and letter see G. Kubler in *Mitteilungen des Kunsthistorischen Institutes in Florenz* XI (1963), pp. 149–52.

Coma's letter was first published in N. Scillacio: *De insulis meridiani atque indici maris nuper inventis*, Pavia 1496. For early descriptions and illustrations of maize see John J. Finan: "Maize in the Great Herbals" in *Annals of the Missouri Botanical Garden* XXXV (1948), pp. 149–91; and for tomatoes, first mentioned in 1544, G. A. McCue: "The History of the Use of the Tomato" in the same periodical, XXXIX (1952), pp. 289–348. For tobacco see Charles Singer: "The Early History of Tobacco" in *Quarterly Review* CCXIX (1913), pp. 125–42, and Egon Caesar conte Corti: *Die trockene Trunkenheit*, Leipzig 1930. The history of the potato is admirably documented by R. N. Salaman: *The History and Social Influence of the Potato*, Cambridge 1949. On the introduction of the pineapple into England see Miles Hadfield: *Gardening in Britain*, London 1960, pp. 126, 166–67. For drawings of plants: Wilfred Blunt: *The Art of Botanical Illustration*, London 1950, and for illustrated botanical books see C. Nissen: *Die botanische Buchillustration*, Stuttgart 1966. The prayer book of Albrecht V is fully described by S. Killermann; *Die Miniaturen im Gebetebuch Albrechts V. von Bayern*, Strasbourg 1911. Höfnagel included miniatures of *Mirabilis jalapa* and *Helianthus annuus* in his *Missale Romanum,* f. 83, 333, 349, in the Österreichisches Nationalbibliothek, Vienna. For Cornut see the facsimile edition of *Canadensium Plantarum* with valuable introduction by Jerry Stannard, New York 1966. The most recent account of the painters and naturalists employed by Maurits of Nassau in Brazil, with extensive bibliography, is P. J. P. Whitehead: "Clupeoid Fishes of the Guianas," Appendix I, with an account of natural history drawings made in Brazil by Frei Christovão de Lisboa in Appendix II, in *Bulletin of the British Museum (Natural History), Zoological Supplement* V (1973), pp. 187–219. Charles Plumier published *Description des plantes de l'Amérique,* Paris 1693; *Filicetum Americanum,* Paris 1703; *Nova plantarum americanorum,* Paris 1703, and *Traité des fougères de l'Amérique,* Paris 1705. Maria Sibylla Merian's book is *Metamorphosis insectorum Surinamensium,* Amsterdam 1705. Drayton mentions the "useful Sassafras"; Marvell in "Bermudas" might seem to refer to no American plants, but his "Apples . . . of such a price,/No tree could ever bear them twice" are apparently bananas! For Buffon and America see A. Gerbi:*Disputa del Nuovo Mondo.*

Chapter 3

For general accounts of sixteenth-century attitudes to American Indians see Romeo: *Le scoperte Americane*; John H. Rowe: "Ethnography and Ethnology in the Sixteenth Century" in *The Kroeber Anthropological Society Papers,* no. 30 (1964), pp. 1–19; Giuliano Gliozzi: *La Scoperta dei selvaggi,* Milan 1971; Sergio Landucci: *I filosofi e i selvaggi 1580–1780,* Bari 1972; E. Dudley and Maximilian E. Novak (eds.): *The Wild Man Within,* Pittsburgh 1972. French reactions are described by G. Chinard: *L'Exotisme Américain* and *L'Amérique et Le Rêve Exotique,* and G. Atkinson: *Les nouveaux horizons.*

The documents relating to Cabral's discovery of Brazil are collected in William B. Greenlee: *The Voyage of Pedro Álvarez Cabral to Brazil and India,* Hakluyt Society LXXXI, London 1938; see also C. R. Boxer: *The Portuguese Seaborne Empire,* London 1969 (also for Portuguese attitudes to the Indians at later periods).

Richard Bernheimer: *Wild Men of the Middle Ages,* Cambridge, Mass., 1952, is the indispensable book on its subject. The remarks of Paracelsus are quoted in the still valuable article by Thomas Bendyshe: "The History of Anthropology" in *Memoirs of the Anthropological Society of London* I (1863–64), p. 353–54. The lines by John Donne are at the beginning of the verse letter "To the Countesse of Huntington" (their authorship has however been questioned).

For the debate on the status of the Indians see Lewis Hanke: "Pope Paul III and the American Indians" in *Harvard Theological Review,* XXX (1937), pp. 65–102, and *Aristotle and the American Indians,* London 1959. In the former Hanke discusses the political background to the bull *Sublimis Deus* which Paul III appears to have seen not only as a measure for protecting the Indians but also as a means of establishing papal control over the ecclesiastical government of the New World, and which Charles V resisted for the same reason.

All Christoph Weiditz's drawings of Mexicans (also one of Cortés) are reproduced in T. Hampe: *Das Trachtenbuch des Christoph Weiditz,* Berlin-Leipzig 1927; see also Howard P. Cline: "Cortes and the Aztec Indians in Spain" in *Quarterly Journal of the Library of Congress* XXVI (1969), pp. 70–90. The account of the Mexican jugglers in Rome is from Bernal Diaz: *Historia de la Conquista,* quoted by Hanke: "Pope Paul III and the Indians," p. 79. Suzanne Collon Gevaert: "L'art précolumbien et le palais des princes-évêques à Liège" in *Bulletin de la Société d'Art et d'Histoire du Diocèse de Liège* XLI (1959), pp. 73–95, suggests that the Liège capitals were inspired by Mexican gold masks, and this interpretation is followed by A. Chastel: "Masques Mexicains à la renaissance" in *Art de France* I (1961), p. 299, who proposes the same source of inspiration for masks on the tomb of Cardinal d'Amboise in Rouen Cathedral. N. Dacos: "Présents américains à la renaissance," accepts Gevaert's thesis but points out that the Rouen masks are closer to Italian grotesque decorations than to New World artifacts. None of these writers considers the possibility that the Liège capitals record the appearance of the Indians brought over by Cortés.

The codex in the Museo de America, Madrid, was described by José Tudela de la Orden: "Las primeras figuras de Indios pintados por Españoles" in *Homenaje a Rafael García Granados: Instituto Nacional de Antropología,* Mexico 1960, pp. 31–329.

For the frieze in Saint-Jacques, Dieppe, see Pierre Margry: *Les navigateurs françaises,* Paris 1867, pp. 371–94, with engraving. The state visit of Henri II to Rouen and the Brazilian village created there are described and illustrated in an illuminated manuscript *Entrée de Henri II à Rouen* in the Bibliothèque Municipale, Rouen, and in the published volume: *C'est la déduction du sumptueux ordre, plaisantz spectacles et magnifiques théatres . . . ,* Rouen 1551. Modern literature on this spectacle includes Ferdinand Denis: *Une fête brésilienne célébrée à Rouen en 1550,* Paris 1850; M. M. McGowan: "Form and Themes in Henri II's Entry into Rouen" in *Renaissance Drama,* n.s. I (1968), pp. 199–251. For other festival occasions in which "Indians" took part see M. Paquot: *Les étrangers dans les divertissements de la Cour, de Beaujoyeux à Molière* (1581–1673), Brussels [1933]. The standard edition of *Hans Stadens Wahrhaftiger Historia* is that by Reinhard Maack and Karl Fouquet, Marburg, 1964; an Italian translation by Amerigo Guadagnin: *La mia prigionia tra i cannibali di Hans Staden,* Milan 1970, has a valuable introduction and bibliography. Staden has been translated into English by R. F. Burton (1874) and Malcolm Letts (1928).

Ronsard's "Complainte contre fortune" is analyzed in E. Armstrong: *Ronsard and the Age of Gold,* Cambridge 1968, pp. 26–29, 134–41, 186–87. On the "noble savage" of Antiquity see A. O. Lovejoy et al.: *A Documentary History of Primitivism and Related Ideas,* Baltimore 1935. For Shakespeare's debt to Montaigne and to travel writers see the introduction and notes by Frank Kermode in *The Arden Edition of the Works of William Shakespeare: The Tempest,* London (1954), revised 1962. There is a stimulating interpretation of *The Tempest* as "Shakespeare's American Fable" in Leo Marx: *The Machine in the Garden,* London-New York (1964), 1967, pp. 34–72.

The career and works of John White are fully described by P. Hulton and D. B. Quinn: *The American Drawings of John White,* London 1964. His drawings of Picts are discussed by T. D. Kendrick in *British Antiquity,* London 1950, pp. 123–25.

For Eckhout the only monograph is Thomas Thomsen: *Albert Eckhout,* Copenhagen 1938; a checklist of his works was published by Enrico Schaeffer in *Dedalo* I (1965), pp. 51–74. See also Whitehead: "Clupeoid Fishes." There is a brief account of Bonaventura Peeters by Erik Larsen: "Some Seventeenth Century Paintings of Brazil" in *The Connoisseur* CLXXV, pp. 129–31, who suggests (without any evidence) that Bonaventura's brother Gilles went to Brazil.

Chapter 4

The best account of allegories of America and of the other continents is by Erich Köllmann, Karl-August Wirth, et al., s.v. "Erdteile" in *Reullexikon zur deutschen Kunstgeschichte*, vol. V, Munich 1967, col. 1107–1202. Among earlier works listed in their bibliography, articles by James Hazen Hyde are still valuable for illustrations and quotations—"L'iconographie des Quatres Parties du Monde dans les Tapisseries" in *Gazette des Beaux Arts* LXVI (1924), pp. 253–72; "The Four Parts of the World as Represented in Old Time Pageants and Ballets" in *Apollo* IV (1926), pp. 232–38, V (1927), pp. 20–26—also Clare Le Corbeiller: "Miss America and Her Sisters, Personifications of the Four Parts of the World," in *Metropolitan Museum Bulletin* N.S. XIX/XX (1960), pp. 209–23. Allegories of America are discussed mainly with reference to the late eighteenth century by E. McClung Fleming: "The American Image as Indian Princess, 1765–1783" and "From Indian Princess to Greek Goddess: The American Image, 1783–1815" in *Winterthur Portfolio* II (1965), pp. 65–81, and III (1967), pp. 37–66.

Etienne Pasquier's remark is in *Les Oeuvres d'Estienne Pasquier*, Amsterdam 1723, vol. ii, p. 55. Francesco Guicciardini's comment is in *Stora d'Italia*, Florence 1561, lib. 6 (ed. C. Panigara, Bari 1929, vol. II, pp. 130–31).

Figures illustrating the four continents had appeared earlier in the corners of maps (e.g., the Sebastian Munster map of 1532) and on the title page of Abraham Ortelius: *Theatrum Orbis Terrarum*, Antwerp 1570. For further examples of late sixteenth- and early seventeenth-century allegories see Hugh Honour: *European Vision of America*. For the Mappamondo room at Caprarola and other similar cycles of fresco decoration, especially those in the Vatican, see R. Almagià: *Le pitture murali della Galleria delle Carte geografiche* and *Le pitture geografiche murali della terza loggia e di altre sale Vaticane*, Vatican City 1952 and 1955. Renato Roli: "Giovanni de' Vecchi" in *Arte antica e moderna* 29 (1965), pp. 53–54 discusses the authorship of the paintings at Caprarola but identifies the figure in the upper left corner as Africa.

Costume books illustrating "Americans" include *Recueil de la diversité des habits*, Paris (Richard Breton) 1567; Pietro Bertelli: *Diversarum nationum habitus*, Padua 1589; Cesare Vecellio: *Degli habiti antichi e moderni di diverse parti del mondo*, Venice 1598.

A general account of the significance of pageants, entries, masques, etc., is given by Roy Strong: *Splendour at Court*, London 1973. Much information is provided by the various contributors to J. Jacquot (ed.): *Les Fêtes de la Renaissance*, 2 vols, Paris 1960. The various Florentine spectacles are fully described by Eve Borsook: "Art and Politics at the Medici Court II: The Baptism of Filippo de' Medici in 1577" and "III: Funeral Décor for Philip II of Spain" in *Mitteilungen des Kunsthistorischen Institutes in Florenz* XIII (1967), pp. 95–114, and XV (1969), pp. 91–114. The *Nave di Amerigo Vespucci* is described by A. M. Nagler: *Theatre Festivals of the Medici*, New Haven 1964, pp. 107–8. The return of Vespucci was again celebrated in Florence in September 1765, see P. Gori: *Le feste fiorentine attraverso i secoli—Le feste per San Giovanni*, Florence 1926, p. 380.

For Rubens and the entry for the Cardinal-Infante Ferdinand into Antwerp in 1635 see J. R. Martin: *The Decorations for the Pompa Introitus Ferdinandus*, London and New York 1972, pp. 189–203. For the French court ballets see M. Paquot: *Les étrangers dans les divertissements*, and Marie-Françoise Christout: *Le ballet du cour de Louis XIV*, Paris 1967. The masque designs by Inigo Jones are described and illustrated by Stephen Orgel and Roy Strong: *Inigo Jones, The Theatre of the Stuart Court*, London and Los Angeles 1973. On Borgonio's designs see M. Viale-Ferrero: *Feste delle Madame Reali di Savoia*, Turin 1965.

The painting by Farinati is documented by Lionello Puppi: *Paolo Farinati Giornale 1573–1606*, Florence 1968, p. 134, and a preliminary drawing for it was published by Terence Mullaly in *Master Drawings* VI (1968), p. 288 and pl. 39.

On Bernini's fountain in Piazza Navona see H. Kauffmann in *Jahresberichte der Max Planck Gesellschaft* (1953–54) pp. 55 ff.; N. Huse in *Revue de l'art*, no. 7 (1970), pp. 7 ff.; and R. Wittkower: *Art and Architecture in Italy 1600 to 1750* (1958), revised ed. Harmondsworth 1973, pp. 169–70. Pozzo's S. Ignazio ceiling is described by Lione Pascoli: *Vite de' Pittori, scultori ed architetti moderni*, Rome 1736, vol. II, p. 259. For various pulpits in the Low Countries see B. Knipping: *De Iconografi van de Contra-Reformatie Nederlanden*, Hilversum 1940, vol. II, pp. 158–66. The mosaic allegories of the continents in the baptismal chapel of St. Peter's are after designs by Francesco Trevisani; see Frank R. Difederico: "Alcuni modelli del Trevisani per San Pietro" in *Arte Illustrata* V (1972), pp. 321–24.

On van Kessel see Ulla Krempel: *Jan van Kessel d.Ä. 1626–1679: die vier Erdteile* (exhibition catalogue, Alte Pinakothek), Munich 1973. The somewhat complicated history of the Gobelins tapestries *Les Indes* is described by Michael Benisovich: "The History of the *Tenture des Indes*" in *Burlington Magazine* LXXXIII (1943), pp. 216–25; M. Jarry: "Les Indes. Série triomphale de l'exoticisme" in *Connaissance des Arts* 1959 (May), pp. 62–66; J. de Sousa Leão: "Du nouveau sur les tableaux du Brésil offerts à Louis XIV" in *Gazette des Beaux-Arts* LVII (1961), pp. 95–104; E. Larsen: *Frans Post, interprète du Brésil*, Amsterdam 1962. There is a great deal of information about tapestries of the four continents in the Marillier tapestry archive in the Victoria and Albert Museum, London.

For other interpretations of Tiepolo's allegories of America see Theodor Hetzer: *Die Fresken Tiepolos in der Würzburger Residenz*, Frankfurt am Main 1943; K. Gerstenberg: "Tiepolos Weltbild in Würzburg und Madrid" in *Zeitschrift für Kunstgeschichte*, XV (1952), pp. 143–62; Barry Hannegan: "The Ceilings of G. B. Tiepolo in the Enlightenment" in *Atti del Congresso internazionale di studi sul Tiepolo*, s.l., s.d.

Chapter 5

The most interesting discussions of late seventeenth- and eighteenth-century European attitudes to the Indians are in works already cited, i.e., A. Gerbi: *Disputa del Nuovo Mondo*, G. Gliozzi: *La scoperta dei selvaggi*, S. Landucci: *I filosofi e i selvaggi*, E. Dudley and M. E. Novak: *Wild Man Within*, and, for French attitudes, G. Chinard: *L'Exotisme Am-*

éricain and *L'Amérique et le Rêve Exotique*. American views on the question are described by Roy Harvey Pearce: *The Savages of America*, Baltimore 1953. B. Bissell: *The American Indian in English Literature of the Eighteenth Century*, New Haven and Oxford 1925, surveys the various appearances of Indians in fiction, drama, and poetry. H. N. Fairchild: *The Noble Savage*, New York 1928, covers the same ground without adding much of consequence (despite the more general title). Although he is concerned with the Polynesians and Australian aborigines, Bernard Smith: *European Vision and the South Pacific 1768–1850*, Oxford 1960, is informative on the notion of the "noble savage." Carolyn Thomas Foreman: *Indians Abroad, 1493–1938*, Norman, Oklahoma, 1943, chronicles the visits of North American Indians to Europe. European and American images of the Indian were shown in *The Noble Savage: The American Indian in Art*, exhibition at the University Museum, Philadelphia 1958, with catalogue by R. C. Smith; see also Ruthven Todd: "The Imaginary Indian in Europe" in *Art in America* LX (1972), pp. 40–47; B. F. Swan: "Prints of the American Indian 1670–1775" in *Boston Prints and Printmakers 1670–1775*, Boston 1973 (Publications of The Colonial Society of Massachusetts), pp. 241–82; and Elwood Parry: *The Image of the Indian and the Black Man in American Art*, New York 1974.

For Le Brun's painting on the Escalier des Ambassadeurs see Roseline Bacou: *Cartons d'artistes du XVe au XIXe siècle* (exhibition catalogue, Cabinet des Dessins, Musée du Louvre), no. 31, Paris 1974.

So pervasive is the influence of Dryden's phrase that Verrazzano's remark about the Indians' "aria dolcie et suave imitando molto l'antico" has been mistranslated "gentle and noble as those of classical sculpture" (cf. J. R. Elliott: *Old World and New*, p. 20). The passage from Hobbes is in *Leviathan*, London 1651, pp. 62–63. Locke's remark, often cited out of context, occurs in his discussion of the origin of money, *Two Treatises of Government*, London 1690, Bk. II, chap. V, para. 49; his reference to Peruvian cannibalism, Bk. I, chap. VI, para 57.

Rousseau's meaning is clarified by A. O. Lovejoy: "The Supposed Primitivism of Rousseau's *Discourse on Inequality*," 1923, reprinted in his *Essays in the History of Ideas*, Baltimore 1948, pp. 14–37. Voltaire presented a ridiculous picture of South American Indians in *Candide* (1759), cited them in covert attacks on Rousseau in *Essai sur Moeurs* (1756–65), yet presented a "savage from Guiana" as a spokesman for common sense in *Entretiens d'un sauvage et d'un bachelier* (1761). The hero of *Le Huron ou l'Ingénu* (1767) is of course a Frenchman who has merely been brought up by Hurons.

The Jesuits tended to be more favorable to the Indians than were the Mendicants, some of whom were hostile, notably the Franciscan Louis Hennepin in his several (increasingly imaginative) travel books: *Description de la Louisiane*, Paris 1683, *Nouvelle découverte d'un très grand pays*, Utrecht 1697, *Nouveau voyage d'un pais plus grand que l'Europe*, The Hague 1704. In dwelling on the less amiable qualities of the Indians, Hennepin was, however, expressing his hostility not so much to them as to the Jesuits who had praised them. Grotius expounded his theory in *De Origine Gentium Americanarum*, Paris 1643. The theory of Jewish origin was first advanced by Gregorio Gracía: *Origen de los Indios del Nuevo Mundo y Indias Occidentales*, Valencia 1607 (for later statements of it see the introduction by Samuel Cole Williams to Adair's *History of the American Indians*, Johnson City, New York, 1930).

Aphra Behn says that Oroonoko's beloved Imoinda was tattooed like "our antient Picts that were figured in the Chronicles" (see A. Behn: *Works*, Montague Summers (ed.), London 1915, vol. V, p. 174), which suggests that she had been looking at the prints in de Bry's *America*: her descriptions of Oroonoko recall the engravings after White and Le Moyne rather than any representations of Africans. For the contrast in attitudes to Indians and Africans the *locus classicus* is J.-B. Labat: *Nouveau voyage aux Isles de l'Amérique*, Paris 1722, in which the author, a Dominican missionary, describes how he flogged his black slaves yet refers to the Carib Indians in the area as "messieurs sauvages." *The Jesuit Relations* have been fully published in the original texts with translations by R. G. Thwaites, 73 volumes, Cleveland 1896–1901.

Lahontan's three volumes are entitled: *Nouveaux voyages de M. le baron de Lahontan*, *Mémoires de l'Amérique Septentrionale ou la suite des voyages de M. le baron de Lahontan*, and *Supplément aux Voyages du baron de Lahontan, où l'on trouve des dialogues curieux entre l'auteur et un sauvage de bon sens qui a voyagé*, The Hague 1703. The first volume includes an account of the arrival in Quebec of deported *filles de joie*—precursors of Prevost's *Manon*. The author of *Arlequin Sauvage* was Louis François de la Drevetière Delisle; it was first performed at the Théâtre des Italiens, June 17, 1721. An English adaptation, *Art and Nature*, was first performed in London in 1738.

Picart's illustrations are in B. Picart and Bruzen de la Martinière: *Cérémonies et coutumes religieuses de tous les peuples du monde*, 11 vols, Amsterdam 1723. For comparative religion see Frank E. Manuel: *The Eighteenth Century Confronts the Gods*, Cambridge, Mass., 1959. The title of Lafitau's book is *Moeurs des sauvages américains comparées aux moeurs des premiers temps*, Paris 1724. There is a curious reference to Lafitau, inspired by the landscape between Ulm and Augsburg, in William Beckford: *The Travel Diaries*, Guy Chapman (ed.), London 1928, vol. I, p. 53.

The visit of the Iroquois to London in 1710 is very fully described by Richmond P. Bond: *Queen Anne's American Kings*, Oxford 1952. Addison's essay is in *Spectator*, no. 50 (April 27, 1711). The *Spectator* (no. 11, March 13, 1711) also included and gave wide diffusion to the story of an Indian girl called Yarico who saves and falls in love with a shipwrecked English merchant Inkle but is subsequently sold into slavery by him—a tale frequently retold, versified, and dramatized.

For the Townshend caricatures see Eileen Harris: *The Townshend Album*, London 1974. Gray's letter is in Paget Toynbee and Leonard Whibley (eds.): *Correspondence of Thomas Gray*, Oxford 1935, p. 657. For Robert Adam see John Fleming: "Robert Adam, Luc-François Breton and the Townshend Monument" in *The Connoisseur* CL (1962), pp. 163–71. Indians also appear on the monument to Cornet Geary (killed 1776) in Great Bookham Parish Church, cf. Ian Nairn and N. Pevsner: *Surrey* (Buildings of England), Harmondsworth 1962, p. 226 and pl. 44a. For the portraits of Brant see J. R. Fawcett Thompson: "Thayendanega the Mohawk and his Several Portraits" in *The Connoisseur* LXX (1969) pp. 49–53.

De Pauw's first volume is *Recherches philosophiques sur les Américains ou Mémoirs intéressants pour servir à l'histoire de l'espèce humaine*, Berlin 1768; Pernety's reply: *Dissertation sur*

NOTES

l'Amérique et les Américains, contre les Recherches Philosophiques de Mr. de P., Berlin 1770; De Pauw's response: *Défense des Recherches Philosophiques sur les Américains*, Berlin 1770; and Pernety's second reply: *Examen de Recherches Philosophiques sur l'Amérique et les Américains et de la Défense de cet ouvrage*, Berlin 1771. For other accounts of the Patagonian giants see Percy G. Adams: *Travellers and Travel Liars*, Berkeley and Los Angeles 1962, pp. 19–43.

Guillaume-Thomas-François Raynal's work is entitled: *Histoire philosophique et politique des etablissements et du commerce des Européens dans les deux Indes*, Paris 1770. Robertson's summary of the Indians is in book IV of *The History of America* (1777), London 1808, vol. II, pp. 49–244. He was the uncle of Robert Adam and it would be interesting to know his views on the figures on the Townshend monument.

The review of Crèvecoeur appeared in the Grimm-Diderot *Correspondence littéraire*, January 1785 (Paris 1830, vol. XII, p. 257). The cruelty of the Iroquois was described in a comic vein in the account of Obadiah Lismahago's adventures in T. Smollett: *The Expedition of Humphry Clinker*, London 1771. On Wright of Derby's *Indian Widow* see Robert Rosenblum: *Transformations in Late Eighteenth Century Art*, Princeton 1967, p. 45. The passage in Adair has not previously been cited as the source for this picture (cf. H. Honour: *European Vision of America*). On Carver see Timothy Severin: *Explorers of the Mississippi*, London 1967, pp. 184–201. Schiller derived the last stanzas of his poem not from the dirge but from the passage which follows it in Carver's book.

Chapter 6

Durand Echeverria: *Mirage in the West*, Princeton 1957, revised 1968, provides an admirably thorough and penetrating account of French reactions to the American Revolution. The most important of the English parliamentary speeches are conveniently assembled by Max Beloff (ed.): *The Debate on the American Revolution 1761–1783* (London 1949, New York 1960). English caricatures relating to the Revolution are fully described in F. G. Stephens: *Catalogue of Political and Personal Satires Preserved in the Department of Prints and Drawings in the British Museum*, vol. IV, London 1883, and M. D. George, *idem*, vol. V, London 1935. See also R. T. Haines Halsey: "Impolitical Prints" in *Bulletin of the New York Public Library* XLIII (1939), pp. 795–828. These and other visual images are discussed by E. McClung Fleming: "American Image as Indian Princess" and "From Indian Princess to Greek Goddess."

For a contemporary comment on Chastellux's essay see *Correspondance Littéraire*, July 1787 (Paris 1830), vol. XIII p. 413. The literature on the Beauvais tapestries after Le Barbier is listed in H. Honour: *European Vision of America*. The print after Fragonard and many other European representations of Franklin are discussed by Charles Coleman Sellers: *Benjamin Franklin in Portraiture*, New Haven and London 1962. Penn had been shown before 1743 holding the book of the laws of Pennsylvania in a painting (destroyed) in one of the garden temples of the great Whig stronghold Stowe; see *Vertue Notebooks* in Walpole Society XXII (1934), p. 133.

Goethe recorded the impact of the outbreak of the American Revolution in *Dichtung und Wahrheit*, Book XVII: "We wished the Americans all success, and the names of Franklin and Washington began to shine in the firmament of politics and war." Cf. J. Urzidil: *Das Glück der Gegenwart: Goethes Amerikabild*, Zurich 1958, who also quotes Klopstock's salute to the Revolution as the "Frühlingsmorgen der neugeborenen Freiheit" and the "Morgenrötes eines nahenden grossen Tages."

The theory that the French peasant soldiers who served in the American war were inspired to stir up revolution in France was proposed by F. McDonald: "The Relationship of the French Peasant Veterans of the American Revolution to the Fall of Feudalism in France, 1789–1792" in *Agricultural History* XXV (1951), pp. 151–61. For a corrective see J. Godechot: *Les Revolutions 1770–99 (Nouvelle Clio XXXVI)*, Paris 1963. Aristocratic enthusiasm for the United States was expressed in a pyramid commemorating American Independence, raised among many Gothic follies in the Jardin de Betz designed by the duc d'Harcourt before 1792, cf. René Lanson: *Le goût de moyen age en France au XVIIIe siècle*, Paris and Brussels 1926, p. 40.

For an earlier epigram on Franklin by Barbeu Dubourg: "C'est l'honneur et l'appui du nouvel hémisphère,/Les flots de l'Océan s'abaissent à sa voix;/Il réprime ou dirige à son gré le tonnerre./Qui désarme les dieux peut-il craindre les rois?" suppressed by the French censor (probably because France was not yet at war with England), see *Correspondance Littéraire*, October 1777 (Paris 1830, vol. IV, p. 432).

For Houdon's portraits of Americans see H. H. Arnason: *Sculpture by Houdon*, exhibition catalogue, Worcester Art Museum, 1964, and L. Réau: *Houdon, sa vie et son oeuvre*, Paris 1964. A marble bust of Washington by Louis-Jacques Pilon, signed and dated 1781, is in the Metropolitan Museum of Art, New York; this sculptor also executed a project for Franklin's tomb and a plaster group, "allégorie de Washington et de la Liberté," both of which were shown in the Paris Salon of 1791 (cf. S. Lami: *Dictionnaire des sculpteurs de l'école française au dixhuitième siècle*, Paris 1911, vol. II, p. 259). For another group of busts of the same period see U. Desportes: "Giuseppe Ceracchi in America and His Busts of George Washington" in *Art Quarterly* XXVI (1963), pp. 140–79.

The literature on slavery is vast and constantly growing. A very helpful summary of eighteenth-century attitudes (with bibliography) is provided by Peter Gay: *The Enlightenment, an Interpretation: The Science of Freedom*, London 1969, pp. 410–23, 670–72. For Blake see David V. Erdman: "Blake's Vision of Slavery" in *Journal of the Warburg and Courtauld Institutes*, XV (1952), pp. 242–52.

Michel-Guillaume Jean (commonly known as J. Hector St. John) de Crèvecoeur published *Letters from an American Farmer*, London 1782, and translated it into French (with the encouragement of Mme. d'Houdetot) as *Lettres d'un cultivateur Américain*, Paris 1784, reprinted 1787. Henriette Lucie de La Tour du Pin: *Journal d'une femme de cinquante ans*, Paris 1913, is available in an abridged English translation by Felice Harcourt as *Memoirs of Madame de La Tour du Pin*, London 1970.

Carlo Botta's history is entitled: *Histoire de la guerre de l'indépendance des États-Unis d'Amérique*, Paris 1809. For Canova's statue of Washington see Philipp Fehl: "Thomas Appleton of Livorno and Canova's Statue of George Washington" in Antje Koesegarten and Peter Tigler (eds.): *Festschrift Ulrich Middeldorf*, Berlin 1968, pp. 521–52; also Hugh Honour in *The Age of Neo-Classicism* (exhibition catalogue, Royal Academy and Victoria & Albert Museum), London 1972, no. 324. M. Missirini: *Della vita di Antonio Canova*, Milan 1825, vol. II, p. 168, records that he read Botta. For Giordani's comments see *Opere di Pietro Giordani: Epistolario*, Milan 1854, vol. IV, p. 196.

For Coleridge's Pantisocratic plans see Mrs. Sandford: *Thomas Poole and His Friends*, London 1888, vol. I, p. 97. The Bonapartist colony in Texas is described by Jesse S. Reeves: *The Napoleonic Exiles in America: A Study in American Diplomatic History*, Johns Hopkins University Studies in Historical and Political Science, Series XXIII, nos. 9–10, Baltimore 1905. For the Owenite, Fourierist, and Icarian communities see Donald Drew Egbert: *Socialism and American Art*, Princeton 1952.

Alexis de Tocqueville: *De la démocratie en Amérique*, Paris 1835, was translated into English by Henry Reeve as *Democracy in America*, London 1835. Both texts had been reprinted several times before the second part appeared almost simultaneously in France and England in 1840. In the vast literature on this work the historical and bibliographical essay by Phillips Bradley in the Vintage Books edition, New York 1945, is particularly helpful.

The Statue of Liberty is set in its historical and artistic context by Marvin Trachtenberg: *The Statue of Liberty* (Art in Context), London and New York, 1975.

Chapter 7

For eighteenth-century and later European reactions to Mexico and Mexican art see D. Heikamp: *Mexico and the Medici* and Benjamin Keen: *The Aztec Image*. Eighteenth-century literary references to Central and South America are discussed by Gilbert Chinard: *L'Exotisme Américain* and *L'Amérique et le Rêve Exotique*.

Jean-François Marmontel's Peruvian fantasy even includes two chapters about free love in the Polynesian islands inspired by Louis-Antoine de Bougainville: *Voyage autour de monde*, Paris 1771. The review of *Les Incas* is in *Correspondance Littéraire*, May 1777 (Paris 1830, vol. IX, pp. 345–48). *Polexandre* was embellished with elegant illustrations by Abraham Bosse but they have even fewer exotic elements than the text; cf. Diane Canivet: *L'illustration de la poésie et du roman français au XVIIe siècle*, Paris 1957, pp. 106–7. Montesquieu discussed the Incas and Aztecs in *De l'esprit des lois*, Paris 1748. For Francesco Algarotti's *Saggio sopra l'impero degli'Incas* (1753) see his *Opere*, Venice 1791, vol. IV, pp. 173–202, and for Frederick the Great's letter about his *Montézuma* libretto, vol. XV, p. 172. Other Montezuma-Cortés operas include those by C. de Majo 1765, Manuel Ferreira 1765, Giovanni Paisiello 1775, Antonio Maria Gasparo Sacchini 1775, N. Zingarelli 1781, an unknown composer with libretto by Fermín del Rey (*Hernan Cortés en Cholula*) 1782, Giuseppe Giordani (*Fernando nel Messico*) 1786, Mariano Berner y Bustos (*Hernan Cortés en Tabasco*) 1790, Marc'Antonio de Portogallo (*Fernando in Messico*) 1797, Henry Rowley Bishop 1822, Ignaz Xavier Seyfried 1825, Giovanni Pacini (*Amazilia*) 1825; cf. José Subirá: "Hernan Cortès en la Música Teatral" in *Revista de Indias* IX (1948), pp. 105–26. J. C. Bach wrote a ballet *Montesuma*.

For the Mexican gods illustrated by Pignoria see R. W. Lightbown in *Journal of the Warburg and Courtauld Institutes* XXXII (1969), p. 243, and Detlef Heikamp: "American Objects in Italian Collections." The history of the gold vessel of which drawings were shown at the Society of Antiquaries is recorded in the minute books of the Society and in William Robertson: *History of America*, vol. III, p. 415. The drawings have not previously been reproduced and the present whereabouts of the object itself is unknown. For the vases and masks see Thomas Pownall: "Observations arising from an Enquiry into the Nature of the Vases found on the Mosquito Shore" in *Archaeologia* V (1778), pp. 318–24, and Charles Rogers: "An account of certain earthen Masks from the Musquito Shore," idem. VI (1780), pp. 107–9 (both articles are illustrated with engravings). For the Guadalajara vases see Alvar Gonzalez-Palacios in *Arte Illustrata* V (1972), pp. 444–46. Marchese Leonardo Ginori Lisci kindly informs me that the vases came into the possession of his family from Spain in the late seventeenth century. Many of these large vases survive in Spain (e.g., Museo di America, Madrid) and there are two in the Palazzo Pitti, Florence, but none is mounted as are the Ginori Lisci pair.

For the regulations regarding emigration and even visits to Spanish America see Richard Konetzke: *America centrale e meridionale: La colonizzazione ispano-portoghese* (1965), Milan 1968, pp. 56–71, and his several articles on this topic mentioned in the notes. On Vico's ideas expounded in *Scienza Nuova* (1725, revised 1744) see Sergio Landucci: *I filosofi e i selvaggi* pp. 272–91. Johann Gottfried Herder devoted a chapter to "Americans" in *Ideen zur Philosophie der Geschichte der Menschheit*, 1784–1791.

The standard biography of Humboldt is Hanno Beck: *Alexander von Humboldt*, Wiesbaden 1959. Douglas Botting: *Humboldt and the Cosmos*, London 1973, provides a stimulating introduction. *Alexander von Humboldt und seine Welt* (exhibition catalogue, Schloss Charlottenburg), Berlin 1969, contains much information on the artists connected with him. See also F. Muthmann: *Alexander Humboldt und sein Naturbild im Spiegel der Goethezeit*, Zurich 1955.

Debret's original watercolors are in the Fundação Raymundo Ottoni de Castro Maya, Rio de Janeiro. For Ender see Gilberto Ferrez: *O Velho Rio de Janeiro através das gravuras de Thomas Ender*, São Paolo n.d. Martius and Spix published *Reise in Brasilien auf Befehl Sr. Majestät Maximilian Joseph I Königs von Baiern*, Munich 1823; *Historia naturalis palmarum*, Munich 1825–50; and *Tabulae physiognomicae*, Munich 1840–46. For a group of interesting watercolors of Peru by an amateur (French consul) see J. Edgardo Rivera Martinez: *Leonce Angrand. Imagen del Peru en siglo XIX*, Lima 1972.

The formation of the British Museum collection of pre-Columbian art is described by J. H. Braunholtz in *British Museum Quarterly* XVIII (1953), pp. 90–93. Lord Kingsborough's publications are entitled *Antiquities of Mexico*, London 1841–48, nine volumes. For Robert Curzon and the Zouche codex see A. N. L. Munby: *Connoisseurs and Medieval Miniatures 1750–1850*, Oxford 1972, p. 103. A set of drawings by Castañeda which belonged to Lord Kingsborough is in the British Museum (Ethnology), Add. MSS 15502. For Galindo see Ian Graham: "Juan Galindo, enthusiast" in *Estudios de Cultura Maya* III (1963); for the discovery of Maya art in general, Elizabeth Carmichael: *The British and the Maya* (British Museum), London 1973; for Catherwood see Victor Wolfgang von Hagen: *Frederick Catherwood, Architect*, New York 1950.

The Linthorpe Pottery vases are described and illustrated in *Christopher Dresser* (exhibition catalogue, Fine Art Society), London 1972. For Gauguin and Peruvian pottery see Werner Schmalenbach: *Die Kunst der Primitiven als Anregungsquelle für die europäische Kunst bis 1900*, Cologne 1961, pp. 134–38. His letters on Martinique are quoted by Douglas Cooper: *Gauguin* (exhibition catalogue, Royal Scottish Academy), Edinburgh 1955, pp. 19–20. For his pottery see Merete Bodelsen: *Gauguin's Ceramics*, London 1964.

For Apollinaire and Rousseau see Apollinaire: *Il y a*, Paris 1925. A remarkably close literary parallel to his "Mexican" scenes is provided by poems of the same period by Leconte de Lisle (who was born in the West Indies), e.g., "Le Rêve du Jaguar."

D. H. Lawrence evoked the atmosphere of Mexico also in his novel *The Plumed Serpent*, 1926, and a disturbing story, *The Woman who Rode Away*, 1928; see also his accounts of Mexico and New Mexico in Aldous Huxley (ed.): *The Letters of D. H. Lawrence*, London 1932.

Chapter 8

Nineteenth-century travel literature on the United States is vast, but there are several studies of and guides to it, notably Henry T. Tuckerman: *America and Her Commentators*, New York 1864; Jane Louise Mesick: *The English Traveller in America 1785–1835*, New York 1922; Frank Monaghan: *French Travellers in the United States 1765–1932*, New York 1933; Andrew J. Torielli: *Italian Opinions of America as Revealed by Italian Travelers*, Cambridge, Mass, 1941; Max Berger: *The British Traveller in America*, New York 1943. There are two useful annotated anthologies—Allen Nevins: *America through British Eyes* (1923), revised, New York 1948; and H. S. Commager: *America in Perspective: The United States through Foreign Eyes*, New York 1947. A brisk survey of references to the United States in imaginative literature is given by Carl Wittke: "The American Theme in Continental European Literature" in *The Mississippi Valley Historical Review* XVIII (1941), pp. 3–26. For the dominant prejudices about America in the nineteenth century see A. Gerbi: *Disputa del Nuovo Mondo*.

The significance of Keats's lines was first elucidated by Harold E. Briggs: "Keats, Robertson and *That Most Hateful Land*" in *Publications of the Modern Language Association of America* LIX.I (1944), pp. 184–99. For Dickens see W. G. Wilkins: *Charles Dickens in America*, London 1911; Angus Wilson: *The World of Charles Dickens*, London 1970; M. House, G. Storey and K. Tillotson (eds.): *The Letters of Charles Dickens 1842–43*, vol. III, Oxford 1974; and of course his own *American Notes for General Circulation* (1842)—the Penguin edition, Harmondsworth 1972, has an informative introduction by John S. Whitley and Arnold Goldman—and *Martin Chuzzlewit* (1842–43).

On Lenau and America, Homer D. Blanchard: "Lenau's Ohio Venture" in *Ohio History* LXXVIII (1969), pp. 237–51, lists the earlier literature and includes new documentary information. The most interesting of the English travel books are H. B. Fearon: *Sketches of America*, London 1819; William Faux: *Memorable Days in America*, London 1823; Basil Hall: *Travels in America*, Edinburgh 1830; Frances M. Trollope: *Domestic Manners of the Americans*, London 1832; Isaac Fidler: *Observations on Professions, Literature, Manners and Emigration in the United States and Canada*, London 1833; Harriet Martineau: *Society in America*, London 1837; Frederick Marryat: *A Diary in America*, London 1839. The standard edition of Mrs. Trollope is that by Donald Smalley, New York 1949; see also Eileen Bigland: *The Indomitable Mrs. Trollope*, London 1953. William Cobbett is in a class apart not only as a writer but also because he was more than a traveler, serving in the British army in New Brunswick 1785–91, living in the United States and working as a political pamphleteer 1792–99, and again returning to farm on Long Island 1817–19. His *A Year's Residence in the United States*, London 1819, provided a balanced practical account of prospects for farmers in America.

Carlyle's anti-emigration remark is in his letter of February 22, 1822, to his brother Alexander; see C. R. Sanders and Kenneth J. Fielding (eds.): *The Collected Letters of Thomas and Jane Welsh Carlyle* (Duke-Edinburgh edition), Durham, North Carolina, 1970, vol. II p. 54, and also vol. I, p. 156, for similar comments in a letter of January 8, 1819, to James Johnston, who emigrated nonetheless.

W. F. Ainsworth's description is in *Wanderings in Every Clime*, London 1872, p. 33. Ford Madox Brown's *Last of England* is in Birmingham City Museum, cf. M. Bennett: *Ford Madox Brown* (exhibition catalogue, Walker Art Gallery), Liverpool 1964, no. 29. For a general account of British emigration to the United States 1846–55 (the peak period) see Terry Coleman: *Going to America*, London and New York 1972.

For English pottery with American views see Ellouise B. Larsen: *American Historical Views on Staffordshire China*, New York 1950, and J. Jefferson Miller II: "Transfer-printed English Earthenware for the American Market" in *Apollo* LXXXI (1965), pp. 46–50. For scenic wallpapers of American subjects see Horace L. Hotchkiss, Jr.: "Wallpapers used in America 1700–1850" in H. Comstock (ed.): *The Concise Encyclopedia of American Antiques*, London 1958, pp. 485–93.

Matthew Arnold's remarks are in his *Civilization in the United States*, London 1888.

For Eyre Crowe who saw the slave market in Richmond when traveling as secretary to W. M. Thackeray, who was lecture-touring and gathering local color for *The Virginians*, see Patricia Hills: *The Painters' America: Rural and Urban Life, 1810–1910* (exhibition catalogue, Whitney Museum), New York 1974, no. 71.

For images of Brother Jonathan and Uncle Sam see Allen Ketchum: *Uncle Sam, The Man and the Legend*, New York 1959.

Svinin's watercolors are discussed and illustrated by Margaret Jeffrey: "As a Russian Saw us in 1812" in *Metropolitan Museum of Art Bulletin* N.S.I. (1942–43), pp. 134–40. For drawings by P. P. Tofft see *The American West* (exhibition catalogue, Los Angeles County Museum), Los Angeles 1972. The watercolors by Edward Fanshawe are in the National Maritime Museum, Greenwich. Interesting sketches and descriptions of Civil War scenes by Henry Yates Thompson (the bibliophile) are in Christopher Chancellor: *An Englishman in the American Civil War*, London 1971.

The main sources for Frank Buchser are H. Ludeke: *Buchsers Amerikanische Sendung*, Basel 1941, and Frank Buchser: *Mein Leben und Streben in Amerika*, ed. G. Wälchli, Zurich-Leipzig 1942. For Degas see John Rewald: "Degas and his Family in New Orleans" in *Gazette des Beaux Arts* 6 XXX (1946), pp. 105–26; M. Guerin (ed.): *E. G. H. Degas, Letters*, Oxford 1947; and *Degas, His Family and Friends in New Orleans* (exhibition catalogue, Isaac Delgado Museum), New Orleans 1965.

Chapter 9

Nineteenth-century European attitudes to the North American Indians are discussed by Carolyn Thomas Foreman: *Indians Abroad*. Though mainly concerned with American attitudes, Roy Harvey Pearce: *Savages of America*, and Ellwood Parry: *Indian and Black Man in American Art*, are informative. Both European and American paintings of Indians are discussed by James Thomas Flexner: *That Wilder Image*, New York 1962.

Chateaubriand's descriptions of Indians appear in his *Essai sur les révolutions*, London 1797, *Atala*, Paris 1801, and its sequel *René*, incorporated in the *Génie du Christianisme*, Paris 1802, *Les Natchez*, Paris 1826, *Voyage en Amérique*, Paris 1827, and the posthumously published *Mémoires d'outre-tombe*, Paris 1849–51 (standard modern text, ed. Maurice Levaillant and Georges Moulinier, Bibliothèque de la Pléiade, Paris 1957). For a general account see Gilbert Chinard: *L'Exotisme américain dans l'oeuvre de Chateaubriand*, Paris 1918. On the many problems surrounding his visit to America, Pierre Martino: "Le voyage de Chateaubriand en Amérique: Essai de mise au point 1952" in *Revue d'Histoire Littéraire de la France* LII (1952), pp. 149–64, and Richard Switzer's critical edition of *Voyage en Amérique*, Paris 1964. For illustrations to *Atala* see Henry Lemonnier: "L' 'Atala' de Chateaubriand et l' 'Atala' de Girodet" in *Gazette des Beaux Arts* 4 XI (1914), pp. 363–71; J.-R. Thomé: "Les Illustrateurs de Chateaubriand" in *Le Courrier Graphique* VII (1948), pp. 23–28; and especially George Levitine: "Some Unexplored Aspects of the Illustrations of *Atala*" in Richard Switzer (ed.): *Chateaubriand. Actes du Congrès de Wisconsin*, Geneva 1970, pp. 139–45.

On the two paintings by Goya see *Goya and His Times* (exhibition catalogue, Royal Academy, London), London 1963–64, no. 103, with full bibliography. The other two paintings in the same series are in the Villagonzalo collection, Madrid; cf. F. Gassier and J. Wilson: *Oeuvre et vie de Francisco Goya*, Fribourg 1970.

For American attitudes to the "wilderness" see Roderick Nash: *Wilderness and the American Mind* (1967), revised, New Haven 1971, and Leo Marx: *The Machine in the Garden*, New York and London 1964. On the legends of Boone, Crockett, and others, see Henry Nash Smith: *Virgin Land* (1950), Cambridge, Mass., 1970, and Richard M. Dorson: *America in Legend*, New York 1973. Accounts of Crockett were published in London, *Sketches and Eccentricities of Colonel David Crockett, of West Tennessee*, 1834, and *Colonel Crockett's Exploits and Adventures in Texas Written by Himself*, 1837, both reviewed by H. W. in *London and Westminster Review* XXXII (1839), pp. 137–45. The frontiersman was given greater prominence in Germany than elsewhere in Europe by the many stories of Charles Sealsfield (alias Karl Postl) and Friedrich Gerstäcker, who had been one himself (as he described in his first book, *Streif- und Jagdzüge durch die Vereinigten Staaten Nord Amerikas*, Bremen 1844). For Millet's drawings and prints see E. Havercamp-Begemann and A.-M. Logan: *European Drawings and Watercolours in the Yale University Art Gallery, 1500–1900*, New Haven and London 1970, pp. 84–87 (with earlier literature).

There is a very thorough study of Fenimore Cooper's influence and reputation in France—Margaret Murray Gibb: *Le roman de Bas-de-Cuir, étude sur Fenimore Cooper et son influence en France*, Paris 1927. His influence in Germany and elsewhere is discussed by Hans Plischke: *Von Cooper bis Karl May*, Dusseldorf 1951. Crabb Robinson's comment is in Edith J. Morley (ed.): *Henry Crabb Robinson on Books and their Writers*, London 1938, vol. I, p. 347. The works of art inspired by Fenimore Cooper's novels include the following paintings shown at the Paris Salon: *The Falls of Glen* (from *The Last of the Mohicans*) by H.-F.-E. Phillipoteaux, 1834; the same by Auguste Jugelet, 1835; a scene from *The Pioneer* by E.-A. Demahis, 1835; *Heyward and the Hurons* by E.-A. Van den Berghe, 1835; *Sioux Hunters* (from *The Prairie*), 1845. (Information derived from the index of Salon pictures compiled by Jon Whitely, Department of the History of Art, Oxford.) Jean Schey exhibited a statue of Uncas at the Salon of 1839.

Several albums of drawings by C.-A. Lesueur are in the Museum d'histoire naturelle, Le Havre. For Rindisbacher see John Francis McDermot: "Peter Rindisbacher: Frontier Reporter" in *Art Quarterly* XII (1949), pp. 129–44; Karl Meuli: "Scythica Vergiliana" in *Schweizerisches Archiv für Volkskunde* LVI (1960), pp. 140–200; N. Feder: "Art of the Eastern Plains Indians" in *The Brooklyn Museum Annual* IV (1962–63), pp. 7–41; Alvin M. Josephy: *The Artist was a Young Man: The Life Story of Peter Rindisbacher*, Fort Worth 1970. For Maximilian, Prince zu Wied-Neuwied, see Horst Hartmann: *Die Plains- und Prärieindianer Nordamerikas*, Museum für Völkerkunde, Berlin 1973. Bodmer's work is described and illustrated in *Karl Bodmer* (exhibition catalogue, Smithsonian Institution, Washington D.C.). For Pettrich see Hans Geller: *Frans und Ferdinand Pettrich*, Dresden 1955. For another Swiss who lived among and depicted Indians see Emil Kurz: "Aus dem Tagebuch des Malers Friedrich Kurz über seinen Aufenthalt bei den Missouri-Indianern 1848–1852" in *Jahresbericht der Geographischen Gesellschaft von Bern*, 13–14 (1894–95).

Catlin published the press comments on his exhibition in England and France in *Notes of Eight Years' Travels and Residence in Europe*, New York 1848. Baudelaire's account of Catlin is in his *Salon de 1846*, Paris 1846. He also wrote a poem, *Le calumet de la paix*, "imité de Longfellow," possibly inspired by Catlin's paintings and troupe; cf. Jean Giraud: "George Catlin, 'le cornac des sauvages,'" et Charles Baudelaire" in *Mercure de France* CVII (1914), pp. 875–82. See also Robert N. Beetem: "George Catlin in France: His Relationship to Delacroix and Baudelaire" in *Art Quarterly* XXIV (1961), pp. 129–44. Louis-Philippe commissioned fifteen paintings from Catlin but only one was delivered (now in musée de Blérancourt). For the paintings bought from him by the King of Prussia see *Alexander von Humboldt und seine Welt*, cit. nos. 75–86.

Theodor Kaufmann's painting is illustrated in Patricia Hills: *The American Frontier Images and Myths* (exhibition catalogue, Whitney Museum), New York 1973, fig. 34. Rosa Bonheur's paintings and drawings of Indian subjects are described (and several reproduced) in A. Klumpke: *Rosa Bonheur: Sa vie et son Oeuvre*, Paris 1908; see also George Holme: "Rosa Bonheur" in *Munsey's*, 1894, pp. 58–65; Lida Rose MacCabe: "How America Made Rosa Bonheur" in *Ladies' Home Journal*, 1911, pp. 11, 63–65.

On Karl May see Klaus Mann: "Karl May, Hitler's Literary Mentor" in *The Kenyon Review* II (1940), pp. 391–400; Hans Wollschläger: *Karl May in Selbstzeugnissen und Bilddokumenten*, Hamburg 1965; and for the illustrated covers for his novels, Hansotto Hatzig: *Karl May und Sacha Schneider*, Beitrage zur Karl-May-Forschung, vol. II, Bamberg

NOTES

1967. Grosz's account of him is in: *Ein kleines Ja und ein grosses Nein*, Hamburg 1955, p. 81. May's remark about the dying Indian race is in the preface to the 1892 edition of *Winnetou I*.

There are many general accounts of Western films, notably Philip French: *Westerns*, London 1973, and Raymond Bellour (ed.): *Le western*, Paris 1966. For Westerns made in Europe see Mike Wallington and Chris Frayling in *Cinema XX*, 6 and 7 (August 1970), and David Austen: "Continental Westerns" in *Films and Filming*, July 1971, pp. 36–40.

For Grey Owl see Lovat Dickson: *Wilderness Man*, London 1973.

Chapter 10

See A. Gerbi: *Disputa del Nuovo Mondo*, for the notion of America as a land without a past, also for analyses of Goethe's poem and Hegel's ideas. The Socialist vision of America is investigated by R. Laurence Moore: *European Socialists and the American Promised Land*, New York 1970.

Wilde's well-known epigram—"The youth of America is their oldest tradition. It has been going on now for three hundred years"—is spoken by Lord Illingworth, the villain of *A Woman of No Importance*. For his spontaneous comments on the United States see Rupert Hart-Davis (ed.): *The Letters of Oscar Wilde*, London 1962, pp. 85–132, and the lectures Wilde delivered there in his *Essays and Lectures*, London 1908.

Makart's ceiling was published by Brigitte Heinzel in *Mitteilungen der Österreichischen Galerie* XV (1971), p. 98. J.-B. Carpeaux, however, in his statues of the Continents for the Fontaine de l'Observatoire, Paris (1872–74), gave America her traditional feather headdress.

Comments on American furniture and machinery by Bucher, Julius Lessing, and the author of the French report on the Philadelphia exposition are quoted by Sigfried Giedion: *Space, Time and Architecture*, Cambridge, Mass., 1941, pp. 258–66.

Edmond and Jules de Goncourt, *Journal*, January 16, 1867, referred to the introduction of "pots de chambre à couvert" as among the unfortunate effects of the Americanization of France.

For European reactions to late nineteenth-century American architecture see Henry Russell Hitchcock: "American Influence Abroad" in *The Rise of an American Architecture*, New York 1970, and Donald Leslie Johnson in *Art Bulletin* LVI (1974), pp. 462–63.

Bing's writings on American art are collected in S. Bing: *Artistic America, Tiffany Glass and Art Nouveau*, intro. Robert Koch, Cambridge, Mass., and London 1970. On Loïe Fuller see Lincoln F. Johnson, Jr.: "The Light and Shape of Loïe Fuller" in *Baltimore Museum of Art News* XX (1956). For (mainly hostile) French comments on modern America see P. Jourda: *L'Exotisme dans la littérature française depuis Chateaubriand*, Paris 1938, vol. II, pp. 159–84.

For the Italian Futurists' admiration of Walt Whitman see Donald Heiney: *America in Modern Italian Literature*, New Brunswick 1964 (though this work is concerned mainly with Italian writers of the interwar period), and Dominique Fernandez: *Il mito dell'America negli intelettuali Italiani dal 1930 al 1950*, Caltanisetta-Rome 1969. He was also much admired by the Russians and Chukovsky called him the real futurist of world literature; cf. Vladimir Markov: *Russian Futurism*, London 1969, p. 220. For Sant'Elia see Reyner Banham: *Theory and Design in the First Machine Age*, London 1960, and L. Caramel: *Antonio Sant'Elia: Catalogo della Mostra Permanente*, Como 1962. Another manifesto of "architettura futurista," written by Umberto Boccioni in 1913 but only recently printed, makes a specific reference to American architecture: "Oggi cominciamo ad avere intorno a noi un ambiente architettonico che si sviluppa in tutti i sensi: dai luminosi sottoranei dei grandi magazzini dai diversi pieni di tunnel delle ferrovie metropolitane alla salita gigantesca dei grattanuvole americani. L'avvenire farà sempre più progredire le possibilità architettoniche in altezza e in profondità." Cf. Zeno Birolli (ed.): *Umberto Boccioni. Altri inediti e apparati critici*, Varese 1972.

The attitudes of Gropius and Le Corbusier to American architecture and engineering are analyzed by Reyner Banham: "Europe and American Design" in Richard Rose (ed.): *Lessons from America*, London 1974, pp. 67–91.

For Picasso's *Buffalo Bill* see C. Zervos: *Pablo Picasso*, Paris 1942, no. 255. A copy of the "catalogue" of Picasso's one-man show at the Photo-Secession Gallery, New York, in 1911 is in the Beinecke Library, Yale University, but it does not, unfortunately and incredibly, list the works exhibited. The main accounts of *Parade* are Douglas Cooper: *Picasso Theatre*, London 1968, pp. 23–30, and Francis Steegmuller: *Cocteau: A Biography*, London 1970, pp. 165–66.

On Picabia see William A. Camfield: "The Machinist Style of Francis Picabia" in *Art Bulletin* XLVIII (1966), pp. 309–22 and Maurizio Fabiolo dell Arco: *Francis Picabia Mezzo Secolo di Avanguardia* (exhibition catalogue, Galleria Civica d'Arte Moderna), Turin 1974–75. For George Grosz see Hans Hess: *George Grosz*, London 1974, in which several of the paintings and drawings done by Grosz after he settled in the United States in 1932 are also reproduced. For Art Deco see Bevis Hillier: *Art Deco*, London 1968, and *The World of Art Deco* (exhibition catalogue, Minneapolis Institute of Arts), Minneapolis 1971.

For Piet Mondrian see M. Seuphor: *Piet Mondrian: Sa vie, son oeuvre* Paris 1970; for Léger see S. Giedion: "Léger in America" in *Magazine of Art* XXXVIII (1945), pp. 295–99. For the comments of both these artists and André Masson and Max Ernst see "Eleven Europeans in America" in *Museum of Modern Art Bulletin* XIII, 4–5 (1946); see also George Heard Hamilton: *Painting and Sculpture in Europe, 1880–1940* (1967), Harmondsworth, revised 1972 *passim*. See also *European Artists in America* (exhibition catalogue, Whitney Museum), New York 1945, with works executed in America during the war by these four artists and by, among others, André Breton, Marc Chagall, Salvador Dali, Marcel Duchamp, Jacques Lipchitz, Yves Tanguy, Pavel Tchelitchew, and Ossip Zadkine. It is remarkable, however, how few of the works included were of American subjects.

Reyner Banham: "Europe and American Design," provides an inside account of the English Pop movement. For Pop in general see Mario Amaya: *Pop as Art*, London 1965, and John Russell and S. Gablick: *Pop Art Redefined*, London-New York 1969. For Hamilton see Richard Morphet: *Richard Hamilton* (exhibition catalogue, The Tate Gallery), London 1970. For Hockney see *David Hockney: Paintings, Prints and Drawings, 1960–1970* (exhibition catalogue, Whitechapel Art Gallery), London 1970; Robert Wennersten: "Hockney in L.A." in *London Magazine*, NS. XIII (1973), pp. 30–49.

List of Illustrations

COLOR PLATES

I. American section of the Cantino world map, body-color on vellum, 1502. Biblioteca Estense, Modena. (Photo: Cav. U. Orlandini)

II. *The Triumph of Maximilian I*, pen and ink, watercolor, and gold on vellum, 1512–16. Attributed to Albrecht Altdorfer. Albertina, Vienna. (Photo: Museum)

III. *English Sailors in a Skirmish with Eskimo*, watercolor, 1577. By or after John White. The British Museum, London. (Photo: Museum)

IV. Western Hemisphere of the "Miller" world map, pen and ink and watercolor on vellum, 1525. Attributed to Lopo Homem. Bibliothèque Nationale, Paris. (Photo: BN)

V. *A West Indian Scene*, oil on panel, c. 1540–50. Jan Mostaert. Frans Hals Museum, Haarlem. (Photo: Museum)

VI. *A Mexican Chieftain with His Entourage*, fresco, 1588. Lodovico Buti. Uffizi, Florence. (Photo: Heikamp)

VII. *A Parrot (Psittacus Araucana)*, watercolor, 1580s. Jacopo Ligozzi. Uffizi, Florence. (Photo: Scala)

VIII. American section of a world map, pen and ink and watercolor on vellum, 1551. Sancho Gutiérrez. Austrian National Library, Vienna. (Photo: Library)

IX. *Marvel of Peru (Mirabilis Jalapa)*, watercolor, 1580s. Jacopo Ligozzi. Uffizi, Florence. (Photo: Scala)

X. *Panorama in Brazil*, oil on canvas, 1652. Frans Post. Rijksmuseum, Amsterdam. (Photo: Museum)

XI. Detail of *Inferno*, oil on panel, c. 1550. Anonymous, Portuguese. Museu de Arte Antiga, Lisbon. (Photo: Giraudon)

XII. *René de Lavdonnière and Chief Athore*, gouache, 1564. Jacques Le Moyne. New York Public Library. Astor, Lenox, and Tilden Foundations. (Photo: Library)

XIII. *A Camp-Fire Ceremony*, watercolor, 1585–87. John White. The British Museum, London. (Photo: Museum)

XIV. *A Tapuya Brazilian*, oil on canvas, 1641. Albert Eckhout. Danish National Museum, Copenhagen. (Photo: Museum)

XV. Western Hemisphere of a world map with allegories of the continents, fresco, 1574. Giovanni de' Vecchi. Palazzo Farnese, Caprarola. (Photo: Scala)

XVI. Ballet costume designs for *Peregrina Margherita*, 1660, and *Fenice Rinnovata*, 1644, watercolor. Tommaso Borgonio. Biblioteca Nazionale, Turin. (Photo: Rampazzi)

XVII. *America*, oil on copper, 1664–66. Jan van Kessel. Alte Pinlakothek, Munich. (Photo: Blauel).

XVIII. *America*, fresco, 1694. Andrea Pozzo. S. Ignazio, Rome. (Photo: Scala)

XIX. *Les Nouvelles Indes*, tapestry, 1737–63. Gobelins. Palazzo del Quirinale, Rome (Photo: Scala)

XX. *America*, porcelain, 1745. Meissen. The Wadsworth Atheneum, Hartford, Connecticut. (Photo: Atheneum)

XXI. *America*, detail of ceiling, fresco, 1753. Giovanni Battista Tiepolo. The Residenz, Würzburg. (Photo: Hepfinger)

XXII. Detail of ceiling, fresco, 1764. Giovanni Battista Tiepolo. The Throne Room, Royal Palace, Madrid. (Photo: Courtesy of the Patrimonio Nacional, Madrid)

LIST OF ILLUSTRATIONS

XXIII. *America*, tapestry panel, and two chairs with tapestry covers, 1786–91. Beauvais tapestry, after designs by Jean-Jacques-François Le Barbier. Artemis S.A.

XXIV. *View of Jalapa and Pico de Orizaba* and *Distant View of Orizaba*, oil on paper, 1831. Johann Moritz Rugendas. Staatliche Graphische Sammlung, Munich. (Photo: Blauel)

XXV. *Tropical Landscape—An American Indian Struggling with an Ape*, oil on canvas, 1910. Henri Rousseau le Douanier. Collection, Mr. and Mrs. Paul Mellon

XXVI. *William H. Seward in His Garden*, oil on canvas, 1869. Frank Buchser. Kunstmuseum, Basel. (Photo: Hans Hinz)

XXVII. *The Cotton Office, New Orleans*, oil on canvas, 1872–73. Edgar Degas. Musée des Beaux Arts, Pau. (Photo: Giraudon)

XXVIII. *Indiens Peaux-Rouges,* colored engraving, 1891. Pellerin & Cie, Imagerie d'Épinal. Bibliothèque Nationale, Paris. (Photo: BN)

XXIX. *Loïe Fuller*, colored lithograph, 1892. Henri de Toulouse-Lautrec. Bibliothèque Nationale, Paris. (Photo: Giraudon)

XXX. *Broadway Boogie Woogie*, oil on canvas, 1942–43. Piet Mondrian. Collection, The Museum of Modern Art, New York. (Photo: Museum)

XXXI. *A Bigger Splash*, acrylic on canvas, 1968. David Hockney. London, Lord Dufferin. (Photo: Courtesy of Kasmin Gallery, London)

BLACK AND WHITE

1. Frontispiece to the first illustrated edition of Columbus's letter, woodcut, Basel 1493. The New York Public Library. (Photo: British Library, from a facsimile)

2. *Columbus Landing in the Indies.* Woodcut frontispiece to Giuliano Dati's *Lettera*, 1493. The British Library, London. (Photo: British Library)

3. Detail of *The Story of Paris,* oil on panel, late fifteenth century. Florentine. The Metropolitan Museum of Art, New York (The Collection of Giovanni P. Morosini, presented by his daughter Giulia, 1932). (Photo: Museum)

4. Frontispiece to Vespucci's *De ora antarctica (Mundus Novus)*, woodcut, Strassburg, 1505. The British Library, London. (Photo: British Library)

5. Illustrations to Vespucci's letter to Soderini, woodcuts, Strassburg, 1509. The British Library, London. (Photo: British Library)

6. (a) Illustration to Vespucci's *Mundus Novus*, woodcut, probably Rostock, 1505. The British Library, London. (Photo: British Library)
   (b) Illustrations to Vespucci's *Mundus Novus*, woodcuts, Dutch translation, c.1506–10. The J. Carter Brown Library, Providence, R.I. (Photo: British Library, from a facsimile)

7. *The People of the Islands Recently Discovered . . .* , woodcut with color wash, German, probably Augsburg or Nuremberg, c. 1505. Bayerisches Staatsbibliothek, Munich. (Photo: Library)

8. Page from the Prayer Book of Maximilian I, pen and ink, 1515. Albrecht Dürer. Bayerisches Staatsbibliothek, Munich. (Photo: John R. Freeman and Co., from a facsimile)

9. (a) Detail from *The Triumph of Maximilian I*, woodcut, 1526. Hans Burgkmair
   (b) *Indian Holding a Mexican Shield*, pen, ink, and wash, post 1519. Attributed to Hans Burgkmair. The British Museum, London. (Photo: John R. Freeman & Co.)

10. *The Silver Mines of Potosi,* woodcut illustration from Cieza de León, *Chronica del Peru*, 1553. The British Library, London. (Photo: British Library)

11. Detail of *The Virgin of the Palm,* oil on panel, 1520. School of Amiens. Musée de Picardie, Amiens. (Photo: Museum)

12. *The Spanish Treatment of Fugitive Black Slaves,* engraved illustration from Theodor de Bry, *America,* Part V, 1595. The British Library, London. (Photo: British Library)

13. *The Assassination of Pizarro,* engraved illustration from Theodor de Bry, *America*, Part VI, 1596. The British Library, London. (Photo: British Library)

14. *The Recovery of Bahia in Brazil*, oil on canvas, 1635. Juan Bautista Maino. The Prado, Madrid. (Photo: Mas)

15. Mexican greenstone mask, fifth–sixth century. In the Medici collection by the mid-sixteenth century. Museo degli Argenti, Palazzo Pitti, Florence. (Photo: Soprintendenza)

16. Mexican turquoise-encrusted mask, Mixtec and Puebla Culture. In the Aldrovandi collection, Bologna, by the mid-sixteenth century. Museo Pigorini, Rome. (Photo: Heikamp)

17. Mexican featherwork shield, probably sent to Europe by Cortés. In the Hapsburg collection at Schloss Ambras by the mid-sixteenth century. Museum für Völkerkunde, Vienna. (Photo: Museum)

18. Detail of frescoed ceiling in the former Grand Ducal Armoury, the Uffizi, Florence, 1588. Lodovico Buti. (Photo: Soprintendenza)

19. Mexican greenstone mask in an early seven-

[284]

teenth-century European silver gilt and enamel mount, probably part of the dowry of Vittoria della Rovere, 1634. Museo degli Argenti, Palazzo Pitti, Florence. (Photo: Heikamp)

20. Brazilian axe in U. Aldrovandi's collection, woodcut illustration from U. Aldrovandi, *Musaeum metallicum,* 1648

21. Ole Worm's museum at Copenhagen, engraved illustration from *Museum Wormianum,* Leyden 1653. The British Library, London. (Photo: British Library)

22. *A Woman of Florida,* woodcut illustration from U. Aldrovandi, *Ornithologia,* 1599.

23. Detail of *St. George Baptizing the Gentiles,* oil on canvas, 1507. Carpaccio. S. Giorgio del Schiavoni, Venice. (Photo: Anderson)

24. Loggetta of Cardinal of Bibbiena in the Vatican, 1516. Raphael and Giovanni da Udine. (Photo: Vatican Fototeca)

25. *A Turkey,* bronze, c.1567. Giovanni da Bologna. Museo Nazionale, Florence. (Photo: Alinari)

26. *A Toucan,* woodcut illustration from André Thevet, *Les Singularités de la France Antarctique,* 1558. The British Library, London. (Photo: British Library)

27. *An Armadillo,* woodcut from N. Monardes, *Auctarium ad Exoticorum libros,* 1605

28. *An Opossum and Cannibals,* woodcut from Martin Waldseemüller's *Carta Marina,* 1516. Bodleian Library, Oxford. (Photo: Library)

29. *An Iguana,* woodcut from Gonzalo Fernández de Oviedo, *Coronica de las Indias,* 1547. The British Library, London. (Photo: British Library)

30. *An Agouti,* watercolor, 1580s. Jacopo Ligozzi. Gabinetto dei Disegni, Uffizi, Florence. (Photo: Soprintendenza)

31. *South American Wildlife,* engraving from Arnoldus Montanus, *De Nieuwe en Onbekende Weereld,* 1671. (Photo: Freeman)

32. *The Evil Effects of Tobacco,* woodcut from Girolamo Benzoni, *La Historia del Mondo Nuovo,* 1565. The British Library, London. (Photo: British Library)

33. *A Tobacco Plant,* pen, ink, and watercolor, c. 1554–55. Konrad von Gesner. From Gesner's *Historia Plantarum* in the University Library, Erlangen. (Photo: Courtesy of Urs Graf-Verlag)

34. Page from the Prayer Book of Albrecht V of Bavaria, watercolor on vellum, 1570. Georg Höfnagel. Bayerisches Staatsbibliothek, Munich. (Photo: Library)

35. *Dyewood Gatherers in Brazil,* woodcarving, c.1550. Anonymous, French. Musée Départmental, Rouen. (Photo: Lauros-Giraudon)

36. *An Agave,* watercolor, 1580s. Jacopo Ligozzi. Gabinetto dei Disegni, Uffizi, Florence. (Photo: Soprintendenza)

37. *A Prickly Pear,* woodcut from Gonzalo Fernández de Oviedo, *Coronica de las Indias,* 1547. The British Library, London. (Photo: British Library)

38. *A Cactus,* woodcut from Giovanni Battista Ramusio, *Navigationi et Viaggi,* 1565

39. *A Pineapple,* watercolor, 1580s. Jacopo Ligozzi. Gabinetto dei Disegni, Uffizi, Florence. (Photo: Soprintendenza)

40. *The First Pineapple to Fruit in England,* oil on canvas, 1720. Theodorus Netscher. Fitzwilliam Museum, Cambridge. (Photo: Museum)

41. *Self-Portrait,* oil on canvas, 1633. Sir Anthony Van Dyck. Duke of Westminster Collection.

42. *Brazilian Fruits,* oil on canvas, 1640–43. Albert Eckhout. Danish National Museum, Copenhagen. (Photo: Museum)

43. *Adoration of the Magi,* oil on panel, c.1505. The Master of Viseu. Museu de Grão Vasco, Viseu. (Photo: Museum)

44. *Inferno,* oil on panel, c.1550. Anonymous, Portuguese. Museu de Arte Antiga, Lisbon. (Photo: Museum)

45. Detail from the Grynaeus world map, woodcut, 1555. Royal Geographical Society, London. (Photo: Freeman)

46. (a) *Mexicans,* pen, ink, and wash, 1529. Christoph Weiditz. Germanisches Nationalmuseum, Nuremberg. (Photo: Museum)
    (b) *Mexicans,* pen, ink, and wash, 1528. Christoph Weiditz. Germanisches Nationalmuseum, Nuremberg. (Photo: Museum)

47. *Mexican Jugglers,* pen, ink, and wash, 1528. Christoph Weiditz. Germanisches Nationalmuseum, Nuremberg. (Photo: Museum)

48. *Mexican Ball Players,* pen, ink, and wash, 1528. Christoph Weiditz. Germanisches Nationalmuseum, Nuremberg. (Photo: Museum)

49. Capitals in the Episcopal Palace, Liège, c.1529. (Photo: ACL).

50. *Mexican Woman,* pen, ink, and wash, c.1550. Anonymous. Museo de America, Madrid. (Photo: Mas)

51. *A Man from Acapulco,* pen, ink, and wash, c.1550. Anonymous. Museo de America, Madrid. (Photo: Mas)

52. *Brazilian Fête at Rouen,* woodcut, 1551. Anony-

LIST OF ILLUSTRATIONS

mous, French. Bibliothèque Nationale, Paris. (Photo: BN)

53. *Hans Staden among the Brazilian Cannibals*, woodcut, 1557. Anonymous, after Hans Staden. From Hans Staden, *Wahrhaftiger Historia und beschreibung einer Landtschaft der Wilden Nacketen Grimmigen Menschenfresser Leuthen in der Newenwelt America*, 1557. The British Library, London. (Photo: British Library)

54. *Brazilian Indians Making Fire*, woodcut from André Thevet, *Les Singularités de la France Antarctique*, 1557. The British Library, London. (Photo: British Library)

55. *Brazilians*, woodcut from Jean de Léry, *Histoire d'un voyage faict en la terre du Brésil*, 1578. The British Library, London. (Photo: British Library)

56. (a) *An Eskimo*, watercolor, 1576. Lucas de Heere. Universiteitsbibliothek, Ghent. (Photo: Library)
    (b) *An Eskimo*, pen, ink, and watercolors, 1576–77. John White. The British Museum, London. (Photo: Museum)

57. (a) "Peru" from *Cosmographie Universelle*, 1555. Guillaume Le Testu. Ministère des Armées, Paris. (Photo: Giraudon)
    (b) "Brazil" from *Cosmographie Universelle*, 1555. Guillaume Le Testu. Ministère des Armées, Paris. (Photo: Giraudon)

58. *A Man of Florida*, pen, ink, and watercolors, c.1588. John White, after Jacques Le Moyne. The British Museum, London. (Photo: Museum)

59. *Outina on a Military Expedition*, engraving after Jacques Le Moyne. From Theodor de Bry, *America*, Part II, 1591

60. *The Flyer or Medicine Man*, watercolor, 1585–87. John White. The British Museum, London. (Photo: Museum)

61. *Indian Woman and Child*, watercolor, 1585–87. John White. The British Museum, London. (Photo: Museum)

62. *The Village of Secoton*, watercolor, 1585–87. John White. The British Museum, London. (Photo: Museum)

63. *The Youth of Florida*, engraving after Jacques Le Moyne. From Theodor de Bry, *America*, Part II, 1591

64. *Brazilians*, woodcut, 1557. Anonymous, after Hans Staden. From Hans Staden, *Wahrhaftiger Historia und beschreibung einer Landtschaft der Wilden Nacketen Grimmigen Menschenfresser Leuthen in der Newenwelt America*, 1557. The British Library, London. (Photo: British Library)

65. *Brazilians*, engraving, 1592. Anonymous, after Hans Staden. From Theodor de Bry, *America*, Part III, 1592. Bibliothèque Nationale, Paris. (Photo: BN)

66. *Cannibal Scene*, woodcut, 1557. Anonymous, after Hans Staden. From Hans Staden, *Wahrhaftiger Historia und beschreibung einer Landtschaft der Wilden Nacketen Grimmigen Menschenfresser Leuthen in der Newenwelt America*, 1557. The British Library, London. (Photo: British Library)

67. *Cannibal Scene*, engraving, 1592. Anonymous, after Hans Staden. From Theodor de Bry, *America*, Part III, 1592. Bibliothèque Nationale, Paris. (Photo: BN)

68. *Spanish Attack on Indians*, engraving from Theodor de Bry, *America*, Part IV, 1594. The British Library, London. (Photo: British Library)

69. *Tapuya War Dance*, oil on canvas, c.1641–43. Albert Eckhout. Danish National Museum, Copenhagen. (Photo: Museum)

70. *Brazilian Woman*, oil on canvas, 1641. Albert Eckhout. Danish National Museum, Copenhagen. (Photo: Museum)

71. *Brazilian Man*, oil on canvas, 1643. Albert Eckhout. Danish National Museum, Copenhagen. (Photo: Museum)

72. *Black Woman with Mulatto Child*, oil on canvas, 1641. Albert Eckhout. Danish National Museum, Copenhagen. (Photo: Museum)

73. *Brazilian Woman and Child*, oil on canvas, 1641. Albert Eckhout. Danish National Museum, Copenhagen. (Photo: Museum)

74. *A West Indian Scene*, oil on canvas, c.1650. Bonaventura Peeters. Private Collection.

75. Detail from *A West Indian Scene*, oil on canvas, 1648. Bonaventura Peeters. Wadsworth Atheneum, Hartford, Conn. (Photo: Courtesy of Wadsworth Atheneum)

76. *America*, etching, 1575. Etienne Delaune. Bibliothèque Nationale, Paris. (Photo: BN)

77. *America*, engraving, 1581–1600. Philippe Galle. Bibliothèque Nationale, Paris. (Photo: BN)

78. *America*, engraving, 1581. Jan Sadeler, after Dirk Barendsz. Rijksmuseum, Amsterdam. (Photo: Rijksmuseum)

79. Pewter tankard. Nuremberg, early seventeenth century. Museum für Kunsthandwerk, Dresden. (Photo: Museum)

80. *America*, engraving, early seventeenth century. Crispijn de Passe. Rijksmuseum, Amsterdam. (Photo: Rijksmuseum)

81. *Vespucci "Discovering" America*, engraving, late sixteenth century. Theodor Galle, after Stradan-

LIST OF ILLUSTRATIONS

us (Jan van der Street). The British Museum, London (Photo: Freeman).

82. *America,* pen, ink, and wash, 1594. Maarten de Vos. Prentencabinet, Antwerp. (Photo: ACL)

83. *America,* etching, 1644. Stefano della Bella. The Metropolitan Museum of Art, New York.

84. *Allegory of America,* engraving, early seventeenth century, François van den Hoeye. (Photo: Bulloz)

85. *The Ship of Amerigo Vespucci,* etching, 1608. After Giulio Parigi. Bibliothèque Nationale, Paris. (Photo: BN).

86. *Archway of the Mint,* oil on canvas, 1635. Peter Paul Rubens. Koninklijk Museum, Antwerp. (Photo: ACL)

87. *The Four Continents,* oil on canvas, c.1615. Peter Paul Rubens. Kunsthistorisches Museum, Vienna. (Photo: Museum)

88. *Allegory on the Abdication of the Emperor Charles V at Brussels, October 25, 1555,* oil on panel, c. 1636. Frans Francken II. Rijksmuseum, Amsterdam. (Photo: Rijksmuseum)

89. (a) *Indian Torchbearer,* pen, ink, and watercolor, 1613. Inigo Jones. Trustees of the Chatsworth Settlement. (Photo: Trustees)
    (b) Costume design, pen, ink, and watercolor, early seventeenth century. Giulio Parigi. Biblioteca Marucelliana, Florence.

90. Ballet designs, pen, ink, and wash, 1626. Daniel Rabel. Musée du Louvre, Paris. (Photo: Museum)

91. American costumes worn at the Carrousel of 1662, engraving 1671. François Chauveau. Bibliothèque Nationale, Paris. (Photo: BN)

92. *America,* fresco, 1595. Paolo Farinati. Villa Della Torre, Mezzane di Sotto, Verona

93. *The River Plate,* 1651. Gianlorenzo Bernini. Piazza Navona, Rome. (Photo: Anderson)

94. *America,* woodcarving, c.1690. Anonymous, Netherlandish. S. Jacob, Bruges. (Photo: ACL)

95. *America,* stone, c.1700. Hendrick Verbruggen. Petrus and Paulus Kerk, Mechelin. (Photo: ACL)

96. *Buenos Aires, Mexico City, Havana, Domingo, Porto Seguro, Vera Cruz,* oil on copper, 1664–66. Jan van Kessel. Alte Pinakothek, Munich. (Photo: Museum)

97. *Les Indes,* tapestry, 1687. Gobelins. Mobilier Nationale, Paris

98. *Les Nouvelles Indes,* tapestry, 1737–63. Gobelins. Palazzo del Quirinale, Rome. (Photo: Alinari)

99. *America,* silver, 1692. Lorenzo Vaccaro. The Cathedral, Toledo. (Photo: Mas)

100. *America,* oil on canvas, 1689–90. Luca Giordano. (Photo: Courtesy of Hazlett Gallery)

101. *America,* oil on canvas, 1742. Jean Dumont. Israel Museum, Jerusalem. (Photo: Museum)

102. *Tea-pot à l'amérique,* porcelain, c.1730. Meissen. The Metropolitan Museum of Art, New York, Gift of the Estate of James Hazen Hyde, 1959. (Photo: Museum)

103. Sledge, carved and painted wood, c.1723. Georg Kaufmann. Städtische Kunstsammlungen, Veste Coburg. (Photo: Museum)

104. *America,* engraving, early eighteenth century. De Launay, after Gravelot. Bibliothèque Nationale, Paris. (Photo: BN)

105. *Amériquain,* pen, ink, and watercolor, 1764. Nicolas Bocquet. Bibliothèque de l'Opéra, Paris. (Photo: BN)

106. *America,* oil on canvas, c. 1750–60. Johann Wolfgang Baumgartner. Städtische Kunstsammlungen, Augsburg. (Photo: Museum)

107. Detail of sketch for Throne Room ceiling, Royal Palace, Madrid, 1762. Giovanni Battista Tiepolo. National Gallery of Art (Samuel H. Kress Collectio). (Photo: National Gallery)

108. Detail of Throne Room ceiling, Royal Palace, Madrid, fresco, 1764. Giovanni Battista Tiepolo. (Photo: Mas)

109. *The Peoples of America,* black chalk, heightened with white, 1674–79. Charles Le Brun. Musée du Louvre, Paris. (Photo: Museum)

110. *Convoi Funèbre des Peuples du Canada,* engraved illustration from Bernard Picart et Bruzen de la Martinière, *Cérémonies et coutumes religieuses de tout les peuples du monde,* 1723. Bibliothèque Nationale, Paris. (Photo: BN)

111. *Indian Courtship,* engraved illustrations, after B. Picart, from Bernard Picart et Bruzen de la Martinière, *Cérémonies et coutumes religieuses de tous les peuples du monde,* 1723. Bibliothèque Nationale, Paris. (Photo: BN)

112. *Le Grand Sacrifice des Canadiens à Quitchi-Manitou ou le Grand Esprit,* engraving after B. Picart, from Bernard Picart et Bruzen de la Martinière, *Cérémonies et coutumes religieuses de tous les peuples du monde,* 1723. Bibliothèque Nationale, Paris. (Photo: BN)

113. Engraved illustration to P. Joseph François Lafitau, *Moeurs des sauvages amériquains comparées aux moeurs des premiers temps,* 1724

114. (a) *Ho Nee Yeath Taw No Row, King of the Generethgarich;* (b) *Sa Ga Yeath Qua Pieth Tow, King of the Maquas;* (c) *Tee Yee Neen Ho Ga Row, Emper-*

[287]

LIST OF ILLUSTRATIONS

or of the Six Nations; mezzotints, 1710. Jean Simon, after John Verelst. Library of Congress, Washington, D.C. (Photo: Library)

115. *Austenaco, Great Warrior, Commander in Chief of the Cherokee Nation,* engraving, 1762. Anonymous, from the *Royal Magazine,* 1762.

116. *Indian,* pen and ink, c.1700. From the *Codex canadensis.* Thomas Gilcrease Institute, Tulsa. (Photo: Bulloz)

117. *Indians, New Orleans,* pen, ink, and wash, 1732. Alexandre de Batz. Peabody Museum, Harvard University, Cambridge, Mass. (Photo: Museum)

118. *Chief Lapowinsa,* oil on canvas, 1735. Gustavus Hesselius. Historical Society of Pennsylvania, Philadelphia.

119. *Outewas Indians,* pen, ink, and wash, 1759. George Townshend. The National Portrait Gallery, London. (Photo: E. Harris)

120. (a) Designs for the Townshend Monument, pencil, pen, and wash, 1760. Robert Adam. Sir John Soane's Museum, London. (Photo: Freeman)
     (b) The Townshend Monument in Westminster Abbey, 1761. Thomas Carter and John Eckstein, to designs by Robert Adam. (Photo: Warburg Institute)

121. Detail from *The Death of Wolfe,* oil on canvas, 1770. Benjamin West. The National Gallery of Canada, Ottawa. (Photo: Gallery)

122. *Thayeadanegea, Joseph Brant, the Mohawk Chief,* oil on canvas, 1775–76. George Romney. The National Gallery of Canada, Ottawa. (Photo: Gallery)

123. *Joseph Brant,* oil on canvas, c.1800. Wilhelm von Moll Berczy. The National Gallery of Canada, Ottawa. (Photo: Gallery)

124. *Californian Indians,* pen, ink, and watercolor, 1769. Alexandre-Jean Noël. Musée du Louvre, Paris. (Photo: Museum)

125. *Indian Parents Mourning over the Grave of Their Deceased Child,* engraving, 1786. P.-C. Ingouf, after Jean-Jacques-François Le Barbier. Bibliothèque Nationale, Paris. (Photo: BN)

126. *L'Enfant Perdu,* black chalk, c.1785. Antoine Borel. Musée de la Coopération Franco-Américaine, Blérancourt. (Photo: Museum)

127. *Sir John Caldwell as an Ojibwa Chief,* oil on canvas, c. 1782. Anonymous, English. F. E. G. Bagshawe collection. (Photo: National Portrait Gallery)

128. *William Augustus Bowles,* oil on canvas, 1791. Thomas Hardy. The National Trust, Upton House. (Photo: Blinkhorns)

129. *Cherokee Indian,* oil on canvas, 1791. William Hodges. The Royal College of Surgeons, London.

130. *The Indian Widow,* oil on canvas, 1783–85. Joseph Wright of Derby. Derby Museum and Art Gallery, Derby. (Photo: Museum)

131. *Liberty Crowning Franklin,* aquatint, 1778. Abbé de Saint Non, after Jean-Honoré Fragonard. Bibliothèque Nationale, Paris. (Photo: BN)

132. *Indépendance des États-Unis,* engraving with colored wash, 1786. L. Roger, after Duplessis Bertaux. Bibliothèque Nationale, Paris. (Photo: BN)

133. *American Independence,* c.1782. Toile de Jouy (plate printed cotton). Musée des Arts Décoratifs, Paris. (Photo: Museum)

134. *William Penn with Lycurgus and Alfred the Great,* detail from *Elysium,* oil on canvas, 1777–83. James Barry. Royal Society of Arts, London.

135. *Quaker Meeting,* engraving, mid-eighteenth century. Anonymous, French. Bibliothèque Nationale, Paris. (Photo: BN)

136. English caricature, engraving 1765. Anonymous. The British Museum, London. (Photo: Museum)

137. *Lord Chatham and America,* c.1766. Derby Porcelain. Victoria & Albert Museum, London. (Photo: Museum)

138. *The Phoenix or Resurrection of Freedom,* engraving and aquatint, 1776. James Barry. The British Museum, London. (Photo: Museum)

139. *The Tea Tax Tempest,* mezzotint engraving, 1778. Carl Gutenberg. Bibliothèque Nationale, Paris. (Photo: BN)

140. English caricature, engraving, 1780. Anonymous. The British Museum, London. (Photo: Museum)

141. French caricature, *Le Destin molestant les Anglois,* engraving 1780. Anonymous. Bibliothèque Nationale, Paris. (Photo: BN)

142. *L'Amérique indépendante,* engraving, 1778. Jean-Charles Le Vasseur, after Antoine Borel. Bibliothèque Nationale, Paris. (Photo: BN)

143. *Louis XVI and Franklin,* 1782–85. Niderviller Porcelain. (Photo: Courtesy of The Henry Francis du Pont Winterthur Museum, Winterthur, Del.)

144. (a) Medal of Washington, bronze, c.1776–82. Benjamin Duvivier. Private Collection, Paris
     (b) Medal of John Paul Jones, bronze, c.1776–82. Augustin Dupré. Private Collection, Paris

145. *The Genius of Franklin,* etching, 1778. Marguerite Gérard, after Jean-Honoré Fragonard. Bibliothèque Nationale, Paris. (Photo: BN)

146. *Benjamin Franklin,* oil on canvas, 1778. Joseph Siffred Duplessis. The Metropolitan Museum of

LIST OF ILLUSTRATIONS

Art, New York. The Michael Friedsam Collection, 1931. (Photo: Museum)

147. *George Washington,* marble, 1785–96. Jean Antoine Houdon. The State Capitol, Richmond, Virginia. (Photo: Virginia State Library)

148. *Homage to Franklin,* oil on canvas, c.1779–82. Christian August Lorentzen. Statens Museum for Kunst, Copenhagen

149. *Traite des Nègres,* engraving, 1794. John Pettit, after George Morland. Bibliothèque Nationale, Paris. (Photo: BN)

150. *Moi Libre,* engraving with color wash, c.1794. Anonymous. Bibliothèque Nationale, Paris. (Photo: BN)

151. French clock, bronze, partly gilt, c.1810. Anonymous. Museo degli Argenti, Palazzo Pitti, Florence. (Photo: Soprintendenza)

152. (a) Illustration to J. G. Stedman, *Revolted Negroes of Surinam,* 1796. William Blake
    (b) Page from *America,* 1973. William Blake

153. (a) Model for statue of George Washington, plaster, 1818. Antonio Canova. Gipsoteca di Possagno, Possagno. (Photo: Fondazione Cini)
    (b) *Lafayette in 1825 Viewing Canova's Statue of Washington,* lithograph, 1840. Albert Newsam, after J. Weisman and Emmanuel Leutze. Hall of History, Raleigh, N. C.

154. "*Les Lauriers seuils y croitront sans culture,*" *Champ d'Asile,* lithograph, c.1818. Anonymous, French. Bibliothèque Nationale, Paris. (Photo: Bulloz)

155. *Owen's Proposed Village,* from *The Cooperative Magazine & Monthly Herald,* 1826

156. *Surrender at Yorktown,* oil on canvas, 1837. Auguste Couder. Château de Versailles. (Photo: Bulloz)

157. *George Washington on Horseback,* oil on canvas, c.1830–40. Ary Scheffer. Museum of Art, Rhode Island School of Design, Providence, R.I., Gift of Mrs. Murray S. Danforth

158. *The Statue of Liberty under Construction in Paris,* oil on canvas, 1883. Victor Dargaud. Musée Carnavalet, Paris. (Photo: Giraudon)

159. (a) *The Sublime Loyalty of the Cacique Henri,* wash/drawing, 1810. Jean-Jacques-François Le Barbier. Musée des Beaux-Arts, Rouen. (Photo: Ellebé)
    (b) *Orozimbo Saving Amazili,* oil on canvas, c. 1820. Pietro Benvenuti. Private collection. (Photo: Alinari)

160. *Les Incas,* 1826. Dufour & Leroy scenic wallpaper. Musée des Arts Décoratifs, Paris. (Photo: Museum)

161. Stage design for Spontini's *Fernand Cortez,* watercolor, c.1820. Karl Friedrich Schinkel. Staatliche Museen zu Berlin. (Photo: Museum)

162. *Montezuma,* oil on canvas, late sixteenth century. Anonymous. Museo di Etnologia, Florence

163. *Montezuma,* watercolor, 1807. Karl Lorenz Gindl. Bildarchiv d. Öst. Nationalbibliothek, Vienna

164. (a) Copy of Mexican codex, 1566–89. Pedro del Ríos
    (b) Page from Lorenzo Pignoria's appendix, "Imagini degli dei indiani," to Vincenzo Cartari, *Le vere e nuove imagini degli dei delli antichi,* 1615

165. Copy of a Mixtec codex, watercolor, 1650. J. Ludolph. Royal Library, Copenhagen

166. Lord Orford's "Cup of Montezuma," pen and ink, 1738. Anonymous. The Society of Antiquaries, London. (Photo: Society)

167. Lord Orford's "Cup of Montezuma," pen, ink, and wash, 1765. Paul or Thomas Sandby. The Society of Antiquaries, London. (Photo: Society)

168. Mexican greenstone mask in a European mount, gold, silver-gilt, gilt-bronze, onyx, precious stones, and enamel, c.1720. Mount attributed to Guillaume de Groff. Schatzkammer der Residenz, Munich

169. Guadalajara vase on a carved and gilded wood stand, early eighteenth-century Florentine. Coll. Conte Leonardo Ginori Lisci, Florence. (Photo: Barsotti)

170. *Humboldt and Bonpland on the Orinoco,* engraving. Anonymous, after Keller. Staatsbibliothek, West Berlin

171. *Chimborazo,* colored engraving, 1810. Bouquet, after Thibault. From Alexander von Humboldt, *Vues des Cordillères . . . ,* Paris 1810

172. *Maranhao Island, Brazil,* watercolor, 1817. Thomas Ender. Akademie der bildenden Künste, Vienna

173. *Brazilian Landscape,* watercolor, 1817. Thomas Ender. Akademie der bildenden Künste, Vienna

174. *Spix and Martius in the Amazonian Forest,* lithograph, 1819. From C. F. P. von Martius, *Flora brasiliensis,* 1840–46. British Museum (Natural History). (Photo: Museum)

175. *Prince Maximilian of Wied-Neuwied in Brazil,* engraving, 1820. From Prince Maximilian of Wied-Neuwied, *Travels in Brazil in the years 1815, 1816, 1817,* 1820

176. *The Sageota Canal, Peru,* wood engraving, 1869. E. Riou. From Paul Marcoy, *Journey across South America,* 1869

LIST OF ILLUSTRATIONS

177. *Primeval Forest, Venezuela,* pencil, 1843–47. Ferdinand Bellermann, Staatliche Museen zu Berlin. (Photo: Museum)

178. *Near Mérida, Venezuela,* oil on canvas, 1843–47. Ferdinand Bellermann. Staatliche Museen zu Berlin. (Photo: Museum)

179. *The Mexican Exhibition, London,* lithograph, 1825. A. Aglio

180. *Jean Frédéric Maximilien de Waldeck Being Carried over the Chiapas,* oil on panel, Salon, 1870. J. F. M. de Waldeck. Robert Isaacson Collection, New York

181. *Maya Stele (C) at Copàn,* ink and wash over pencil, 1843. Frederick Catherwood. Yale University Art Gallery (Gift of Henry Schnackenberg), New Haven, Connecticut. (Photo: Museum)

182. *The Mouth of the Wells of Itzá,* ink and wash over pencil, 1843. Frederick Catherwood. The Brooklyn Museum, Brooklyn. (Photo: Courtesy of The Brooklyn Museum)

183. *Archway, Casa del Gobernador, Chichén Itzá,* ink and wash, 1843. Frederick Catherwood. The Brooklyn Museum, Brooklyn. (Photo: Courtesy of The Brooklyn Museum)

184. *The First Conference between the Spaniards and the Peruvians, 1531,* oil on canvas, 1840. Henry Perronet Briggs. The Tate Gallery, London. (Photo: Gallery)

185. Brazilian Forest, Exposition Universelle, Paris, 1867, from *L'Exposition Universelle de 1867 illustrée,* after a drawing by M. Lancelot

186. Replica of the Temple of Xochicalco, Exposition Universelle, Paris, 1867

187. Peruvian section of the Central and South American Pavilion, Exposition Universelle, Paris, 1878

188. Central and South American and other exhibits in the Ethnographical section of the Exposition Universelle, Paris, 1878

189. *Fruit Pickers, Martinique,* oil on canvas, 1887. Paul Gauguin. Rijksmuseum Van Gogh, Amsterdam. (Photo: Museum)

190. *Joyeux Farceurs,* oil on canvas, 1906. Henri Rousseau le Douanier. Philadelphia Museum of Art, Philadelphia

191. *Emigrants on the St. Lawrence,* engraving, 1872. Gustave Doré. From W. F. Ainsworth, *Wanderings in Every Clime,* London, 1872. (Photo: Freeman)

192. *The European Dream; The American Reality,* aquatint, c.1830. Anonymous, German. Bibliothèque Nationale, Paris. (Photo: BN)

193. *The Thriving City of Eden as It Appeared on Paper* and *The Thriving City of Eden as it Appeared in Fact,* 1844. "Phiz." From Charles Dickens, *Martin Chuzzlewit*

194. *The Emigrants' Last Sight of Home,* oil on canvas, 1858–59. Richard Redgrave. (Photo: Courtesy of Messrs. Sotheby)

195. *A Mormon Evangelist Visiting a Danish Carpenter's Family,* oil on canvas, 1856. Christen Dalsgaard. Statens Museum for Kunst, Copenhagen

196. *The Emigrants,* engraving, 1861. After Théophile Schuler. Bibliothèque Nationale. (Photo: BN)

197. *Emigrants Waiting to Embark,* oil on canvas, 1896. Angelo Tommasi. Galleria d'Arte Moderna, Rome. (Photo: GFN)

198. *Niagara Falls,* Staffordshire pottery dish, c.1830. The Smithsonian Institution, Washington D.C.

199. *Slave Market at Richmond, Virginia,* oil on canvas, 1852. Eyre Crowe. Private collection

200. *Punch* cartoon, 1848. John Leech. (Photo: Freeman)

201. *Les Noirs, avant, pendant et après l'Emancipation,* lithograph, c.1839. Anonymous, French. Bibliothèque Nationale, Paris. (Photo: BN)

202. *Mines d'Or de la Californie,* hand-colored engraving, c.1850. Dembour et Gangel. Bibliothèque Nationale, Paris. (Photo: BN)

203. *Punch* cartoon, August 9, 1862. John Tenniel

204. *"Worldlyfolk" with Chimney Sweeps before Christ Church, Philadelphia,* watercolor, 1812. Pavel Petrovich Svinin. The Metropolitan Museum of Art (Rogers Fund, 1942), New York. (Photo: Museum)

205. *A Philadelphia Anabaptist Immersion During a Storm,* watercolor, 1812. Pavel Petrovich Svinin. The Metropolitan Museum of Art (Rogers Fund, 1942), New York. (Photo: Museum)

206. *At the Theatre,* lithograph, c.1830. August Hervieu, from Frances Trollope, *Domestic Manners of the Americans,* 1832

207. *Buffalo, New York,* watercolor, 1844. Eduard Hildebrandt. Staatliche Museen zu Berlin. (Photo: Museum)

208. *Broadway, New York,* oil on canvas, c.1855. Hippolyte Sebron. Musée de la Coopération Franco-Américaine, Blérancourt. (Photo: Hutin)

209. *Johann August Sutter,* oil on canvas, 1866. Frank Buchser. Museum der Stadt Solothurn, Solothurn. (Photo: Schweizerisches Institute für Kunstwissenschaft)

210. *Eternal Plains, August 22, 1866,* pencil, 1866.

Frank Buchser. Oeffentliche Kunstsammlung Basel. (Photo: Gallery)

211. *Crossing the River Platte,* oil on canvas, 1866. Frank Buchser. Oeffentliche Kunstsammlung Basel. (Photo: Gallery)

212. *The Volunteer's Return,* oil on canvas, 1867. Frank Buchser. Oeffentliche Kunstsámmlung Basel. (Photo: Gallery)

213. *Woodstock, Virginia,* oil on canvas, 1867. Frank Buchser. Stiftung Oskar Reinhart, Winterthur (Zurich). (Photo: Gallery)

214. *A Black Man,* oil on canvas, c.1867. Frank Buchser. Private Collection. (Photo: Schweizerisches Institut für Kunstwissenschaft)

215. *General Sherman,* oil on canvas, 1869. Frank Buchser. Museum of Fine Arts, Berne. (Photo: Museum)

216. *New York Bay,* oil on canvas, 1867–68. Frank Buchser. Museum der Stadt Solothurn, Solothurn. (Photo: Schweizerisches Institut für Kunstwissenschaft)

217. *William Cullen Bryant,* oil on canvas, 1867–68. Frank Buchser. Oeffentliche Kunstsammlung Basel. (Photo: Gallery)

218. *Indian Emcampment,* oil on canvas, 1868. Frank Buchser. Museum der Stadt Solothurn, Solothurn. (Photo: Schweizerisches Institut für Kunstwissenschaft)

219. *An August Morning in Virginia,* oil on canvas, 1869. Frank Buchser. Private Collection, Switzerland

220. *The Ballad of Mary Blane,* oil on canvas, 1870. Frank Buchser. Museum der Stadt Solothurn, Solothurn. (Photo: Schweizerisches Institut für Kunstwissenschaft)

221. *Mme René de Gas, New Orleans,* oil on canvas, 1872. Edgar Degas. National Gallery of Art (Chester Dale Collection), Washington, D.C. (Photo: National Gallery)

222. *Femme à la Potiche,* oil on canvas, 1872. Edgar Degas. Musée du Louvre, Paris. (Photo: Museum)

223. *Enfants assis sur le perron d'une maison de campagne à la Nouvelle-Orléans,* oil on canvas, 1872–73. Edgar Degas. Ordrupgaardsamlingen, Copenhagen. (Photo: Ordrupgaardsamlingen)

224. (a) Sketch for *The Cotton Office, New Orleans,* oil on canvas, 1872–73. Edgar Degas. The Fogg Art Museum, Cambridge, Mass. (Photo: Museum)
(b) *M. H. de Clermont, New Orleans,* black chalk heightened with white, 1872–73. Edgar Degas. Kongelige Kobberstik Samling, Copenhagen. (Photo: Courtesy of Royal Collection)

225. *Strike on the Baltimore-Ohio Railroad,* engraving, 1877. Anonymous, French. Bibliothèque Nationale, Paris. (Photo: BN)

226. *Aux Etats-Unis—Lynching Negroes,* reproductive engraving, c.1890. After L. Carrey. Bibliothèque Nationale, Paris. (Photo: BN)

227. *The Burial of Atala,* oil on canvas, 1808. Anne-Louis Girodet-Trioson. Musée du Louvre, Paris. (Photo: Lauros-Giraudon)

228. *The Death of Atala,* oil on canvas, 1830. Cesare Mussini. Galleria d'Arte Moderna, Florence. (Photo: Soprintendenza)

229. *Chactas,* bronze, 1836. François-Joseph Duret. Musée des Beaux-Arts, Lyons. (Photo: Museum)

230. Illustration to *Atala,* engraving, 1860. Gustave Doré

231. *Les Natchez,* oil on canvas, 1824–35. Eugène Delacroix. Collection Lord Walston, Cambridge. (Photo: Réunion)

232. *American Indians Capture a Monk,* brown ink and wash, c.1812. Francisco Goya. Brod Gallery, London

233. *Scenes of Cannibalism,* oil on canvas, c.1812. Francisco Goya. Musée des Beaux-Arts, Besançon. (Photo: Giraudon)

234. *The Rescue of the Daughters of Daniel Boone and Richard Calloway,* charcoal and sepia chalk, 1850. Jean-François Millet. Yale University Art Gallery (Everett V. Meeks Fund), New Haven, Conn. (Photo: Joseph Szaszfai)

235. Illustration to *The Last of the Mohicans,* engraving, 1827. Tony Johannot. Bibliothèque Nationale, Paris. (Photo: BN)

236. Costume designs for *Les Mohicans,* watercolors, 1837. P. Lormier, Musée de l'Opéra, Paris. (Photos: BN)

237. *The Oneidas in Paris,* lithograph, 1819. Anonymous. Bibliothèque Nationale, Paris. (Photo: BN)

238. *The Osages in Paris,* lithograph, 1827. H. V. (Horace Vernet?) Bibliothèque Nationale, Paris. (Photo: BN)

239. *Indian Hunters Pursuing the Buffalo in the Spring,* watercolor, c.1825. Peter Rindisbacher. Peabody Museum, Harvard University, Cambridge, Mass. (Photo: Museum)

240. *Leather Tents of the Assiniboins, near Fort Union,* watercolor, 1833. Karl Bodmer. Northern Natural Gas Company Collection, Joslyn Art Museum, Omaha, Nebraska. (Photo: Museum)

LIST OF ILLUSTRATIONS

241. *Mandan Indian Buffalo Dancer,* watercolor, 1833. Karl Bodmer. Northern Natural Gas Company Collection, Joslyn Art Museum, Omaha, Nebraska. (Photo: Museum)

242. *Bison Dance of the Mandan Indians,* lithograph, 1833. Alexander Manceau, after Karl Bodmer. (Photo: Freeman)

243. *The Dying Tecumseh,* marble, 1856. Ferdinand Pettrich. National Collection of Fine Arts, Smithsonian Institution, Washington, D.C. (Photo: Smithsonian)

244. *Catlin's Ioway Indians,* lithograph, 1845. Henry Emy. Bibliothèque Nationale, Paris. (Photo: BN)

245. *Catlin's Ojibway Indians,* pen and ink, 1845. Eugène Delacroix. Musée du Louvre, Paris. (Photo: Museum)

246. Study for *Pony Express,* pencil, c.1860. Jules-Emile Saintin. Musée Nationale de la Coopération Franco-Américaine, Blérancourt. (Photo: Réunion)

247. *Chief Kicking Bear,* bronze, 1892. Carl Rohl-Smith. Statens Museum for Kunst, Copenhagen

248. *Buffalo Bill on His White Horse,* oil on canvas, 1889. Rosa Bonheur. Buffalo Bill Historical Center, Cody, Wyoming

249. *The Buffalo Hunt,* oil on canvas, 1889. Rosa Bonheur

250. *Indian Encampment,* oil on canvas, c.1890. Rosa Bonheur. The Thomas Gilcrease Institute of American History and Art, Tulsa, Okla.

251. *Peaux Rouges,* oil on panel, c.1895. Pierre Bonnard. Amon Carter Museum of Western Art, Fort Worth, Texas. (Photo: Courtesy of Amon Carter Museum, Fort Worth, Texas)

252. (a) Covers for Karl May's *Winnetou,* 1893 and c. 1900 editions. Archiv Karl-May-Verlag, Bamberg
(b) Designs for covers of Karl May's *Winnetou* and *Am Rio de la Plata,* 1904–5. Sascha Schneider. Archiv Karl-May-Verlag, Bamberg

253. Poster for Puccini's *La Fanciulla del West* at La Scala, Milan, 1910–11. Giuseppe Palanti. Museo Teatrale alla Scala, Milan

254. *Indian Scalping an Enemy,* engraving, c.1860. Anonymous, French. Bibliothèque Nationale, Paris. (Photo: BN)

255. Red Indians and U.S. soldiers, painted lead or tin figures c.1900. Germanisches National Museum, Nuremberg. (Photo: Museum)

256. *Grey Owl,* photograph, 1931. (Photo: Courtesy of Ontario Archives)

257. (a) *American Strikes,* from *Illustrazione Italiana,* May 23, 1886
(b) *Chicago "Haymarket" Executions,* from *Illustrazione Italiana,* December 4, 1887

258. *To Brother Jonathan,* 1902. Max Beerbohm, from *Cartoons, The Second Childhood of John Bull*

259. *America,* detail of a ceiling decoration, oil on canvas, c.1870. Hans Makart. Österreichische Galerie, Vienna. (Photo: Gallery)

260. *Consuelo, Duchess of Marlborough, and Lord Ivor Spencer-Churchill,* oil on canvas, 1906. Giovanni Boldini. The Metropolitan Museum of Art, New York. Gift of Consuelo Vanderbilt Balsan, 1946. (Photo: Museum)

261. Designs for *Nuova Città,* pencil, 1913. Antonio Sant' Elia. Commune di Como

262. *Buffalo Bill,* oil on canvas, 1905. Maximilien Luce

263. *Buffalo Bill,* oil on canvas, 1911. Pablo Picasso. Formerly Müller Collection, Solothurn

264. The New York Manager in *Parade,* photograph, 1917. Pablo Picasso

265. *Memory of New York,* pen and ink, 1916. George Grosz. From *Erste George Grosz-Mappe,* Berlin 1917

266. Stills from *Metropolis,* 1926. UFA, sets by Otto Hanke. (Photo: National Film Archive, London)

267. Still from *Things to Come,* 1936. Alexander Korda. (Photo: National Film Archive, London)

268. Theater Program, 1935. "Hicks"

269. *Adieu New York,* oil on canvas, 1945. Fernand Léger. Musée National d'Art Moderne, Paris. (Photo: Archives)

270. *Just what is it that makes today's homes so different, so appealing?* collage, 1956. Richard Hamilton. Edwin Janss, Jr., Thousand Oaks, California

271. *The Solomon R. Guggenheim,* screenprint, 1965. Richard Hamilton. Petersburg Press, London

272. *Savings and Loan Building,* acrylic on canvas, 1967. David Hockney. Kasmin Gallery, London. (Photo: Geoffrey Clements)

273. *Rocky Mountains and Tired Indians,* acrylic on canvas, 1965. David Hockney. Kasmin Gallery, London. (Photo: John Webb)

274. *A Lawn Sprinkler,* acrylic on canvas, 1967. David Hockney. Kasmin Gallery, London. (Photo: Geoffrey Clements)

Index

Acosta, José de, 78
Adair, James, 135–6
Adam, Robert, 129, 277, 278
Adams, John, 192
Addison, Joseph, 125, 277
Africans, compared with Indians, 121
agave, 41, 45
Aglié, Filippo conte d', 94
Aglio, Agostino, 178
Aimard, Gustave, 240, 244–5
Ainsworth, William Francis, 194, 280
Albrecht V, Duke of Bavaria, 30, 42, 47
Aldrovandi, Ulisse, 32, 34–5, 41, 274
Alexander VI, Pope, 56
Algarotti, conte Francesco, 162–3, 279
allegories of continents, 84–117, 276
alligator, 41, 89, 109, 113
Altdorfer, Albrecht, 13, 15, 273
Amazon, river, 85, 172, 174
Amiens, painting for cathedral, 20–1
Amman, Jost, 85
Amsterdam, town hall, 109
Ango, Jacques, 63
Angrand, Leonce, 279
Anne, Queen of Great Britain, 125, 277
Antonioni, Michelangelo, 265
Antwerp, festival decorations in, 91–2
Apache Indians, 240, 242, 245
Apollinaire, Guillaume (Wilhelm de Kostrowitzky), 186–7
Arauca, 99
Archadia, 16
Argentina, 176. *See also* Patagonia
Arizona, 262
armadillo, 39–40, 89, 97
Armstrong, Louis, 260
Arnold, Matthew, 197, 280
Art Deco style, 259, 282
Art Nouveau style, 253
Asia, America seen as part of, 4, 13, 15, 39, 60
Assiniboin, 232–3
Atahualpa, Inca, 162

Atlantis, 3
Auberteuil, Michel-René Hilliard d', 149
Augsburg, silver made at, 89
Azores, 4
Aztecs, 18, 21, 58, 87, 124, 162–5, 170, 259

Bach, Johann Christian, 279
Bacon, Francis, 1st Baron Verulam, 162
Baffin Island, 67
Bahamas, 4
Bahia (Brazil), 27, 274
Balboa, Vasco Núñez de, 16
ballets, America and Americans represented in, 93–5, 101–3, 111, 276, 279
Balzac, Honoré de, 157
Banham, Reyner, 255, 262
Baradère, Jean-Henri, 179
Barendsz, Dirk, 87
Barlow, Joel, 150
Barlow, Roger, 39
Barry, James, 142, 144–5
Bartholdi, Frédéric-Auguste, 160
Bartlett, William Henry, 197
Batz, Alexandre de, 127
Baudelaire, Charles-Pierre, 237, 281
Baumgartner, Johann Wolfgang, 113
Beauvais tapestry factory, 138–9, 151
beaver, 21, 40, 246
Bebel, August, 249
Beckford, William, 277
Beerbohm, Sir Max, 250
Beham, Hans Sebald, 273
Behn, Mrs. Aphra, 121, 277
Belasco, David, 244
Bella, Stefano della, 89
Bellermann, Ferdinand, 175–7
Belon, Pierre, 37
Benvenuti, Pietro, 161–2
Benzoni, Gerolamo, 25, 42–3, 66, 77, 274

Berchem, Claes (or Nicolaes), 99
Berczy, Wilhelm von Moll, 130–1
Berkeley, George, Bishop of Cloyne, 22
Berlin, Sir Isaiah, 141
Berlioz, Hector, 163
Bermuda, 51, 141, 190
Berner y Bustos, Mariano, 279
Bernini, Gianlorenzo, 97, 276
Bertelli, Pietro, 276
Best, George, 67
Betanzos, Domingo de, 57
Betz, Jardin de, 278
Biard, Auguste-François, 215
Bibbiena, Bernardo Dovizi, Cardinal of, 35
Bimini, 18
Bing, Samuel, 253, 257
Bingham, Hiram, 187
Birkbeck, Morris, 190
Bishop, Henry Rowley, 279
"Black Legend," 23, 77, 95
Blake, William, 154–5
Blanc, Louis, 159
Blanchard, Claude, 148
Blarenberghe, Louis-Nicolas van, 147
Boccage, Marie-Anne Le Page, Mme du, 99
Boccioni, Umberto, 282
Bocquet (or Boquet), Louis-René, 111
Bodmer, Karl, 229, 232–4, 236
Bogotá, 44
Boldini, Giovanni, 251–2
Bologna, Giovanni (Jean Boulogne), 39
Bologna, botanical gardens at, 35
Bolivia, 176
Bonheur, Rosa, 238–41, 281
Bonincontri, Lorenzo, 4
Bonnard, Pierre, 240–1
Bonpland, Aimé, 170
Boone, Daniel, 227–9
Bordeaux, 64
Borel, Antoine, 133, 147
Borgonio, Tommaso, 95, 103, 276

[293]

INDEX

Bosse, Abraham, 279
Boston (Mass.), 148, 202
Boswell, James, 120, 131
Botero, Giovanni, 92
Botta, Carlo, 156, 159, 278
Boturini Benaduci, Lorenzo, 168–70
Bouchardon, Edmé, 113
Bougainville, Louis-Antoine de, 131, 279
Bourget, Paul, 253
Bourquet, Henry, 129
Bowles, William Augustus, 134–5
Bramhall, John, 118
Brandt, Sebastian, 272
Brant, Joseph (Thayendanega), 125, 130, 225, 277
Brazil, discovery of, 7–8, 53, 55; Dutch colony in, 48, 80–1; French colony in, 55, 63–5, 141; natural products of, 34, 44, 50, 183; nineteenth-century travelers in, 172–6, 232
Brazilians, 53, 80, 83–4, 90. See also Tapuya, Tupinamba
brazilwood (dyewood), 21, 44–5, 63
Brébeuf, St. Jean de, 227
Brecht, Bertolt, 260
Brendan, St., 4
Breton, André, 282
Breton, Richard, 276
Briggs, Henry Perronet, 180, 182
Brissot de Warville, Jacques-Pierre, 152, 155
Brokoff, Ferdinand Maximilian, 98
Bronzino, Agnolo, 39
Brooke, Rupert, 197
Brown, Ford Madox, 194, 280
Bruges, church of St. Jacob, 98
Bry, Theodor de, 24–5, 70–1, 75–8, 92, 122, 125, 200, 274, 277
Bryant, William Cullen, 210
Bucher, Lothar, 251, 282
Buchser, Frank, 203–15, 238
Buenos Aires, 99, 100
Buffalo, 202
"Buffalo Bill" (William Cody), 239–40, 244, 255–6
Buffon, Georges-Louis Leclerc, comte de, 51, 131–2, 171, 190–1
Bullock, William, 177
Burgkmair, Hans, 14, 272
Burke, Edmund, 141
Bute, John Stuart, 3rd Earl of, 144
Buti, Lodovico, 31–2
Byron, George Gordon, 6th Baron, 227
Byss, Johann Rudolf, 113

Cabet, Etienne, 157
Cabot, John, 8, 13
Cabral, Pedro Alvarez, 7, 55, 275
cactus, 45–6
Caldwell, Sir John, Bt., 134

California, 132, 265–8
Calloway, Richard, 228
Caminha, Pedro Vaz de, 55
Camoẽs, Luis de, 273
Campbell, Thomas, 225
Canada, 125, 194, 231, 246
cannibals, 5, 7–8, 10, 12, 40, 56–8, 64, 66, 81, 89, 97, 109, 115, 119, 146, 170–1, 227
Canova, Antonio, 156–7, 278
Cantino, Alberto, 8, 272
Cape Breton, 62
Cape Cod, 47, 141
Cape Fear, 16
Caprarola, Palazzo Farnese, 85, 276
Carli, Giano Rinaldo, 170
Carlyle, Thomas, 193, 280
Carpaccio, Vittore, 35
Carpeaux, Jean-Baptiste, 282
Carrey, Louis-Jacques, 218
Cartari, Vincenzo, 165
Cartier, Jacques, 16, 273
Carver, Jonathan, 136, 221, 223, 278
Cassatt, Mary, 251
cassava, 44, 66
Castañeda, Luciano, 170, 279
Catesby, Mark, 51
Cathay, 3, 16
Catherwood, Frederick, 179–82
Catlin, George, 232, 236–8, 281
Cavalieri, Tommaso de', 30
Caxés, Eugenio, 26
Ceracchi, Giuseppe, 278
Chagall, Marc, 282
Champ d'Asile (Texas), 157, 196
Champlain, Samuel de, 47
Chapman, George, 5, 93
Chappe d'Auteroche, Jean, 132
Charles II, King of England, 46, 92
Charles V, Holy Roman Emperor, 18, 28–30, 59–60, 92, 274, 275
Charles IX, King of France, 64
Charles X, King of France, 231
Charlevoix, Pierre-François-Xavier de, 141
Charlottesville (Va.), 211
Chastellux, François-Jean, marquis de, 138, 147, 278
Chateaubriand, François-René, vicomte de, 220, 262, 281
Chatham, William Pitt, 1st Earl of, 144–6
Chauchetière, Claude, 121
Chauveau, François, 96
Cherokee, 125, 134–5, 219
Chicago, 249, 254
Chichén Itzá, 181–2
Chickasaw, 135
Chile, 44, 90, 176
Chimborazo, 172
chocolate, 44, 115
Choctaw, 219
Cholula, 170

Christy, Henry, 178
Chukovsky, Kornei, 282
Cieza de León, Pedro, 44
Cincinnati, 192
Civil War, American, 203, 249
Clavigero, Francisco Javier, 170
Clement VII, Pope, 61
climate, American, 5, 16, 51, 131, 190
Clusius (Charles de l'Ecluse), 44
Cobbett, William, 280
Cocteau, Jean, 256
cod, 8, 21
Codex canadensis, 127
codices, Mexican, 30, 62, 165–7, 172, 178, 275
Cody, William. See "Buffalo Bill"
Coleridge, Samuel Taylor, 157, 279
Coligny, Admiral Gaspard de, 141
Colombia, 44
Columbus, Christopher, 13, 37, 41, 43, 45, 59, 121; aims of, 3–5, 21, 56; representations of, 85, 90, 99, 114, 116–7; writings of, 6–8, 34, 271–2
Coma, Guglielmo, 41, 274
Comanche, 240
Concord, 146
Condorcet, Marie-Jean-Antoine-Nicolas Caritat, marquis de, 152
Considérant, Victor, 157
Cook, James, 175
Cooper, James Fenimore, 229, 235, 240, 242, 244, 281
Copán, 180
Cope, Walter, 33, 274
Cornut, Jacques-Philippe, 48, 275
Corte-Real, Gasparo, 8, 13
Cortés, Hernando, 15, 21, 34, 60–1, 85, 163, 273
Cosimo I, Grand Duke of Tuscany, 30
Couder, Louis-Charles-Auguste, 158–9
Cowper, William, 153–4
Creek Indians, 125, 134
Crèvecoeur, Hector-St. Jean de, 133, 150, 155, 190, 278
Crockett, David, 228, 281
Crowe, Eyre, 198, 280
Cuba, 5, 90
Cumberland, Henry Frederick, Duke of, 146
Curzon, Robert, 14th Baron Zouche, 178, 279
Custer, George, 238
Custine, Adam-Philibert, comte de, 147
Cuzco, 168

Dali, Salvador, 282
Dalsgaard, Christen, 195
Dargaud, Victor, 160
Dati, Giuliano, 6–7, 11

[294]

Davenant, William, 95, 162
Debret, Jean-Baptiste, 172, 279
Dee, John, 33, 274
Defoe, Daniel, 121. See also *Robinson Crusoe*
Degas, Edgar, 213–7, 280
Delacroix, Ferdinand-Victor-Eugène, 223, 225, 237
Delaune, Etienne, 85
Delisle, Louis-François de la Brevetière, 277
Demahis, Etienne-Achille, 281
Derby porcelain factory, 144
Desceliers, Pierre, 39
Desportes, Alexandre-François, 102
Diaghilev, Serge, 256
Diaz del Castillo, Bernal, 21, 273
Dickens, Charles, 191–2, 194, 197–8, 219, 280
Diderot, Denis, 161
Dieppe, church of Saint-Jacques, 63, 275
Doesborch, Jan van, 12, 272
Donne, John, 58, 275
Doré, Gustave, 194, 223
Drake, Sir Francis, 26
Drayton, Michael, 6, 27, 51, 190, 275
Dresser, Christopher, 185, 279
Dryden, John, 118, 163, 277
Duchamp, Marcel, 257, 282
Dufour et Leroy, 162
Duhamel, Georges, 253
Du Maurier, George, 250
Dumont, Jean, 108
Dupaix, Guillermo, 170
Duplessis, Joseph Siffred, 149
Duplessis-Bertaux, Jean, 139
Dupont, Pierre-Samuel, 149
Dupré, Augustin, 148
Dürer, Albrecht, 13, 28–9, 274
Duret, François-Joseph, 223
Duvivier, Pierre-Simon-Benjamin, 148
Dvorak, Anton, 260
Dyck, Anthony van, 47–8
dyewood. See brazilwood

Eckhout, Albert, 48, 50–1, 78–83, 99, 102, 275–6
Eden, Richard, 272
Egyptian Hall (London), 177, 236
Elcano, Juan Sebastián de, 16
emigrants to America, 193–6
Emy, Henry, 236
Encyclopédie, 131, 143
Ender, Thomas, 172–3
Engels, Friedrich, 248–9
Epinal, imagerie d', 214, 245
Ernst, Max, 262, 282
Eskimo, 16–17, 67–8, 89–90
Essomericq, 62
Estaing, Charles-Hector, comte d', 146

Evelyn, John, 46
Exposition Universelle (Paris), 1867, 183–4
Exposition Universelle (Paris), 1878, 185

Fabyan, Robert, 272
Fanshawe, Sir Edward George, 202, 280
Farinati, Paolo, 97, 276
fauna, American, 8, 11, 34–42, 51, 131, 171, 187, 190, 274. *See also* armadillo, beaver, iguana, llama, muscovy duck, opossum, parrot, penguin, tapir, toucan, turkey
Faux, William, 192, 280
Fawcett, Colonel, 187
Fearon, Henry Bradshaw, 192–3, 280
featherwork, Mexican, 28, 34, 115
Fenton, Geoffrey, 84
Ferdinand I, Holy Roman Emperor, 30
Ferdinand, King of Aragon, 3, 6–7, 46, 56
Ferdinand II, Archduke, 30
Ferdinand, Archduke of Tyrol, 39
Ferdinand, Cardinal Infante, 92
Fernández de Enciso, Martin, 39
Fernández de Oviedo, Gonzalo, 18, 41, 45, 59, 131
Ferreira, Manuel, 279
Ferry, Gabriel, 240
Fidler, Isaac, 192, 280
Filson, John, 227
Flint, Timothy, 227
flora, American, 5, 7–8, 11, 34, 41–51, 171, 176, 187, 190, 274–5. *See also* brazilwood, cactus, cassava, maize, pineapple, potato, prickly pear, sunflower, tomato
Florence, festival decorations in, 91, 276
Florida, 18, 25, 68, 70–2, 90, 141
Florio, John, 66
Fontenelle, Bernard le Bovier, Sieur de, 163
Fort Dearborn, 238
Fort Kearney, 205
Fourier, Charles, 157
Fragonard, Jean-Honoré, 139, 149–50
Frampton, John, 42
Franken, Frans, II, 92–3
Franklin, Benjamin, 139, 147–9, 152, 155, 278
Frederick II (the Great), King of Prussia, 131, 162–3
Frederick William IV, King of Prussia, 176, 202, 237
Frobisher, Martin, 16, 18, 67–8
Fuller, Loïe, 253, 263, 282
Fulton, Robert, 150
Furly, Benjamin, 142

Fuseli, Henry (Johann Heinrich Füssli), 153
Futurists, 254, 282

Galindo, Juan, 179, 279
Galle, Philipp, 87
Gama, Vasco da, 13
García, Gregorio, 277
Garcilaso de la Vega, el Inca, 161
Gauguin, Paul, 186
Gautherot, Pierre, 222
Geary, Cornet, 277
Genoa, Palazzo Ducale, 99
George III, King of Great Britain, 146
George VI, King of Great Britain, 246
Gérard, Marguerite, 149
Gerstäcker, Friedrich, 281
Gesner, Konrad von, 39, 42–3, 99
Giedion, Siegfried, 260
Gilbert, Sir Humphrey, 16, 27
Gindl, Karl Lorenz, 165
Ginori, marchese Carlo, 168
Giordani, Giuseppe, 279
Giordani, Pietro, 156–7
Giordano, Luca, 108
Giovanni da Udine (Giovanni Ricamatore), 37
Girodet-Trioson, Anne-Louis, 221–3
Gobelins, Manufacture royale des, 83, 99, 101–2, 106, 276
Goethe, Johann Wolfgang von, 136, 248, 253, 278
gold, 6, 18, 21, 28, 90, 171, 200
golden age, myth of, 5–6, 24, 56, 120, 142, 272
Goldsmith, Oliver, 190, 195
Gomberville, Martin Le Roy de, 162
Goncourt, Edmond and Jules de, 159, 253, 282
Gonneville, Binot Palmier de, 62
Goya y Lucientes, Francisco José de, 225–7, 281
Grainger, James, 111
Graun, Karl Heinrich, 165
Gravelot, Hubert, 109, 111
Gray, Thomas, 128, 277
Great Bookham, Surrey, 277
Great Exhibition (London), 1851, 183, 251
Greuze, Jean-Baptiste, 149
Grey Owl (Archie Belany), 246–7
Gropius, Walter, 255, 282
Grosz, George, 242, 257
Grotius, Hugo, 120, 277
Guadalajara, Mexico, 168–9
Guiana, 5, 21
Guicciardini, Francesco, 84
Guise, Louis-Joseph de Lorraine, duc de, 95–6
Gutenberg, Carl, 145
Gutiérrez, Sancho, 38, 40

[295]

INDEX

Haggard, Sir Henry Rider, 183
Hakluyt, Richard, 18, 25, 42, 63, 273
Hall, Basil, 192, 201–2, 219, 280
Hamilton, Richard, 262, 265, 282
hammock, 11, 65–6, 101, 274
Hanke, Otto, 258
Harcourt, duc d', 278
Hardy, Thomas, 135
Hariot, Thomas, 25, 66, 71, 73
Harrison, William Henry, 234
Havana, 90, 99, 100
Hawkins, William, 62
Hearne, Samuel, 137
Heere, Lucas de, 67
Hegel, Georg Wilhelm Friedrich, 248
Heine, Heinrich, 248
Hennepin, Louis, 277
Henry VIII, King of England, 63
Henty, George Alfred, 182
Herder, Johann Gottfried, 170, 279
Heriot, George, 231
Hernandez, Francisco, 48
Herrera y Tordesillas, Antonio de, 161
Hersent, Louis, 222
Hervieu, August, 201–2
Hesperides, 4
Hesselius, Gustavus, 127
Hildebrandt, Eduard, 175, 202
Hispaniola, 43, 56
Hobbes, Thomas, 118, 277
Hockney, David, 265–8, 282
Hodges, William, 134–5, 175
Hoeye, François van den, 90
Höfnagel, Georg, 39, 42, 43, 48, 275
Homem, Lopo, 18, 19
Homer, Winslow, 215
Hopi Indians, 262
Houasse, René-Antoine, 101
Houdon, Jean-Antoine, 150, 278
Hudson Bay, 122
Hugo, Victor-Marie, 159, 223
Humboldt, Alexander von, 170–1, 176, 179, 237, 279
Hume, David, 152
hummingbird, 37, 39, 274
Hunt, Richard Morris, 253
Hunter, John, 134
Huron, 122, 124, 277
Hyde de Neuville, Jean-Guillaume baron, 158
Hyndman, Henry Mayers, 249

Icaria, Iowa, 157
iguana, 11, 41, 274
Incas, 18, 124, 162
Independence, declaration of, 145
Indians, American, 53–83, 118–37, 219–47; communism of, 5, 12, 122; compared with Greeks and Romans, 56, 75–7, 120, 124, 233, 236–7; nudity of, 8, 11, 65; religion of, 5, 8, 122, 124; sex life of, 8, 12, 56–7, 59, 131. See also Apache Indians, Assiniboin, Cherokee, Chikasaw, Choctaw, Creek Indians, Hopi Indians, Huron, Iowa Indians, Iroquois, Leni-Lenâpé, Mandan, Mohawks, Mohicans, Natchez, Ojibwa, Oneida, Osage, Seneca, Sioux, Tapuya, Tupinamba.
Ingram, David, 18
Innocent X, Pope, 97
Iowa Indians, 236
Iroquois, 124–5, 128, 141, 227, 277
Isabella, Queen of Castile, 3, 6, 56

Jamaica, 199
James I, King of England, 67, 93
Jamestown, 93
Jay, Antoine, 155
jazz, 259
Jefferson, Thomas, 150, 152, 191, 211
Jesuit Order, 121, 131, 277
Jews, supposed descent of American Indians from, 121, 135, 178, 277
Jiménez de Quesada, Gonzalo, 44
Johannot, Alfred and Tony, 229
Johnson, Andrew, President of U.S., 205
Johnson, Guy, 130
Johnson, Richard M., 234
Johnson, Samuel, 44, 120, 153
Jones, Inigo, 93–5, 276
Jones, John Paul, 148, 150
Jonson, Benjamin, 84
Jouy, toile de, 140
Jugelet, Auguste, 281

Kafka, Franz, 254
Karl of Steuermark, Archduke, 30
Karlsbrücke (Prague), 98
Kaufmann, Georg, 111
Kaufmann, Theodor, 238, 281
Keats, John, 190, 280
Kellermann, Bernhard, 259
Kenton, Simon, 228
Kessel, Jan van, 99–101, 104–5, 276
King, Charles Bird, 219, 235
Kingsborough, Edward King, Viscount, 121, 178–9, 279
Klinger, Friedrich Maximilian, 143
Klopstock, Friedrich Gottlieb, 278
Korda, Alexander, 259
Kotzebue, August von, 162
Krenek, Ernst, 260
Kürnberger, Ferdinand, 191
Kurz, Friedrich, 281

Labat, Jean-Baptiste, 277
Laboulaye, Edouard-René Lefebvre de, 159, 252
Labrador, 16, 134

La Condamine, Charles-Marie de, 170
Lafayette, Marie-Paul-Joseph-Gilbert, Motier, marquis de, 148
Lafitau, Joseph-François, 123–5, 233, 277
Lahontan, Louis-Armand de, 122, 221, 277
Lake Superior, 210
Lallement, St. Gabriel, 227
La Martinière, Bruzen de, 277
Langsdorff, Baron von, 176
Lapowinsa, 127
Laramie, Wyoming, 206
La Salle, Robert Cavelier de, 93, 101
Las Casas, Bartolomé de, 34, 62, 66, 274; as protector of the Indians, 24, 58–9, 78, 131; representations of, 161
La Tour du Pin, Henrietta-Lucy, marquise de, 155, 278
Laudonnière, René de, 68, 71
Lawrence, David Herbert, 187, 280
Lawrin, Charles, 249
Le Barbier, Jean-François, 133, 138–9, 147, 151, 161
Le Blanc de Guillet, 162
Le Brun, Charles, 118–9, 277
Le Clerc, Jean, 142
Leconte de Lisle, Charles-Marie-René, 280
Le Corbusier (Charles-Edouard Jeanneret), 255
Lee, Robert E., 209
Leech, John, 199
Léger, Fernand, 260–1, 282
Le Moyne de Morgues, Jacques, 68, 70–2, 75, 277
Lenau (Nikolaus Kranz Niembsch von Strehlenau), 191, 280
Leni-Lenâpé, 127
Lenin, Vladimir Ilich Ulyanov, 250
Leo X, Pope, 58
Léry, Jean de, 55, 65, 81
Lescarbot, Marc, 120
Lessing, Julius, 252, 282
Lesueur, Charles-Alexandre, 231, 281
Le Testau, Guillaume, 68–70
Levinge, Sir Richard Graham Augustus, 228
Lexington, 146
Liberty, Statue of, 160, 279
Liebknecht, Wilhelm, 248
Liège, episcopal palace, 61
Ligozzi, Jacopo, 36–7, 41, 45–6, 49, 274
Lincoln, Abraham, 159, 200
Linnaeus (Carl von Linné), 48
Linthorpe pottery, 185, 279
Lipchitz, Jacques, 282
llama, 40, 85, 274
Locke, John, 46, 119, 145, 277
Loos, Adolf, 253, 255
López de Gómara, Francisco de, 3, 272

[296]

INDEX

Lordon, Pierre-Jérôme, 222
Lorentzen, Christian August, 152
Lormier, P., 229–30
Los Angeles, 265–8
Loti, Pierre, 253
Louis XIII, King of France, 92
Louis XIV, King of France, 89, 93, 95, 99–101
Louis XVI, King of France, 138–9, 147
Louis XVIII, King of France, 158
Louis-Philippe, King of the French, 236, 238
Louisiana, 93, 101, 125, 127, 203
Luce, Maximilien, 255
Ludolph, J., 167

Macaulay, Thomas Babington, 1st Baron, 180
Mackenzie, Henry, 125, 135
Madrid, Palacio Real, 115–7
Magellan (Fernão de Magalhães), 16, 85
Magellan, Straits of, 16
Maine, 16
Maino, Juan Bautista, 27, 274
maize, 41, 274
Majo, C. de, 279
Makart, Hans, 250–1
Manco Capac, 162
Mandan, 232–4
Mandeville, Sir John, 3–5, 12, 272
Manet, Edouard, 215
maps, 8, 35, 68, 273; "Cantino," 9; "Grynaeus," 57; Gutiérrez, 38; "Miller," 19; Waldseemüller, 13, 40
Marcgrave, Georg, 50
Marcoy, Paul (L. Saint Cricq), 175
Marin, Joseph-Charles, 133
Marinetti, Filippo Tommaso, 254
Marlborough, Consuelo Vanderbilt, Duchess of, 251–2
Marlowe, Christopher, 85
Marmontel, Jean-François, 161, 279
Marquez, Pedro José, 170
Marryat, Frederick, 192, 280
Martineau, Harriet, 192, 219, 280
Martinique, 186
Martius, Carl Friedrich Philipp von, 172, 174
Martyr, Peter (Pietro Martire d'Anghiera), 6, 18, 28–9, 37, 40, 57, 65, 272
Marvell, Andrew, 6, 48, 141, 190, 275
Marx, Karl, 22, 249
Masson, André, 262, 282
Maurits (Johan) of Nassau-Siegen, count, later prince, 48–50, 80–1, 99–101, 275
Maximilian I, Holy Roman Emperor, 13

Maximilian, Emperor of Mexico, 186
May, Karl, 242–4, 257, 265, 281–2
Maya, 179–82, 279
McCullough, Major, 228
McKenney, Thomas L., 235
Meissen porcelain factory, 109–10
Mendieta, Gerónimo de, 21
Merian, Maria Sibylla, 51, 275
Mexico, artifacts of, 28–34, 165–6, 168, 177–8; conquest of, 15, 18, 21, 57; inhabitants of, 60, 59–62; landscape of, 176, 186–7; natural resources of, 172. See also Aztecs, codices, Mexican
Michelet, Jules, 159
Milhaud, Darius, 259
Millais, Sir John Everett, 180
Miller, Alfred Jacob, 236
Millet, Jean-François, 228–9, 281
Minaya, Bernardino de, 58
missionaries, Christian in America, 56, 98, 120, 277
Mitla, 187
Mohawks, 130
Mohicans, 125, 229
Molina, Giovanni Ignazio, 99
Monardes, Nicolás, 40, 42, 47–8
Mondrian, Piet, 260, 264, 282
Monnoyer, Jean-Baptiste, 101
Montaigne, Michel Eyquem, seigneur de, 64–7
Montalboddo, Fracanzio, 8, 18
Montanus, Arnoldus, 41–2
Monte Pascoal, 7
Montesquieu, Charles-Louis de Secondat, baron de, 142, 152, 162, 279
Montezuma (or Moctezuma) II, 21, 28, 34–5, 162–3, 165, 279
Monticello, 211
Moore, Thomas, 190
More, Sir Thomas, 27
Morison, Samuel Eliot, 16
Morland, George, 153
Morton, "Jellyroll," 260
Mostaert, Jan, 22–4
Munich, Residenz, 97
Muscovy ducks, 39
Museo Pigorini (Rome), 33
Mussini, Cesare, 222–3

Napoleon Bonaparte, 155–6, 158
Napoleon III, Emperor of France, 159
Nashoba, 202
Natchez, 127, 220, 223, 225
Nebel, Carlos, 179
Netscher, Theodorus, 47
New Andalusia, 170
Newfoundland, 4, 8, 62
New Harmony (Indiana), 157, 231–2

New Orleans, 127, 213–7
New York, 161, 199, 203, 210, 215, 253–4, 257–60, 265
Niagara, 131, 197, 201, 203, 220–1
Nicaragua, 58
Niderviller porcelain factory, 147
Noble Savage, use of term, 118, 275, 277
Noël, Alexandre-Jean, 132
Norsemen, 4, 272
Northwest Passage, 16, 220
Norumbega, 18

Occom, Sampson, 125
Ohio River, 197
Ojibwa, 134, 236–7
Oneidas, 219, 231
operas on American subjects, 102, 163, 279
opossum, 40
Orford, Edward Russell, Earl of, 167
Orinoco, 5, 171
Orizaba, 164
Ortelius, Abraham, 85
Ortiz, Tommaso, 57
Osage, 125, 231, 234, 238
Ostenaco, 125
Owen, Robert, 157–8, 231
Oxford, Ashmolean Museum, 34

Pacific Ocean, 15
Pacini, Giovanni, 279
Padua, botanical garden at, 34
Paisiello, Giovanni, 279
Palafox de Mendoza, Juan, 121
Palanti, Giuseppe, 244
Paolozzi, Edoardo, 262
Paracelsus (Theophrastus Bombast von Hohenheim), 58, 275
Paraguay, 168
Parigi, Giulio, 91, 94–5
Paris, Treaty of, 138
parrot, 6–7, 9, 34–7
Pasquier, Etienne, 84, 276
Passe, Crispijn de, 47, 87–8
Patagonia, 16, 90, 131, 278
Paul III, Pope, 58, 275
Pauw, Cornelius de, 131–2, 138, 168, 190, 277–8
Pedro I, Dom, Emperor of Brazil, 172
Peeters, Bonaventura, 82–3, 276
Pellerin & Cie., 214, 245
penguin, 39
Penn, John, 127
Penn, William, 129, 142, 278
Pennsylvania, 141–3
Penobscot, 18
Pernety, Antoine-Joseph, 131, 168, 277–8

[297]

INDEX

Peru, allegories of, 90–1; artifacts from, 30, 167, 184–6, 274; conquest of, 21, 29, 162; inhabitants of, 57, 119; landscape of, 176, 279; map of, 69; riches of, 18
Pettrich, Ferdinand, 233, 235
Philadelphia, 201; Centennial Exposition at, 252, 260
Philip II, King of Spain, 40, 48, 91
Philippoteaux, Félix-Henri-Emmanuel, 40
Phiz (Hablot Knight Browne), 194–5
Piazza Navona (Rome), 97
Picabia, Francis, 257, 282
Picart, Bernard, 120, 122, 124
Picasso, Pablo, 186, 256–7, 282
Pigafetta, Antonio, 16, 40, 66, 273
Pignoria, Lorenzo, 165
Pilgrim Fathers, 141
Pilon, Louis-Jacques, 278
pineapple, 45, 47, 65, 274
Pinzón, Vicente Yáñez, 40
Piron, Alexis, 163
Piso, Gulielmus (Willem Pies), 50
Pizarro, Francisco, 25, 29, 161, 180
Pizarro, Hernando, 30
Plate, River, 91, 97
Platte, River, 206
Platter, Thomas, 33
Plumier, Charles, 51, 275
Pocahontas, 67
Poggini, Gianpaolo, 40
Polo, Marco, 3, 4
Pommersfelden, Schloss, 113
Ponce de León, 18, 273
Pontiac's conspiracy, 129
Pop art, 265, 282
Popayán, 44
Pope, Alexander, 131
Port-Vendres, 147
Porto Seguro, 99–100
Portogallo, Marc' Antonio de, 279
Portuguese school, 53–5
Post, Frans, 48, 52, 98–9, 102
potato, 34, 43–4, 274
Potosí, 18, 92
Powhattan, 33
Powis, Dr., 40
Pownall, Thomas, 279
Pozzo, Andrea, 98, 109, 276
Prescott, William Hickling, 179–80, 182–3
Prévost d'Exiles, Antoine-François, 277
prickly pear, 45
Protestants, America as haven for, 98, 141
Puccini, Giacomo, 244
Punch, 199–200, 250
Purchas, Samuel, 165

Quakers, 129, 142–3, 148–9
Quebec, 227
Quoniambec, 64

Rabel, Daniel, 95
Rabelais, François, 39
ragtime, 259
Raleigh, Sir Walter, 21, 26, 40, 272
Raleigh (N.C.) State Capitol, 156
Rameau, Jean-Philippe, 102
Ramusio, Giovanni Battista, 18, 46, 273
Raphael (Raffaello Sanzio), 37
Rastell, John, 273
Raynal, Guillaume-Thomas-François, 131–2, 138, 170, 278
Redgrave, Richard, 195
Reid, Thomas Mayne, 242, 244
Reunion (Texas), 157
Revolution, American, 132–5, 138–52, 161, 227, 278
Revolution, French, 155, 278
Ribero, Diego, 39
Richardson, Henry Hobson, 253
Richmond (Va.), 198
Rindisbacher, Peter, 231–2, 281
Rio de Janeiro, 172, 202
Rios, Pedro del, 165
Riou, Edouard, 175
Ripa, Cesare, 89
Roanoake, 68
Roberts, Lloyd, 246
Robertson, William, 132, 141, 167, 170, 190, 278
Robinson, Henry Crabb, 229
Robinson Crusoe, 121, 153
Rochambeau, Donatien de Vimeur, comte de, 138, 148, 220
Rochester (N.Y.), 202
Rogers, Charles, 279
Rohl-Smith, Carl, 238
Rolfe, John, 67
Romney, George, 130–1
Ronsard, Pierre de, 65, 275
Rossi, Franco, 265
Rouen, 44, 63–4, 275
Rousseau, Henri "le Douanier," 166, 186–8, 280
Rousseau, Jean-Jacques, 119–20, 131, 162, 277
Royal Society of Arts (London), 142
Rubens, Peter Paul, 92, 276
Rudolf II, Holy Roman Emperor, 30
Rugendas, Johann Moritz, 164, 175–6
Ruskin, John, 198

Sacchini, Antonio Maria Gaspar, 279
Sacramento, 202, 205
Sackville, Lord George, 128
Sadeler, Jan, 87

Saguenay, 18
S. Ignazio (Rome), 98, 106, 109
St. Lawrence River, 16, 193
St. Louis, 232
Saint-Gelais, Melin de, 51
Saint-Martin, Grenier, 222
Saint-Non, Jean-Baptiste-Claude-Richard de, 139
St. Peter's (Rome), 98, 276
Saintin, Jules-Emile, 238
Sand, George (Amadine-Aurore-Lucie Dupin, baronne Dudevant), 236–7
Sandby, Paul and Thomas, 167
Santa Cruz, Alonzo de, 40
Sant' Elia, Antonio, 254
Santo Domingo, 99–100
Satie, Erik, 256
Scheffer, Ary, 159
Schey, Jean, 281
Schiller, Friedrich, 136, 278
Schinkel, Karl Friedrich, 163
Schneider, Sascha, 243
Schoor, Ludvig van, 102
Schuler, Théophile, 195
Scillacio, Niccolò, 7
Scioto Company, 155
Sealsfield, Charles (Karl Postl), 281
Sebron, Hippolyte, 203
Ségur, Louis-Philippe, comte de, 143
Selkirk, Thomas Douglas, 5th Earl of, 231
Seneca, 231
Servi, Costantino de', 95
Seton, Ernest Thompson, 245
Seward, William H., 204–5
Seyfried, Ignaz Xavier, 279
Shakespeare, William, 37, 44, 66–7, 275
Shebbeare, John, 125
Sheridan, Richard Brinsley, 162
Sherman, William, 205, 209
Silone, Ignazio, 268
Sioux, 245
skyscrapers, 253
slaves, African, 25, 56, 152–5, 191–2, 198–9, 278; Indian, 56, 59
Smith, Adam, 152
Smith, Charlotte, 134
Smith, John, 26
Smith, William, 129
Smollett, Tobias, 278
Society of Antiquaries (London), 167–8
Soderini, Pier, 10
Solimena, Francesco, 99, 113
Solis y Ribadenyra, Antonio de, 164
Southey, Robert, 182
Spenser, Edmund, 85
Spix, Johann Baptist von, 172, 174
Spontini, Gaspare, 163
Staden, Hans, 25, 64, 75–7, 275

[298]

INDEX

Stael, Mme. de (Anne-Louise-Germaine Necker), 152
Stamp Act, 144
Stedman, John Gabriel, 154–5
Stein, Gertrude, 256
Stephens, John Lloyd, 179
Stewart, Sir William Drummond, Bt., 236
Stowe (Bucks.), 278
Stradanus (Jan van der Straet), 41, 88–9
Stuart, Gilbert, 131
Stuchs, G., 272–3
Sullivan, Louis Henry, 253
sunflower, 47–8
Surinam, 141, 154–5
Sutter, Johann August, 205
Svinin, Pavel Petrovich, 201, 280

Tajín, 170
Tanguy, Yves, 282
tapir, 40, 89
Tapuya, 78–81
Taunay, Nicolas-Antoine, 172
Tchelitchew, Pavel, 282
Tecumseh, 234–5
Tenniel, Sir John, 200
Tenochtitlán, 21, 168
Teotihuacán, 187
Texas, 157
Thackeray, William Makepeace, 280
Thevet, André, 39, 55, 64–5, 99
Thompson, Henry Yates, 280
Ticonderoga, 129
Tiepolo, Giovanni Battista, 112–6, 276
Tiffany, Louis Comfort, 253
Tippecanoe, 234–5
tobacco, 41–3, 274
Tocqueville, Alexis de, 158–9, 210, 219, 279
Tofft, Peter Petersen, 202
Toledo, Cathedral treasury, 109
tomato, 44, 274
Tommasi, Angelo, 195–6
Tordesillas, treaty of, 8
Torelli, Giacomo, 94
toucan, 39
Toulouse Lautrec, Henri de, 253, 263
Townshend, George, 4th Viscount and 1st Marquess, 128, 277
Townshend, Roger, 129
Tradescant, John, 33
Trevisani, Francesco, 276
Trollope, Anthony, 192

Trollope, Mrs. (Frances Milton), 191–3, 197, 219, 280
Trotsky, Leon, 250
Troyes, 64
Tupinamba, 13, 62, 64, 76–7
Turgot, Anne-Robert-Jacques, 149–50
turkey, 37, 39
Turner, Joseph Mallord William, 198

Uffizi (Florence), 31–2
"Uncle Sam," 200, 280
Uruguay, 176

Vaccaro, Lorenzo, 108–9
Valverde, Vicente, 161
Van den Berghe, Charles-Auguste, 281
Varèse, Edgard, 260
Vatican, 35, 37, 234, 276
Vecchi, Giovanni de', 85–6, 276
Vecellio, Cesare, 276
Venezuela, 8, 176–7
Vera Cruz, 99–100
Veragua, 37
Verbruggen, Hendrik, 98
Verelst, John, 125–6
Verrazzano, Giovanni da, 16, 56, 118, 273, 277
Versailles, Château de, 109, 118, 158
Vespucci, Amerigo, 8, 10–13, 27, 56, 65, 131, 272; representations of, 85, 88, 90–1, 276
Vico, Giambattista, 170, 279
Victoria, Queen of Great Britain, 236, 238, 244
Vienna, Kunsthistorisches Museum, 168; Museum für Volkerunde, 30
Villegagnon, Nicolas Durand de, 55, 63, 65
Vincent de Beauvais, 4
Vinland, 4
Virginia, first colony named, 71–4, 85
Virginia, second colony, 27, 51
Virginia Company, 67, 93
Viseu, 53
Vitoria, Francisco de, 58
Vivaldi, Antonio, 163
Voltaire (Françoise-Marie Arouet), 119–20, 131–2, 142, 152, 162, 277
Vos, Maarten de, 89

Wagner, Richard, 163, 260

Waldeck, Jean Frédéric Maximilien de, 179
Waldseemüller, Martin, 13, 40, 163, 260, 273
Wall, William Guy, 197
Waller, Edmund, 51, 190–1
War of 1812, 227, 234, 238
Washington, George, 155–6, 220; representations of, 139, 148, 150–1, 156, 158–9, 278
Washington, D.C., 191, 205, 212
Waugh, Evelyn, 187
Webster, Daniel, 238
Weiditz, Christoph, 59–61, 275
Weil, Kurt, 260
Wells, Herbert George, 249–50, 259
Wernigerode, 89
West, Benjamin, 129–30, 251
Western films, 245, 265, 282
Westminster Abbey, 129
Whistler, James Abbot McNeill, 251
White, John, 17, 25, 67–8, 70–5, 77, 275
Whitman, Walt, 254, 282
Wied-Neuwied, Maximilian Prinz zu, 174–5, 232
Wilberforce, William, 153
Wilde, Oscar O'Flahertie, Wills, 248, 282
Wolfe, James, 128–9
Woodstock (Va.), 208–9
Woolner, Thomas, 194
Worde, Wynkyn de, 272
Wordsworth, William, 137
Worm, Ole (or Olaeus), 33, 166
Wright, Frank Lloyd, 255
Wright, Joseph, of Derby, 135–6, 278
Wunderkammer, 30, 99
Württemberg, 92, 111
Würzburg, Residenz, 113

Xochicalco, 170, 184–5

Yeats, William Butler, 253
Yorktown, 147, 158–9
Yucatan, 179

Zadkine, Ossip, 282
Zingarelli, Nicolà Antonio, 279
Zuber, Jean & Cie., 197

ABOUT THIS BOOK

In *The New Golden Land*, Hugh Honour, the distinguished English art historian, explores the changing image of America as it has evolved in the European mind over the last four centuries. The book draws upon a vast variety of material to show how the landscapes of the New World, its flora and fauna, its peoples and their customs, have been seen by European artists from the early explorations to the present day. Hundreds of reproductions of art works are included, from the woodcut illustrations for Columbus's and Vespucci's letters and the often vivid and beautiful figures of men and animals on early sixteenth-century maps, to John White's watercolors done on the spot at Raleigh's first Virginia colony, to Tiepolo's fantastic allegory of America on the ceiling of the Archbishop's palace in Würzburg, to Picasso's cubist *Buffalo Bill*. These are accompanied by a rich and varied literary background: Montaigne, Shakespeare, Blake, Byron, Goethe, Keats, Karl Marx, down to Hitler's favorite author, Karl May, and his Red Indian stories. Part fact, part fantasy, the whole is a fascinating mirror of the American experience.

The New Golden Land is based on the bicentennial exhibit prepared by Hugh Honour for the National Gallery in Washington and the Cleveland Museum of Art. However, this brilliant and highly enjoyable book goes beyond the exhibit to include a great many pictures that could not be shown in the museums.

Hugh Honour was educated at the King's School, Canterbury, and at St. Catharine's College, Cambridge. After working in the Department of Prints and Drawings at the British Museum in London, he became Assistant Director of the Leeds City Art Gallery and Temple Newsam House. Since 1945 he has lived in Italy. He is the author of many highly praised books, including *Chinoiserie*, *The Companion Guide to Venice*, *Neo-Classicism*, *The Penguin Dictionary of Architecture* (with Nikolaus Pevsner and John Fleming), and the forthcoming *Dictionary of Decorative Arts* (with John Fleming).